WILLIAM CAXTON AND
ENGLISH LITERARY CULTURE

The Pilgrims, from Caxton's second impression (1484)
of *The Canterbury Tales*, fo. c iiii.

WILLIAM CAXTON AND
ENGLISH LITERARY CULTURE

N.F. BLAKE

THE HAMBLEDON PRESS
LONDON   AND   RIO GRANDE

Published by The Hambledon Press, 1991

102 Gloucester Avenue, London NW1 8HX (U.K.)

P.O. Box 162, Rio Grande, Ohio 45672 (U.S.A.)

ISBN 1 85285 051 5

British Library Cataloguing in Publication Data

Blake, N.F. (Norman Francis)
  William Caxton and English Literary Culture.
  1. England. Printing. Caxton, William, 1422-1491.
  I. Title.
  686.2092

Library of Congress Cataloging-in-Publication Data

Blake, N.F. (Norman Francis)
  William Caxton and English Literary Culture/N.F. Blake
  1. Caxton, William, ca. 1422-1491.
  2. English literature – Middle English,
     Criticism, Textual.
  3. Printing – England – History – Origin and antecedents.
  4. Literature, Medieval – Criticism, Textual.
  5. Literature publishing – England – History.
  6. Printers – Great Britain – Biography.
  7. Incunabula – England.
  8. England – Civilization – Medieval period, 1066-1485.
  I. Title.
  Z232.C38B65   1991
  686.2'092 – dc20 [B]   91-705 CIP

Printed on acid-free paper and bound in Great Britain
by Bookcraft Ltd., Midsomer Norton, Somerset.

Contents

Introduction		vii
Acknowledgements		xi
1	William Caxton: A Review	1
2	William Caxton: the Man and his Work	19
3	Some Observations on William Caxton and the Mercer's Company	37
4	A New Approach to William Caxton	51
5	The Spread of Printing in English during the Fifteenth Century	57
6	Dating the First Books Printed in English	75
7	Continuity and Change in Caxton's Prologues and Epilogues	89
8	Caxton's Reprints	100
9	Caxton and Courtly Style	119
10	Caxton's Language	137
11	Caxton and Chaucer	149
12	John Lydgate and William Caxton	167
13	Caxton's Copytext of Gower's *Confessio Amantis*	187
14	Caxton prepares his edition of the *Morte Darthur*	199
15	The Biblical Additions in Caxton's 'Golden Legend'	213
16	William Caxton's *Reynard the Fox* and his Dutch Original	231
17	English Versions of *Reynard the Fox* in the Fifteenth and Sixteenth Centuries	259
18	Manuscript to Print	275
Index of Manuscripts		305
Index of Names		307

Introduction

Over the last thirty years or so Caxton studies have undergone a profound shift in emphasis. Before that time research was conducted on three separate levels which rarely intersected with one another. These approaches may be defined broadly as editorial, historical and typographical. Many of Caxton's works were edited in modern editions by those whose primary interest was in medieval English literature and the links it had with Continental literature at that time. Little attempt was made to fit Caxton into the context of English literature because the fifteenth century was regarded as a period of little literary merit. Even Caxton's output which consisted of so much translation of late medieval texts was not rated very highly from a critical point of view, partly because there is a common, if not always fully articulated, prejudice against translation as not creative and partly because the late Middle Ages preceded the classical revival of the Renaissance and was regarded as the unhappy tail-end of fourteenth-century creativity which formed a dip before the literary upsurge of the Tudor and Elizabethan periods. Caxton was thus seen as doing rather inferior literary work, translation, in a period which in itself represented the nadir of English literary creativity.

From a historical point of view the focus was on Caxton's life which was studied through whatever documentary evidence could be found in England and the Low Countries and through the statements made in his prologues and epilogues which were understood to be honest and accurate accounts of what had led him to produce the works which he printed and published. The trouble with the documentary evidence is that it is scattered through various sources and it is not always possible to understand what the evidence amounts to unless the context of the whole document is studied in depth to prevent faulty conclusions from being reached. Certain apparent facts were thereby discovered, but they hardly added up to a picture of the man although he was clearly a successful merchant. As for the prologues and epilogues Caxton represents himself as satisfying the whims of his patrons and so he was seen by many as someone who merely did what he was told and had little imagination or initiative. The second half of his life seemed to be the complete reverse of the first half: a successful and dynamic businessman had become the lackey of others. The prestige he had from bringing the printing press to England appeared to be insignificant when compared with the rather weak man who pampered the old-fashioned tastes of those who demanded translations and editions from him. A few scholars did try to suggest that he had shown some initiative by printing English literary works, but the tone was inevitably defensive and negative.

The typographical research was particularly concerned with establishing how many books were printed in the fifteenth century and how many copies of each survived. The books were in their turn arranged according to type, and some attention was given to chain and wire lines and to paper sorts. The aim was to produce general catalogues (which remain important research tools even today) rather than to study individual editions in depth. For a bibliographer a book is a concrete artefact which can be described and compared with other books. The stages which led to its production may well seem less important, not to say controversial, and it was the detailed facts of the physical entity which were significant.

The last thirty years have seen attempts to study individual aspects of Caxton's life and work in greater detail and to consider them as a whole so that one side of his work can help to explain another. This change in attitude can be seen in this book, for some of the earlier articles reflect the attitudes prevailing when I first started to study Caxton and these have gradually given way to a more rounded approach to his career. This development was assisted by research carried out in related areas which have led to a re-evaluation of the fifteenth century. In literature the critical credit of the fifteenth century has been rising steadily. Authors like Lydgate who were previously disparaged have now had substantial books devoted to them and the whole fifteenth-century literary scene is much better understood and appreciated. Equally there has been considerable interest in the processes of manuscript production and transmission in the fifteenth century, prompted in part by the study of the manuscripts of such authors as Chaucer. The way in which texts were prepared for copying, the way in which they were copied by being broken down into stints for different scribes, the relationship between those who produced and those who acquired manuscripts, and the way in which small texts in booklet form could be assembled together to form one large manuscript have all been the subject of intense research. All this has had its impact on Caxton studies because it has revealed that the way he worked and the relations he established with others were not so different from those which were already found in the manuscript culture both before and during his working life. There is a continuity between the manuscript culture and the production of early printed books, and there was co-operation between those who produced the written and the printed word. It is also clear from studies in Caxton's attitude towards English authors, such as are printed in the latter half of this collection, that he was a literate man who was quite familiar with the best writing of his time. He knew the works of people like Lydgate and Chaucer well, and he could echo their words in his own writings. The realisation that he was so familiar with English literature has modified our attitude to him and his publishing policy.

The knowledge of the historical background to Caxton's life and work has also been greatly widened in the recent past. Studies of individual figures in English fifteenth-century history, of English relations with the Continent, and of the Burgundian dukes have made us more familiar with the historical context in which Caxton lived. Studies in depth of some of the historical sources, such as the examination of the Wardens' Account Book of the Mercers' Company, have resulted in a fuller appreciation of what such sources can tell us. The growing understanding of English literary culture in the fifteenth century and Caxton's place in it has modified our interpretation of his publishing policy as represented in his own prologues and epilogues. Caxton is no longer seen as the unimaginative responder to the imperious demands of ignorant patrons. It is clear that what he wrote in his prologues and epilogues was designed to market the books, and consequently they are to be understood not so much as historical records as publisher's blurbs. He was a merchant who had something to sell, printed books, and he followed the example of people like Lydgate in devising prologues and epilogues which would make his books attractive to potential customers. It follows from this that it was Caxton who was responsible for choosing books to publish and for working out a policy which would enable him to survive in business. He was clearly an astute businessman all his life, and there is no need to assume a sharp break between his early and his later career. The products he sold may have changed, but he remained a salesman with a keen flair for marketing. Unlike most of those who invested in a printing press in the fifteenth-century, Caxton made a commercial success of his venture – a success which tells us a lot about his financial and business acumen. Although he was clearly interested in books and literature, he remained a merchant and a mercer all his life. As such his services were often used by those in power, but he was not a courtier or a salaried official. Our respect for the man has grown as we have come to understand that he shaped his own destiny by exploiting his own talents. Inevitably there are many facts that we would still like to know, but the picture of the man has become more complete and convincing.

A similar development has taken place in bibliography: wide-ranging studies of the background have supported in-depth investigations of individual Caxton editions. The former have enabled us to understand the development of printing in Cologne and the Low Countries in particular so that the early years of Caxton's publishing career could be fitted into its proper context. Detailed investigations of individual texts have often been able to identify how the editions were set up, how many compositors there were, who some of them may have been, and what the relative dates of each edition were. The important dates in Caxton's career are now more firmly established. At the same time our confidence in the dating of the editions and our knowledge in how texts were prepared for the press have enabled us to relate Caxton's literary interests to his finished products. These in turn have enabled us to build up a more convincing picture of his publishing policy. Whereas in the past particular attention was paid to a few selected texts, recent study has taken a look at all his output including his reprints. A publishing policy and the preparation of editions cannot be determined solely by a consideration of one or two big works; every edition has something to tell us about the press and its owner. Changes in type, the introduction of woodcuts, the regularisation of capitals and other linguistic features all have something to tell us about the working of the printing office. Equally we need to bear in mind that Caxton acted as printer, publisher and bookseller. In the past we concentrated too much on his role as a printer, but it is more as a publisher and to a lesser extent as a bookseller that he deserves to be remembered. That he introduced the printing press into England has tended to underplay his role as publisher and bookseller to the detriment of our understanding his life more completely.

The essays in this volume illustrate different aspects of Caxton's life and work and I hope they underline how essential it is to consider all aspects of his career if we are to come to a just evaluation of it. Because he was so immersed in English literary culture he appears to represent the final flowering of the late Middle Ages. But as a businessman and entrepreneur he represents the new spirit which was sweeping Europe and so he symbolises the changes which were going to take place. The printing press is itself a great promoter of change. Caxton must be appreciated against the context of the times in which he lived. In this introduction I have not provided references to the many studies which have clarified that context for us, but full details may be found in my *William Caxton: A Bibliographical Guide* (New York: Garland, 1985). Naturally, scholarship continues to provide further information and insights, but the picture of the man which has been built up over the recent past seems unlikely to be drastically modified, though there still remain many investigations into individual editions and other aspects of his work to be undertaken to fill in the gaps in our understanding and appreciation of this fascinating and important figure.

Sheffield
December, 1990

Acknowledgements

The articles in this volume were originally published in the journals or books listed below. The author and publisher would like to thank editor, publisher or society for permission to reprint individual pieces.

1 *From Script to Book, A Symposium*, edited by H. Bekker-Nielsen, M. Borch and B.A. Sorensen (Odense: Odense University Press, 1987), p-. 107-26.

2 *Eight Papers presented to the Caxton International Congress 1976: Journal of the Printing Historical Society* 11 (1976-77): 64-80.

3 *The Book Collector* 15 (1966): 283-95.

4 *Collector* 26 (1977): 380-85.

5 *Gutenberg-Jahrbuch* (1987): 26-36.

6 *Gutenberg-Jahrbuch* (1978): 43-50.

7 *Gutenberg-Jahrbuch* (1979): 72-77 and (1980): 38-43.

8 *The Humanities Association Review*, 26 (1975): 169-79.

9 *Essays and Studies* n.s. 21 (1968): 29-45.

10 *Neuphilologische Mitteilungen* 67 (1966): 122-32.

11 *Leeds Studies in English* n.s.l. (1967): 9-36.

12 *Leeds Studies in English* n.s. 16 (1985): 272-89.

13 *Anglia* 85 (1967): 282-93.

14 *Journal of Librarianship* 8 (1976): 272-85.

15 *Traditio* 25 (1969): 231-47.

16 *Bulletin of the John Rylands Library* 46 (1963-64): 298-325.

17 *Studies in Philology* 62 (1965): 63-77.

18 *Publishing in Britain 1375-1475*, edited by Jeremy Griffiths and Derek Pearsall (Cambridge: Cambridge University Press, 1989), pp. 403-32.

1

William Caxton: A Review

William Caxton remains a somewhat shadowy figure outside England and the Low Countries, and so it is desirable to begin this review by briefly surveying his life if only because it provides a convenient lead into the scholarship which has developed around the introduction of printing into England. Nothing is known of his parents or early life before he became apprenticed to Robert Large, a mercer in London, who was later to become Lord Mayor. It is reasonable to suppose that his parents were themselves merchants or officials of one kind or another. His enrolment as an apprentice by Large which took place by 1438 was the most important event in his life for it shaped the pattern of his future career. The mercers constituted one of the most influential guilds in London in the fifteenth century and they dominated the trade between England and the Low Countries. This was technically in the hands of the Merchant Adventurers Company, a loose conglomeration of merchants engaged in the overseas trade. The Merchant Adventurers had little formal organisation and, as they used the Mercers' Hall in London as their administrative centre, the mercers formed the controlling group in the Merchant Adventurers Company. Inevitably a boy who enrolled as an apprentice with the mercers would drift into the overseas trade with the Merchant Adventurers. This trade was less regulated than that within England. Whereas the mercers in England were restricted to handling items of 'mercery' which included haberdashery, cloth and silks, those engaged in the overseas trade could deal in almost any item they chose except wool. At a later period, for example, we find Caxton involved in transactions in pewter. It was also in the overseas trade that the largest fortunes were made.

By joining Large, Caxton became associated with a powerful man in an important guild which dominated the trade with the Low Countries. He naturally acquired influential and rich friends among the merchant class; he learned how to handle money, how to float a loan, and how to arrange complicated financial transactions; and he became involved in some of the political and diplomatic events of the time. The merchants traded with the Low Countries and with France, where some of them lived. They were naturally involved in negotiations with the local authorities there in an effort to improve their trading conditions. Because of this expertise, merchants were frequently used by the crown to conduct negotiations at a national level. One of England's major exports at this time was wool, which was in great demand in the Low Countries by the many weaving establishments. The Low Countries were part of the Duchy of Burgundy, a large conglomeration of possessions acquired through dynastic succession and marriage which stretched from Switzerland through north-eastern France to embrace much of modern Holland and Belgium. For his French possessions the Duke owed feudal allegiance to the French crown, and the dukes were princes of royal French blood with pretensions to the French throne. Their Low Countries territories were outside French royal authority and encouraged the dukes to pursue a more independent political policy, which included the possible creation of a kingdom of Burgundy. These possessions were also among the most lucrative and made the dukes perhaps the richest and most powerful rulers in Northern Europe. In their efforts to achieve independence from France and in an attempt to protect the supply of English wool, the dukes were often encouraged to form an alliance with the English against the French. The political realities of the time led to the constant re-grouping of alliances among the English, French and Burgundians.

It was this political situation which operated when Caxton first went to Flanders, probably in the late 1440s. English merchants were attracted to Flanders and the Low Countries in general by the international markets held there, particularly the one at Bruges. There they were able to buy many exotic items to import into England. In addition, Flanders was at the centre of the production of de luxe manuscripts which were sought after both inside the Low Countries and beyond. Important libraries were owned by the dukes themselves and by Louis de Gruuthuse, who was made Earl of Winchester by Edward IV. Edward was said to be very impressed by Louis's library which he saw during his exile in the Low Countries in 1471. Many Flemish manuscripts now form part of the Royal collection of manuscripts in the British Library; and no doubt some joined the collection in the fifteenth century. One of these, Royal 19 A ix, has been identified as the copy used by Caxton to make his translation, *Mirror of the World*, which he subsequently printed. The mercers were involved in the import of such manuscripts into England, and although definite proof is lacking in Caxton's case there seems little doubt that he also took part in this business. Certainly many manuscripts passed through his hands and he had sold some to important clients in England, such as the manuscript containing the French version of *Blanchardin and Eglantine*. After he returned to England to establish his press in Westminster, he imported many books, printed and manuscript, into England, and it is reasonable to assume that this was a continuation of what he had been doing for a long time. It is even possible that he gave commissions to Flemish scriveners for texts which he wished to sell in England. Shortly after acquiring a press and setting up in Bruges, he entered into a publishing association with a former scrivener, Colard Mansion, which may reflect previous business contacts between the two.

According to his own account in the prologue to *History of Troy*, the first book published in English, Caxton started to translate this work in 1469 and after completing a few quires gave up the project. There is no evidence that Caxton had made any translations before this time, and the question naturally arises as to why he should have started translating then. The most acceptable hypothesis is that he did so with a view to publishing, presumably through printing, the finished translation. If this were so, it would have important implications for our understanding of the man. By 1469 printing had spread as far as Cologne, but it had not yet reached the Low Countries. Yet Caxton foresaw its possibilities and had already made plans to capitalise upon them. Furthermore, it would imply that he had also thought out a publishing policy long before he had acquired the means of printing. If so, this implies a man who did not enter printing accidentally through some fortunate coincidence, but who went out of his way to acquire a press. This point we may return to later. In 1471 he took up the translation again and went to Cologne where, as we know from Wynkyn de Worde, he was involved in the printing of a Latin version of the *De proprietatibus rerum* by Bartholomaeus Anglicus. The only edition that was printed in the early 1470s in Cologne is attributed to the printer of the *Flores Sancti Augustini*, now identified through typographical and other evidence as Johannes Veldener, who subsequently practised as printer and typecutter at Louvain. It is from Veldener that Caxton acquired his press and presumably the workmen to operate it. What is of particular importance is that *De proprietatibus* is the largest work printed by Veldener in Cologne and indeed the biggest book produced in Cologne by that date, where small quartos rather than large folios were the order of the day. It is clear that Veldener had an additional source of capital to finance the volume, and the most likely source for that money is Caxton. As a merchant he could have financed the project out of his own resources or he would have known how to borrow the necessary capital.

When he left Cologne at the end of 1472 he returned to Bruges where first he printed *History of Troy*, the book he had translated from French. This work was written in French by Raoul Lefèvre, a secretary at the Burgundian ducal court, and had been dedicated to Duke Philip. Caxton's version was dedicated to Margaret, the sister of Edward IV and now the wife of Charles Duke of Burgundy. From typographical investigations into this edition, it has been shown that four compositors worked on it. One of these who worked on the start of the first two books of *History of Troy* has been identified as Johannes Veldener because of the printing in red found only there which is elsewhere such a characteristic feature of Veldener's work. It seems probable that Veldener assisted in the setting up of the press, lent a hand in the early compositorial work to get it off to a good start, and then went off to re-establish his own business elsewhere, presumably Louvain. Caxton meanwhile continued at Bruges where he issued another of his translations, *Game of Chess*, which was dedicated to George Duke of Clarence. Then he issued four editions in French. In 1476 he returned to England where he established his printing press in the precincts of Westminster Abbey. There he continued with his publication work, issuing perhaps a further hundred editions of different texts, many of which were his own translations. Many of these editions were dedicated to various members of the nobility and some to merchants and officials. He continued as a printer, publisher and translator till his death. According to Wynkyn de Worde, Caxton completed his translation of the *Lives of the Fathers (Vitas patrum)* only just before he died. It was printed by de Worde after Caxton's death, which took place in 1492.

The following points emerge from this resumé of his career and have been at the centre of some of the controversies in Caxton studies. Caxton was a successful printer and publisher; he did not go bankrupt as so many early printers did. If we include his Cologne period, he was in the printing and publishing business for twenty years and issued over a hundred editions. He clearly had sufficient commercial acumen to survive where so many others foundered; and the question that has been asked is in what precisely the secret of his success lay. Most attention has been focussed on his choice of texts to print, for in such a long career there are sufficient texts to make analysis worthwhile. To many of his editions Caxton added a prologue and/or epilogue. These often provide his reasons for printing a particular text and his remarks have been accepted as accurate accounts of what happened. They have also been admired as writings in their own right, and therefore he has come to be accepted by some as a literary figure rather than as just a printer. He lived off and on in Bruges for well over twenty years and Bruges was in the dominions of the Dukes of Burgundy. He translated works written for the dukes and dedicated his first printed book to the then duchess. Scholarship has naturally focussed on the influence exerted on him by Burgundian literary taste and to what extent he was trying to capitalise on the fashion for things Burgundian in England. The problem with this view has been to fit his publication of English works, such as the poems by Chaucer, into such a theory. When he includes a prologue and/or epilogue he often introduces the name of a patron who is made to seem responsible for the volume in question. The many patrons mentioned have provoked dispute as to how far Caxton was responsible for the choice of the works he printed or whether he was following the whims of individual patrons. In other words, did he lead or follow public taste? Finally, there is the question of the sort of man he was: printer, merchant, scholar, diplomat and politician have all been put forward. They are not necessarily mutually incompatible, though individual scholars have emphasised one aspect to the exclusion of others. Many of these points are interrelated and I shall not attempt to keep them separate in what follows.

In England Caxton is generally honoured as the man who introduced printing into England – indeed, to many he still remains (erroneously) the man who invented printing. Although he is remembered as a printer, most of the scholarly argument about him has been over his role as publisher. He is not usually criticised for the quality of his printing, his use of particular type, his choice of woodcuts, or the layout of his page, though in all these points his record is poor. He is generally criticised or praised for the choice of texts he chose to print, though occasionally it is his command of English which is brought into question. An anonymous writer of 1766 complained that he »was but an illiterate man, and of small judgement, by which means he printed nothing but mean and frivolous things«.[1] Gibbon a little later noted that »In the choice of his authors, that liberal and industrious artist was reduced to comply with the vicious taste of his readers; to gratify the nobles with treatises on heraldry, hawking, and the game of chess, and to amuse the popular credulity with romances of fabulous knights« and legends of more fabulous saints«.[2] Caxton had not produced any classical or humanist texts. Although nineteenth-century scholars tried to salvage his reputation from the attacks of their predecessors, they did so by excusing or explaining his choice of material to print. It is regarded as a mark of his good taste that he should have printed so much English poetry. Naturally to modern ages like our own which do not read the

---

[1] *Anonymiana* (London, 1809), p.136.

[2] *The Miscellaneous Works of Edward Gibbon, Esq.*, edited by John, Lord Sheffield (London, 1814), III, 563-4.

classics in the original language, it may not seem too reprehensible that a printer should have omitted classical texts from his list.

The problem of this dispute has been establishing the data which can form the basis of the discussion. Most scholars work from modern bibliographical lists of Caxton's output, though these can differ as to what they include. This arises not so much because it is uncertain whether a particular edition was printed by Caxton as from the differing premises of such lists. For example, should the *De rerum proprietatibus* printed in Cologne about 1472, which I referred to earlier, be included in a list of Caxton's printed books? The problem is that in the fifteenth century specialisation in the production of books to which we are accustomed today had not yet arisen. This specialisation has since affected almost all products: goods are not made and sold on the same premises. For example, now when you buy a loaf of bread you would not expect that it had been baked in the shop where you purchased it. Similarly today a publisher chooses books to print, edits them and markets the finished product. The actual printing is entrusted to a printer, who simply sells his services to the publisher. The printer will expect to be reimbursed for his labour fairly promptly, but the publisher will only see a return on his capital investment as the books are sold. For publishers the problem of cash-flow is important, for investments may be of a long-term nature. The financial demands of the two occupations are very different. A printer will have made a capital investment in his equipment and he will employ staff to help him carry out the diverse tasks of the printing process. He will need to keep his equipment and staff busy by acquiring a constant stream of work. A publisher can publish as many books as he wants to: it can be a few or it may be a large number. He need not employ staff if he can handle the volume of business himself. But each edition that he publishes is a financial gamble: he may lose heavily or he may make a fortune. In any event he is not likely to get his money back quickly, and he can easily be beaten to the post by another publisher and find he has a stock of unsaleable books on his hands.

It is important to bear this distinction in mind, because it is clear that Caxton was both a printer and a publisher. He printed at least seven indulgences while he was at Westminster. In producing these he was acting only as printer, for he must have printed them for whoever was going to sell and distribute them. Caxton had no right to sell indulgences, which were issued by some ecclesiastical authority with a view to raising money for a particular clerical purpose. We may assume that Caxton was paid for these indulgences in much the same way as any printer is paid today. On the other hand, he acted on some occasions as publisher. Guillaume Maynial, a Paris printer, printed a Sarum *Missal* and

Legenda for Caxton in 1487-88. Apparently after these books arrived at Westminster Caxton added his mark, which here does duty as a publisher's sign. Caxton presumably paid Maynial for the printing of these volumes and he took the financial risk involved in distributing (i.e. publishing) them.

Bibliographers are concerned with the printed book, because it is something tangible which can be described: a book has type, paper and watermarks, which can be objectively analysed and catalogued. They therefore group books under the printer rather than under a publisher. A publisher is too shadowy a concept for most bibliographers. In most lists of Caxton's books, therefore, the indulgences are included, but not the two books printed by Maynial. Yet if Caxton is being criticised for his choice of books to print and publish, then the indulgences should be discounted because he did not choose to publish them; he simply printed them. However, the Sarum *Missal* and *Legenda* ought to be taken into account because Caxton made the decision that these books should be printed and published, even though he farmed out the actual printing to someone else. Inevitably there are books for which it will be more difficult to decide how far Caxton's involvement extended. Thus if one wished to refute Gibbon's claim that Caxton had published no classical or humanist texts, one might point to three works in particular: the *Nova rhetorica* and its *Epitome* by Lorenzo Guglielmo Traversagni and the *Sex epistolae* or letters sent between Pope Sixtus IV and Venice, provided of course that these works were *published* by Caxton.

The *Nova rhetorica* and the *Epitome* were printed in 1479 and 1480 respectively, and *Sex epistolae* appeared in 1483. The first of these texts is of particular interest for it has now been shown that it was set up from Vatican Library MS Latin 11441: the compositor's marks are clearly visible and correspond to the pages in the printed edition. This manuscript was Traversagni's personal copy. Traversagni was an Italian who had come to England to teach rhetoric and had established himself in Cambridge. That Traversagni should have known there was a printer working in Westminster is more probable than that Caxton should have known there was an Italian rhetorician teaching in Cambridge who had written a new book. The *Nova rhetorica* would itself be used as a text book, and it is likely that its author, a teacher, would want to provide his pupils with copies. Since the copytext was his personal copy, the conclusion seems inescapable that it was Traversagni who asked Caxton to print the text. Whether Traversagni or some of his friends in Cambridge distributed the text and so acted as publishers is less easy to determine, though it is quite probable. In other words for this text we may assume Caxton was acting more in the role of printer than of publisher. The *Epitome* was not set up from Latin 11441, though a copy of it is in that manuscript. Traversagni left England after *Nova rhetorica* was printed and before *Epitome* went to press. He may well have allowed a copy of the *Epitome* to be made from his own manuscript to act as the printer's copytext. Again we should probably conclude that Caxton's part in the edition was that of printer. This text, like *Nova rhetorica*, was probably going to be distributed in Cambridge and other university towns where Traversagni taught. Their distribution is likely to have been in the hands of the author and his friends, who to that extent were acting as publishers. *Sex epistolae* contains letters between Sixtus IV and Venice, and since few Englishmen were likely to be very interested in the subject matter the interest of the edition probably lay in its style. Presumably the edition was used as a teaching aid to provide models of epistolary rhetoric. In the colophon to the edition it is stated that the letters were *diligenter emendate* by Pietro Carmeliano, another Italian who had come to teach in England though he had settled in Oxford. This phrase can only mean that Carmeliano corrected the proofs of the letters as they were going through the press, and therefore he had some special interest in the edition. Presumably his interest sprang from the fact that he had asked Caxton to print the volume and may also have contributed financially to the printing. He may also have distributed the printed copies. For this text as well Caxton probably acted as printer rather than as publisher. Consequently it is insufficient to work from a list of books attributed to the printer Caxton by bibliographers if we want to consider his work as a publisher. As we have seen the three books which have the best reason to be labelled as humanist texts among his printed editions were probably not chosen by him and he may not even have published or distributed them. Caxton the printer needed a constant flow of material to keep his presses busy; if he had no material of his own, he would have to take work in from outside. But the financial dictates of the printing business should not influence our understanding of what was going on in the publishing business.

On the other hand, Caxton dedicated many of his books to patrons, who in some cases had asked (according to Caxton) for the work in question to be printed. This point has been seized on by defenders of Caxton. Gibbon and the eighteenth century attacked him for the trivial nature of the books he published. But Caxton the man was excused because he was, in Gibbon's words, "reduced to comply with the vicious taste of his readers". Many have followed this lead to suggest that he had to print what members of the aristocracy demanded. If this were so, it would reduce his role as publisher since the choice of texts would be taken out of his hands and even his financial involvement may have been reduced. It should be emphasised that this defence accepts that the books were bad ones; it simply shifts the blame for publishing them on to different should-ers. However, the most recent scholarship has tended to increase the part played by Caxton in the choice of these texts at the expense of his patrons.

This may seem a surprising trend for there is much to support the general idea of patronage and specifically in England. Patronage seems to have been an important feature in early printing and there is frequent reference to patrons of early printers in almost all countries. Literature, especially poetry, is associated with the court in the period immediately before and during the first age of print-ing, and court poetry is often a patronised poetry. In English this is apparently substantiated by such facts as the picture of Chaucer reading his poetry to the assembled court in Corpus College Christi Cambridge MS 61 of *Troilus and Criseyde*. Lydgate also mentions many aristocrats who had commissioned poems from him. The patronage of printers would follow on naturally from the patron-age of poets, and there are presentation pictures of books (printed or manus-cript) being offered to patrons. In Caxton studies the most famous is the woodcut in the Huntington copy of *History of Troy* showing the presentation of the volume to Margaret of Burgundy. A manuscript copy of the printed version of *Dicts or Sayings* in Lambeth Palace Library MS 265 contains a frontispiece illustrating the presentation of the book to Edward IV. Caxton for his part frequently refers to his patrons and claims that they had requested individual volumes. Finally, he was employed on diplomatic missions by the crown and it is thought he may have been in more permanent employment with Margaret of Burgundy. If this were so, it is natural to assume that his employers were his patrons as well.

These arguments are, however, far from conclusive. That many early prin-ters had patrons is hardly surprising since they were artisans who lacked finan-cial expertise and often had little literary sophistication. Caxton was a different kind of person – a publisher rather than a printer, a merchant rather than an artisan. He did not work in the printing shop himself; he employed others to do it. The role which patrons played for other early printers was filled by Caxton himself. He had the capital and literary knowledge to direct a publishing house; and it was others who did the work of printing. How far the poetry of the hundred years before Caxton was a court poetry is difficult to decide for England. For example, Chaucer did not dedicate any of his poems to a member of the aristocracy, though one might assume the *Book of the Duchess* was written for John of Gaunt since it is a consolatory poem for the death of his wife Blanche. The picture in Corpus MS 61 dates from after Chaucer's death and is based on iconographical models depicting preachers; it may therefore have little basis in reality. Although Lydgate mentions patrons in his works, he was not a courtier since he was a monk at the Abbey of Bury St Edmunds. What the relation between Lydgate and these patrons was is difficult to decide, though we have been too quick to decide that it was the patrons who took the initiative in deciding what poem Lydgate should write. Since many of his poems were translations from Latin and French, and since Lydgate is more likely to have had access to the originals than his patrons, the primary impetus for the translations is likely to have come from the poet. That Caxton acted for the crown in various negotiations is no more proof that he was employed permanently by the crown than it would be today if a university professor, for example, served on a government commission. Caxton was employed, just as a professor would be employed, on a temporary basis because of the particular expertise he had. It has, however, been frequently claimed that he was in the employment of Margaret of Burgundy and went to Cologne on her behalf to acquire a printing press. The reasons given for this are that in the prologue to the *History of Troy* he described himself as her 'servant', he said he has often received a fee from her, and she had commanded him to complete the translation which he had put aside when it was barely started. In the fifteenth century the word 'servant' was used by the member of one class to express deference to a member of a higher class and does not signify an employer-employee relationship. It was still used like this till the nineteenth century, and even today this usage is reflected in those letters which end 'Your obedient servant'. Caxton used the word to express his deference to several 'patrons', and no one has dared to claim he was an employee of all these other people. The fee is equally without value as evidence. Caxton received fees from other patrons. A fee was a payment for services rendered, although it could also be given to those who occupied influential positions as a mark of favour. Caxton had been Governor of the English Nation, in which position he had received many fees, and it is likely that the Duchess of Burgundy would wish to show particular favours to a countryman in such an important job. In addition, the duchess dabbled in the overseas trade herself and she is likely to have sought advice about her financial ventures from such people as Caxton. A fee would be a natural reward for such advice, though it need not have been paid in cash. The fee he received from the Earl of Arundel consisted of a buck in summer and a doe in winter. Although it is true that he said Margaret had ordered him to complete the translation, she clearly knew nothing about the project at its inception. Caxton started to translate the text in 1469 and then put it to one side for two years after completing a few quires. If he showed the incomplete translation to Margaret, it can have been only in 1471. Margaret can have had nothing to do with the choice of text, or presumably, with the underlying project of setting the finished translation up in type. This point, however, needs to be considered in relation to why Caxton wrote his prologues and what he included in them.

Not all of Caxton's editions have a prologue or epilogue. All his translations from the French contain one, as does his edition of Malory's *Morte Darthur* which had been written only fifteen years before it was printed. In addition some reprints, such as the second edition of the *Canterbury Tales*, contain a prologue. A few other texts also have one. From this it seems likely that a prologue or epilogue was included when a text was less well known or where it might be in competition with another text such as the first edition. The inclusion of a prologue or epilogue was designed, in part at least, to introduce a new text or new edition to the potential purchasers to encourage them to buy it. It is likely that the use of the names of patrons was designed to accomplish this end. However, individual patrons are not named in all prologues. In addition to the prologues or epilogues which name individual patrons, there are those which refer to anonymous patrons. These latter may be generalised in such references as 'diverce gentlemen' or 'all noble ladies and gentlemen' or they may be specific as the 'noble lady' who is referred to as the patron of the *Knight of the Tower* (1484). These types of reference are not mutually exclusive. The *History of Troy* was completed at the request of Margaret of Burgundy, though in the epilogue Caxton wrote that he had asked for copies by *dyverce gentilmen* (p.100).[3] The *Order of Chivalry* (c.1484) had been requested by an anonymous *gentyl and noble esquyer* (p.126) who provided Caxton with the French original to translate, though the edition is presented to Richard III. Malory's *Morte Darthur* (1485) was printed after a *copye unto me delyverd* (p.108-9), but the book was presented *unto alle noble prynces, lordes and ladyes, gentylmen or gentylwymmen* (p.109). This mixing of categories is significant, for it suggests that in trying to increase the appeal of his editions Caxton felt a single patron (whether named or not) was insufficient. It was important for him to make as general an appeal as possible; the patrons were only part of a wider policy. He was using them to sell his books. This does not necessarily mean that what he wrote about his patrons was fictitious, though it should alert us to that possibility.

Let us consider the *Game of Chess*. This text was translated from French by Caxton and printed twice: once in Bruges on 31 March 1474 and once in West-

---

[3] References in brackets after quotations from the prologues and epilogues are to N.F. Blake, *Caxton's Own Prose* (London, 1973).

minster about 1483. The second edition contains woodcuts, but is otherwise reprinted from the first. Both editions contain a prologue, though each one is different. The prologue to the first edition commences with an elaborate dedication to George Duke of Clarence by his *most humble servant* (p.85), William Caxton. Clarence is devoted to promoting English interests and therefore Caxton has translated a book which came into his hands recently. "Whiche booke, right puyssant and redoubtid Lord, I have made in the name and under the shadewe of your noble protection not presumyng to correcte or enpoigne onythynge ayenst your noblesse" (p.85). Caxton asks Clarence not to scorn this book from his *humble and unknowen servant* (p.85). Evidently it was Caxton who had chosen the book which he had published without Clarence knowing anything of it. What is more Caxton was unknown to Clarence, who presumably knew nothing of the edition until he received a copy. Caxton had chosen an English nobleman to act as dedicatee and patron of his edition without that person's knowledge or even his acquaintance. He was quite prepared to exploit other people's positions for his own commercial ends. Presumably he thought the introduction of any noble name would help to make his edition better known.

Clarence was the brother of Margaret of Burgundy and of Edward IV, and it was doubtless for this reason he was chosen. However, after the first edition was printed Clarence was beheaded for treason in 1478, and so his name became a liability. When Caxton issued the second edition of *Game of Chess*, he composed a completely new prologue. In this second prologue he extols all writing as moral, and among the moral books available there was one written by a Hospitaller of St John's in France. Caxton then adds that he had come across a copy of this book when he was living in Bruges and he had decided to translate it into English. The translation had been printed and then sold. Because it contains such wholesome wisdom he has reprinted it, including in the reprint pictures of the people who appear in the game of chess. He concludes by asking the reader for his indulgence as regards the translation. There is no patron to this edition, which is recommended because of its moral value and of its woodcut illustrations. These two attributes perform the same function as Clarence's name. Caxton was evidently sensitive to local developments and wrote his prologues with care and attention. He may have felt another patron's name would not be apposite at this time, and so relied on more general recommendations. He was prepared to use a name and to drop it again as circumstances warranted. The second prologue contains genuine information which could have been used earlier, whereas the first edition has a prologue which is pure propaganda. The patron had nothing to do with the book and his name was introduced to increase the book's sales. Caxton was quite unscrupulous in his use of such names. He alone was responsible for the edition.

By the same token when he refers to anonymous patrons it seems likely that he was often inventing little stories to make his edition more attractive. When the second edition of the *Canterbury Tales* was printed he claimed he had been asked by an unnamed gentleman to print a better text from a manuscript in his father's possession. This was probably a way of suggesting that those who had bought the first edition should also buy the second since it had a better text, and that was a more important recommendation than a noble name would have been since the second edition was in direct competition with the first. Similarly when Caxton refers directly to a named patron, we cannot always trust his word that the patron had asked for the edition. In the prologue to *Charles the Great* (1485) he wrote "for to satisfye the desyre and requeste of my good synguler lordes and specyal maysters and frendis, I have enprysed and concluded in myself to reduce this sayd bood into our Englysshe" (p.67). Yet in the epilogue he wrote "I Wylliam Caxton was desyred and requyred by a good and synguler frende of myn, Maister Wylliam Daubeney, ... to reduce al these sayd hystoryes into our Englysshe tongue" (p.68). Here we have two contradictory statements: one that Caxton decided to make the translation, and the other that he was asked by Daubeney to do so. Perhaps we may assume that Caxton actually hit upon the text and decided to translate it, and then at some state he asked Daubeney to be its patron, or perhaps just as likely, he used Daubeney's name without permission. The introduction of a patron's name is no evidence that the patron took any initiative in getting a text into print or even that he knew anything about it. We must be cautious in accepting anything that Caxton wrote in these prologues and epilogues as genuine. He needed names to recommend his books, but that does not imply that the patrons had formally given permission for their names to be used or even that they knew their names were being used in this way. It is only when fairly precise details of the commission are given, as in the case of his formal audience with Henry VII to receive a commission to translate *Feats of Arms*, that we may give credence to what he writes.

If we return to the *History of Troy* I think we might reasonably conclude that Margaret's part in it was much less than is at first implied. Caxton thought of the translation, completed it, acquired a press, and printed the finished translation. Margaret may at best have encouraged him in his venture and she may have made recommendations as to his style. The volume was dedicated to her, but her involvement was otherwise very limited. If the humanist texts were commissioned and perhaps published by others, the translations from French were very much Caxton's own initiative. He is responsible for their choice and marketing.

This conclusion leads naturally to a consideration of whether in his publishing policy which these translations from French represent Caxton was trying to promote Burgundian culture in England. Ever since Huizinga's *The Waning of the Middle Ages* we have been fascinated by Burgundian culture and sensible of its influence elsewhere. More recent studies have built on his foundations to fill in the debt that England owed to Burgundy. It was natural therefore that it should be supposed that Caxton himself shared with his countrymen a respect for Burgundian literary and chivalric taste. His association with Margaret of Burgundy and his translation of books by secretaries to the dukes were taken as proof of this thesis. Furthermore, the contents of the Burgundian ducal library were catalogued on the deaths of each duke, and two of these catalogues from the fifteenth century have survived and been printed. It was therefore relatively easy to compare Caxton's output with the contents of that library. One important feature of the ducal library was that the majority of its holdings were in French rather than Latin; it was a vernacular library devoted to didactic and romance works rather than a scholarly library devoted to scholastic learning and intellectual dispute. The duke's secretaries made translations of Latin works for them. It was one of these that Caxton began translating in 1469, his first attempt at translation.

That Caxton should have made translations from French does not in itself prove that he was directly influenced by Burgundian taste as represented in the ducal library. Now that his link with Margaret has been shown to be rather tenuous, his knowledge of its contents would have been limited. He may have known scriveners like Colard Mansion who produced de luxe manuscripts for the library, including those of texts made by the ducal secretaries, but this would provide him with a restricted idea of the contents. Furthermore, some studies have revealed that many of the books Caxton translated were also found in many other libraries in the Low Countries, and it is equally true that others were not to be found in the ducal library at all if we can trust the extant inventories. While Caxton was in Bruges it was natural that he should translate texts that were readily accessible there and which had recently become available. Translations by Raoul Lefèvre fall into this category, and his position as ducal secretary can only have increased the attraction of the works he translated. Yet when Caxton returned to England, he did not continue to produce works which had a close connection with Burgundy. He was on the look out for works in

French that had recently appeared. Since the majority of works in French appeared in France, it is naturally to France that he looked to satisfy his demand. Many vernacular texts were printed in Lyons and the trade links between England and France were so well developed that books printed there could be published in an English translation within a couple of years. Lyons editions lie behind Caxton's versions of *Paris and Vienne* (Westminster 1485, Lyons 1480), *Four Sons of Aymon* (Westminster c.1489, Lyons 1480), and *Eneydos* (Westminster c.1490, Lyons 1488). This may also apply to other texts like *Book of Good Manners*, *Doctrinal of Sapience* and *Feats of Arms*. From this it would seem as though he chose French texts which were readily available rather than those which had a particular link with Burgundy. Furthermore when he returned to England he did not continue referring to Burgundian ideas or people in his prologues and epilogues. *History of Troy* is dedicated to Margaret of Burgundy, and *Jason* which is a continuation of it and which appeared shortly after his return to England refers to Duke Philip's castle at Hesdin, though the book is dedicated to the Prince of Wales. References to France and French people are frequent in the later books, usually because they are translations of books written there. For example, the *Royal Book* refers to Philip the Bold, King of France, for whom the French original had been written. Finally, we may note that even in his prologue to *History of Troy*, which might be considered a Burgundian text, he mentions that he was not sophisticated because he had never been to France. It was France that was the true home of French language and culture.

If Caxton was not directly motivated by the wish to introduce Burgundian texts to his English readers, what were the principles he was following? Where did he get his inspiration? Undoubtedly he did look for foreign texts to translate into English and for the most part these were French texts because they were among the foreign texts most readily accessible in England. Yet in acting thus Caxton was not behaving very differently from his predecessors in English cultural life. We have ignored the continuity that exists between the manuscript culture of the fifteenth century and the incunable period. After all many of the texts Caxton translated had been available in earlier translations. The *Royal Book* was available in six pre-Caxton English translations, though clearly many of them had only a local circulation since these earlier translations were unknown to him. The *Knight of the Tower* is the second translation of this work into English; the first one, made at the beginning of the fifteenth century, is now considered not to have been used by Caxton. However, for his translation of the *Golden Legend* Caxton used the Latin and French versions as well as the earlier English translation, now referred to as *Gilte Legende* to distinguish it from his own translation. Caxton also knew that translations had been a staple part of literary life in England before his time, for he refers to many translators and translations. It is probable that he knew many more than those he mentioned, for he tends to refer only to courtly translations by name. Among earlier translations he printed one may pick out Chaucer's version of Boethius's *De consolatione*. Since he praised Chaucer so highly as a stylist, he must have approved of translation in general and this translation in particular. Lydgate made a poetic version of the Troy story, which Caxton describes in his *History of Troy* as a translation. Here is another famous poet making a translation. In his prologue to the *Polychronicon* he refers to John Trevisa, chaplain to Thomas Lord Berkeley, who translated (according to Caxton) the Bible, *De proprietatibus rerum* and *Polychronicon* into English. Caxton printed Cicero's *De amicitia* translated by John Tiptoft Earl of Worcester and his *De senectute* in a translation made for Sir John Fastolf of Norfolk, though he does not give the name of the translator. It does not follow, of course, that Caxton knew of the existence of all these translations before he commenced his own first translation in 1469, though it is likely that he knew of some of them such as Lydgate's *Troy-Book* which is referred to in that work. English literary life in the Middle Ages thrived on translation, and there had been a great spate of translation from French since at least the early fourteenth century. These translations were made by nobles and great poets as well as by obscure clerics. For the most part they consisted of romances, in poetry or prose, and of moral and didactic tracts, usually in prose. There was a well developed literary tradition with which Caxton was surely familiar, since his choice of material to translate is similar to that which was being translated by others in the fifteenth century. If he differs from his predecessors it is only in having greater access to French originals through his links with the Continental booktrade. Translation is only one aspect of English literary life; the other is the composition of courtly poetry by Chaucer, Gower and Lydgate. If we accept that Caxton was responding to the English tradition in his publishing policy, there is no need to question why he published both English poetry and translations of French prose works.

It is evident that Caxton knew quite a lot about the literary scene in England. Equally he seems to have had connections with scribes and booksellers. He imported many books and manuscripts which he must have passed on to others. More important perhaps are his links with the producers of Malory's *Morte Darthur*. Only one manuscript of this work survives. It was discovered at Winchester in 1934 and is now British Library MS Additional 59678; its date is uncertain. Malory completed his work in 1469/70 and Caxton printed it in 1485.

Editors of the text have claimed, convincingly I feel, that Caxton's edition was not set up from Additional 59678, but from a manuscript which is no longer extant. However, it has recently been shown that Additional 59678 was in Caxton's workshop because it contains offsets of Caxton's type on some folios. It may have been in the workshop form about 1480 until 1489, which of course covers the time when Caxton printed his version of *Morte Darthur*. It has usually been argued that Additional 59678 and Caxton's copytext were closely related copies of the same original. In other words it is posited that there were at least three manuscripts of this work, the original, Caxton's copytext and Additional 59678; and now it might be claimed that of those three at least two were in Caxton's workshop at the same time. Why this should be so we cannot tell, though it has been accepted for some time that Caxton ran a bookshop as well as a publishing business. It is possible, therefore, that Caxton had an association with the scriptorium that produced two copies of the *Morte Darthur* – a sign that he had very close links with other providers of fashionable reading matter. Such links would provide him with material to print as well as giving him some insight into the sort of material which it would be worth his while to translate.

These conclusions have an important bearing on the question of patronage and on the sort of man Caxton was. Here was a man who ran a printing and publishing business as well as a bookshop. He imported books and disposed of these as well as his own output. He had links with other producers of literature and could acquire manuscripts produced in England, though he cannot have known all that was being produced on literature. He was familiar with the main lines of literary development in England and he directed his business in a traditional way, that is he produced English courtly literature and translations of romances or moral and didactic texts just as many before him had done. He had a publishing policy and he was uniquely placed to chart literary developments in England and abroad. It would therefore be natural to suppose that it was Caxton who was responsible for the choice of texts coming off his press rather than the nobles or merchants who are mentioned in them. The continuity in his choice of books can be explained only on the basis of a single controlling mind; it is not reasonable to assume that he was responding to the whims of many various patrons.

There is also the question of the sort of man Caxton was. The important features of his career are his period as a merchant, his success as a printer, and his knowledge of the publishing business. For many years he was thought to have been a kind of hack who responded to the poor taste of his patrons and initiated little himself. Then it was proposed he was a scholar. Neither of these views now seems tenable. There is nothing to support the idea that he took an academic interest in the texts he printed and we have just seen that patronage was part of the method of book promotion and had little to do with the publishing policy. It has also been suggested that he was a political person who entered into publishing in order to promote particular political views. This also seems unlikely, although it is true that he moved on the fringes of political circles for many years and had considerable diplomatic experience. It is difficult to see what political message is encapsulated in his prologues and epilogues or even in the actual books he printed which fall in so easily with what was being read in the fifteenth century. Political advocacy demands a little more clarity than is found in his books. It still seems most acceptable to regard Caxton as a merchant, as a man that was interested in buying and selling. Early in his life he dealt in many goods, but later in his life he confined his entrepreneurial activities to books and manuscripts. He probably acquired a press because it enabled him to control the means of production and so to impose his own policy on the material he sold. It was his mercantile experience that enabled him to survive both by planning a policy in his buying and selling operations and by obtaining the necessary credit and loans. Naturally a rich man who had control of one means of communication might well have been drawn into political and other activities, but these should be regarded as secondary to the main purpose of his life and work.

Naturally over the recent past research has also been carried out into the typographical aspects of Caxton's production, and important new discoveries have been made in dating and related matters. Yet these discoveries have followed traditional paths of investigation and perhaps hold less interest in methodology to the delegates at this conference. What is important about Caxton's career is what it can tell us about the relation between producer and buyer, about the processes involved in the choice of texts – in a word about those details which we today associate with publishing rather than with printing. But discussion about publishing is always bedevilled by the presentation of the extant material in a manner which suits the bibliographer, who catalogues the actual books. Yet it is in the publishing aspects of incunables that the greatest controversies are likely to continue.

2

William Caxton: The Man and his Work

THE quincentenary of printing in England is a fitting occasion in the scholarship of Caxton's life and work to look back as well as forward, and that is what I propose to do in this paper. Scholarly investigation of Caxton and his influence started only with William Blades's magisterial study.[1] What I should like to consider is whether from Blades's time to our own we have reached any firm conclusions about the man and his work, what have been the pitfalls in outlook that we should seek to avoid from now on, and in what directions future research is likely to proceed most profitably.

It is important to remember that as a man Caxton has aroused little interest among historians. His work has never been studied in depth by an historian and his interest for them is that of a minor influence in the cultural scene. This lack of interest is partly because he played such a small part in the economic and intellectual life of the country and partly because there has been a natural antipathy towards biographical enquiry of people of his rank in the enquiry into wider social, constitutional and political issues. It may also be that Gibbon's uncomplimentary remarks about his production have reduced his importance in their eyes.[2] This vacuum left by the historians has been filled by bibliographers, men of letters and literary historians, few of whom have the necessary expertise in sifting through the historical documentation. Not unnaturally the result has been a tendency towards romanticising Caxton and his life, for often a complete biography has seemed more attractive than a survey of possible hypotheses. Hence the records have become the basis for fanciful elaboration. Unfortunately one scholar's suggestion has become the next's fact. A good example of this is Caxton's reference to his being the 'servant' of Margaret of Burgundy. Until it was pointed out that this word was used in a literary and not a literal sense, biographers had a field day deciding what job Caxton occupied in Margaret's household. The two most favoured were secretary and librarian; often he occupied both positions. What started out as suggestions soon became accepted as part of Caxton's biography. It never occurred to the biographers to question whether in view of his earlier career he would be a suitable choice for either position, or whether it

---

[1] *The Life and Typography of William Caxton*, 2 vols. (London, 1861–3).
[2] For a summary of earlier scholarship about Caxton see N. F. Blake, *Caxton and his World* (London, 1969), pp. 194–216. References to matters discussed in that book and alluded to here are not given in this paper.

was normal for merchants to be employed as secretaries or librarians by members of the aristocracy. But then to many Caxton has always appeared to be a special case for whom the normal historical parallels were inapplicable. Indeed, it could be claimed that one of the major advances in Caxton scholarship has been the realization that his life and work were not as extraordinary as was formerly thought.

SOURCES FOR CAXTON'S LIFE

The types of evidence available for the study of Caxton's life have influenced the way scholars have tried to reconstruct it. In his biography Blades used three sources: contemporary records, remarks made by Caxton himself in his own writings, and later documentary evidence which was held to apply also to the time at which Caxton lived. The third type, which Blades himself used sparingly, is now discounted because our knowledge of the fifteenth century is much greater and it has revealed that conditions then differed considerably from those at a later date. Even where there are gaps in our knowledge it is dangerous to fill them from evidence culled from later periods. The other two types of evidence are still the major sources for Caxton's biography, but even today we fail to realize sufficiently clearly their differing nature and importance. One aspect of this twofold nature of the sources is that most of the documentary records come from the period before 1473 and refer to Caxton's life as a merchant, whereas naturally his own writings start only in 1473 though they may refer to events which occurred before then. His own writings concentrate on books and patronage. This division is illustrated by Crotch's volume for the Early English Text Society. Ostensibly an edition of Caxton's prologues and epilogues, this volume contains a biography of Caxton which is followed by transcripts of all the documentary sources – and these form a quite separate section of the book from Caxton's own writings.[1] The difference in the nature of the two types of source and the fact that one type is early and the other late encouraged earlier scholars to think that Caxton's life fell into two quite distinct halves. There was Caxton the merchant before and Caxton the scholar-printer after 1473. It has been increasingly appreciated that this division is a false one encouraged by the dual nature of the sources. The discovery, for example, of Caxton's name in the Port of London accounts after he settled in Westminster has enabled us to grasp that Caxton continued to act as a merchant after he began to print.[2] The realization that there is no sharp break in his career has important implications for both periods of his life – and we shall return to this in a moment.

[1] W. J. B. Crotch, *The Prologues and Epilogues of William Caxton*, E.E.T.S., o.s. 176 (London, 1928). The sources are printed on pp. cxxxiii–clxiii as an appendix to the life. This book remains the primary edition of the documentary sources.

[2] See N. J. M. Kerling, 'Caxton and the Trade in Printed Books', *Book Collector*, iv (1955), 190–9.

DOCUMENTARY EVIDENCE

The two sources are very different in kind and produce quite different answers. The documentary evidence from contemporary records refers to his life as a merchant and public official. As an important merchant and later as governor of the English Nation at Bruges he had contact with local officials and corporations, by and for whom records are kept. Public bodies have to keep a record of their expenses and negotiations. This is quite different from Caxton's later life for in his work as a printer and publisher he had little impact on those who keep accounts or records. The rent paid for his premises is naturally recorded, but individuals would not record that they had bought a book or even, in the days before diaries were common, that they had had interesting conversations on literature. The documentary records are factual and prosaic, and their exact significance is often difficult to gauge. They can only be studied against the background in which they were written; and this means studying similar documents of the same time to understand the purpose and vocabulary of the records. It is wrong to extract information from them out of context.

Thus early biographers assumed that because 1438 was the date in the Warden's Account Book of the Mercers' Company where the fee for his enrolment as an apprentice was recorded, that Caxton became an apprentice in the company in that year. However, a close study of the Account Book revealed that the accounts merely recorded when the money *was* paid, and not when it *should have been* paid.[1] Many of the records in which Caxton's name appears have still to be investigated and correctly interpreted. Typical of these records is the pardon issued to Caxton in the name of Edward IV in 1472 by which all his crimes were forgiven. Until a thorough analysis of all the pardons issued at this time is made we shall remain uncertain as to the true significance of this document: whether it is merely a standard pardon issued as a kind of safeguard or whether it implies something more important.

Other documents are now ripe for study in depth: although the various accounts of the officers at Westminster Abbey have been known and published, it is not clear even today what their exact relationship to one another was. What parts of the Abbey were in the domain of which officers? Is there any significance in the different words used for the premises Caxton rented, such as *shopa, tenementum* etc? Where are the various places located? Who were the other tenants and do they give us any indication as to the nature of the businesses carried on there? Answers to questions such as these might enable us to draw more definite conclusions as to why Caxton settled in Westminster Abbey, to what extent he was still a merchant, and how the printing and publishing were organized.

[1] N. F. Blake, 'Some Observations on William Caxton and the Mercers' Company', below, pp. 37-49.

It is necessary to understand the limitation of this type of contemporary record. In the first place it is not always easy to decide whether some of the early documents do in fact refer to the mercer and future printer. Caxton is a common surname and William an even more familiar Christian name. We have in the past been too ready to assume that any document which mentioned a William Caxton referred to the future printer. It is only when a document mentions that William Caxton was a mercer or even governor of the English at Bruges that we are on firm ground, for we have no records of other mercers of that name. In the second place as documents are mostly official they can tell us only of public events. They can be understood only against the historical background of the time, and so they naturally tend to create the picture of a conventional merchant rather than that of an individual. The discovery of more documents from his early life might enable us to say that he was in a particular place at a particular time, but would not add to our understanding of the man himself and what led him to develop his interests in the way he did. The parallels of Chaucer's and Malory's lives are worth pointing out. We have a great number of documents concerning Chaucer which give us a fairly full picture of his 'official' life; but the more we study them the less we seem to understand the poet.[1] The documents concerning the life of Thomas Malory of Newbold Revell are so unlike the ethos of *Le Morte d'Arthur* that some biographers have felt obliged to look for a different Malory whose life would harmonize more with the book.[2] Indeed the pursuit of biography may be the wrong approach for medieval writers since in medieval literature there is no cult of the individual.[3] The study of official records is likely to tell us more about the general background than about the individual – more about buying and selling in Caxton's case and about the Civil Service in Chaucer's than about either's attitude to life or to literature. Because the records are such we cannot assume that Caxton only became interested in books in 1469 when he began his translation of the *Recuyell of the Histories of Troy* any more than Chaucer only became interested in writing about 1370.

CAXTON'S OWN WRITINGS: A. ADDITIONS TO TRANSLATIONS

Caxton's writings have their own difficulties of interpretation, though their limitations are of a different nature from those associated with the documentary evidence. They may conveniently be divided into two groups: the prologues and the epilogues on the one hand and the

---

[1] See M. M. Crow and C. C. Olson, *Chaucer Life-records* (Oxford; Austin, 1966). The case of the 'rape' of Cecilia Chaumpaigne is one that has created particular problems for Chaucerian biography; see P. R. Watts, 'The Strange Case of Chaucer and Cecilia Chaumpaigne', *Law Quarterly Review* lxiii (1947), 491–515.

[2] See for example W. Matthews, *The Ill-framed Knight* (Berkeley, 1966).

[3] Cf. G. Kane, *The Autobiographical Fallacy in Chaucer and Langland Studies* (London, 1965).

additions made to translations on the other.[1] It is important to remember this distinction for whereas the prologues and epilogues were written in the full glare of publicity which would naturally affect what was included and how, the additions are of a more informal nature. They can hardly have attracted any attention among his contemporaries, partly because their sense of textual variation was not developed and partly because they were unaware of the originals from which the translation was deviating. Although some of the inclusions may have been inserted for literary reasons, such as the complaint about the state of England in the *Game of Chess*, they are in general likely to be more accurate than the prologues and epilogues because they are less premeditated. They refer back to Caxton's earlier life and are normally fairly factual. Even so the information they provide can be important. Sister Mary Jeremy has shown that a careful reading of his *Golden Legend* can produce many examples of additions by Caxton. In one of them he mentions he had been to Cologne. This discovery was made after the publication of the evidence in the Cologne Register of Aliens and so it aroused little attention.[2] But if one reflects about the arguments that raged over whether Caxton had learned printing in that city or not, one realizes the importance of such details. Thus Blades, who rejected the Cologne theory which in his opinion was based only on the 'statement of Wynken de Worde, unsupported by any corroborative evidence', might have felt his remark to be injudicious if he had known that Caxton had been to Cologne.[3] While Caxton does not say in the *Golden Legend* when or for what purpose he was there, the knowledge that he had been there would have transformed earlier argument about his learning to print – and the information was readily available. Unfortunately collections of Caxton's prologues and epilogues too readily give the impression that we now have all that he wrote about himself. But many of Caxton's works remain to be made available in modern editions; and it will only be in such editions where his translation is compared with its source that these references will come to light. Even the *Golden Legend* is in this state, and since Sister Mary did not manage to find all the additions made by Caxton, it is possible that this text itself still has much to reveal. Too much attention has been focused on the prologues and epilogues, the most frequently edited of his writings; we can easily forget that his translations also contain his reminiscences embedded in them. It may well be that future advances in Caxton's biography will come from the humdrum work of editing.

---

[1] Now edited in N. F. Blake, *Caxton's Own Prose* (London, 1973).

[2] Sister Mary Jeremy, 'Caxton's Original Additions to the *Legenda Aurea*', *Modern Language Notes*, lxiv (1949), 259–61. The Cologne material was published in H. Thomas, *Wilh. Caxton uyss Engelant* (Cologne, 1928).

[3] Blades, *Caxton*, i, 57.

B. PROLOGUES AND EPILOGUES

Because the prologues and epilogues were designed to publicize the works in which they are included, they tend to be topical. The relatively few references to his early life are chiefly introduced for particular literary effects. In order to make use of them biographically one needs not only to appreciate the literary theme being exploited, but also the implications of the language used. Caxton's reference to his being born in Kent in his prologue to the *Histories of Troy* is a case in point. This reference has always been taken at its face value and biographers have scoured Kent and Kentish records for a potential birthplace for him and a home for his parents. But he introduced the reference to Kent together with that to his thirty-year stay abroad as part of the writer's humility formula by which he throws his attainments into the worst possible light in order that the reader's indulgence could be won over. A study of contemporary literature indicates that to be born in Kent was regarded in the fifteenth century as the brand of a non-standard speaker. This raises the question whether 'to be born in Kent' had become a proverbial saying which could be used of anyone no matter where he was born – just as we today can send a man to Coventry without his actually going there. There are at this time several examples of people claiming to be born in Kent in a way that can only be taken apologetically. Some of these are fictitious characters and so they cannot help us, but one is an author called Peter Idley who wrote a poem now known as *Instructions to his Son*. In this poem the author writes:

> And thoughe myn Englysshe be symple to your entent,
> Haue me excused – I was born in Kent. (ii, 1425–6.)

The editor of this poem, Professor D'Evelyn, was of the opinion that the reference to Kent was proverbial for she thought that Peter Idley came from an Oxfordshire family and that he was almost certainly born in that county.[1] While I do not think that this example by itself is sufficient to prove that 'to be born in Kent' was a proverbial saying, it certainly makes it possible. We have, therefore, to accept that Caxton may in this instance have been using a proverbial phrase which need not be understood as literally true. For likewise when in the same sentence he writes 'in France was I never' this probably means not that he had never been to any part of the Continent in which French was spoken as a first language, but rather that he had never been to central France where Parisian French was spoken which was the prestige dialect of French. This example shows that a study of the literary and linguistic background, like the study of the documentary background, leads to the abandonment of earlier biographers' certainties about detailed facts in Caxton's life. This is perhaps compensated by a growing awareness of the importance of his life and his place in the fifteenth century.

[1] C. D'Evelyn, *Peter Idley's Instructions to his Son* (Boston and London, 1935), pp. 3–4.

RELATIONSHIP OF BIBLIOGRAPHICAL AND LITERARY CRITERIA

The prologues and epilogues are for the most part devoted to the circumstances surrounding the publication of the various volumes and the printer's attempt to make his books seem desirable to his clients. They have therefore been subjected to extensive scrutiny particularly in relation to three topics: the choice of books to translate and print, whether Caxton led or followed public taste, and his relations with members of the aristocracy. These three themes are so closely interrelated that it is not always easy to keep them apart, and in the rest of this paper I do not pretend to do so. The way our attitudes to these topics have changed has been occasioned by our own training and outlook. Blades was himself a printer and he meticulously catalogued the books printed by Caxton. He knew their typography and was familiar with their make-up. But his interest in the literary background and the more general problems of authorship associated with the fifteenth century was limited, so he tended to the view that Caxton merely printed what his patrons demanded. The implication was that he was subservient to them. Blades rarely looked beyond the particular texts to consider the wider problems of what it meant to be a publisher in the fifteenth century; indeed he hardly considered Caxton to be a publisher. Twentieth-century scholars have been motivated by the desire to vindicate Caxton against Blades' rather disparaging attitude. Many have been literary scholars without that familiarity with Caxton's individual texts which Blades had. They have worked by considering the titles of Caxton's books which they arranged into different categories in order to show why he may have printed the works he did.[1] The implication was that Caxton chose to publish a particular text because it belonged to one of the categories he favoured, such as courtly romance, and that he was therefore much more independent of his patrons and their demands than Blades allowed. The arguments put forward have certain weaknesses. As the categories chosen are both arbitrary and general, such as 'romance' or 'satire', they are more apparent to us than they may have been to the fifteenth-century reader; it is doubtful whether we can attach much weight to them. As such scholars argued about his choice of texts without considering his relations with his patrons, it is difficult to accept some of their conclusions. Finally they completely ignored bibliographical details so that they are sometimes guilty of ignoring important evidence which could materially affect their views.

THE REPRINTING OF THE CANTERBURY TALES

It is important that in future both bibliographical and literary criteria are considered together. Let me give a couple of examples how a con-

---

[1] See particularly H. B. Lathrop, 'The First English Printers and their Patrons', *The Library*, 4th ser. iii, (1922–3), 69–96, and D. B. Sands, 'Caxton as a Literary Critic', *Papers of the Bibliographical Society of America*, li (1957), 312–18.

sideration of a book's make-up may influence our attitude why the text was chosen and what the printer's relationship with his patrons was. The first concerns the reprinting of Chaucer's *Canterbury Tales*. Literary critics have noted that Caxton's editions of Chaucer's works fall into two groups: one about 1477/8 and the other about 1483/4. The *Canterbury Tales* appears in each group, but none of Chaucer's other works is reprinted. Literary historians have been quick to suggest that Caxton was here responding to the popularity of Chaucer's works in the fifteenth century (amply confirmed by the numerous manuscripts) and as the *Canterbury Tales* was the most popular of those poems it was naturally the one to be reprinted. Each edition served as the main item in each of his periods of Chaucerian publication and helped to sell the other poems issued at the same time. It was reasonable therefore to assume that the *Canterbury Tales* was reprinted partly because of its popularity and partly because it was designed to promote the other texts by Chaucer. Unfortunately this straightforward argument runs up against the claim made by Caxton in his prologue that he was asked to print the second edition by a gentleman who was distressed by the textual inaccuracy of the first. The text of the second edition is in many respects inferior to that of the first, though Caxton did introduce a certain number of textual modifications. One of the biggest differences between the editions, though, is that the second has woodcuts, a feature of this edition's make-up which is ignored by literary critics.

EARLY WOODCUTS IN CAXTON'S WORKS

Here it is necessary to review the use of woodcuts in Caxton's printed books. He started to use them in 1481; all previous books are without illustration. It is not certain whether the third edition of Benedict Burgh's poem *Cato*[1] or Caxton's own translation of the *Mirror of the World* was the first book to contain woodcuts. The former contains only two; the latter contains a whole series including the two found in *Cato*. This series is based on the manuscript illuminations in British Library MS. Royal. 19.A.ix., although the two *Cato* woodcuts are not copied from it. It is certain that the same artist made the cuts in both books, and it is likely that whereas he copied those for the *Mirror of the World* direct from the manuscript, he based those for *Cato* indirectly upon it. Both works were probably printed in 1481 and which came first is unimportant for our purpose. The important consideration is Caxton now realized that illustrations could help to sell his books. But the use of woodcuts imposed certain limitations upon the choice of books he could print. The English artists that he employed did not read the texts they were to illustrate and then create pictures out of their imaginative reaction to those texts. They may indeed never have read the texts.

---

[1] The first two editions are without illustrations. The first edition has recently been edited: F. Kuriyagawa, *Paruus Cato Magnus Cato*, Seijo English Monographs, xiii (Tokyo, 1974).

They simply copied or adapted illustrations from other manuscripts or books available. The other texts issued with woodcuts by English artists, *Game of Chess*, *Canterbury Tales*, *Golden Legend* and *Æsop*, are alike in that in their manuscript or printed versions they are more often than not provided with illustrations. On the other hand, a text like *Reynard the Fox* which he printed shortly after the *Mirror of the World* was not illustrated because the Dutch printed book he used had no illustrations. Although French manuscripts of the *Roman de Renart* are often illuminated Caxton was obviously not prepared to go out of his way to find suitable models for his artists.

The dates of the second editions of the *Game of Chess* and *Canterbury Tales* are not included in their respective prologues. The former is dated by bibliographers from 1481 to 1484; the latter is usually attributed to 1484. I have suggested elsewhere that the second edition of the *Canterbury Tales* is better dated to early 1483 or even late 1482, and that it was printed shortly after the *Game of Chess* which is best placed in 1482.[1] These two texts show certain similarities as against the *Golden Legend* and *Aesop*. They both contain woodcuts but no printed paragraph marks or initial capitals which Caxton first used in *Aesop*. They both contain a standard size of woodcut, which is half the size of a folio page; neither has cuts which are larger or smaller than this. The woodcuts are all executed by the same artist though this is not the same man who made the cuts for *Cato* and *Mirror of the World*. This second artist also made the majority of the cuts in the *Golden Legend* and *Aesop*, though both series in these books were completed by different artists. The woodcuts in *Game of Chess* and *Canterbury Tales* are re-used extensively. There are sixteen separate cuts in the former, one of which is used three times and seven others are used twice. In the latter the woodcuts are used in the General Prologue and again for the tales themselves, and several do duty for more than one pilgrim. In view of these similarities it is natural to think that *Canterbury Tales* was printed after *Game of Chess* but before *Golden Legend*, which appeared in November 1483.

The case of the *Game of Chess* is itself quite instructive. Caxton made his translation and printed it in 1474 while he was still in Bruges. It was dedicated to George Duke of Clarence. But Clarence was imprisoned for treason in 1477 and he died in the Tower in the following year. While his name may have added tone to the first edition in 1474, it could clearly not be used for the second about 1482. In fact Caxton scrapped the original prologue and epilogue, thus completely removing Clarence's association with the work. He wrote a new prologue for the second edition. In this he mentioned that he had printed an edition in Bruges and that this printing is the second edition. But this edition is different because it contains illustrations: 'the figures of suche persones as longen to the playe' (the representation of those people who appear

[1] N. F. Blake, *Caxton: England's First Publisher* (London, 1976).

in the game). It could be said that where the first edition had been promoted by a patron's name, the second was promoted by the inclusion of woodcuts. For we must remember that reprints of courtly works like *Game of Chess* were infrequent in Caxton's output precisely because such works rely on their novelty for their sale. The introduction of the woodcuts would make the second edition as novel as the first had been and so encourage people to buy it.

THE PROLOGUE OF THE SECOND EDITION OF
THE CANTERBURY TALES

With this example in mind let us turn to the second edition of *Canterbury Tales*. There is no prologue or epilogue in the first edition and so there is no way of telling exactly why Caxton printed it. The second edition contains a prologue which like that in the second edition of *Game of Chess* after some general remarks about the book and its author goes on to discuss the first edition and the new edition being issued. The following points are the most notable. 1. The first edition was printed six years earlier from an incorrect version which had been brought to him. 2. A gentleman who had bought a copy of this edition complained that it was inaccurate. 3. This gentleman's father had a copy of the poem which was textually sound. 4. If Caxton agreed to issue a reprint this gentleman would try to prevail on his father to lend the printer his copy although he knew that his father was so attached to it that he would be loath to let it out of his hands. 5. The gentleman got the copy from his father and gave it to Caxton who then produced this corrected version.

We have always taken all that Caxton wrote at its face value and so this story has been accepted as genuine. The question is whether we are right to do so. Publishers are not usually regarded as among the most veracious of men – at least as far as their promotional literature is concerned. Let us try to put ourselves in Caxton's position. He was going to reprint *Canterbury Tales* with woodcuts. But he had just reprinted a work which was specifically recommended because of its new illustrations. He could have made the same claim with *Canterbury Tales*, though the novelty value of this claim would be much less when reused – and indeed Caxton rarely recommends different books for identical reasons. *Canterbury Tales* differs from *Game of Chess* in that the former is an English poem by the acknowledged master of English poetry; the latter is simply a translation by Caxton, who following the conventions of the time throws his efforts into the worst possible light. It would therefore be quite possible to recommend *Canterbury Tales* by suggesting that the second edition was textually more accurate than the first since this would redound to Chaucer's fame and the printer's carefulness. Caxton does not give specific details of the superiority of the second edition to the first and it is doubtful whether many of his readers would have been aware of the difference themselves. But if he invented a story in which a gentleman asked for a corrected second edition, Caxton could readily suggest that his clientele, i.e. gentlemen and merchants who wanted to be thought such, ought to be interested in the accuracy of the editions; and therefore they would need to buy the second edition to show their concern for the great poet. As it happens because the second edition has woodcuts which are modelled on what might be called the major tradition of illumination in the manuscripts of the *Canterbury Tales*, it would seem to his clientele to be a more authentic version than the first edition since it *looked* much more like the manuscripts of the poem which were circulating at the time. It was the inclusion of the illustrations rather than the accuracy of the text which would have aroused a contemporary's attention immediately. Caxton's story suggesting improvements in his text would have met a responsive echo in his clients through the inclusion of the woodcuts. After all *Canterbury Tales* was not like the small English poems such as *The Churl and the Bird* which were reprinted almost immediately, no doubt to satisfy a demand which had not been foreseen when the original printing was run off. It was a lengthy poem which was reissued after a six-year gap, and his public had to be convinced that they ought to have a second, improved copy. The implication of this would be that there was no popular demand for another edition; Caxton was himself creating the demand for the new edition.

If we examine Caxton's prologue in detail most of his claims seem at best rather dubious. He says that the first edition was printed from a manuscript which had been brought to him. As far as I am aware no one has ever given this statement much credence. For the first edition was printed shortly after he set up his shop in Westminster, and his remark if true would mean that on his return to England people were coming along with major pieces of work for him to print. Our knowledge of the press suggests that this is unlikely; and if it were true why did he not use it to promote the first edition? A patron at that early date would have been welcome. Yet the suspicious nature of this statement has never encouraged scholars to doubt the rest of the prologue's accuracy. The first edition was sold to various gentlemen, one of whom came to see him. We may note that Caxton uses a phrase like 'diverse gentlemen' in many other prologues when he is indicating the type of people he hoped would buy his work; it is too vague to be reliable. And to name his caller a gentleman seems too general an anonymous description to suggest a real person. His other anonymous patrons are more sharply characterized: a noble lady, who had given birth to many daughters, and an earl. This gentleman complained of the text of Caxton's first edition. Yet he did not own a correct version – only his father did. He must have been the first gentleman to complain about the state of a text in the medieval period, for then both poetry and prose were continually modified during the course of copying. Only authors themselves are known to have worried about the state of their written works – and few of them expressed concern about what was a daily occurrence. Finally the gentleman promised to get the manuscript from his father who would not want to loan it since he loved it so much. Here we can understand why Caxton made the gentleman rather than his father come to him. In this way he can get across two important points: that one gentleman wants to have a correct version printed and that another loves his Chaucer so much that he will not gladly part with it. Who could resist buying the second edition after this build-up?

Our picture of Caxton as honest, hardworking and undevious is so ingrained that many will react in amazement to the suggestion that he invented this story. Indeed it could be argued that in my *Caxton and his World* I provided a good reason why he withheld the gentleman's name; for in that book I suggested that 1483–5 was a period of anonymous patronage for Caxton on account of political conditions: he was obliged to conceal the names of people like Earl Rivers and Elizabeth Woodville as they were either dead or in disgrace.[1] But when I wrote that book I accepted the date customarily provided by bibliographers of Caxton's works for the second edition, namely c.1484, for this date puts it firmly in that troubled period following Edward IV's death on 9 April 1483. This is why the date of this edition is so important and why I spent time showing that it may have been printed early in 1483 or even in 1482. If it was printed in 1483, the early part of the year is the most likely time since we happen to know that many other texts were printed later that year. Clearly if it appeared before 9 April 1483, the political distur-bances after that date could not have been the reason for concealing the gentleman's identity, for Edward's death when it came was sudden. A date for this edition before April 1483 makes it more likely that Caxton's prologue enshrines a publisher's fiction. At least I hope it is clear that it is not sufficient for literary critics to say that *Canterbury Tales* was popular and that Caxton therefore naturally reprinted it. The story is much more complicated than that. The possibility of including woodcuts was an important, perhaps the most important, factor in his decision to reprint. And the care which Caxton gave to the promotion of this second edition shows that there cannot have been (at least in his opinion) a ready market for more copies of the *Canterbury Tales*; potential clients had to be per-suaded that they needed the second edition if they wanted to be con-sidered cultured.

THE KNIGHT OF THE TOWER

The second example which underlines how important it is to keep bibliographical details in mind concerns the *Knight of the Tower*. This book was translated by Caxton from the French. The translation was completed on 1 June 1483. In his prologue Caxton says that the book came into his hands 'by the request and desyre of a noble lady which

[1] Op. cit. pp. 92–5.

hath brought forth many noble and fayr doughters.' She also requested him to translate the work. In the colophon, however, no mention is made of this lady, though Caxton does say there that he finished the translation on 1 June 1483 and printed it on 31 January 1484. This lady has been identified as Elizabeth Woodville and that identification is still in my opinion correct. Consequently in my book *Caxton and his World* I assumed that he had indeed been requested by Elizabeth to make the translation and that the gap between the completion of the translation and its printing was caused by the circumstances following Edward IV's death which led his queen to take sanctuary in Westminster Abbey. It was her desperate condition which led him to allude to her instead of naming her directly. This interpretation seemed to make good sense within the literary and historical framework I suggested; but if we take the bibliographical details into account the position appears to be rather different.

The collation of *Knight of the Tower* is four folios with no signature (though 'ij' appears on the second recto), a–m⁸ n⁶. The initial folios were obviously added after the rest of the book was in print and they contain Caxton's prologue and the table of contents. Without this unsigned opening gathering, the rest of the volume follows the standard practice of the workshop. Indeed if one were to leave out the first gathering, the book would be a typical product of the press beginning on a1ʳ 'Here begynneth the book whiche the knyght of the toure made' and ending on n4ᵛ with the colophon. The colophon would provide all the information one might expect: the name of the translator, the date of translation and printing, and the place of publication. It is difficult to escape the conclusion that the initial gathering was added after the book was complete and that it was an afterthought. This is why there is no reference to the lady in the colophon. No doubt the table of contents was added to the prologue in order to fill out four folio pages instead of the normal eight of a quaternion.

If my interpretation of the collation is correct (and in view of similar features in others of his works I find it difficult to understand it in any other way), the implications are far-reaching. Caxton made the translation of the *Knight of the Tower* entirely on his own initiative and had actually set up the text in print before thinking about its promotion. As chance would have it Elizabeth Woodville had become his neighbour at Westminster Abbey where she was in sanctuary. Since the book consisted of advice by the knight to his daughters, it would be quite appropriate if Elizabeth were made its patron since she had several daughters. Caxton merely took advantage of the situation which presented itself to him and referred to his 'patron' obliquely, but clearly enough for any perceptive reader to know who was meant. When Caxton finished his translation on 1 June 1483, Elizabeth was already in sanctuary and Edward V remained with her till later that month.

His mother was still an important person even if her position was daily becoming more precarious. Her brother Antony was not executed till 25 June, although he had been imprisoned in April. If she had requested the translation, it seems likely that he would have gone on to print it as soon as it was finished, even though the political situation was uncertain; surely he would wish to exploit such an important patron. The reason for the delay in the book's printing was simply that several large volumes like *Confessio Amantis* and *Golden Legend* were waiting to be printed; the *Knight of the Tower* just took its turn in the queue. In this case also we must accept that Caxton was not being entirely truthful in his remarks about the translation, since in the interpretation which I am putting forward Elizabeth could not have asked for the work to be translated as Caxton claimed because she was not aware of the book or its translation until she was in sanctuary at Westminster.

THE WIDER INTERPRETATION OF THESE TWO EXAMPLES

These two cases must stand as examples for the rest of Caxton's output which there is not space to consider here. It may be accepted that often there are reasonable grounds for assuming he was not responding to a patron's request in printing a given volume no matter what he actually writes in his prologue and epilogue. His relations with his patrons were very different from our normal picture of them. His accounts of conversations with members of the aristocracy or with those who came along to request certain books are largely, if not wholly, fictitious. His association with the nobility was distant. Either he had a formal audience at court, as suggested in *Feats of Arms*, or else the nobles communicated their wishes to him through their servants and officers. The dedication or patronage of a book no doubt flattered some, but it can never have been of such importance for them that it called for a personal visit to the press. After all Caxton was only one of the many people who were soliciting for the favours of the powerful. Arundel sent his servant John Stanney to take care of the printer, and Rivers sent his secretary. Only his merchant friends, like William Pratt, remain important as far as suggesting books is concerned; and this is perhaps what we might expect.[1] The choice of books to translate or print and the overall control of the publishing policy were more firmly in Caxton's hands than we previously realized. His was the guiding hand behind every facet of the project, though it is unlikely that he took any practical part in the more technical side of printing. Since he was at all times the presiding genius the question why he as a merchant turned to printing and publishing becomes more pressing. If much of what is included in the prologues and epilogues is fictitious, paradoxically it becomes more interesting precisely because it is more imaginative. The less truthful his accounts are, the more creative he becomes as a writer. He is no longer

[1] See N. F. Blake, *Caxton's Own Prose* (London, 1973), pp. 28–31.

the unimaginative chronicler of the steps which led to the appearance of a particular volume. He can be seen as a publisher trying to interest his clients in his wares and using various means of persuasion. He did not always use the same argument but showed a nice sense of discrimination in his variety. Even when he relied on fictitious anonymous characters at one stage in his career, the people so represented differ in their status and interests. His choice of promotional ideas is also revealing. While illumination has always been used to increase a book's appeal, claims for an authentic text or the historicity of a person like Arthur, such as he used in his promotion of Malory, are much more characteristic of the Tudor age than of the medieval period, and show that Caxton was more farsighted than we have given him credit for. At the same time if the claim for the accuracy of a text is merely a promotional idea, we can more easily understand why the text is in fact no better than the one it superseded and why this promotional idea is not repeated in other volumes he printed.

WHY CAXTON TURNED TO PRINTING

Why Caxton learned to print is an important question which is given a new focus as the importance of his patrons recedes. Earlier I suggested that the absence of any sharp break in Caxton's life about 1473 had significance for our understanding of both his earlier and later life; it is time now to develop that thought. We commonly refer to Caxton as a merchant, but since that word is today somewhat archaic it might be better if we referred to him as a salesman. Because it is so often assumed that to be a merchant is a genteel profession which allows little room for initiative and flair. I am sure that this is one reason why writers believe that Caxton's patrons were more important in the history of the press than their printer. A salesman does not produce goods, but makes his money by selling them. He has to live by his wits, to know how to interest his clients and to be able to clinch a sale. In selling books Caxton used stories which were designed to make his wares attractive; and he clearly knew something about books and manuscripts since his stories make good sense in literary and historical terms. This knowledge cannot have been acquired overnight; indeed the more imaginative his writing is, the more likely it becomes that he took an interest in literary affairs over a long period.

THE IMPORTANCE OF MS. ROYAL 19. A. IX.

It is at this point that we need to reconsider the evidence of the *Mirror of the World*. Caxton translated and printed this work in 1481 using a French manuscript, now British Library Royal 19. A. ix., which had been written in Bruges in 1464. The text of the French manuscript is so close to that of Caxton's own and the illustrations in Caxton's print are so clearly modelled on those in the manuscript that there can be little doubt that this is the original French copy he used. But whereas the French prologue says that the manuscript was written in Bruges in 1464, Caxton says in his own prologue that it was completed in Bruges in June 1464. How did he know that the manuscript was written in June that year since this information is not in his original? One solution is that he bought the manuscript from 'Jehan le clerc librarier' as soon as it was finished, though this seems no good reason why he should remember the month so clearly. I would suggest a more likely explanation is that he actually commissioned the writing of this manuscript from the Bruges shop and was therefore quite familiar with the date at which it was executed. In other words Caxton not only sold in England manuscripts written in French in Bruges, but also he commissioned them to be written so that he could sell them to his clients. And by 'commissioned' I mean not that he simply asked for any manuscript to be written, but that he asked for manuscripts of particular texts to be copied. Hence when he came to sell them in England he could claim that they were fashionable not so much because they were recently copied in Bruges, but because they had been specially ordered by him from his knowledge of what was then being read in fashionable quarters there. This is one reason why the choice of texts for translating caused him few problems later. He may have acquired his French manuscripts of such texts as *History of Troy*, *Jason*, and *Game of Chess* in this way. The evidence to support this view is slight, but it is quite compelling. If it is accepted, it may help to explain why he took to printing.

THE ADVANTAGES TO CAXTON OF PRINTING

If he commissioned manuscripts, he already was involved to that extent in the production of literature. But there were limitations to this form of business. Manuscripts were luxury goods which could be sold only to the wealthy. As Caxton did not own a scrivener's shop, he would have to put out his order at a work shop, take his place in a queue of orders, and have his choice limited perhaps by the available exemplars. The copies would all be written in French and would be that much less saleable in England. For although it would be easy enough for Bruges copyists to copy texts in English, there would be little point in Caxton commissioning them to do so. English courtly literature, such as Chaucerian poems, were already being produced abundantly in manuscript form in England itself. To translate courtly French works into English and then have them copied singly or in small quantities would not provide Caxton with sufficient remuneration for his own labour. Hand-written copies of Caxton's translations may occasionally have been produced as de luxe presentation volumes, as is possibly the case with Ovid's *Metamorphoses*, but such examples are exceptional. As a salesman who commissioned manuscripts Caxton had little alternative to asking for copies of works in French. It is hardly surprising that his business was of limited scope.

Caxton could well have found it irksome and seen in printing a way of circumventing so many of his difficulties. Provided he himself made the translations, he would have control over the whole process of book production. He could choose the books to translate, then translate and print them, and finally sell them. At the same time printing would demand that he use translation: it may have been difficult to dispose of manuscripts in French in England; it would have been impossible to sell multiple copies of French books there. The advent of printing would enable Caxton to develop his business without restraint and so hopefully to make a handsome profit. I would also suggest that he became a printer rather than just a publisher more by force of necessity than by inclination. Since the concept of a printer as distinct from a publisher had not emerged at this time, he had naturally to become both. But I doubt whether he was really interested in printing as such.

CONCLUSION

We come back in the end to the man himself. The view I have outlined here increases my own admiration for Caxton. He is not a cypher merely carrying out the whims of arbitrary patrons. He is a man of foresight, energy and determination. He is astute and knowledgeable enough to make money from selling various kinds of goods in ways best suited to each particular ware. He is above all a man of more imagination than we have previously allowed. Perhaps as our knowledge of the historical man grows less certain, our appreciation of the man of letters will increase.

3

Some Observations on William Caxton and the
Mercers Company

THE DATE OF Caxton's birth is not known, though since *The Life and Typography of William Caxton* by William Blades was published in 1861–63 most writers on Caxton have accepted that he was born about 1422. Up till then the matter had remained open, though William Oldys, the 18th-century antiquarian, suggested in the *Biographia Britannica* that Caxton's birth should be dated about 1412.[1] His reason was that in 1471 when Caxton made his translation *The Recuyell of the Historyes of Troye* he wrote of himself, 'that age crepeth on me dayly and febleth all the bodye'.[2] Oldys deduced from this that Caxton must have been about 60 at this time and so he suggested 1412 as a suitable date for his birth. But this date was by no means universally accepted and Dibdin dismissed it as 'mere conjecture'.[3]

Blades in his epoch-making book approached the problem from a different angle. He decided to work out Caxton's date of birth from the first known date in Caxton's life which is 16 Henry VI.[4] His name is found under that year in the Wardens' Account Book of the Mercers' Company. The entry records that the two shillings for his entry into an apprenticeship with Robert Large had been paid. Blades contended that the terms of an apprenticeship were always so arranged that a boy issued from his service at the age of 24, when he would attain his civic majority. Since most apprentices served their masters for from 7 to 14 years, Caxton must have been anything from 10 to 17 years old in 1438.

[1] *Biographia Britannica*, 2nd ed., 1784, vol. III, p. 351.
[2] W. J. B. Crotch, *The Prologues and Epilogues of William Caxton*, EETS o.s. 176, 1928, p. 7. [Henceforth referred to as Crotch.]
[3] J. Ames, W. Herbert and T. F. Dibdin, *Typographical Antiquities*, London, vol. I, 1810, p. lxxv.
[4] In this context 16 Henry VI is from 25 June 1437 to 24 June 1438; see further below.

But, Blades goes on, as Caxton had built up a considerable position for himself in Bruges by the end of the 1440s, it is more likely that Caxton was nearer 17 in 1438. Consequently Blades concludes that Caxton was born about 1421.[5] Since then most commentators have accepted a date between 1421 and 1424 for Caxton's birth,[6] though Crotch, the most authoritative biographer since Blades, thought 1422 the most probable date.[7]

Quite recently the Mercers' Company decided to appoint an archivist[8] and thus to make their records more generally available to scholars. Taking advantage of this, I decided to re-study the Mercers' records in order to set the Caxton entry of 16 Henry VI within the general framework of entry into and issue from apprenticeship in the Mercers' Company. The Wardens' Account Book of the Mercers' Company contains the accounts from 1391 to 1464.[9] The wardens, usually four in number, held office for a year. At the end of their year of office, which began and ended at the Feast of the Nativity of St John the Baptist i.e. 24 June, the wardens entered their accounts (which presumably had been kept during the year on loose slips of paper or possibly in another book) into the Account Book. This is the only contemporary record of the Mercers' Company in existence for the majority of this period.[10] But the Mercers' Company also possesses a register of all the freemen of the company. This register was begun in the 16th century; but the first compiler included all the earlier freemen of the company in the 14th and 15th centuries whose names he could discover. It is not known what sources this compiler drew upon, for his list of freemen is not identical with the lists of apprentices who are recorded as issuing from apprenticeships

[5] W. Blades, *The Life and Typography of William Caxton*, London, 1861–63, pp. 3–4. [Henceforth referred to as Blades.]

[6] R. Hittmair, *William Caxton Englands erster Drucker und Verleger*, 1931, p. 8: ' . . . das Jahr, das zwischen 1421 und 1424 liegen muss'. H. R. Plomer, *William Caxton (1424–1491)*, 1925, pp. 18–19, prefers 1424 for Caxton's birth.

[7] Crotch, p. xxviii.

[8] The first archivist is Miss Jean Imray, to whom I am greatly indebted for constant advice and encouragement.

[9] There is a certain amount of miscellaneous material in the Account Book earlier than 1391, though that is when the regular series of accounts begins.

[10] The Acts of Court of the Mercers' Company begin in 1453.

in the Wardens' Account Book. Caxton, however, is not mentioned in this Register of the Freemen of the Mercers' Company.

As mentioned above, Caxton's name is to be found in the Wardens' Account Book under the entry of the apprentices for 16 Henry VI. The accounts were drawn up at the end of each fiscal year and they were dated in accordance with the regnal year of the King of England. The two years do not correspond: the Mercers' fiscal year ran from 25 June to 24 June, whereas the regnal year of Henry VI, whose reign we shall mainly be concerned with here, ran from 1 September to 31 August. So the accounts of 16 Henry VI were drawn up on 24 June 1438, and they embrace the period 25 June 1437–24 June 1438, even though some of this period is actually within the 15th regnal year of Henry VI. During the course of this article I shall refer to the accounts made in 16 Henry VI by the single year 1438 (and all other years on a similar basis), though it should not be forgotten that by 1438 is meant the fiscal year ending on 24 June 1438. As Caxton's entry as an apprentice is given under the year 1438 in the Wardens' Account Book, I decided first to compile a card-index of all the apprentices who were recorded as having entered upon their apprenticeship during the first 30 years of Henry VI's reign (1423–52), Caxton's entry falling roughly in the middle of this period. I then made a separate card-index of all the apprentices who issued from their apprenticeship throughout the whole of Henry VI's reign (1423–61). I was then able to compare these two indices to see how long each apprentice served. The results so obtained are set out in Table 1.

This Table reveals some interesting facts. It is noticeable, for example, that there is no record of any issue for an overwhelming proportion of the apprentices who enter. It is, however, often thought that Caxton's issue was not recorded because he left for the Low Countries soon after the death of his master Robert Large in 1441. But the real reason may well be the incompleteness of the Wardens' Account Book, for we know from the Register of Freemen that many of the apprentices whose issue is not recorded in the Account Book did in fact issue from their apprenticeship and take up the freedom of the company. Similarly many apprentices are recorded as having issued from their apprenticeship, even though I can find no corresponding entry

TABLE I

Regnal Year Henry VI	Apprentices		Years of Apprenticeship													
	Total	No issue recorded	0	1-4	5	6	7	8	9	10	11	12	13	14	15	16-21
I	20	12				I	I	I		3	I					I
2	21	7				I	3	2	2	I	I	3				I
3	13	9						2	I	I						
4	I					I										
5	47	30	I			I	2	4	6		I				I	I
6	15	7		I		I	2	I		2	I					
7	5	2					2				I					
8	30	17	2		I		4	2	2				I			I
9	21	13		I	I		I		I	2	I		I			
10	5	3						I	I							
11	2							I		I						
12	18	12	2				I		I							2
13	9	4	4						I							
14	52	33	I		I	I	5	5			3			2	I	
15	11	8	I						I				I			
16	25	14			I	4			I		I	3	I			
17	16	13								I	2					
18	24	16		I		I	I	3	I			I				
19	10	7							I		I			I		
20	15	8	2						2		2				I	
21	50	29	2	I	I	4	4	4			2	I	I	I		
22	68	44	3			5	3	3	2	I	I	I	4			I
23	4	I			2		I									
24	22	17				I	I		I		2					
25	35	20				I		3	3	4	2		2			
26	53	34		2	2	I	2		7	3	I		I			
27	17	10				I	I	I	I	I		I	I			
28	29	20	I			I	I	2	2	I			I			
29	8	6							2							
30	24	15			I	I	4	I			2					
Total	670	411	19	6	10	25	40	40	35	25	22	10	14	3	3	7

which records their entry into it. It is doubtful, therefore, whether any significance can be attached to the omission of Caxton's name from among those who issued from their apprenticeship.

Another point of interest is that the Table shows the two-shilling fee for an apprentice's issue was often paid in the same year as the two-shilling fee for his entry. This raises an important question about the authority of the Wardens' Account Book. It was decreed by the Mercers' Company that two shillings should be paid to the company for each boy who started work with a mercer as an apprentice. But it does not follow that it was obligatory to pay this two shillings immediately. And in many cases it was clearly many years after a boy had started as an apprentice that the fee was paid, perhaps because the master felt that if his apprentice died or failed to complete his apprenticeship he might save the two shillings. No doubt also the master waited until it was convenient to pay the fee. Thus we often find that a master pays the entry fees of two, three, four or even five apprentices at once. In these cases, as the years in which these apprentices issue are often so far apart, it is more reasonable to assume that the master decided to pay off all the outstanding fees at once rather than that he actually took on two, three, four or five apprentices at one time. It is important, therefore, to em-phasize that the Wardens' Account Book records only when the entry fee of two shillings was paid; it does not record when a boy actually embarked upon his apprenticeship. This means, of course, that the entry in 1438 that records Caxton's entry into the apprenticeship only tells us that the two-shilling entry fee was paid in that year. It may well be that Caxton had in fact started on his apprenticeship much earlier.

Our suspicions that the Wardens' Account Book cannot be used for accurate dating of an apprentice's entry or issue are strengthened by an examination of all of Large's apprentices whose entry fees were paid within the first 30 years of Henry VI's reign. His apprentices are listed below in Table 2:[11]

---

[11] The names bracketed together are entered jointly in the accounts. Because the entry for Caxton's first livery payment is erased, I have put it in square brackets. The system of livery payments is explained later in my article.

TABLE 2

Name	Year of entry	Year of issue	First year of livery payment
John Harowe (Harwe)	1423	1454	1450
⌈Robert Halle	1428	—	—
⌊Randolf Strete	1428	1438	1452
⌈James Heton	1431	—	—
⌊Richard Bonifaunt	1431	1442	1444
Thomas Nyche (Neche)	1431	1441	1452
Henry Dukmanton	1436	—	1444
⌈William Caxton	1438	—	[1453]
⌊John Large	1438	—	—
Christopher Heton	1443	1443	—

Under all the respective entries for the entry into or issue from apprenticeships these boys are all said to be the apprentices of Robert Large. Yet Christopher Heton's year of entry is 1443, which is remarkable because Robert Large died on 24 April 1441. Heton had been an apprentice of Large long before 1443, for in the Will which Large made on 11 April 1441 he refers to a 'Christopher my apprentice' and this Christopher can be no other than Christopher Heton.[12] It is clear that Large had put off the payment of Heton's entry fee during his own lifetime and that this was only paid after his death. It shows convincingly that Large did not bother to pay an apprentice's two shillings in the same year as a boy actually started working as an apprentice for him. Despite the fact that Large had been dead for about two years when Heton issued from his apprenticeship, Heton is nevertheless described as being Large's apprentice. Similarly when John Harowe and Richard Bonifaunt issue, they are also described as Large's apprentices even though they are recorded as issuing after Large's death.[13] This is worth noting because many of Caxton's biographers assume that Caxton would have been transferred to

---

[12] P. C. C. Rouse 16. A translation is printed by W. Blades, *The Biography and Typography of William Caxton*, 1882, pp. 153–8. The section dealing with the apprentices referred to here and later is on pp. 155–6.

[13] There may be a special explanation for this as far as Harowe is concerned which I deal with later.

another master automatically after Large's death and some have
gone so far as to suggest that it was for this assumed new master
that Caxton went as a factor to the Low Countries.[14] It is true
that in the Wardens' Account Book many apprentices issue with
a new master (presumably because the old one had died), and
sometimes it specifically records that an apprentice had served
first one master and then another. But because Heton issues as
Large's apprentice in 1443 it is possible that Large made some
arrangement for his apprentices to finish their term of service in
his house or that his wife carried on the business in his name. We
know from the Plea and Memoranda Rolls of the City of London
that a widow did, or at least was expected to, carry on her hus-
band's trade and teach his apprentices.[15] It is not necessary to
assume that Caxton was transferred to another master automatically on Large's death; it is just as feasible that Caxton finished his
apprenticeship in Large's house and then left for the Low Countries as an independent merchant. It must be accepted, however,
that Caxton was still an apprentice on 11 April 1441, for in his
Will which he made on that day Large refers to Caxton as 'my
apprentice' (*apprentico meo*). This is the expression he uses to
describe all his apprentices who, as we can tell from the Wardens'
Account Book, had not issued from their apprenticeship by that
date. But Thomas Nyche, on the other hand, who issued in 1441
presumably shortly before the Will was made, is referred to by
Large as 'my servant' (*seruienti meo*).

Robert Large's Will contains one further piece of information
which also helps to show how incomplete the Wardens' Account
Book is. He refers in his Will to 'Robert Dedes my apprentice'.
But there is no reference to a Robert Dedes in the Account Book.
Yet he, like William Caxton, receives 20 marks as a bequest from
Large, and it would seem unlikely that as he received so large a
sum he had started on his apprenticeship only shortly before Large
made his Will. One must assume that Large never paid the two-
shilling entry fee for his apprentice Robert Dedes, although Dedes
may well have been his apprentice for some time by 1441. His

[14] Crotch, pp. xxxvii–xxxviii.
[15] *Calendar of Plea and Memoranda Rolls 1413–1437*, edited by A. H. Thomas,
1943, pp. 230–1; *Calendar of Plea and Memoranda Rolls 1437–1457*, edited by
P. E. Jones, 1954, pp. 31, 46, etc.

case is similar to Christopher Heton's, whose fee was likewise not paid by Large during his own lifetime. We cannot avoid the conclusion that an apprentice's entry fee was not necessarily paid as soon as he became an apprentice. Similarly it would appear that the two-shilling fee payable on the issue of an apprentice was not necessarily paid in the same year that an apprentice issued. This is shown by the various payments made for John Harowe. According to the Wardens' Account Book he entered in 1423, issued in 1454 and made his first livery payment in 1450. This is completely irregular for one could naturally only be admitted into the livery after one had issued from apprenticeship and become a freeman of the company. I think we must here accept that Robert Large did not bother, or he forgot, to pay the necessary two shillings when Harowe issued. Later when this omission was discovered, Harowe was asked to pay the two shillings which he accordingly did. If this is so it would mean that his apprenticeship did not last 21 years, but that it lasted only 17 years or even less,[16] which is in any case a more reasonable period for an apprenticeship. If the payment for an apprentice's issue was delayed in this case, it is likely to have been delayed in others as well, and it would indicate that we should treat the dates in the Wardens' Account Book for both issue from and entry into apprenticeship with great reserve.

We cannot, therefore, calculate the date of Caxton's birth from the date 1438 and all attempts to do so must be regarded as suspect. Indeed even if it could be proved that Caxton actually began his apprenticeship in that year, it would not be correct to say, as some do,[17] that the normal period of apprenticeship can be shown from

---

[16] That Harowe had in fact issued from his apprenticeship before 1454 as given in the Account Book is proved by the record of the entry of apprentices for 1443. In that year Harowe is himself given as the master of two apprentices, and if he were still an apprentice it would have been impossible for him to enrol others as his apprentices.

[17] Crotch, p. xxvii states: 'The customary age at which a youth was apprenticed in the Fifteenth Century can be ascertained with some accuracy from other records not in themselves bearing upon the life of Caxton himself and particularly from similar entries in the books of the Company embracing this period: from a study of which it is found that the period of apprenticeship most usual was a term of ten years; in no case was the term less than seven years.' Cp. Blades, p. 4.

the Wardens' Account Book to have been from 7 to 14 years. A glance at Table 1 will show that according to the accounts the period of apprenticeship is anything from none to 21 years, although the average period is from 5 to 13 years. As no clear pattern emerges from these figures and as many of them, as I have shown, do not reveal the true period of apprenticeship, it is not possible for us to decide from this source how long Caxton's period of apprenticeship is likely to have lasted. But it may be noted that in other records, as for example the Plea and Memoranda Rolls of the City of London,[18] the usual period of apprenticeship seems to have been from 7 to 15 years. If we could assume from this that no apprentice served less than seven years— but this would be a doubtful assumption—it would mean that of the 259 apprentices whose issue from the Mercers' Company is recorded in the period under discussion (see Table 1) 60 are said to have served less than this length of time. In other words, a little more than 23 per cent of the entries recording entry into an apprenticeship could be regarded as not representing the actual year when the apprenticeship began. It would merely confirm our doubts about the reliability of the accounts for providing a date for an apprentice's beginning of his term of service.

Finally, we ought to look at Blades's contention that an apprenticeship was so arranged that it should terminate when the apprentice was 24 and had thereby attained his civic majority. I have been unable to find any support for this claim and, indeed, there is evidence to show that this definitely did not happen in some cases. For example, one boy who became an apprentice before he was 14 years of age was to serve only eight years.[19] S. L. Thrupp has shown by comparing the Registers of the Freemen of the Mercers' and the Grocers' with wills and inquisitions that apprentices took up the freedom of the company at ages ranging from 21 to 26.[20] And, no doubt, these examples could be multiplied. Blades's view can no longer be accepted.

To sum up then, it may be asserted that there is no guarantee

---

[18] *Op. cit., passim.*

[19] *Calendar of Plea and Memoranda Rolls 1413–1437*, edited by A. H. Thomas, 1943, pp. 28–9.

[20] S. L. Thrupp, *The Merchant Class of Medieval London [1300–1500]*, 1948, p. 193.

that Caxton actually began his apprenticeship in 1438 even though his two-shilling entry fee was paid in that year. The 'about 1422' given by most biographers as the date of his birth must be regarded as 'mere conjecture', for not only is it calculated from the year 1438 but also the steps by which the year 1438 is made to produce the year about 1422 for his birth cannot be substantiated. We can say no more than that Caxton had begun his apprenticeship by 24 June 1438 and that he had not concluded it by 11 April 1441. The date of his birth, however, is still unknown and will have to be arrived at by other methods.

Caxton's name occurs again in the Wardens' Account Book under 1453. His biographers differ in their interpretation of this reference, though it is to be doubted whether many of them have actually consulted the Account Book for many improbable theories have been advanced. Blades, for example, claims that William Caxton, Richard Burgh and Edmond Redeknape were admitted into the livery in 1453, and adds: 'We may remark also that the usual fees on their taking up the livery seem to have been remitted, as the whole passage in the volume of accounts is erased by pen'. He suggested further that Burgh and Redeknape were mercers living in Bruges who had travelled with Caxton for the ceremony.[21] Crotch accepts that Redeknape, Burgh and Caxton 'had evidently journeyed from Bruges together to be admitted to the Livery. The sum paid in each case was 6s. 8d., but the whole entry is erased with a pen and beneath is the memorandum "Qz int. debitores in fine c̄opotˢ", from which have arisen many unnecessary theories.' He rejects the theory that the fees were remitted by the company. On the basis of Ordinance 45 of the Mercers' Company,[22] which states that all livery dues are to be paid within a fortnight on pain of a penalty of *6s 8d*, he suggests that the wardens thought these three had not paid within the specified term and so entered their names in the book, but on discovering their mistake they erased the entry again.[23] More recent biographers seem to have forgotten that the entry has been erased from the Account Book and merely assume that Caxton

[21] Blades, p. 12.
[22] The ordinances were confirmed by Act of Parliament in 1504, and it is not known how long the individual ordinances had already been in force.
[23] Crotch, pp. xliv–xlv.

was admitted into the livery in 1453. Thus James Wells writes: 'In 1453 he returned to London to be formally admitted into the Mercers. He paid a fee of 40s. for his entry into livery, which he was commanded to have ready by the following Easter and to wear, on pain of fine, upon all occasions set by the Court of the Company'.[24]

The position, however, is this. After an apprentice had issued from his service and become a freeman of the company, he was entitled to take up the livery on payment of 20s. In almost all cases this payment was divided up into three annual instalments of 6s 8d each to be paid in consecutive years. The Wardens' Account Book records faithfully the payments made in each case and states whether it was for the first, second or third year. In 1453 there are no payments for the second and third years, but only payments for the first year. Seventeen names are entered under the appropriate heading. But one mercer, Henry Lytelton, paid 20s for all three years and there is a note against his name which reads 'pur toutz iij Ans... xx s.' Fourteen of the others paid their 6s 8d as their first livery payment and their names are duly recorded under 1454 and 1455 for their second and third instalments. Among these 14 is Redeknape, whose name is *not* erased in the Account Book. Two names only are crossed out and these are those of William Caxton and Richard Burgh. Against their names there is written in the margin 'quia inter debitores in fine compoti' (i.e. because they are among the debtors at the end of the account). At the end of the account for that year we find the entry:

Dettours pur lour primer An pur lentre en la lyveray

Richaert Burgh	vj s.	viij d.
William Caxton	vj s.	viij d.

Probably when the clerk who was copying out the accounts came to write the names of the debtors he remembered that he had already recorded the names of William Caxton and Richard Burgh among those who had paid their first instalment. So he turned back a page to cross out their names and to put the note in the margin.

One or two facts about this entry should be noted. It is impossible that the fees could have been remitted, as Blades suggests,

---

[24] J. Wells, *William Caxton*, The Caxton Club, Chicago, 1960, p. 9. See also H. W. Larken, *At the Sign of the Red Pale*, [privately printed, no date], p. 18.

because the two appear among the company's debtors. There is no evidence that William Caxton was ever admitted into the livery at all, as so many assume. The example of Henry Lytelton shows that he could have paid the three instalments in one if he had so wished. Consequently it cannot be suggested that it was because he was normally resident in Bruges and so would be unable to pay the other instalments that he did not pay the first one in 1453. Finally, it should be emphasized that Redeknape's name is not erased in the Account Book and there is thus no reason to link Caxton's name with his rather than with that of any of the other 14 mercers who were admitted into the livery in 1453.

The problem of why these two names were entered into the Account Book and then erased will probably never be satisfactorily solved. Any answer necessarily involves a certain amount of speculation, though if we knew more about Burgh we might come nearer to a solution. It is the only occasion in the Wardens' Account Book that a livery entry was subsequently crossed out. The debt is not referred to in the following years, but it appears to have been the practice in these accounts to carry only the total amount forward. It is hardly satisfactory to suggest that Caxton merely changed his mind, for presumably if he had not intended to join the livery after all, he ought not to have owed the company 6s 8d. It may be that when he was in England he merely forgot to pay his dues and returned to Bruges without paying. He may then have decided to wait for a suitable opportunity to pay, an opportunity which never arose. There would be nothing unusual about this, for we have seen that dues payable to the company were frequently not paid with any promptness. The wardens, for their part, when they realized the dues had not in fact been paid entered Caxton's name among the debtors. As we know so little about Burgh, it is difficult to tell whether this suggestion is feasible or not. We shall have to wait for further evidence before coming to any decision.

There is a second reference to Caxton in the accounts for 1453.[25]

---

[25] Although this entry follows the one discussed above in the accounts, we need not assume that Caxton was fined on a date which was later than that on which he was supposed to pay his livery dues. The entries in the Account Book are entered in a set order and have no reference to the particular date in the year on which they actually occurred.

Because unwarranted inferences have been drawn from this entry, I should like to conclude this article by discussing it briefly. Crotch writes of this entry:

> 'Caxton remained in England to the end of the year, for when Geoffrey Fielding was elected Mayor (on the day of the Feast of St. Edward, 13th October), he, Burgh, Thomas Bryce, and Wm. Pratt were fined three shillings and fourpence each for not attending his riding to Westminster to be presented and admitted before the Barons of the Exchequer. This ceremony took place on the day after the swearing-in at the Guildhall, that is, on October 29th. It is interesting to find him so early connected with this latter pair, for they remained his friends throughout their lives and took no small interest in his later work as a Printer.'[26]

Crotch mentions only four mercers who were fined and this he has taken over directly from Blades.[27] But under the heading 'Fynes deux *que* les ne chivacherent ouesq*ue* Le maier Geffre Feldyng' we find that there are 36 names entered, among whom are the four mentioned by Crotch. All 36 were fined 3*s* 4d each. It is impossible, therefore, to link Caxton's name closely with those of William Pratt and Thomas Bryce at this date. This entry does not prove that there was any special relationship between Caxton and the other two. Nor is this entry in any way unusual, for almost every year some mercers were fined for not attending the mayor.

During the course of this article then I have tried to show that scholars have read too much into the limited material available in the Wardens' Account Book of the Mercers' Company. No doubt because we know so little about Caxton's early life, we tend to make large inferences about that little we have; and unfortunately what is merely suggested by one scholar becomes accepted as fact by the next. But Caxton's life must be studied against the background of his times and the reliability of the available sources must be tested by studying them in depth. It is foolish to extract the references to Caxton without considering the rest of the source and the type of information it has to offer, particularly as the passages which refer to Caxton have been misread or misinterpreted so frequently.

[26] Crotch, p. xlv.
[27] Blades, p. 12.

4

A New Approach to William Caxton

Mr Painter's new quincentenary biography of Caxton[1] is to be welcomed for it concentrates on an aspect of his career which has been unduly neglected in the past. A man who was a merchant, a negotiator, a royal factor and who moved on the fringes of aristocratic society in a delicate political period can hardly have failed to be a political animal. Previous biographies have concentrated on his scholarly or mercantile activities; this one restores the balance by presenting Caxton the politician. However, the author does not give us a comprehensive view of Caxton's political activities, and his political beliefs are never examined in detail; it is simply that his career is examined from the political standpoint. Unfortunately this leaves the impression, which Mr Painter wishes to dispel, that Caxton was a man who trimmed his sails to every wind for he survived, and prospered, under such different monarchs as Edward IV, Richard III and Henry VII. This new interpretation necessarily means that the prologues and epilogues are looked at in a new light. They are considered to be political documents which to be understood have to be read between the lines. Although this approach is perfectly valid, it involves certain general considerations which ought to have been aired in the book.

The most important of these is the relationship between the prologues and the works in which they occur. Recently it has been suggested that the prologues were added as publisher's blurbs to help sell the volumes, a theory which involves a close relation between the two. But if the prologues are hidden political statements, even propaganda, they become divorced from the works to which they are prefixed unless those works are themselves politically motivated. Mr Painter never suggests that the latter is so, though many of them were recommended to Caxton by his patrons according to the printer. Mr Painter is generally prepared to believe Caxton in such matters. But if the books were really recommended, are the texts important for political reasons? Or do they merely reflect a patron's individual taste? And if the prologues are a kind of propaganda, is it immaterial to what book this

[1]G.D. Painter,*William Caxton, A Quincentenary Biography of England's First Printer*. (London: Chatto & Windus, 1976. £7.50.) Pp.xi + [i] + 227. Illus. Index.

propaganda was added or would it have made a greater impact if it was added to a particular type of work? Furthermore, it is not quite certain what the financial implications of this theory are. If the prologues are blurbs, we realize they were meant to sell the text in question. If they are veiled political statements, we would have to assume that the texts were sufficiently popular to sell by themselves so that the buyer would absorb the political message of the prologue. What audience was going to understand these political messages is never explained. What audience needed to be informed and swayed by the political considerations which motivated Caxton? What was the result of this propaganda supposed to be? Did other printer-publishers of the 15th century behave in the same way? By raising general considerations like these I do not seek to imply that it is wrong to consider Caxton as a political animal. The theory is attractive and ought to be considered. But it cannot be the whole explanation, and as a theory it needs to be fitted into other aspects of Caxton's work which tend to be minimized here.

Another major concern of the book is to examine all relevant documents and sources for Caxton's life which 'have not as yet been adequately studied and interpreted' (p. vii). In many ways this concern for detail and precise dating is closely related to the author's interest in Caxton's political life, since the timing of individual actions is often an important element in suggesting that a given document is relevant in understanding Caxton's political career. In this way Mr Painter is able to link the two halves of Caxton's life together, for he shows how Caxton remained a diplomat and politician throughout his life. There is no doubt that by concentrating on the details of the documentary evidence Mr Painter has made important contributions to our knowledge of the printer's life and work. This book, which never takes anything for granted, corrects many misunderstandings and assumptions that have been made in the past. His work also makes clear that it is time a new collection of Caxton documents was made; it is a pity that this was not launched as a quincentenary project. Nevertheless, although many Caxton documents do still need detailed discussion, one may wonder whether this is the right kind of book for that type of work. There is the danger that the book will deteriorate into disconnected examinations of disparate documents which obscure the overall interpretation of the life and work. Mr Painter has not entirely avoided this pitfall. Methodologically it also leads to the difficulty of deciding what is of primary and what of secondary importance. Often this is decided rather haphazardly, and the relationship between the text and the footnotes is erratic. In addition the premisses on which the book is based will lead the reader to assume that Mr Painter has seen and studied all the documents. It sometimes seems as though this is not the case, for if the document is not printed or not immediately available it may be discussed at second hand. Thus in his discussion of the documents now at Lille discovered by Thielemans (pp. 19-20) it is clear that he has not acquired photostats of them. He interprets them rather cavalierly on the basis of what he would like to see in them. This hardly seems satisfactory in a book of this nature. Finally many of the documents can be understood only against the background in which they were produced, and this means that other documents of the same type have to be examined and the purpose for which the documents were produced has to be investigated. While he is good on the mercantile sources whose background he fills in clearly, he is less happy on the more political variety. It may be that it was lack of space which prevented him from including this background.

This problem of incompleteness can be highlighted by two quite different examples. The first concerns the origins of Caxton's family. Mr Painter decides, probably correctly, that the family name comes from the place-name. But instead of looking at all the possible place-names in the country, he confines his attention to those in East Anglia and Kent. It is never explained why Caxton's family must originate from one of these areas, for there are no reasons why his family should not have originated in the Midlands, for example, even if Caxton himself was born in Kent as he claimed. Furthermore, new references to Caxtons are being discovered every day, and Professor R. R. Griffith in his American Typophiles volume[2] introduced us to many hitherto unknown ones. Mr Painter in his introductory chapter merely mentions the more familiar ones and claims to be able to detect a pattern in them. This pattern is quite illusory. Where so much is uncertain it is dangerous to claim too much, for those with less specialist knowledge than the author will assume that the problem has been solved. Though Mr Painter's views about Caxton's family and its origins are perfectly reasonable, they remain pure speculation.

The second example concerns *The Mirror of the World* and its French original, which has been taken to be the manuscript now British Library Royal 19.A.ix. Of this Mr Painter writes that the Royal manuscript 'belongs to the same group as Caxton's, originating at Bruges with a manuscript written in June 1464 to the order of Jehan Le Clerc bookseller, but omits various illustrations and the manuscript captions

2 See Typophile Chap Book 52, 1976, ed. S. O. Thompson, pp. 20-54.

to the diagrams which are all present and correct in Caxton's edition;
so Caxton must have used a different and better manuscript, now lost'
(pp. 108, 110). Here it is possible that Mr Painter is correct, but he is so
brief that the less specialized reader could hardly understand what the
problem was. Since Mr Painter is a man who deals with details, many
readers might assume that the details here were so self-evident that they
did not need to be put forward in the book. His case may appear
stronger because he has not argued it in detail. The French text of the
Royal manuscript is identical textually with Caxton's English and the
two of them differ against all other French manuscripts. The problem
therefore is whether Caxton used this manuscript and eked out the
illustrations from another source or whether he used a lost manuscript
which was written at the same time and which was otherwise identical
with the Royal one except for added illustrations. The problem is more
complicated and the solution less straightforward than Mr Painter
suggests.

One of the most important theories advanced in this book concerns
the reasons which led Caxton to Cologne and printing in 1471-2. Mr
Painter suggests that Caxton had no prior intention to learn printing
and that it was a series of coincidences which turned him into a printer-
publisher. These views are expounded in his chapter which is significantly called 'The Exile'. While Mr Painter does not argue the point
explicitly, the implication of his approach is that Caxton was always a
politician and a man of affairs who happened to come across printing
by chance while in exile in Cologne. As a political animal he realized
the advantages of printing for propaganda and related activities, and so
learned how to print and acquired a press. Because he came to printing
by chance, Mr Painter is able to suggest that Caxton was little interested
in the literary and economic aspects of the press. The theory involves
many assumptions about what happened to Caxton around 1471. It is
claimed that he was ousted from his governorship of the English Nation
in Bruges as a result of a change in political fortunes in England. Since
nothing is known of why or when Caxton left the governorship, this
view is quite possible. It is supported by reference to his election to the
governorship, since it is generally accepted that his predecessor was
ousted from office. Although this was ostensibly for maladministra-
tion, Mr Painter assumes that this was merely a cover-up for political
manœuvring. Even if this is so, it is doubtful whether there was as much
political chicanery as the author suggests, for the services of the ousted
governor were still used. Nor is it necessary to assume that all governors
lost their jobs as a result of political upheaval because one may have

done. In fact, Caxton's successor as governor, John Pickering, appears to have had the same political outlook as Caxton so that politics may not be the answer to the end of Caxton's appointment. One wonders also that if he were ousted whether this would not have led to records being made of the episode and to further trouble in later appointments to the job.

After being 'expelled' from the governorship, Caxton went to reside with Margaret of Burgundy in her house at Ghent. Here he continued with his translation of *The History of Troy*, which she had encouraged him to complete. His stay here with Margaret is inferred from his statement in *The History of Troy* that he started the work in Bruges, continued it in Ghent and finished it in Cologne. The explanation is ingenious, though it must be remembered we have evidence that Caxton did stay with the White Friars in Ghent and none that he stayed with Margaret. This theory also produces its own difficulties. We are never told exactly what the relationship was between Margaret and the future printer. Margaret was his patron, but not his employer, though she was prepared to give him house-room. It is further suggested that because Margaret moved away from Ghent in June 1471 Caxton was forced to seek alternative accommodation; this is why he decided to go to Cologne. This solution is quite unacceptable. There is no reason why Caxton should not have accompanied Margaret to her next residence, as other members of her household did, or why he could not have remained where he was. Protection and patronage did not have to be so personal that a protégé lived in the same building. The trouble may be that Mr Painter looks for too many explanations why Caxton went to Cologne and so weakens his case. At one stage he suggests the trip may have been partly official, as though he was encouraged to go there to conduct private negotiations connected with the Hanseatic dispute. At another it is intimated that he had to find a new home when Margaret left Ghent. Finally it is suggested that he went to Cologne in a protective self-exile, which in the author's opinion is not unconnected with the pardon issued to him in 1472. These multifarious reasons are an indication of the theory's weakness and some are contradictory. It must be emphasized that no English king could exile Caxton from Bruges. As Mr Painter himself informs us, the Lancastrians Somerset and Exeter had been able to live unmolested in Flanders during the Yorkist ascendancy. It would be no different with Caxton, particularly if he was Margaret's protégé. It was quite unnecessary for him to go to Cologne for self-protection, for it could be argued that he would be much safer under Margaret's protection. It is equally unlikely that he was in Cologne for diplomatic reasons since the entries in the Cologne Register of Aliens are so curt as to suggest that Caxton was there in a private capacity. It still seems reasonable to accept the older view that Caxton went there to learn how to print.

Indeed, Mr Painter ignores a lot of evidence which supports this view and which he introduces in different contexts in his book. Why did Caxton start to translate *The History of Troy* already in 1469, if it was not done with a view to learning to print? Mr Painter suggests that Margaret was interested in Caxton because he was a supremely literate merchant, and yet he discounts any concern in literary matters in the Cologne visit. The author shows that Caxton had a long association with Colard Mansion and that this association probably started long before he went to Cologne. Is it not likely that the Bruges scrivener and the future printer discussed the benefits of printing before 1471? Finally he suggests that Caxton was acquainted with printed books at an early stage in his career and that he may have been present when John Russell, one of his future 'patrons', bought a copy of *De officiis* in Bruges in April 1467. Yet he does not think that Caxton went to Cologne with any idea of acquiring a press. Scattered through this book are many indications as to why Caxton should have deliberately gone to Cologne to learn printing, but they are disregarded in favour of the larger theory of Caxton's political involvement.

In this review I have considered some of the general attitudes to Caxton which have inspired its composition, since these are matters of wide concern which will be discussed for many years to come. It might, however, be argued that this book makes a greater contribution to Caxton studies in its detail rather than through its overall approach. Certainly no one in future will be able to disregard what it says for it makes so many advances in documentary and typographical material. The dating of the many undated editions through the various states of Caxton's mark is masterly. Important as these new details are, they are less controversial than the more general theories. No one can doubt their importance and the great advance they have made in Caxton studies. But Mr Painter, I am sure, would like to feel that the book as a whole is important for the way in which he sees Caxton and tries to bring him to life. As I have indicated, this aspect of the book is likely to be the subject of debate for many years to come. In it the author has given a fresh insight into Caxton and his work, an insight that will have to be accommodated in future evaluations of the printer-publisher, even if some of the more extreme views are finally discarded.

5

The Spread of Printing in English during the Fifteenth Century

In the incunable period printing in England was largely confined to London and Westminster, though presses were also operative for short times at Oxford and St Albans.[1] William Caxton had introduced printing into England in 1476 when he set up his presses at Westminster. He continued operations till his death in 1492, when his business was taken over by Wynkyn de Worde, who was Caxton's principal helper and foreman. This publishing house was to continue its activities until de Worde's death in 1535. The press established by Caxton may, therefore, be said to have dominated the publishing scene in England during the fifteenth century. The businesses in Oxford and St Albans were evidently much smaller and certainly each survived for only a few years. As a start to a consideration of the spread of printing in the vernacular, it may be helpful to consider the differences among these three publishers before going on to consider the position in London more fully. I shall commence by evaluating the policies of the two presses at Oxford and St Albans. Both these presses started operating after Caxton and so it is possible that there was some link between him and them; the St Albans printer, for example, used some Caxton types for his later productions.

The first book printed at Oxford was the *Expositio symboli* of Tyrranius Rufinus. Although dated 17 December 1468, it is agreed that this date is a misprint for 1478. The book has no name of publisher in it, though it may have been produced by Theodoric Rood who was active in Oxford from 1481; it is printed in a Cologne type associated with Gerard ten Raem in 1477 and 1478. Recently the researches of Dr de la Mare and Dr Lotte Hellinga have considerably increased our understanding of the publication of this book.[2] This book survives in many copies. The

---

[1] For bibliographical details of English books printed in the fifteenth century see E. Gordon Duff, *Fifteenth Century English Books*. Bibliographical Society Illustrated Monographs 18. (Oxford: Oxford University Press, 1917.)

[2] A.C. de la Mare and L. Hellinga, 'The First Book printed in Oxford: the *Expositio Symboli* of Rufinus', *Transactions of the Cambridge Bibliographical Society* 7.2 (1978): 184-244.

Cambridge University Library copy has been extensively decorated to make it resemble a manuscript, a form of decorative treatment which does not occur too often in English incunables. This decoration is based on Italian humanistic vine-stem style and includes the arms of the Goldwell family. It is based upon the decoration found in British Library MS Sloane 1579, which is itself a copy of the *Expositio symboli* attributed once more to Jerome. An examination of this manuscript showed that it had been discreetly cast off, and a comparison of the two texts revealed that Sloane 1579 was indeed the copytext for the Oxford 1478 edition. The Cambridge University Library copy must be a presentation copy which was perhaps prepared for the patron of the edition. It is therefore imporant to determine which member of the Goldwell family was the recipient of this copy. The most likely person is James Goldwell, who was Bishop of Norwich from 1472 to 1499. Many books survive from James Goldwell's library, including manuscripts of Italian provenance as well as incunables. He is the first Englishman who is recorded as the owner of an incunable. He had travelled to Italy on several occasions and he picked up books and manuscripts on these travels. One of these manuscripts was Sloane 1579, which had been made in Italy and was earlier owned by Vespasiano da Bisticci.

The evidence would suggest that it was this James Goldwell who was instrumental in establishing the first press at Oxford. With his links it would not have been too difficult for him to persuade some Cologne printer, perhaps Theodoric Rood, to come to England to establish a printing press at Oxford, which was Goldwell's old university. Goldwell would have provided the impetus for this venture as well as making the first text available to the printer. The *Expositio symboli* was very popular in the fifteenth century, although written of course much earlier, for many manuscripts and incunable editions of it survive from that century from many parts of Europe. Naturally some of the impetus for this press may have come from the Cologne printer, but under any consideration a substantial part of the credit for the establishment of the press belongs to Goldwell. The initiation of printing in Oxford is consequently not dissimilar from what happened in so many places in Europe. A printer of German origins, who was trained in one of the major printing centres there, was encouraged to move to a city with a university in another country under the prompting of an eminent churchman and man of learning. The result was a book in Latin belonging to the standard Western intellectual tradition, but the edition itself was in competition with many others that were produced in Italy, Germany and Switzerland during the fifteenth century.

For information about the Oxford press see E. Gordon Duff, *The English Provincial Printers, Stationers and Bookbinders to 1557* (Cambridge: Cambridge University Press, 1912), pp. 1-22, and H. Carter, *A History of Oxford University Press* (Oxford: Clarendon 1975) I. 4-12.

Two further Latin texts were produced in the same type and without printer's name in Oxford, one a copy of Aristotle's *Ethics* in the Latin version of the humanist Leonardo Bruno and the other a treatise on original sin by Aegidius de Columna. The latter contains a colophon in red ink, which is the only time red-ink printing was used in Oxford. Both texts contain many misprints, some of which have been corrected by hand in the extant copies. These two texts were printed in 1479. From 1481 a series of other editions were printed at Oxford, but these were issued under the imprint of Theodoric Rood, a printer who came from Cologne and continued to use Cologne type. But the type used after 1481 is quite different from that used in the first three Oxford books. Not all these later books identify Rood as the printer, but the type makes it clear that the same printer was involved in all of them. It is natural to suppose that the editions produced after 1481 came from the same press as those produced in 1478 and 1479, though this cannot be proved. There is some continuity in the type of material produced, though there are certain obvious differences as we shall see. Also there is the problem of why there is the gap in production from late 1479 to early 1481 and why the printer should have added his name to some editions appearing after 1481 but not to any of those which were issued earlier. A possible solution to this problem is that Goldwell may have been instrumental in establishing the press in 1478 and he may have supported it for the next year, after which he lost interest. The gap would be caused by this cessation of patronage and the attempt by the printer to decide how to proceed. Possibly he looked for support among the academics of the university or even branched out on his own with the intention of capturing the academic market. The texts printed after 1481 have a strong English association as well as noticeable educational links. Many of them were by English authors, such as Alexander of Hales, John Lathbury, John Anwykyll, William Lyndewode and Richard Rolle. Several of these are religious texts, but others are school texts. John Anwykyll was a master at Magdalen College School, Oxford, who died in 1486 and who is credited with the authorship of a grammar which became the basis of most Latin grammars for many years to come. Other Latin texts produced by the press could also be used as school texts, such as Cicero's *Pro Milone*. One text which is of some passing interest is *Epistolae* of Phalaris in the Latin translation of Franciscus Aretinus, since this edition contains some verses by way of a prologue written by the court poet Petrus Carmelianus. This man prepared the edition of *Sex epistolae* for the press in the edition which was printed by Caxton about the same time (i.e. 1485) as this Oxford work appeared. The texts printed after 1481 are more local and educational and less humanist than those printed earlier, though they continue the general publishing policy established by those first texts. One text, the *Vulgaria* of Publius Terentius Afer, contains English translations of the Latin sentences, but this was clearly intended as a help to students learning Latin and was often issued with Anwykyll's grammar. However, one text from the later period is entirely in English. This is the last text attributed to Rood's press, and although it is dated 14 October 1486, it contains no printer's name or place of publication. The text is the *Liber festivalis*, which despite its title is a collection of sermons in English written by John Mirk, an Austin canon. of Lilleshall, Shropshire, at the end of the fourteenth century. This text is interesting since it is in English and it had by 1486 already been printed by Caxton at Westminster. It is also found in a large number of manuscripts.[3] Rood's text is not, however, printed from Caxton's edition and Rood did not include with the *Liber festivalis* the text known as *Quattuor sermones* which usually appeared as part of the printed editions. But when Caxton re-issued the text about 1491 he set up his second edition from the Oxford one, which was in some respects fuller than his own first edition.

The question naturally arises as to why Rood should have turned to an English work for his final printed edition since he had been content to produce Latin religious and educational material until then. We may assume that if Goldwell was instrumental in setting up the press he withdrew his financial and moral support at some stage, even if not after the publication of the first three editions. We must also assume that the printer then turned to material which had an English link, but which was still basically in the same mould as that produced in 1478 and 1479. It appears as though the market for this material was not large enough to sustain a press in operation. Once the academic market in Oxford and Cambridge was satisfied, there would not be many outlets for the type of book being produced since there is not much evidence that religious houses would necessarily wish to acquire this type of material. In any case similar material, though not necessarily by English authors, was available from Continental publishers and the book trade between England and the Continent was sufficiently well developed for books from presses in Europe to be readily available in Oxford. Furthermore many academics, like Goldwell himself, travelled abroad and acquired books and manuscripts on their travels. One may also wonder whether Oxford was a good distribution centre for books either to the rest of England or indeed to Europe. At all events the change from Latin texts to this English text would suggest a change of policy which may have been dictated by financial considerations. The Oxford printer could see that Caxton was active in Westminster and that his press was flourishing. The bulk of books produced by him were in English, and the publication of the *Liber festivalis* looks like a desperate attempt to change direction to prevent bankruptcy by imitating a policy that was already well established elsewhere. Even the book chosen was one which had already been

---

[3] On the various editions and manuscripts see R.E. Lewis, N.F. Blake and A.S.G., Edwards, *Index of Printed Middle English Prose* (New York: Garland, 1985), item 734.

published at Westminster. It has been suggested that the Oxford press was going to publish other more popular material, perhaps in English, because most of the woodcuts which were used in the edition of *Liber festivalis* are more suitable for works like the *Golden Legend*. Other woodcuts in this edition seem intended for a *Book of Hours*, though no edition is known of from the Oxford press. These woodcuts show links with those used by Caxton and it may well be that there was some co-operation between the presses at this level. In any event the Oxford press stopped producing editions after the *Liber festivalis*, and it is probable that it succumbed to financial insolvency as so many other early printers did. No one in Oxford or nearby was prepared to support the press financially, and this perhaps is hardly surprising since there was an active printing industry in Westminster and London and since academic books from the Continent could be obtained without much difficulty. The market for English books of an academic or religious nature was not large enough to keep the press afloat, even though these books were in Latin and could in theory be distributed throughout Europe.

One final point about the Oxford press needs to be mentioned. One of the books published by Rood, the *Epistolae* of Phalaris which appeared in 1485, has a colophon stating that it was printed by Theodoric Rood and Thomas Hunt. This Hunt was an Englishman and a stationer at Oxford. It may well be that Hunt was associated with Rood in all the later books printed by the Oxford press, for the last books appeared in a different type which include a *w* character as though it was a fount that was intended for the printing of books in English. Perhaps Hunt replaced Goldwell as a financial backer of the press when Goldwell withdrew his patronage, and as a stationer in Oxford it may be that Hunt was also interested in printing English books. However, as many of the later books of the Oxford press exist only in fragments it is not possible to tell when Hunt joined Rood. And there seems no reason to doubt the basic position which has been outlined earlier, namely that the press turned to English material as a panic measure to stave off financial insolvency caused by the production of Latin texts which did not sell well enough, but the resort to English came too late to save the press from going under.

Much less is known about the press at St Albans, though it has some interesting points of comparison with the press at Oxford.[4] It is not known who was responsible for establishing the press at St Albans, but as there was a large Benedictine abbey there, it seems likely that the Abbot had a hand in it. Wynkyn de Worde was later to refer to this printer as 'sometyme scole master of saynt Albons' and so he is usually known as the schoolmaster-printer. The first work attributed to the St Albans press is

---

[4] E. Gordon Duff, *op. cit.* pp. 34-42. The view of J. Moran, 'The Book of St Albans and the "Schoolmaster Printer"', *Black Art* 2 (1963-64): 117-24 that St Albans may refer to the Abbot of St Albans' house in Westminster has not been widely accepted.

the *Libellus super Tullanis elegantiis* by Augustinus Datus (Agostini Dati, a fifteenth-century Italian writer) which appeared *apud Sanctum Albanum,* probably in 1479 – just a little later than the press at Oxford. No other works by Augustinus Datus were produced in England in the fifteenth century, but several of his writings were printed on the Continent. The choice is in no way exceptional. The type of this edition is an elegant gothic letter which looks to have links with Italy, though there is no particular reason to assume that the printer was a foreigner. However, he abandoned this type in his later books which contain type modelled on Caxton's type. This may indicate that the printer felt Caxton's type sorts which mostly imitate Burgundian *bâtarde* script were most suitable for books printed in England. He may have felt the Italianate type was too foreign. The next book, which is dated in the colophon to 1480, is the *Nova rhetorica* by Laurentius Guglielmus de Saona, which had been printed a year or two earlier by Caxton at Westminster, from whose edition the St Albans version appears to have been printed. This seems to be no more than opportunism on the part of the printer. His next four books are still in Latin and are either religious or academic in content. These texts are not patristic, but are by authors from a more recent time. Apart from the *Nova rhetorica*, these books were not issued by other presses in England during the fifteenth century. However, the last two editions from the St Albans press show a marked difference from what had gone before because both are in English. The first of these, which is undated but is generally attributed to 1485, is an edition of the *Chronicles of England* a prose text based on the history of England known as the *Brut.* This text was available in a large number of manuscripts, many of which show additions as the historical account is brought further up to date. It had already by 1485 been printed twice by Caxton at Westminster, in 1480 and 1482. However, the St Albans edition is not a reprint of either of Caxton's editions.[5] It was clearly set up from a different textual tradition and it was interpolated throughout with details of the popes and other ecclesiastical matters. The interpolations are those that one might expect from a press which had links with a powerful abbey. After all, St Albans Abbey had a long and distinguished historical tradition. Wynkyn de Worde tells us that the compilation of this edition took place in St Albans itself. The last text issued by the St Albans press is less expected.[6] It contains two parts: one an account of hawking and hunting attributed in the edition to 'Dam Iulyans Barnes', and the other an account of the blasing of arms to enable

---

[5] On the manuscripts and printed editions of this text see particularly now L.M. Matheson, 'Printer and Scribe: the *Polychronicon,* and the *Brut*', *Speculum* 60 (1985): 593-614.

[6] For a facsimile and discussion see R. Hands, *English Hawking and Hunting in The Boke of St Albans* (London: Oxford University Press, 1975).

people to distinguish gentlemen from other people. The first part exists in manuscript, though it had never been printed earlier; the second part was translated and compiled at St Albans. Its whole appeal is different from the books published earlier by the St Albans press, since it is directed more towards the secular nobility and middle classes rather than to the academic and religious community.

Once again one is forced to ask why a press which seems to have intended to publish works in Latin for the academic and religious market should suddenly, before it ceases publication altogether, have turned to works in the vernacular which were no doubt aimed at a rather different audience. St Albans is even closer to Westminster than Oxford is, and it is likely that the St Albans press and Caxton's press had some association. Caxton was established at the Almonry in Westminster Abbey, which was also a Benedictine house. Even if the St Albans press was not installed in the Abbey there, it was almost certainly set up with the encouragement and perhaps financial support of the abbots and other members of the community. The St Albans printer reprinted one of Caxton's Latin editions, he used type which is very similar to Caxton's, and he modelled his first English book on another of his editions. Even his turning to English works at the end of the press's life suggests an imitation of what was happening at Westminster. Although the texts in Latin produced by the St Albans press are not so insular as those emanating from Oxford, we may assume that the market for them was not great enough to keep the press solvent. Equally the competition from foreign presses for books of this type was likely to be severe. St Albans did not even have the benefit of an academic community on its doorstep, though both Oxford and Cambridge were within easy travelling distance. It may well be, though, that the trade routes from St Albans to these two universities were not well established, and the number of people who visited St Albans was perhaps not sufficient to make the press economic. At all events the St Albans press went out of business in the same year as the Oxford press, and it is probable that both succumbed to the same pressures: lack of a sufficient market along established trade routes and foreign competition. The production of vernacular texts by these two presses at the end of their brief existence may be attributed to a belated attempt to find a different market when it became apparent that their original market was not sufficient to keep them financially viable. In both cases it is likely that the impetus for this change came from the apparently successful press operated by Caxton in Westminster, a notable feature of which was a large production of texts in English. It is unlikely that the choice of these English texts by the presses at Oxford and St Albans was made after mature reflection and as part of an overall policy. Their publication gives the appearance of being a panic reaction to a desperate financial situation. The choice was governed by what Caxton had already done or by what was immediately available.

It is time now to turn to Caxton and his press.[7] Caxton differs from the other printers in England and indeed from many abroad in that quite a lot is known of his life and that he was active as a printer for a very long time. His life is significant for his printed output and so it is helpful to review it briefly. Although nothing is known of his birth and parentage, it is probable that his parents were merchants or officials. Caxton was enrolled as an apprentice with Robert Large, a mercer who subsequently became Lord Mayor of London; and the payment of his enrolment fee is recorded in the Mercers' Account Book for 1438. The mercers formed the most important section of the Merchant Adventurers Company, through which the overseas trade was organised. Hence by becoming a mercer, particularly to such an important man as Large, Caxton inevitably became involved in the overseas trade which in the fifteenth century revolved around trade between England, the Low Countries and France. Inevitably he became a rich man and he became involved in the diplomatic relations among the kings of England and France and the dukes of Burgundy. The Low Countries were controlled by the dukes, and the English were attracted there by the important trade fairs there and by their outlets to wider markets. However, Flanders was also at this time an important centre of manuscript production, and many of these manuscripts found their way to England – no doubt through the good offices of the merchant adventurers. There seems every reason to believe that Caxton himself engaged in this trade in manuscripts. At all events he became a governor of the English nation in Bruges about 1462, and this is a sign of his status and his wealth. As governor he would have become even more closely involved in the negotiations between England and Burgundy, which took a more optimistic outlook with the marriage of Margaret, Edward IV's sister, to Charles Duke of Burgundy in 1468.

In late 1473 or early 1474 Caxton printed an edition of *History of Troy*, which was his own translation of the prose version by Raoul Lefèvre who had been a kind of secretary to Duke Philip of Burgundy, for whom the French version was made in 1464. The *History of Troy* is the first book to be printed in English. According to his own account in the prologue of *History of Troy*, Caxton started to translate the French text in 1469 but gave up the project after translating only a few quires. There is no evidence that Caxton had made any previous translations, and the comparison in the prologue of his activity to the fate of 'blind Bayard' suggests that he was inexperienced as a translator. It is consequently necessary to enquire why he should have started to make a translation at this time. Why should an experienced, influential and wealthy merchant suddenly start to make a translation, when he was probably fifty and may even have been older? As that merchant went on to print the translation and others which he

[7] For a comprehensive bibliography see N.F. Blake, *William Caxton: A Bibliographical Guide* (New York: Garland, 1985).

subsequently made, it is difficult to avoid the conclusion that the translation was undertaken with a view to its being printed. Caxton did not have a press in 1469 and may not have known how he was going to acquire one, but he was clearly planning to do so. The abandonment of the translation, which turned out to be only temporary, may reflect his difficulties in bringing these plans to fruition. Printing had of course already reached Cologne by this time and so Caxton would have been familiar with the press and its output since Cologne had such close links with Flanders and other parts of the Low Countries.

If Caxton did start his translation with the intention of acquiring a press and printing it, then his approach is very different from that found among almost all other printers. Even before he had acquired a press he had formed some idea as to what he was going to print; in other words he was moving towards devising a publishing policy, and that policy involved vernacular material. The acquisition of the press is, if anything, subordinate to that overall policy. How different that is from the average situation. More often than not a printer, often of German extraction, is encouraged to set up his press in an academic or religious environment through the good offices of a patron. Some books are produced by the printer before he is overwhelmed by financial insolvency and forced to take his press elsewhere to try his luck there. This insolvency may be caused by the patron withdrawing his support or by the inability of the printer to sell his finished books, since a considerable amount of capital would be locked up in each edition. As we have seen, both presses at Oxford and St Albans went out of business after operating for about seven years. Caxton survived in the publishing business, for he was still operating as a publisher when he died in 1492. It is, therefore, important to analyse what his publishing policy was and how he carried it out.

It is now accepted that Caxton acquired his press in the office of Johannes Veldener in Cologne, where Caxton was resident for about eighteen months in 1471-1472. Several books can be ascribed to Veldener's press there, though Caxton is particularly associated with the *De proprietatibus rerum* of Bartholomaeus Anglicus.[8] It need not be assumed that Caxton was responsible for the choice of this particular text or for any of the other texts printed by Veldener there. What is important to notice is that all Veldener's Cologne editions were of Latin texts, as indeed is true of Cologne printing in general up to the time of Caxton's visit. The importance of this is that Caxton was perfectly familiar with what I may call traditional publishing, that is a press established in a diocesan or university centre issuing books which are in Latin and which would appeal to an academic or religious audience. In arriving at a publishing policy which was very different from this, he was not motivated by

---

[8] S. Corsten, 'Caxton in Cologne', *Journal of the Printing Historical Society* 11 (1976-77): 1-18.

ignorance; his choice of a different approach was clearly positive.

In this connection we should remember what happened in the early years of his press. After printing *History of Troy* Caxton then issued another of his translations from French, *Game of Chess*, in 1474. But before he returned to England in 1476 he issued no further books in English; instead he issued four books in French, including the French texts of *History of Troy* and of *Jason*, the first of which he had already printed in English and the second he was to issue in English at Westminster on his return to England. These French texts are therefore the same sort of material that he was issuing in English. What is significant here is either that it would appear he had run out of material in English to publish or that he felt he could not distribute his English texts from Bruges successfully. He did not, however, resort to printing texts in Latin which might have seemed the obvious thing to do, if only because that was what most printers were publishing. To turn to French may indicate a small crisis in the production of English material, whatever caused it, but the refusal to turn to Latin material also suggests a confidence in his basic publishing policy which consisted in the provision of texts in the vernacular to members of the nobility and the middle classes.

What then were the principles which guided Caxton in his publishing policy? He could have chosen to issue works in English, French or Latin, and he deliberately opted for English. In this way he could establish a monopoly, for Continental publishers were not printing English books yet. Although his books would not be saleable on the Continent, this would not matter if his print-run was not too large. It would restrict his market outlets, but make his marketing easier because his books would not have to travel so far. The developments in education meant that his potential audience would be more than sufficient to buy the number of copies he would produce. There was already in existence in England a well-developed system of manuscript production and there is evidence that some entrepreneurs had established businesses that were the equivalent of small bookshops. The texts produced by a man like John Shirley were in English, and so it is possible to see in Caxton the successor to people like Shirley who had produced multiple copies of manuscripts during the earlier part of the fifteenth century.[9] A press is, nevertheless, very different from a manuscript scriptorium not only in the number of copies it produces but also in the need to keep the presses busy so that the workmen are kept employed. So although someone like Shirley could be largely satisfied with reproducing courtly poetry by such authors as Chaucer and Lydgate, this would not be sufficient to keep a press occupied. If Caxton intended to publish material in English, this raises the question of what was available.

[9] C. Greenberg, 'John Shirley and the English Book Trade', *The Library* 6th ser. 4 (1982): 369-80.

It is naturally possible to think in terms of what exists already or what can be created. Among existing material one can isolate four main categories that Caxton could have exploited: courtly poetry, alliterative poetry, historical prose and religious prose. The Bible in English is not to be reckoned as a possible book to print, since in the fifteenth century it was still associated with the Lollards and hence heretical. Caxton published no alliterative poetry, presumably because he considered it unfashionable and provincial; it is associated in England with the north and west rather than with London. He published only general religious prose; he published no specialist religious texts like those by the mystical writers. His audience was not attuned to this kind of material. He published a great deal of the courtly poetry and historical prose which was available, but we need to remember that the amount of this type of literature which was available was limited. It was certainly not sufficient to keep a publisher fully active for more than a few years. Hence he had to rely on new texts: he had to create material to keep his presses busy. This did not mean patronising young writers whose work could then be published; new books meant translation. This naturally raised two further considerations: what was to be translated and who was to make the translation?

In the fifteenth century men's eyes were turned towards the court of Burgundy which was considered the most elaborate and sophisticated one north of the Alps. England had close ties with the duchy through trade, but English people tended to look to it also as a model for behaviour.[10] And the rise of the middle classes meant that people were much more conscious of behaviour than hitherto as the flood of courtesy books indicates. The marriage of Margaret to Duke Charles had encouraged even further cultural links between England and Burgundy. The dukes of Burgundy had a magnificent library which contained numerous works in French, many of which had been made for the dukes from Latin versions. Naturally such texts were also to be found in other libraries, for the manuscript shops were able to produce copies of them. So one does not need to assume that Caxton was influenced by ducal taste alone in so far as that taste was also imitated in many other households in Burgundy.[11] What he does seem to have thought is that he could fill a gap in the English market by providing English translations of fashionable reading matter in French from Burgundy. Later after his return to England he translated texts which had been printed in France, particularly in Lyons. The basic policy was the same; the source of supply was different. He provided

[10] G. Kipling, *The Triumph of Honour. Burgundian Origins of the Elizabethan Renaissance* (Leiden: University Press, 1977).

[11] L. Hellinga, 'Caxton and the Bibliophiles', *Actes du XIe Congrès International de Bibliophile Bruxelles 1979* (Brussels, 1982): 11-38.

English versions of texts that could be presented as recently made available in French and so he was able to capitalise on the novelty of the material as well as on its sophistication. This did, however, present a problem about the translation. Caxton did not publish alliterative poetry because it was unsophisticated in its style. It would not be sensible to go out of one's way to use material in translation which could be termed unsophisticated. Since style seems to have been a matter partly of content and partly of the translator, this meant in effect that Caxton had to use translators who would carry a certain amount of prestige through the position they occupied. Consequently he never employed a professional translator or hack writer. Although Wynkyn de Worde was in Caxton's employment for many years, he was never invited to make a translation for Caxton. Although he must have been a native speaker of Low German, he was not even asked to translate the Dutch *Reynard the Fox* into English. Translators had to have a certain social standing to guarantee the quality of their style.

It was probably for this reason that Caxton introduced the story of the makings of his own translation in the prologue to *History of Troy*.[12] There he said he had completed a few quires of the translation and then put it aside in despair because he was so dissatisfied with it. Later he showed the translation to Margaret Duchess of Burgundy and she ordered him to make some improvements to his style and then to complete the translation. This he proceeded to do. This story is surely meant to disarm criticism. Although some people might assume that a mere merchant would not be able to translate elegantly, Caxton is able to assure them that his style has been purified of any infelicities by Margaret's advice and that it may be said to have the approval of such a noble lady as Margaret. From now on his style could be accepted as courtly. Other translations which Caxton printed were either by members of the nobility or by those closely associated with such people. Translations printed by Caxton include those by John Tiptoft, Earl of Worcester, and Anthony Wydeville, Earl Rivers. When he printed *Of Old Age*, which had been translated by William Worcestre, he devoted the major part of its prologue to a discussion of the life of Sir John Fastolfe who was the original patron of the edition. Similarly when he published Trevisa's translation of Higden's *Polychronicon* he devoted part of the prologue to Lord Berkeley, who had been Trevisa's employer.

Although books in Latin were printed on Caxton's presses, it seems likely that in these instances he was usually acting as a printer rather than a publisher and consequently they should not be regarded as part of his publishing programme. They were bespoke texts to keep his presses busy. Thus, for example, the edition of *Nova rhetorica* by Lorenzo Guglielmo

---

[12] Caxton's prologues and epilogues are edited in N.F. Blake, *Caxton's Own Prose* (London: Deutsch, 1973).

Traversagni of 1478-79, which was set up from the author's holograph, was almost certainly printed at the request of the author or his friends in Cambridge, and one may assume it was distributed by them.[13] As far as Caxton was concerned his publishing policy consisted of providing material in English for the nobility and for the middle classes. This material consisted of poetry and prose already available provided it was of sufficient stylistic quality and of translations which reflected as far as possible current reading matter either in Burgundy or more generally in France. At first the source for these French texts was the scriptoria in Flanders; later it became the printing presses in France, particularly Lyons. It is important to emphasise that this policy was devised by Caxton before he had even acquired a printing press and was adhered to by him throughout his career as printer and publisher. It was evidently successful since he survived financially until his death. But that survival may also be attributed to his knowledge of financial matters, since his experience as a merchant would have given him the knowledge and expertise to float large capital projects. It is also to be noted that he established his press near the royal court at Westminster which was also close to the trade routes which ran from London. The presses at Oxford and St Albans perhaps failed because of their location, though they were imitating the placing of many presses on the Continent. Caxton's press showed that it was not academics or religious who would provide the best support for a press; on the contrary it was courtiers and merchants who had the money for book buying and who were prepared to indulge their taste for what was fashionable and ephemeral reading matter. But because they contained what was fashionable and ephemeral, new printed books were always saleable since each one represented a new example of a traditional genre. Caxton could never produce sufficient books to satiate this market.

Several other printers did establish themselves in England during the last two decades of the fifteenth century.[14] It is noteworthy that they all settled in London, which became and has since remained the centre of publishing and bookselling in England. These other printers have not been studied as extensively as Caxton, and they were naturally very much under his influence. At least two of them appear to have worked for Caxton, Wynkyn de Worde and Richard Pynson, and all were foreigners. This latter fact is of some importance as it prevented them from following

[13] J. Ruysschaert, 'Les manuscrits autographes de deux œuvres de Lorenzo Guglielmo Traversagni imprimées chez Caxton', *Bulletin of the John Rylands Library* 36 (1953-54): 191-97.
[14] H. Plomer, *Wynkyn de Worde and his Contemporaries from the Death of Caxton to 1535* (London: Grafton, 1925) contains some information about these printers. On de Worde and his publishing policy see N.F. Blake, 'Wynkyn de Worde: the Early Years' and 'Wynkyn de Worde: the Later Years', *Gutenberg Jahrbuch* (1971): 62-69 and (1972): 128-38.

Caxton's publishing policy exactly. Caxton himself made many of the translations which he printed and because his style had had the approval of Margaret of Burgundy it could be presented as courtly. This would clearly be impossible for these foreigners who had set themselves up as printers in London. The type of material which Caxton had exploited would not be available to them unless they could find courtly translators. The result was that they developed other strategies. The first was that they frequently reprinted texts which had been printed by Caxton and which had presumably gone out of print sometime earlier. The second was that they printed material which could in some ways be linked with the kind of material which Caxton had printed. For example, the printing of the lives of St Katherine of Siena and St Elizabeth of Hungary in English by Wynkyn de Worde can be seen as providing a text which could be associated with the *Golden Legend*, which had been printed by Caxton and subsequently re-issued by de Worde. Caxton printed a few works by Lydgate, but de Worde printed many more as well as a number of romances. The third was that they tapped sources which had largely been ignored by Caxton. As we saw, Caxton did not print much specialised religious material. But Wynkyn de Worde did. He printed such devotional texts as Hilton's *Scale of Perfection*, *The Mirror of the Life of Christ* erroneously attributed to St Bonaventura, and the English translation of Ruysbroek's *The Chastising of God's Children*. Caxton did not print contemporary writings in English, but de Worde printed many works which had just been written, and some of which may even have been written for the press. Many of the writings by John Alcock, Bishop of Ely, were printed by de Worde as soon as they were written. Caxton printed only one edition of the statutes issued through Parliament. But de Worde and Pynson issued many editions of various statutes or year-books.

Some of these printers did publish books in Latin, but for the most part these were either liturgical or grammatical. English printers did not try to compete with the Continental printers by providing Latin academic or scholastic text. They also tended to avoid humanist texts. The example of Caxton lay like a heavy shadow across the English publishing scene and encouraged other printers to produce only work in English. This became the basic policy of all English printers after the collapse of the Oxford and St Albans presses. How they realised that policy depended upon their own status and the material which they could either acquire or manufacture for themselves. In this respect England differs from most other European countries; and this difference is to be explained through the work of a single man – William Caxton. Without him the history of printing in the fifteenth century in England would surely have been very different.

It is now time to put some of these conclusions into a wider perspective. English printing in the fifteenth century was dominated by Caxton and this meant that it concentrated on printing in the vernacular from the beginning. The very first text to be printed in English was made to be printed. Although the presses at Oxford and St Albans did have a policy of issuing texts in Latin, these were short lived, and the production of classical material was not to be attempted seriously in England for many years to come. In the eighteenth century Gibbon could complain that the world owed England no first edition of a classical text. It is perhaps a sign of the times that we should now have a colloquium on the spread of vernacular printing and concentrate on the production of texts in the vernacular languages.

London was the dominant centre of printing in England and was to remain so. There was no printing in Scotland, Ireland or Wales in the fifteenth century. When printing was introduced into Scotland in the early sixteenth century, the printers there imitated the general policy that can be discerned in London. There was no general development of printing in Ireland or Wales in the early sixteenth century, largely owing to the political domination of England. England had been for many centuries a very centralised kingdom and this prevented the development of printing in provincial centres and accounts in many ways for the relatively small number of printed books as compared with France, Germany or Italy. The centralisation was even further promoted by the dissolution of the monasteries in the 1530s, since they had up till that time provided alternative sources of patronage for writers and alternative homes for localised orthographies. After this period there was no other centre which could challenge the predominance of London in literary or linguistic matters.

It is sometimes suggested that there was competition between church and state in the production of early material in the presses in that the former encouraged the printing of Latin texts. Whatever the position may have been in other countries, this cannot be shown to have been the case in England. After all Caxton established his press within the confines of Westminster Abbey and the St Albans printer must have had some link with the abbey there. Some printers like de Worde used manuscripts in English from the monastic foundations as copytexts, and this probably happened much more frequently than we can tell. Some orders in England are associated with providing religious material in English usually through translation. This applies especially to the Carthusian and Brigettine orders. They would have seen the press as a natural ally in the provision of material in English, and it is not probable that they would have been opposed to the production of material in English. It would only be in one or two delicate areas such as the Bible in English that the church is likely to have kept any close eye on what the presses produced. Otherwise as far as England is concerned, there is no reason to suppose that there was any pressure from the church authorities on the printers to produce material in Latin rather than in English.

It is difficult to provide statistics of what was produced because one needs to know precisely to what any statistics refer. A publisher like

Caxton was also a printer, and he produced material at the request of other people. These can hardly be said to be part of his overall publishing policy, and if allocated to Caxton as part of his publishing output they would give a misleading impression. What can be said is that England did not produce as many texts as its Continental neighbours. Duff lists 431 incunables connected with England,[15] but this is a misleading total as some of the books contain more than one title. Of these books 72 were printed abroad: 4 in French (by Caxton), 9 in English and 59 in Latin. The bulk of the Latin incunables are liturgical and some were produced for English publishers and booksellers. Of the nine English texts two were produced by Caxton in Bruges, four by Gerard Leeu in Antwerp, and the other three in Rouen. The Rouen texts are copies of Mirk's *Liber festivalis*, and were probably produced in association with an English publisher or bookseller, though we cannot be certain of this. These editions are reprints of English editions and may, of course, have been produced speculatively. Of Leeu's four editions in English three were reprints of English editions and one was a new text which he had translated specially. But Leeu was well informed about the English market and he seems to have worked in association with people in England. The books in English printed abroad do not represent new departures in publishing policy.

Of the texts printed in England it is possible to break them down between various centres as follows, though the numbers do not quite fit Duff's totals because of the occasional appearance of two titles in the same edition.

Westminster	Caxton	93	
	de Worde	103	
	Notary	5	Total 201
London	Notary	2	
	Lettou	5	
	Lettou & Machlinia	6	
	Machlinia	22	
	Pynson	101	Total 136
Oxford		17	
St Albans		8	
Others		2	Total 27

It may be simplest to analyse the number of books printed by Caxton and to break those down into vernacular and other texts. But to do so it may be helpful to consider whether the books were published or printed by Caxton. In my *William Caxton: A Bibliographical Guide*[16] I have attempted a basic division of his printed material along lines of this sort. The figures do not tally exactly with Duff's because of new discoveries

---

[15] Duff, *Fifteenth Century English Books, passim*.
[16] Blake, *A Bibliographical Guide, passim*.

about Caxton which have been made since Duff compiled his index. I divided Caxton's works up in the following ways:

Books printed and published by Caxton	97
Books printed by Caxton	10
Books translated by Caxton	3
Books published by Caxton	4

The books published by Caxton are all in Latin, and those translated by him (which have been printed) are all in English. The texts printed by Caxton are all small pieces, most of which are in Latin like *Indulgences*, though some are in English like the *Advertisement*. Of the works printed and published by Caxton, he translated 22, though some of these were issued in more than one edition. The remaining books printed and published by Caxton represent fifteen poetic works in English, nineteen prose texts in English, and twelve Latin texts. Many of the works in English were reprinted, though this was rare for the Latin texts other than the *Horae* which appeared in six editions. It should also be remembered that the English books were often far longer than the Latin texts. Books like *History of Troy, Canterbury Tales* and *King Arthur* are probably each as long as all the combined texts printed in Latin by Caxton. If we include all the editions printed on Caxton's presses and ignore the relative length of each book, we could say that four are in French, twenty-six in Latin and seventy-five in English. The proportion of editions in English is at least 60% of the total printed output, but if one was to consider the volume of pages being produced the percentage of English would be far higher. These statistics would be generally applicable to the other big printers in the fifteenth century like de Worde and Pynson, though they naturally do not apply to the Oxford and St Albans presses. It would probably not be too inaccurate to assume that in England in the fifteenth century the ratio of English to Latin printed material was of the order of sixty to forty.

Finally we ought to remember that the introduction of printing did not lead to any big changes in the literary and intellectual scene. England has a well-developed literature in the medieval period, and the production of translations whether by secular or monastic scriptoria was regular. Caxton built upon the traditions which were already established. Furthermore, scribes remained active after the introduction of printing, though there is no reason to assume that there was any antagonism between scribes and printers. What is characteristic of England is the relatively large number of scribal copies of printed books that were made in the fifteenth century. This presumably reflects an interest in the books that were being produced by the English printers. An interesting case is provided by the historical accounts of England such as the *Chronicles of England*. These were sometimes copied out as the basis for a further historical continuation. In this respect the printed text was fulfilling the same function as a manuscript.

6

Dating the First Books Printed in English

The first book printed by Caxton with a date for its printing widely accepted as unambiguous is *Dicts or Sayings*, which was completed on 18th November 1477. Caxton had started to print several years earlier. The absence of agreed dates for his earlier books has meant that the date when he began to print is disputed, the dates of the earliest books are undecided, and the number of editions which preceded *Dicts or Sayings* at Westminster is uncertain. *History of Troy*, which is accepted to be Caxton's first printed book, contains no date or place of printing, though it is widely accepted that it was printed in Bruges. Many of the standard bibliographical guides have dated it to 1475 or even occasionally to 1476.[1] More recently the discovery of two important sources has modified our attitude to the date of this text. The first, the Register of Aliens at Cologne, showed that Caxton was in that city in 1471/2. Although the interpretation of the entries is not straightforward, it seems beyond reasonable doubt that he left Cologne not later than the end of December 1472. The second is an indulgence printed by Caxton at Westminster. Since the date written in by hand is 13 December 1476, it follows that he had set up his shop at Westminster in 1476 and not in 1477 as previously believed.[2] These two dates (December 1472 and, say, September 1476) now provide the limits within which his Bruges output has to be dated. Not unnaturally these limits have encouraged a trend to date his first editions earlier than had previously been done. Hence *History of Troy* was dated to late 1473 or early 1474 and *Game of Chess* to 1474.[3] In his recent biography, however, Mr Painter has

---

[1] As, for example, E. Gordon Duff, *Fifteenth Century English Books*. Bibliographical Society Illustrated Monographs 18. (Oxford: Oxford University Press, 1917).

[2] As fully discussed in G.D. Painter, *William Caxton: A Quincentenary Biography* (London: Chatto & Windus, 1976), pp. 48, 83-84 and in S. Corsten, 'Caxton in Cologne', *Journal of the Printing Historical Society* 11 (1976-77): 1-18. Because it used to be thought that Caxton had returned to England in 1477, the quatercentenary of the introduction of printing into England was held in 1877, whereas the quincentenary was celebrated in 1976.

[3] N.F. Blake, *Caxton: England's First Publisher* (London: Osprey, 1976), p. 26ff.

reopened the whole question by dating *History of Troy* to late 1474 or early 1475 and *Game of Chess* to the middle of 1475.[4] In this dating he has been followed by the British Library and the John Rylands Library in their quincentenary exhibitions.[5] It therefore seems desirable to look at the dating again, particularly as new evidence which may be of assistance was published in the papers of the Caxton International Congress.

Painter's arguments are briefly as follows. In his epilogue to *Game of Chess* Caxton says he finished the book on 31 March 1474. Painter takes this date to signify 1475 in our modern reckoning and he understands Caxton's *finished* to refer to the work of translation. If this volume was translated only on 31 March 1475, it cannot have been printed till about June 1475. It was printed on the same paper as had been used for the final sections of *History of Troy*, which must therefore have been printed immediately beforehand. This means that *History of Troy* is not likely to have been printed till the early part of 1475. This in turn indicates that there was a long gap between Caxton's departure from Cologne in December 1472 and the commencement of the printing of *History of Troy*, say about August 1474. Painter accounts for this gap by assuming it took Caxton a longer time to build his press and train his workmen than has usually been thought. It would also be easier for Johann Veldener, who by 1474 was in Louvain and not in Cologne, to supervise the setting up of the press since Louvain was so much closer to Bruges. It may not be without significance that also in 1474 Veldener helped the Brothers of the Common Life establish their press in Brussels.

The crucial support of this argument is the date of *Game of Chess*. Right at the very end of the epilogue after the word *Amen* we find this concluding sentence: 'Fynysshid the / last day of marche the yer of our lord god .a. thousand / foure honderd and lxxiiii.' William Blades interpreted this '1474' as 1475 in modern reckoning and was followed in this by many scholars until it was pointed out that the interpretation was unlikely.[6] By reviving this theory Painter has put the clock back. The arguments against it have been set out fully elsewhere and hardly need detailed recapitulation here. Apart from this disputed example Caxton is known to have used two calendars or systems of reckoning the year: one in which the year began on 1 January (as now) and the other in which it started on 25 March (Lady Day). By either of these calendars the 1474 of *Game of Chess* would be 1474 by our reckoning also. But Blades knew that in some documents in the Low Countries the new year was calculated from Easter

---

[4] Painter, *op. cit.* pp. 59-71.

[5] William Caxton, *An Exhibition to commemorate the Quincentenary of Printing into England* (London: British Library, 1976), pp. 30-32; and *Caxton in the Context of European Printing 1476-1976* (Manchester: John Rylands Library, 1976), no. 28.

[6] The arguments against this interpretation are set out most fully in N.F. Blake, *Caxton's Own Prose* (London: Deutsch, 1973), pp. 11-19.

and he assumed Caxton was using this reckoning here, though he is not known to have used it on any other occasion. Since in 1474 Easter fell on 10 April, Blades deduced that in *Game of Chess* Caxton's date meant 31 March 1475 by our reckoning. This particular calendar in which the new year is reckoned from Easter was in very restricted use in the Low Countries and appears to have been completely unknown in England. Since *Game of Chess* was in English and hence designed for an English audience, it is highly improbable that Caxton used a system of reckoning that had only limited currency in the Low Countries. Although *Game of Chess* was printed in Bruges, this is not sufficient to claim that its dating was based on the less familiar of the two calendars in use there. The burden of proof rests with those who claim that he used this calendar, and until they bring forward more convincing arguments it is wiser to accept that the date in *Game of Chess* is 31 March 1474 by our reckoning.

As it happens although Easter fell on 10 April 1474, it fell on 26 March in 1475, a fact which supporters of Blades' theory ignore. So in accordance with this Low Countries calendar there was no 31 March 1474, because 1474 began on 10 April of one year and ended on 25 March of the next. Although a serious objection, it might be argued that this is not an insuperable one since Caxton actually wrote the 'last day' of March. It could be suggested that by this wording he meant 25 March 1475 by our reckoning. This would surely be desperate and assuming too much. How could English people, unused as they were to this particular system of reckoning, understand that the last day of March 1474 was really 25 March 1475? Caxton's wording and common sense militate against this supposition.

The question whether Caxton's *finished* refers to the translation or the printing of the text is more complicated and it may be impossible to reach a final decision. Painter has a few words on the subject which are worth quoting.

> It has been suggested that the word 'finished' in Caxton's colophon to *Reynard* refers to the completion of printing, not of translation. Caxton does indeed use 'finished' in either sense according to context, and *Reynard* is not the only book for which scholars have been tempted to misinterpret as a printing date what is really only a translation date. In fact Caxton's practice is absolutely consistent and unambiguous. He uses the formula 'emprinted and finished' or the like to mean completion of printing, and 'translated and finished' to mean completion of translation. In two books only – *Game of Chess I* and *Polychronicon* – the word 'finished' is used by itself; but here likewise the context, which concerns solely matters of writing and does not mention printing, shows that the date relates to completion of text, not to printing.[7]

---

[7] Painter, *op. cit.* pp. 110-11.

He is, however, incorrect in his details here. *Cordial* and *Description of Britain* both use *finished* by itself to mean printed. The latter is particularly instructive since at the end of the brief epilogue the final sentence reads: 'Fynysshed by me William Caxton the xviii day of August, the yere of Our Lord God MCCClxxx and the xx yere of the regne of Kyng Edward the Fourthe'.[8] This is exactly the same type of formula in the same place as the one in *Game of Chess* and ought to alert us to the possibility of the meaning printed there. In *Description of Britain* this concluding sentence is preceded by an account of the translation by Trevisa almost a hundred years earlier and has no bearing on the meaning of Caxton's *finished*, which has been accepted by all to refer to the printing.

In regard to *Game of Chess* and *Polychronicon* it is difficult to see how the context proves that Caxton's *finished* relates to the translation. Although the former was translated by Caxton, there is no reference in the epilogue to this, for it consists of a reference to the Duke of Clarence, the dedicatee, and of a request for the prosperity of England. There is nothing in the epilogue which prepares us for the final sentence. The *Polychronicon* was not even translated by Caxton; he merely added material from other English books to supplement an existing translation. This is no doubt why Painter refers so cautiously to 'matters of writing', by which he must mean Caxton's editorial work. Whereas he would have us believe that Caxton's *finished* normally indicates the translation, here it embraces only his editorial activity. It may be questioned whether there is a context for the *finished* in this case since the formula 'Fynysshed per Caxton' is put on a separate line by itself after a small gap. It is in this way quite divorced from the rest of the epilogue. So Caxton's use of *finished* is not quite so unambiguous as Painter claims. There is good reason to suggest that when used by itself it could refer to the printing, though it does not follow that this is true of the example in *Game of Chess*.

It should, however, be emphasized that his formula with *finished* comes at the end of the epilogue to *Game of Chess* and is unrelated to the material in the rest of the epilogue. In this it is similar to several other texts and it may well be that all these refer only to the printing. The word *finished* was replaced by *emprinted* in later examples of this formula. Perhaps early in his career the concept *printed* had not become sufficiently established to appear in such an exposed position. Until printing became respectable it is likely that *finished* seemed more appropriate. It was certainly the word he used in *History of Troy*, where he said that all copies of it were finished on the same day.

It may not be without significance to note the order in which the various parts of *Game of Chess* were made. The epilogue opens: 'And therfore, my ryght redoubted Lord, I pray Almighty God to save the Kyng our soverain lord . . .'. This 'redoubted Lord' is the Duke of Clarence who

---

[8] Quotations from prologues and epilogues are from Blake, *Caxton's Own Prose* (1973).

is not even named in the epilogue. It follows that the epilogue was written after the prologue was in existence, since Clarence is there fulsomely acknowledged. The order of the book's parts would therefore seem to be: the translation of the text itself, the prologue and finally the epilogue. The relevance of this order may be gauged by comparing *History of Troy*. This text is more complicated in that it contains a preface as well as a prologue at the beginning and an epilogue to book II as well as an epilogue to the whole work at the end. The prologue contains references only to the genesis of the translation and the incompetence of the translator; there is no reference to printing. It also contains no reference to Ghent or Cologne. It is therefore reasonable to assume that it was written first. The epilogue to book II mentions Bruges, Ghent and Cologne in reference to the translation, but it has no dates and no reference to printing. The preface, which is modelled on that found in the French original contains the principal dedication to Margaret of Burgundy and the date of the completion of the translation at Cologne. There is no reference to printing in it. The epilogue to the whole book is the only place which contains a reference to the book's printing, though it contains no dates. I think it likely that these four parts were composed in this order: prologue, epilogue to book II, preface, and epilogue to the whole book. It seems to me equally probable that the prologue was written in Bruges, where the translation was begun (since this would account for the absence of any reference to Cologne), and the epilogue to book II and the preface in Cologne, which is why there is frequent reference to Cologne in them. The epilogue to the whole book cannot have been written till Caxton was back in Bruges, for although he was in Cologne to learn printing he cannot have been so certain at that stage of the completion of the printing of *History of Troy*. The epilogue to the whole book is best seen as some kind of afterthought written in Bruges when the printing was nearing completion. It may have been written anything up to two years later than the rest of the work. Since *History of Troy* was the only other translation Caxton had made before *Game of Chess*, it is likely that this second text followed the pattern of the first.[9] After the translation was completed he wrote the prologue, which in *Game of Chess* corresponds to the preface in *History of Troy*. The epilogue may not have been added till the book was more or less complete in print. This would mean that the *finished* of the epilogue would refer to the printing rather than to the translation. Indeed, if we accept that 31 March 1474 refers to the printing, it may be that the translation of *Game of Chess* itself was made much earlier than this, possibly even in Cologne. After all *History of Troy* was finished on 21 September 1471 and Caxton still had another fourteen months to while away in that city.

---

[9] The order of the parts of each edition is a subject which has been insufficiently studied; see now (1991) Chapter 7 below, pp. 89-106.

While I am prepared to admit that the arguments advanced above do not prove conclusively that Caxton printed *Game of Chess* on 31 March 1474, I would like to suggest they provide a strong case for that view. Whether one accepts it or not depends on how well this date fits into the history of printing in Cologne and the Low Countries. This is what we must now consider.

At the Caxton International Congress in London (1976) two important papers dealt with the early period of Caxton's printing career, the first by Professor Corsten and the second by Professor and Mrs Hellinga.[10] Professor Corsten focussed his research on the records from Cologne and examined how they might be interpreted. Over the past few years it has become widely accepted that Johann Veldener was the printer of the *Flores Sancti Augustini* and that he also had a brief career as a printer in Cologne before establishing a workshop at Louvain in 1473. Through his investigations Professor Corsten was able to suggest that the order of Veldener's printed books in Cologne was as follows: Burley: *De vita philosophorum*; Pius II: *De duobus amantibus*; Bartholomaeus Anglicus: *De proprietatibus rerum*; and *Gesta Romanorum* (p. 16). The important point about these books is that *De proprietatibus* is a very much larger volume than anything which Veldener had hitherto printed and indeed than anything which had appeared in Cologne. It contains 248 leaves, whereas the two earlier books had only 58 and 22 leaves respectively. Corsten deduces, quite correctly I am sure, that in order to finance such a large project Veldener had access to a new source of capital to provide the money to buy the requisite paper and to pay the workmen while the book was at press. Since we know from de Worde that Caxton learned to print in Cologne on the Latin edition of *De proprietatibus*, this source must be Caxton himself. If so, it is possible he had a hand in the choice of the volume since it was written by an Englishman. In other words, although he may have learned some of the techniques of printing at Cologne on the *De proprietatibus*, he was essentially the publisher of that volume whereas Veldener was its printer. There was presumably some kind of partnership between the two men, in which one must assume that Caxton had the dominant say since he controlled the financing of the edition. It was a situation not unlike that which existed between Fust and Gutenberg almost twenty years previously. The importance of Professor Corsten's paper is that it reveals the essential contribution Caxton made to the appearance of *De proprietatibus* and it underlines Caxton's role as a financier and publisher rather than as a printer.

Professor and Mrs Hellinga examined *History of Troy* in detail to see

---

[10] See Corsten, *op. cit.*, and L. and W. Hellinga, 'Caxton in the Low Countries', *Journal of the Printing Historical Society* 11 (1976-77): 19-32.

what one could deduce from the way it was set up. They discovered that there were four compositors who worked on it and they labelled them A, B, C, D. Their respective contributions they analysed as follows :

Book I		Book II		Book III	
Gathering	Compositor	Gathering	Compositor	Gathering	Compositor
a	A	A	C	aa	A
					C
b	A	B	C		B
c	A,C	C	C	bb	B
d	A,C	D	C	cc	B
e	C	E	C	dd	B
			D		
f	C	F	D		
g	C	G	D	ee	B
	B				
h	B	H	D	ff	B
i	B	I	D	gg	B
k	B	K	D	hh	B
l	B	L	D	ii	B
m	B			kk	B
n	B				
o	B				
p	B				

Of particular interest is compositor A who started books I and III and then apparently disappeared. Since he used certain distinctive abbreviations and since he also did the red-ink printing, the Hellingas suggested that it was Veldener, whose interest in red-ink printing is well known. This suggestion seems very probable. As the paper used in *History of Troy* shows that three presses were in operation for its printing,[11] one can say that compositor A or Veldener helped to start off the first and last books and then dropped out of the project altogether.

The work by the Hellingas raises the question where *History of Troy* was printed, since Veldener is not known to have been to Bruges and since no place of printing is included by Caxton. If compositor A is Veldener and

---

[11] Painter, *op. cit.* p. 62.

as the translation was made by Caxton, three places have to be considered as possible sites for its printing: Bruges, with which Caxton was associated, Cologne, with which both were associated, and Louvain, with which Veldener was associated. Of these Cologne is the least likely since Caxton's permission to reside in Cologne was not renewed after Deicember 1472. To make Cologne at all possible, we would have to assume that Veldener printed the volume for Caxton after he had returned to Bruges. The later history of Caxton's press and even Caxton's earlier presence in Cologne make this view implausible.

Louvain has much to recommend it and was suggested as a possible site by the Hellingas, because Veldener had moved there by 30 July 1473 when he was matriculated in the University. He could naturally have been in the city earlier than this date. If Veldener was compositor A it would be natural to think that he established a large printing workshop in Louvain where several texts were being produced independently, though simultaneously. Veldener would take a hand in any text as need arose and as opportunity permitted. There are, however, several objections to Louvain. We know from the second edition of *Game of Chess* that the first one was printed at Bruges. If *History of Troy* was printed at Louvain, it would mean that Caxton's presses were dismantled and taken off to Bruges after the completion of a single text so that they would be ready in Bruges for the printing of his second text. One may wonder whether the continuity in paper between *History of Troy* and *Game of Chess* would have survived under those conditions. The paper dictates the theory that both texts were printed in the same place. If compositor A is Veldener, it is odd that he should appear only at the beginning of books I and III if the work was printed at Louvain. One might have expected him to appear sporadically as a compositor if the book was set up in his workshop. The disappearance of compositor A from the work indicates that he was no longer physically present where the book was set up. If that was Louvain, we would have to explain Veldener's absence by a trip to Brussels to establish the press of the Brothers of the Common Life. This is hardly likely since it would mean dating the beginning of *History of Troy* to 1474, which would naturally mean the problem of what Caxton was doing there all this time. And Veldener himself is hardly likely to have gone off somewhere else when he had just embarked on one major project in his workshop. Finally, we may ask what need there would be for Caxton to go to Louvain. He could have learned as much as he needed to know about printing at Cologne and it was there, not in Louvain, that he could recruit assistants. If Veldener had been the principal compositor of the edition, there might have been some point in Caxton going to Louvain. But he was not; so Caxton evidently had sufficient helpers. Furthermore we may recall the situation which existed in Cologne: Caxton had the money and Veldener the expertise. The history of printing reveals that the money was the crucial element. Caxton had no association with Louvain and is hardly likely to have wanted to go there. Surely he would want to return to Bruges. As he controlled the purse-stings, he could easily persuade Veldener to accompany him. There was good reason for Veldener to go to Bruges; there was none for Caxton to go to Louvain.

The most acceptable hypothesis is that *History of Troy* was printed in Bruges as has usually been accepted and that, therefore, Veldener also spent a period in Bruges helping Caxton set up his press. Since we know so little about Veldener, this hypothesis is quite likely. If Veldener was in Bruges, we are able to date the earliest works in English more closely and to give some body to this rather shadowy partnership that existed between the English merchant and the printer.

Since Veldener was matriculated in Louvain on 30 July 1473, his section of *History of Troy* must have been in print by then. We would not be far wrong if we assumed that the printing of *History of Troy* commenced in April/May 1473. We do not have to assume that Veldener accompanied Caxton from Cologne to Bruges at the end of 1472 (for he could always have followed independently later), but it is simpler to assume he did. Then we could posit that in the early part of 1473 Veldener made the matrices of Caxton's type I from a Flemish script, perhaps written by Colard Mansion. At the same time Veldener and Caxton would have made the presses, recruited and trained further helpers, and acquired the necessary materials. When *History of Troy* was safely under way, Veldener left Bruges and went to Louvain. There are so many possible explanations for Veldener's departure, that it is useless to speculate why he went. All we can deduce is that the parting was amicable for the two remained business associates for many years: Veldener continued to supply Caxton with his type. In an earlier paper Professor Corsten suggested that political conditions and increasing competition from other printers were the reasons which led Veldener to leave Cologne.[12] I would like to suggest that Veldener left Cologne because Caxton paid him to do so; he accompanied Caxton to Bruges. When he left Bruges, he did not go back to Cologne as we might expect; he went to Louvain. Perhaps Professor Corsten's reasons explain why he did not return to Cologne after parting from Caxton. He went to Louvain, another University town like Cologne, where he could print the books he was interested in and where he could develop his market in the Low Countries which had been so propitiously set up for him.

If we accept the order of Veldener's Cologne output as given by Professor Corsten it is important to note that *Gesta Romanorum* was printed after *De proprietatibus*. If Veldener and Caxton were in partnership for *De proprietatibus* and if Veldener was compositor A of *History of Troy* in Bruges, we can hardly escape the conclusion that Caxton was involved, if only

---

[12] S. Corsten, 'Köln und die Ausbreitung der Buchdruckerkunst in den Niederlanden', *Quaerendo* 1 (1971): 5-17, 179-90.

financially, in *Gesta Romanorum* as well. It has always been accepted in the past that he was involved in only one text while at Cologne, because de Worde mentions *De proprietatibus* but no other texts. It was, however, natural for him to do so since his reference to Caxton's involvement in printing occurs in his own edition of the English translation of *De proprietatibus* (c. 1495). There was no reason for him in that context to refer to any other work printed by Caxton at Cologne. It does not follow, therefore, that he was not a partner in any other text. There is every likelihood that he was. He was in Cologne for about eighteen months, which would probably have given him enough time to be involved in more than one text. *Gesta Romanorum*, like *De proprietatibus*, is a large volume in comparison with Veldener's earlier work for it contains 120 leaves and this may indicate external financing. Since *De proprietatibus* was a large volume and possibly expensive, some time might have elapsed before the partners saw a return on their money. In the meantime Veldener would need more capital to finance his next work, and Caxton could supply it. If the partnership was working smoothly, as it seems to have done, we would be unwise to assume there was a break in it.

If *History of Troy* was begun in April/May 1473, it could have been finished by the end of the year or early in 1474. That at least seems a reasonable inference, though it might be admitted that we know little about the number of copies printed or how long it took to set up and run off a page. Yet if we remember that Caxton had three presses working on the edition, eight to nine months would seem ample time to finish even such a substantial book as this one.[13] Little allowance need be made for the fact that *History of Troy* was his first printed book. For if compositor A was Veldener, one can assume that the workshop was running smoothly by the time he left. If *History of Troy* was completed about the turn of the year 1473/4, this would allow time for *Game of Chess*, a much smaller text, to be printed by 31 March 1474. However, as we know so little about the speed of printing, it may be that *History of Troy* was finished later than I have suggested, which would imply that *Game of Chess* was translated, and not printed, on 31 March 1474. In this case it would not have been printed till about June 1474. Perhaps a couple of months' difference is not so important, though I feel that the evidence points strongly to the completion of printing by March. What is surely beyond dispute is that the date Caxton gave in the epilogue of *Game of Chess* is 31 March 1474 by our reckoning, whether by that date he referred to the printing (as I suggest) or the translation.

If *Game of Chess* was printed on 31 March 1474 (or even for that matter by June of that year), we have to explain what Caxton did between then and his return to England in 1476. There is a period of between two and

---

[13] Painter, *op. cit.* p. 62 suggests it took only five to six months to print.

two and a half years to account for. The problem is that the period from December 1472 when he left Cologne till September 1476 when he returned to England is really too long simply to print the six texts which are assigned to the Bruges period. Mr Painter tried to fill in some of this gap by putting *History of Troy* a year later than is usual and by suggesting it took Caxton rather longer than we had assumed to set up his workshop in Bruges. As we have seen, this solution is not feasible. The answer may be sought in this way.

As *History of Troy* and *Game of Chess* are both in English, they were clearly intended for sale in England for there cannot have been enough English-speaking people on the Continent who would want to buy copies of these editions. Indeed, as one of them, *History of Troy*, was produced in a French version for sale on the Continent in this period (1474-6), it shows that the English version was not available there. What happened after the completion of *Game of Chess* is that Caxton started to print works in French. These may have been produced in partnership with Colard Mansion. The reason for this switch in policy is probably that Caxton found the distribution and sale of books in England while he was resident in Bruges too cumbersome and frustrating. He would need retail outlets and these could not have been easy to find for the sort of books he was publishing. His mercantile connections may not have been as much help to him in this matter as he had anticipated, if only because they were not used to handling this type of goods. He consequently decided to stop printing English texts in Bruges and to make preparations to return to England to set up the workshop there. While making these arrangements, the workshop turned to printing books in French which could be sold direct from the workshop or from Mansion's shop.

The return to England from Bruges cannot have been so easy as the return to Bruges from Cologne – and this may account for that gap of over two years. He had to choose where to settle in England. He chose Westminster, a place he had never lived in before, whereas Bruges had been familiar to him for many years. He had to find and hire premises, persuade his workmen to cross the channel, and wind up whatever financial arrangements he had with Mansion. More importantly he had to decide what material to print as soon as he arrived in England. We should recollect that he started to translate *History of Troy* two years before going to Cologne and he finished it fourteen months before he left that city to start printing by himself. This shows that he had taken care to provide suitable copy before setting up his press. It would be unnatural for him not to take the same trouble when he established his workshop in England. One can hardly imagine him going out to look for suitable copy as soon as he arrived at Westminster.

When the situation is presented in this way, it is clear that he must have translated *Jason* in Bruges for it is the only text he translated which was printed in the period 1476-7 at Westminster. A closer look at *Jason* confirms this theory.[14] Like *Game of Chess* it consists of prologue, text and epilogue. As is true of *Game of Chess*, the epilogue was written after the prologue. In the prologue the book is dedicated to the Prince of Wales, who was still a mere infant. In the epilogue there is reference only to 'my said Lorde Prince', who is not named. The epilogue clearly refers back to the prologue which must, therefore, have already been written. It is likely that *Jason* was composed in the same order as *Game of Chess*, viz text, prologue and epilogue. However, the epilogue must in this case have been written immediately after the prologue and not after a gap of some time, since it also contains comments on those parts of the text which Caxton is anxious to correct in his French original. Such comments are unlikely to have been made any considerable time after the translation itself. So one must assume that text, prologue and epilogue were written in close succession. The prologue is interesting since it contains a reference to *History of Troy* and to Margaret Duchess of Burgundy. Although it would be quite possible to think that this reference was included in England after he had printed several other texts, it is more natural to assume that it was included in Bruges when *History of Troy* and its dedicatee were still very fresh in Caxton's mind. Furthermore, the prologue also contains a description of Duke Philip's castle at Hesdin. Again this description is natural enough in a book dealing with Jason and the Golden Fleece, the emblem of the Burgundian chivalric order. But it is more likely to occur to a man writing in Flanders, where it will seem more immediate and important, than it is to someone writing in England. Caxton was not to include descriptions of any other Burgundian features in his prologues and epilogues written in England. Finally, the French version of *Jason* was one of the French texts issued by Caxton's workshop in that period 1474-6 when he had stopped printing English books in Bruges. Since the French text was available at the workshop in Bruges, it is natural to think that he should have made his translation with prologue and epilogue there. It may be for this reason that no dates are given in prologue or epilogue, for the date of printing would be so uncertain at that stage.

There is good reason then to claim that Caxton translated the whole of *Jason* in Bruges and that he brought it to Westminster in a ready-to-print state. If so, it must have been the first edition to be printed at the press there and it should be dated to 1476. It may have been the only text to precede the indulgence of December 1476. The only objection to this view is the statement by Robert Copland in his preface to *King Appolyn of Tyre*, printed by de Worde in 1510, that he had followed the example of his master Caxton by 'begynnyng with small storyes and pamflettes'. It has been accepted by many that Copland was here referring to the editions of

---

[14] It has often been suspected that Caxton started to translate *Jason* in Bruges, cf. Painter *op. cit.* pp. 78-79, but the case for the place of translation and the date of printing has never been argued in detail. Painter dates *Jason* to 1477.

small poems like *Horse, Sheep and Goose*, which must indeed have been among the early texts to be printed at Westminster. Nevertheless, too much reliance has been placed on these words of Copland, who mentions no text by name and who was writing about events almost thirtyfive years earlier which he may not even have witnessed. When Caxton came back to England he was an established printer-publisher who had hitherto printed relatively substantial works. There is no reason why he should flinch from starting at Westminster with a big book; after all he had started in Bruges with *History of Troy*. Surely he would want to introduce his public to his special type of book immediately. He had never published English poetry in Bruges and it does not seem to have been part of his original policy to do so. In Bruges it would be natural to translate books from French into English since so many French books were available there. It is unlikely that his decision to print English poetry occurred to him as soon as he arrived in Westminster; it is more natural to accept that the idea came to him during the printing of *Jason* as a result of selling poetry at his shop there. The printing of English poetry at Westminster represents a change in his original plans, just as the printing of French texts at Bruges does. Caxton survived so long as a printer-publisher precisely because he planned ahead and yet had sufficient character to adapt his plans to new circumstances as they arose.

7

Continuity and Change in Caxton's Prologues and Epilogues

I. Bruges

In the past it was so normal to consider Caxton a relatively uncomplicated man who could tell only the unvarnished truth that whatever he wrote was taken at face value without any regard to what was included or how it was arranged. More recently we have come increasingly to accept that he was a sophisticated businessman who was prepared to elaborate on the truth to sell his products. This realisation should encourage us to reconsider his prologues and epilogues as a whole. For even if he was as uncomplicated as earlier scholars believed, he was nevertheless the first printer to introduce a series of prologues and epilogues in his works. He had no model for them in printed form, and so we need to locate the models he may have used and the influences, whether technical or not, to which he was subjected in order to grasp how he developed.

Although I have elsewhere mentioned several examples of his fabrication of stories, the examples were often from rather contentious volumes and so it has not been accepted by all that Caxton worked in this way as a general rule.[1] I would therefore like to offer an example of his fabrication from a less contentious volume, since the knowledge that he used his prologues and epilogues as selling aids is essential to an understanding of how he set about compiling the information they contain.

On 2 September 1483 he published the first edition of Gower's *Confessio Amantis* and he opened his prologue like this: 'This book is intituled *Confessio Amantis*, that is to saye in Englysshe *The Confessyon of the Lover*, maad and compyled by Johan Gower squyer, borne in Walys, in the tyme of Kyng Richard the Second.'[2] What is noteworthy about this opening is the statement that Gower was born in Wales. As far as I am aware this view has not been repeated or even considered worth discussion by any

---

[1] See above, Chapter 2, and below, Chapter 14.

[2] N.F. Blake, *Caxton's Own Prose* (London: Deutsch, 1973), p. 69. Future quotations from the prologues and epilogues are taken from this edition and the relevant page numbers are given in brackets after the quotation.

biographer or editor of Gower. Most scholars assume that Gower was a member of one of two families, one in Yorkshire and the other in Kent, with the latter being the more probable.[3] Why then did Caxton include this detail? Either he had information which was not available before or since, or else he tried to deceive his customers.

Since he had no need to include this information, no other explanation seems feasible. Caxton published his edition about seventy years after the poet's death. Since he had lived as a young man in London where Gower worked it is possible that he had access to some information not otherwise available. But as he gives us no other details of Gower's life or work in London and as Gower is not known to have had any association with Wales and his language certainly shows no signs of Welsh influence, it is more likely that Caxton invented this information. The name Gower was itself sufficient to suggest a Welsh birthplace.

But why should Caxton wish to suggest that Gower was born in Wales if that was not true? The answer may be as follows. He may have accepted, as many of his contemporaries apparently did, that Gower came from Kent. But Kent was a county that had very unfavourable connotations at the end of the medieval period and Caxton was himself particularly sensitive to those connotations. When in the *History of Troy* he wanted to refer to himself disparagingly in the traditional humility formula, he referred to his own birth in Kent since Kent was associated with barbarous speech.[4] There are, as it happpens, several Kentish features in Gower's writings, for the London dialect had originally been a Southern one. The change in London English to a more Northern colouring at the end of the fourteenth century and the rise of London English as the standard language led to a fall in status of Kentish.[5] Caxton evidently felt it desirable to shield Gower's reputation from any possible contamination from that association. He therefore introduced a reference to Wales to deflect his customers' attention away from Kent. A harmless fabrication served his own commercial policy.

In order to appreciate how Caxton developed it is necessary to consider his output on a chronological basis. In this section I shall consider his Bruges volumes; his Westminster texts will be tackled after that. When he translated *History of Troy* he used the French version by Raoul Lefèvre. The genesis of Lefèvre's edition is not clear, but it may be that he used an earlier translation of the first two books which he adapted and to which he added the third and final book himself, for some manuscripts contain only the first books and do not mention Lefèvre's authorship. His own translation when completed consisted of a dedication to Philip of

---

[3] J.H. Fisher, *John Gower: Moral Philosopher and Friend of Chaucer* (New York: New York University Press, 1964) contains the relevant details.

[4] N.F. Blake, *Caxton and his World* (London: 1969), pp. 16-22. [See also p. 24 above.]

[5] N.F. Blake, 'Born in Kent', *Lore and Language* 2.5 (1975): 3-9.

Burgundy, his prologue, the first two books, a prologue to book 3, and then book 3. When Caxton printed his translation of Lefèvre's work, it contained a dedication to Margaret of Burgundy, his prologue, a translation of Lefèvre's prologue, the first two books, an epilogue to book 2, book 3, and a final epilogue. It is clear that for the most part Caxton was influenced by his source as to what to include and where. Since his dedication includes the date when the translation was completed, it was written after the completion of book 3. The epilogue to book 2 was surely written when book 2 was finished, for else there is no reason why there should be an epilogue to book 2 because Lefèvre had a prologue to book 3 and clearly Caxton felt there had to be some break between books 2 and 3, even though there was no real reason for Caxton to have any break there since he (unlike Lefèvre) translated all three books from one source and as one unit. This epilogue refers to 'her that is cause of this translacion' (p. 99) and it thus presupposes that the prologue with its account of the translation's genesis was already in existence. This suggests that the prologue was written first. The epilogue to the whole book is the only place which refers to the printing of the translation and so was perhaps not written until the printing of the work was under way; it seems probable that it was written at least after Caxton's return to Bruges, and it would appear to be much later than the rest of the work. The pieces that go to make up the book may have been prepared in this order: Caxton's prologue, Lefèvre's prologue, books 1 and 2, epilogue to book 2, book 3, dedication, epilogue to the whole work.

This sequence presupposes that his own prologue was written before book 1 even though that prologue states that he had completed a few quires before showing them to Margaret of Burgundy for her approval. In view of the example from Gower's *Confessio Amantis*, we need to remember that Caxton could invent stories and so this little episode need not be taken at face value. As *History of Troy* was his first translation, we would naturally expect him to be under the influence of his model, Lefèvre's original. That work contains a dedication and a prologue, in which the two main points are that the translator is unworthy and that the translation had been commissioned by the duke despite the translator's mediocrity. To Caxton it may well have seemed imperative that the book should contain a dedicatee who should be held largely responsible for the book's appearance. The dedication was no problem. Margaret, Edward IV's sister, was married to the present duke. The choice was an obvious one in view of the earlier dedication. But the problem was to explain how she had come to ask him to make the translation. To put it bluntly no aristocrat in his right mind would ask a successful businessman and governor of the English nation at Bruges, particularly if (as Caxton claimed) he had lived so long abroad and had been born in Kent, to make a fashionable English translation of a French book. Lefèvre was a cleric and occupied some kind of secretarial position in the ducal household; he belonged to that class from whose members translations were naturally demanded. It is this difficulty which has led many scholars to make Caxton into some kind of secretary or librarian in order to facilitate the demand that he make a translation. This is to approach the problem from the wrong end, since there is no evidence that he ever occupied such a position or was even a member of Margaret's household. The situation demanded that he invent an episode in which a commission to translate appeared reasonable. He solved the problem successfully. He claimed that he had made a start at translating on his own initiative, but had given up in despair. Then two years later he by chance showed this translated part to Margaret who commanded him to complete the whole work. The work was thus commissioned by the dedicatee. But if he was so disgusted with his own efforts for two years, it is surprising that he should mention the matter to her or that she should wish to see it. The story smacks of invention. The genesis of the translation is more likely to be reflected in what he relates in the first part of his prologue: the book was recently translated into French and he felt it should be made available in England. As far as we know Margaret had no interest in English translations. Consequently we may have to abandon the story in the prologue as largely a fiction.

In his prologue Caxton first mentions the true reasons for the translation as noted above. He then goes on to mention his incompetence as a translator, which led him to include select biographical details of himself. These details go beyond the merely conventional and reveal that he had a knack for breathing life into medieval conventions and that he was apt with story-making. Next he relates the account of Margaret's involvement with the translation. We may note in passing that the complete list of Margaret's titles given here shows that the prologue was written before the dedication, for they are clearly meant as a first reference to this noble lady. They are abbreviated or omitted in later references to her, including the dedication itself. Possibly he intended at this stage that his prologue should fill the role of the dedication. It is natural to assume that Margaret was acquainted with such an important man as Caxton and that she had given him gifts of one kind or another. But we do not need to assume that she asked for the translation or that her gifts had anything to do with it. Then Caxton goes on to say he fulfilled her commands and he asks his readers for their indulgence. No details of where or when the translation was made are given, because at that stage he may not have realised that the progress of the translation would be so long and so chequered. One may note that Caxton decided to have his own separate prologue in this volume; he did not adapt Lefèvre's prologue to make it his own. This may be a sign that he had as yet insufficient experience in handling other people's work – natural enough in a first attempt.

To include a translator's break between books 2 and 3 was a problem. Lefèvre had naturally included a prologue to book 3 because of the way his translation appears to have come about. Caxton could have simply omitted any personal comment here. That he did not suggests how subservient to his model he was. He did not yet have sufficient literary independence to decide what needed to be omitted or included. He had already given details of his translation's genesis and he could at this stage only repeat briefly details of his own unworthiness and of Margaret's commission. He also added a few remarks about the progress of the translation in Bruges, Ghent and Cologne. He then did what he was often to do: he fell back upon English literary history, which for him meant particularly Lydgate. He included remarks about Lydgate's own version of the Troy story, though the result is somewhat mixed. He claims there is no need for him to translate the third book because it forms the material of Lydgate's poem, but he has decided to do so because the two accounts are different and anyway some people prefer prose to verse. We see how cumbersome his work could get when he had no prop to lean on. The warmth of his reference to Lydgate makes one wonder whether he had a copy of Lydgate's *Troy-Book* in Cologne while he was making the translation.

When he finished the translation Caxton wrote the dedication. The first part of this is closely modelled on Lefèvre's dedication and he added to it details of his own translation. A few points may be noted. In this dedication Caxton describes himself as 'mercer of the cyte of London' (p. 97). As Lefèvre had explicitly mentioned that he was in the employ of Duke Philip of Burgundy and as Caxton had repeated that information, we may be certain that if Caxton had been in Margaret's service he would have referred to it here. He did not, and his words show that he had no other occupation than mercer. He had ceased to be governor of the English nation at Bruges and he never was in Margaret's employ. He states that the translation was begun in Bruges on 1 March 1469[6] and finished at Cologne on 19 September 1471. We know from the Register of Aliens at Cologne that he was first granted permission to stay in that city on 17 July 1471, though he no doubt arrived there a little earlier in the month. Even so, the whole of book 3 and some of book 2 were translated in Cologne between July and September, whereas the rest of the book took him over two years. The rate of translation for the final book was very fast indeed and shows that he did have 'good leyzer beyng in Coleyn' (p. 100). The slow progress of the first two books suggests that while he was working in Bruges as governor he had little time for his translating activities. This may have been another reason which prompted him to go to Cologne.

The epilogue to the whole work is rather different from the rest of the

[6] The date given is 1468; but as Caxton reckoned his years from 25 March, his 1 March 1468 is our 1 March 1469.

book for it is more concerned with its printing. Caxton produces two reasons for the printing: firstly his age and general weariness, and secondly the request by friends for copies of the translation. He then states that he has arranged for the book to be printed at his own expense and he adds the odd detail as to how printing differs from manuscript production. It is only then that he repeats that the work is dedicated to Margaret who has accepted the dedication. This order underlines his difficulty in coming to terms with printing within the traditional presentation formula. Normally little or no reference was made to the technical details of manuscript production within manuscripts, for to the author the important details were who composed the work and who commissioned it. Hence although Caxton's translation was clearly made to be printed, as its completion in Cologne reveals, he makes it appear (because such was the tradition) that Margaret had commissioned the translation alone. He himself was responsible for the printing, which was done for the two reasons noted, though neither is likely to be actually the truth. The result is sufficiently incongruous to throw doubt on the veracity of the story as a whole. But in the matter of printing Caxton had little to guide him and he may also have wanted to take some of the credit for himself, even though this may appear to contradict his own claim to incompetence. That Margaret came in for such small praise in this epilogue may be another indication that it was written some time after the other parts of the book. The epilogue continues with an apology for both the translation and the contents of the book, because stories about Troy differ. This enables him to have a different version of the humility formula and shows that he did not like to repeat himself too much. He does not mention Lydgate again, but mentions other writers on the Troy story. He concludes by saying that all agree that Troy was destroyed even if the details differ.

Although there are no signatures in this edition, the quiring is such as to suggest that all the material was available to the printer before he started work – except perhaps the epilogue. This confirms what has already been suggested. What then may we conclude from this first volume of Caxton's press? As a novice translator and publisher he was naturally feeling his way in this book and so leaned heavily on his model: he responded to the pattern provided in it. That model could help him explain his translation, but naturally as a manuscript it could offer no help on the printing side. Hence he offers a more coherent account of the translation which fits in the traditional mould even though it produces a feeling of incongruity with the references to printing. It is also clear that under the influence of his model and traditional practice Caxton was quite willing to invent stories to make his own work fit into the accepted patterns of literary production. We for our part must be willing to read between the lines of what he wrote and we may accept that he was motivated more by a desire to make his books acceptable than by a desire to pass on factual information.

The translation of *Game of Chess* may have been made in Cologne as I have suggested elsewhere.[7] He finished *History of Troy* on 19 September 1471 and probably left the city in December 1472. His rate of translation of book 3 of *History of Troy* shows that he had plenty of time available for translation. *Game of Chess*, like *History of Troy*, has no signatures, but the quiring shows that all the pieces were available to the printer when he started work. Although there are some short interpolations in the body of the work, for our purpose the book consists of three pieces: the prologue, the text and the epilogue. Although it is not possible to be certain of the order of their composition, probably the text was translated first with the prologue and epilogue added later. The epilogue opens with a reference to 'my ryght redoubted lord' (p. 87), though he is not named in the prologue. The absence of the name in the epilogue and the uniformity of the material in prologue and epilogue suggest that it was written immediately after the prologue and as a continuation of it. If so, the prologue was written after the text was translated. If the prologue and epilogue were written as a pair, it may be that they were written long after the rest of the work was completed, perhaps even after Caxton's return to Bruges. Since prologue and epilogue contain no details of the translation, the contents of the book were clearly not in Caxton's mind when he wrote them. In this regard they differ from both the epilogue of book 2 and the final epilogue in *History of Troy*.

That the situation described may be correct is suggested by the probable state of Caxton's copy. The manuscript he used has not been identified, but he used a version of the intermediate text.[8] Generally the manuscripts of this version are less informative about the text's authorship and often contain no details of the work's genesis. It seems likely that Caxton's source was a text with no prologue or epilogue since he shows no signs of being influenced by his copy. If so, this presented him with a new problem: how to present his translation when he had no model to follow. He was naturally forced to rely on the model provided by his first book, *History of Troy*. The most noticeable feature of *Game of Chess* is that it contains both prologue and epilogue because both had been included in *History of Troy*, even though it was not usual to have both in contemporary manuscripts and no epilogue is found in Lefèvre's version of *History of Troy*. Although he had no need for both a prologue and an epilogue in *Game of Chess* and although he compiled the two as a single unit, he could not break away so easily from the model he had set up for himself. He did, however, amalgamate the dedication and the prologue into one in *Game of Chess*. The opening sentence of its prologue contains the name of the dedicatee with all the titles that went with it and the name of the translator; this was the standard formula. From there on Caxton was in a

---

[7] See above, Chapter 6.
[8] C. Knowles, 'Caxton and his Two French Sources', *Modern Language Review* 49 (1954); 417-23.

quandary. He had decided to have a different patron for reasons explained elsewhere.[9] Since the patron he chose was in England and was not known personally to Caxton who was in Bruges or thereabouts, he could hardly invent any convincing story to explain how the dedicatee had commissioned the translation. He therefore included almost no details about the book or what it contained; there is no explanation of the translation's genesis. Instead he launched into rather extravagant praise of Clarence which is expressed in laudatory platitudes. The epilogue differs only in that the focus shifts slightly from Clarence to his brother the king, though as both are considered guardians of the kingdom and the praise is so general the shift is not very marked. Since the epilogue adds nothing substantive to the prologue, one can realise how strong was the influence of the model which dictated he should have an epilogue. The result is a very unsatisfactory prologue and epilogue. It may, however, be emphasised that Caxton was prepared to have another patron, even though it would have been easier to keep the same dedicatee as in *History of Troy* and that he looked for a different angle for this prologue and epilogue as though he was consciously trying not to repeat the same material in succeeding volumes.

The four French texts printed in Caxton's workshop in Bruges contain no additions by the publisher. But *Jason*, which was printed at Westminster, was almost certainly prepared in Bruges and may be considered here.[10] When this volume was printed it is clear that all its parts were available to the printer even though there are no signatures. Those parts are the translator's prologue, the author's prologue to which the translator added a few words, the text itself, and the epilogue. Although the manuscript Caxton used has not been identified, the French text of *Jason* was one of the four issued at the press in Bruges and we may assume that it accurately reflects the state of his copy. That contains the author's prologue and the text which concludes with a sentence asking for the readers' indulgence, although there is no separate epilogue as such. In *Jason* Caxton's epilogue is very different from his prologue, for it contains comments on the author's remark that he had discovered nothing further about Jason than he gives in his work. But Caxton had access to Boccaccio's *De genealogia deorum* and mentions some details from it. He then finishes his epilogue by recommending the book to 'my said Lorde Prince' (p. 106) who is not identified there. It was the Prince of Wales to whom the book was dedicated in the prologue. The epilogue was thus written after the prologue and after the text itself had been translated. The question is to decide when the prologue was written. It may have followed the pattern of *History of Troy* and been written first or the pattern of *Game of Chess* and been written after the text but before the epilogue. The former is

9 Blake, *Caxton and his World*, p. 64.
10 See above, p. 85f.

on balance more likely.[11] This is partly because the prologue and epilogue deal with such different topics and partly because in the prologue Caxton wrote 'I entende to translate the sayd *Boke of th'Istories of Jason*' (p. 104) as though he is announcing an intention rather than an achievement.

Jason contains nothing about its printing, perhaps because the work was completed with prologue and epilogue in Bruges and printed only after Caxton's return to Westminster. Furthermore he had not yet developed any satisfactory way of indicating details of printing because of the tradition of concentrating on authorship and patronage alone. *History of Troy* had details of the new art of printing and *Game of Chess* had the date of printing; but *Jason* has nothing. Clearly Caxton was sufficiently under the influence of the traditional model of the author's (or translator's) prologue to feel that printing was not a worthy subject for discussion. The text and the patron were the important points. With *Jason* Caxton returns to the model of *History of Troy*, perhaps because *Jason* can be thought of as a continuation of the earlier work and partly because the French text was written by the same man, Raoul Lefèvre. The prologue concentrates upon two elements: the connection of *Jason* with *History of Troy* and the dedication of the work to the Prince of Wales, though both have ramifications which are explored.

The prologue opens with a reference to the dedication of *History of Troy* to Margaret of Burgundy and then brief details of that first work are given. This introduction is natural enough, though it makes Margaret more prominent than the dedicatee, the Prince of Wales. It also serves to promote the earlier work as well as the present volume, and it may be that Caxton learned from this to present books of similar material and to use his prologues to refer to his previous output – a theme he was to use frequently later. This introduction naturally enables him to present his reason for making the traditional epilogue. Lefèvre had translated and presented both books to Duke Philip, but he had made two separate works out of them although they both deal with destructions of Troy. Caxton therefore translated the book as a natural continuation of his earlier one. This translation is made under the protection of Edward IV, but as he was in England and Caxton in Bruges he did not feel it advisable to invent any story about being commanded to make the translation. The prologue then goes on to refer to the Golden Fleece, which was the Burgundian order of chivalry to which Edward himself belonged. This enables Caxton to refer to the mechanical contrivances of the castle at Hesdin which were associated with the order – a lively digression which implies how interesting and appealing the story is since it had generated such fascinating contrivances. The prologue then turns to its patron. The book is not dedicated to Edward IV who probably has a copy in French; it is

[11] I suggested the latter above, p. 86, but on reconsideration this seems less likely for the reasons given here.

dedicated to the Prince of Wales. This dedication shows that Caxton remained quite happy to dedicate volumes to people quite unknown to him and who were hardly fit to receive them, since in this case the prince was probably well under seven when the dedication was written.

Caxton also added a few remarks to the author's prologue. He did not amalgamate that prologue with his own. He still has insufficient experience in translating to do that, but his own addition may have opened his eyes to this possibility. It was an approach he was to adopt in later volumes since it relieved him of the problem of finding something different to say with every new work.

The epilogue has little to do with the prologue in that it contains additional details about the Jason story that Caxton took from Boccaccio. It is not certain whether he wanted to show his erudition or whether he felt that there should be an epilogue (as there had been in his two previous translations) and looked around for something suitable to include. The epilogue is rounded off by an allusion to the prince.

What then had Caxton learned in his Bruges period about the presentation of his books? Following the models found in contemporary manuscripts, he accepted that each book should have a patron and that the details of why the translation had been made should be indicated. If possible these two should be linked, though force of circumstances led him to realise that this was not essential, however desirable it might be. Although a dedicatee was needed, a formal dedication was discarded and after *History of Troy* the dedication was made part of the prologue. The patrons were important nobles, but not necessarily known to Caxton or with any interest in the book. Since he had no models to guide him in his role as printer-publisher, he naturally concentrated on his own contribution as a translator – to the dismay of modern scholars who would have preferred more details of his printing. Where he did not have a suitable story about the translation's genesis, he was prepared to decorate the details that were to hand in an inventive way to make his translation fall into the pattern of contemporary requests. These accounts reveal his latent abilities as a story-teller and his concern for lively publication of his works. In Bruges he accepted that each translation should have a prologue and epilogue, but he had not yet sufficient experience to amalgamate his prologue with the original one where one was found. Hence there is a proliferation of prefatory matter. Even where there was no prologue or epilogue he added one, and he followed his sources in adding material to his books in his role as translator. Those books which were not translated by him had no prologue or epilogue and hence no details about their printing or publication. By the time he left Bruges he had not yet learned that printed books need a separate system of presentation from manuscripts.

II. Westminster

I have discussed what Caxton had learned while in Bruges about text presentation from the manuscripts he had used to make his translations. By the time he returned to Englnad to set up his press at Westminster, he had already translated *History of Troy, Game of Chess* and *Jason*. The first batch of books he issued in England presented him with a new problem, for they were editions of English poetic works. These were not translations by Caxton, but poems by well-known English poets which were available in manuscript in England. He had not printed anything of this kind in Bruges and so he had no experience of how to present such a work to his public. He reacted in an understandable way: he followed his exemplars. Since the works of poets like Chaucer and Lydgate generally have no titles, prologues or epilogues in the manuscripts, Caxton included none in his editions. The occasional poem is given an explicit, but no doubt the compositor copied that direct from his copytext. No attempt is made to improve the works' appearance, to find a dedicatee, or to encourage potential purchasers by pointing out the merits of individual poems. Presumably the books were considered well enough known to need no further introduction, or it was felt that poems as such were sufficiently attractive in their own right. There is no distinction between works by Chaucer and those by other poets.

None of these early editions from Westminster have dates and so it is not easy to decide on their order of publication. Only one edition of a Chaucer work, his translation of Boethius's *De consolatione philosophiae*, needs discussion; but as that is usually dated to 1478, it is best to leave consideration of it for the moment. For there is one dated book from 1477: the edition of Earl Rivers's translation of *Dicts or Sayings* appeared on 18 November. Caxton's relations with Rivers constitute one of the most puzzling aspects of his whole career.[12] Caxton printed three of his translations: *Dicts or Sayings* (1477), *Moral Proverbs* (1478) and *Cordial* (1479). It is also often thought that the 'noble and vertuous Erle' (p. 72) who asked for the translation of the *Curial* (c. 1484) is to be identified as Rivers, though this identification is not without problems. Whether Caxton knew Rivers personally, as he claims, is also doubtful, for certainly as far as *Moral Proverbs* is concerned Rivers's secretary acted as the link between the two men.

When the copy of Rivers's translation of *Dicts or Sayings* was delivered to Caxton it already had a prologue. This contains a fairly relaxed account by Rivers of the translation's genesis. To the book as a whole Caxton added an epilogue. At first sight this seems strange. Since the translator had already provided all the necessary information about the book and

---

[12] A new biography of Rivers is being written by Professor R.R. Griffith of C.W. Post Center, New York.

since the translator was a nobleman, any involvement by the book's publisher seems quite unnecessary for the book's promotion. What then prompted him to add an epilogue to *Dicts or Sayings*, and also later to *Moral Proverbs* and *Cordial*? The answer may well be that Rivers was the only nobleman at this time who showed any interest in translating and in having his translation printed. He was unique and Caxton may well have wanted to identify with him as much as possible. Indeed, he may have succeeded in deceiving his clients and modern scholars that his relations with Rivers were much closer than was in fact the case.

Since Rivers had already made the translations, Caxton's rôle was largely limited to that of printer-publisher. He attempted to make that rôle more important by giving details about the book's printing. He had never bothered before to give information about when a book was published or how long it had taken the press to print it. Even after these books were issued such information was far from becoming a regular feature of his editions and so we may accept that he had special motives for introducing it here. In addition the epilogues to these translations by Rivers contain other interesting features. According to Caxton, when Earl Rivers gave him his translation of *Dicts or Sayings*, he mentioned that he had not translated some of the contents of the French version. Caxton himself made a translation of the sayings of Socrates, but not of the other missing parts. These sayings he added as part of his own epilogue; he did not include them in the body of the text where they belonged. In this way he was able to draw attention to his own work as translator and thus associate himself with Rivers as the translator of the book. His rôle became more than that of a mere printer. When he issued *Moral Proverbs* he added the details of printing in a stanza in the same metre as that used for the translation. Since Rivers had finished with a stanza about the poem's translation, Caxton was able to associate himself with Rivers as a poet. This stanza is one of only three short poetic passages that can be attributed to Caxton with confidence, and it is the only one that deals with the printing of a volume. There is no prologue to *Moral Proverbs* and Caxton did not add one. *Cordial*, however, had a translator's prologue and so once more Caxton was forced to include an epilogue with extensive details of the printing. Since he could not add anything to a translation which was complete, he was forced to elaborate upon the life and good deeds of Earl Rivers and upon the moral content of the work being published. It was thus only the force of circumstance which led him to comment on his rôle as printer, and even so it is clear that he felt translation carried more prestige. Nevertheless he was often to indicate his contribution as printer-publisher. Earl Rivers's intervention has had a happy outcome for modern scholars.

When Caxton came back to England he seems to have forgotten all that he learned in Bruges about the presentation of books. At first he included no prologues and epilogues, and then he reacted to the special situation of printing translations by Earl Rivers by including epilogues only. He responded to the situation he was in; he did not develop any general policy of text presentation. As we have already noted he treated Chaucer's translation *Boethius* differently from the other works by Chaucer and Lydgate: he added an epilogue to it. No extant manuscript contains an epilogue and it is very unlikely that any fifteenth-century version had any details which might have given Caxton the idea. Why he included an epilogue to this text is a matter of speculation. If the edition is dated to 1478, as is usual, then it followed *Dicts or Sayings* (18 November 1477) and probably *Moral Proverbs* (20 February 1478), both of which have Caxton epilogues. It could be that he was influenced by these texts to add an epilogue to *Boethius*, though as he did not do so for other texts this seems an unsatisfactory reason. The epilogue consists of Caxton's own contribution in English and the Latin eulogy to Chaucer by Stefano Surigone which Caxton found on a pillar by the poet's tomb in Westminster Abbey.[13] It may be the chance discovery of this eulogy which led Caxton to include an epilogue. He added to the eulogy a Latin quatrain which he himself composed extolling his own merits in printing works by Chaucer. In this way he identified himself with Chaucer and Surigone in this work in much the same way as he had identified himself with Rivers in the three translations discussed above. In the English part of the epilogue Caxton mentions that he was asked to issue the edition 'atte requeste of a singuler frende and gossib of myne' (p. 59). This friend is not named but is often identified as William Pratt (or Praat). If this identification is correct then he may have included the epilogue to honour this *patron*. But since so little is made of this friend and since the book is printed 'in hopying that it shal prouffite moche peple to the wele and helth of their soules and for to lerne to have and kepe the better pacience in adversitees' (p. 59), it may well be that the friend is a convenient fiction. If so, it shows that Caxton no longer felt it necessary to have a named aristocratic dedicatee any more even though it was desirable to intimate that someone wanted the book. Perhaps he felt that an unnamed friend and Surigone's eulogy were sufficient to guarantee the book's sale.

That he added an epilogue rather than a prologue to *Boethius* may be because of the example of the Rivers's translations, manuscript practice or even ease of working. For it is easier to add material to the end after the book is at press; and to wait until the book is printed allows more time to consider what to include in this extra material. The policy, if one may call it such, of having an epilogue was broken with the publication of *Chronicles of England* on 10 June 1480. This book is the first to have signatures and also a new arrangement of presentation. At the end of the work, which existed already in English in manuscript versions, Caxton added a few words in the form of an epilogue and noted the date of printing. But the

---

[13] See below, Chapter 11.

book also contains a prologue and table of contents. These are in the first gathering which has a different signature from that used in the rest of the book which runs as might be expected from *a* to *y*. As the first leaf of gathering *a* is a blank, it is likely that this gathering was intended to come first in the edition. In other words the evidence suggests that the first gathering, in which the leaves are numbered with roman numerals, was added after the rest of the book was complete and probably as an afterthought.

The reasons which led Caxton to include a table are unknown, for it is likely the prologue was included only because a table was added. The manuscript he used as copytext has not been located and so one cannot say whether a table occurred in it, though that seems improbable. It is possible that he got the idea from the *Polychronicon* which he used in this year to make his *Description of Britain*. Alternatively he may have learned the practice from foreign incunabula, as he did the use of signatures. At all events the new method of presentation is important for it is found fairly regularly from this point onwards in his output. Indeed it may be said to mark the switch from the back to the front of the table of contents in English printed books. Certain important implications arise from this new presentation. The first is that, although many books have the introductory material added in a gathering with different signature numbers, this does not become a universal practice. Thus, although the *Description of Britain* published on 18 August 1480 has no signature, it has a prologue and table which fill only part of the first gathering with the text following immediately without break. The prologue and table cannot have been added later. Similarly in the second edition of *Canterbury Tales* (c. 1483) Caxton's prologue is part of the first gathering. In other words Caxton sometimes prepared his prologue sufficiently early so that it was ready for the compositor before he started work. This happens for the most part with reprints or with works already available in English which were not modified. More usually he added an additional gathering after the rest of the book was in type. Even when he did this he also often included an epilogue at the end. It seems likely that there was a gap, perhaps quite a long one, between the completion of the translation with epilogue and the composition of the prologue. This gap allowed Caxton time to reflect on what he should include in his prologue, which could be rather different from what he put in the epilogue. In *Chronicles of England*, for example, he mentions both that he printed the book 'atte requeste of dyverce gentilmen' (p. 69) and that he had included a table for ease of reference. Since the gentlemen are not referred to in the epilogue and since the prologue may be an afterthought, it is likely that they are a publisher's fiction introduced like the friend in *Boethius* to make the book more attractive.

A further implication of this procedure is that after a time Caxton would anticipate adding prefatory material after he had completed his translation and epilogue. However, this extra material may occasionally never have been completed either through an oversight or through a change in policy. This may have happened with *Æsop* printed on 26 March 1484. It contains an incipit after an initial blank in the first gathering together with an epilogue at the end. The edition is also provided with folio numbers throughout – an indication that a table was to be added later at the beginning. In such circumstances it is probable that Caxton would have added a prologue when the table was included, though what it would contain we naturally have no way of knowing.

A new departure may be noted in 1481 with the appearance of the composite volume *Of Old Age*. This edition consists of *Of Old Age*, translated by William Worcestre for Sir John Fastolf, and translations of John Tiptoft, *Of Friendship* and *Declamation of Noblesse*. The latter two translations have separate signatures from those in *Of Old Age*, which has itself an odd set of signatures and gatherings. The first gathering is numbered with arabic numerals and is a ternion; the second gathering with signature *a* is also a ternion with its final leaf blank. The text proper begins of bl^r and *b* is a quaternion as are all the following gatherings. It appears as if the compositor was instructed to leave signature *a* free for the introductory material which was to follow. When it came, however, it was too long to be accommodated in one gathering, and so an extra gathering upsetting the signatures had to be included. This introductory material consists of a lengthy prologue and a *remembrance* of the contents of the book. Among other things the prologue relates how the translation came to be made and gives details of Fastolf's career. It is evident that these details were taken out of the manuscript Caxton was using as his copytext. To this information he added his own reasons for printing the text with the other two translations in one edition. Caxton no longer felt obliged to preserve the integrity of the translator's prologue. Whereas up to now he had always added his own prologue in addition to any already available, he now felt free to amalgamate what was there with what he wanted to include. Naturally this made for simplicty in that it prevented the proliferation of prologues. It also meant that the patron of the original version or translation figured in Caxton's own prologue and so lent a lustre to his own edition. It relieved him of the necessity of looking for a dedicatee since the volume could already be said to have aristocratic patronage. Hence from 1481 onwards one must be careful to distinguish in a Caxton prologue what is his own and what he had simply inherited from his copytext.

The same approach is adopted in *Mirror of the World* (1481) in which he adapted the prologue which existed in the French manuscript he used, BL Royal 19 A ix, and made it his own. In this volume, however, he kept the arrangement of the French text by having the table of contents before the prologue. This work was translated for Hugh Bryce, a mercer, who intended to present it to Lord Hastings. These details are mentioned in both prologue and epilogue. As there is no break in the sequence of signatures, it seems likely that the prologue was written at the beginning when Caxton started his translation. It is perhaps for this reasons that the prologue and epilogue have the same story.

Since we can identify the manuscript Caxton used to make his translation of *Mirror of the World* there is no problem in showing that he adapted the author's prologue. Other texts are not so straightforward. The *Siege of Jerusalem*, also a Caxton translation from French, contains a prologue and table of contents outside the main signature sequence of the edition. The style in which the prologue is written and its length suggest that it is translated from French. As the manuscript Caxton used has not been discovered it is not known whether his copytext contained an equivalent prologue or not. As far as *Polychronicon* (2 July 1482) is concerned, however, it is very unlikely that the prologue Caxton added to his edition was part of the copytext he used to set up the text. This prologue which expatiates on the virtues of history comes from the *Historical Library* of Diodorus Siculus possibly through a French version. It is not found in any extant manuscript of the *Polychronicon* and so was almost certainly included by Caxton who also modified it by adding details about Trevisa. This prologue and its accompanying table of contents were added to the edition after the rest was in type for they have their own separate quire signatures. As it happens this prologue was plundered by Caxton when he came to write the prologue to the second edition of the *Canterbury Tales* (c. 1483).

Thus the period 1480-83 saw important changes in the way Caxton presented his texts. The problem of how to include a table of contents led him to delay including the prefatory material in an edition. He did this by adding an extra quire (or quires) at the beginning after the rest of the text was in print. This quire usually has a different signature letter and is often of a different format from the rest of the edition. As he was adding a table of contents Caxton often took the opportunity to add a prologue too. This prologue was probably written shortly before it was printed. This could mean that the rest of the volume including Caxton's epilogue had been available for printing some considerable time before the prefatory matter was composed. Hence differences arose between prologue and epilogue. At first the prologues added at the beginning were fairly brief, amounting to little more than platitudes. Then he began to use the prologue which already existed in the volume he was preparing for the press as the basis for his own prologue. The resulting prologues are much longer and contain a mixture of material and styles. It is sometimes difficult to decide how much of these composite prologues was actually written by Caxton. When the texts he was printing had no prologues which he could use, he took to borrowing prologues from other works or he adapted those he had used already in a different text. In this way he was able to include longer and more elegant prologues while also saving himself the trouble of writing them himself.

The implications of this method of working can be appreciated from some of the books published in 1483-4. The *Golden Legend* has a prologue and table of contents in an introductory quire with a different signature from the rest of the volume. The prologue is based on that found in the French *Legende Doree*, though it was substantially modified by Caxton. This volume contains woodcuts which also appear in the introductory quire. As the prologue is divided into two by a woodcut, it is often claimed that there are two prologues; that is an erroneous assumption which takes no account of how Caxton was using the prologues in his originals by this time. There is also a brief epilogue by Caxton in this volume. No doubt the epilogue was written before the prologue. But both epilogue and prologue refer to the patronage of William Earl of Arundel, although the account in the prologue of the Earl's intervention in the edition is the longer of the two. However, that both refer to the same person implies that they were both written fairly close to each other and that the earl actually did involve himself in the volume before the translation was complete.

This situation contrasts with that in the *Knight of the Tower* which Caxton translated on 1 June 1483 and printed on 31 January 1484. This text is in its make-up identical with the *Golden Legend* in that it has a prologue and table of contents in an introductory quire which has a separate signature from the rest of the volume. This prologue refers to the book's genesis, which was brought about by a *noble lady* (p. 111) who had asked Caxton to translate it. The edition also contains an epilogue which simply mentions that Caxton made the translation; it has no reference to the noble lady. The implication of this is that Caxton made the translation on his own initiative. It was only the chance arrival of Elizabeth Woodville, Edward IV's widow (who has been identified as the noble lady[14]), at Westminster to seek sanctuary which led him to introduce her involvement in the edition. The gap in time and the difference in the accounts of how the translation arose between epilogue and prologue make this interpretation the most probable.

Although it was quite common for Caxton to include a prologue and table of contents after the work was completed, it was not his only manner of working. Neither *Charles the Great* nor *Order of Chivalry* has irregular quiring at the beginning; both were evidently set up with the prologue first. Each has a prologue based on that in the French original, though the one in *Charles the Great* has been considerably modified. Yet in this prologue there is no reference to William Daubeney who figures in the epilogue as the friend who asked for the book to be produced. In the prologue Caxton says simply that the book was printed 'to satysfye the desyre and requeste of my good synguler lordes and specyal maysters and

---

[14] N.F. Blake, 'The "noble lady" in Caxton's *The Book of the Knyght of the Towre*', *Notes and Queries* 210 (1965): 92f.

frendes' (p. 67). However, when he came to the epilogue he claimed the book 'was desyred and requyred by a good and synguler frende of myn, Maister Wylliam Daubeney, one of the Tresorers of the Jewellys of the noble and moost Crysten kyng . . . Edward the Fourth' (p. 68). In this case we may naturally conclude that Daubeney became involved in the edition only during the course of the book's translation or its printing.

It is not necessary to examine other editions in detail for they all fall into one of the two main methods now established by Caxton. Either all the material was ready for the compositor before he started work and so he began from the very beginning, or else the introductory material was left to the end and was added in an irregular quire (or quires) after the rest of the text was in type. It is not always possible to tell why Caxton chose one method of presentation rather than the other. It is important, though, to bear in mind how an edition was set up before trying to interpret the evidence which the prologues and epilogues contain. Caxton was not a simple printer who simply told the unvarnished truth. He was a clever promoter of books who took advantage of whatever material or circumstance prevailed at the time an edition was set up. He was also a pragmatist. He did not develop a routine system of text presentation: he was not sufficient of a scholar-printer for that.

8

Caxton's Reprints

Although a greal deal of scholarship has been expended on the reasons behind Caxton's choice of texts to print, this subject has always been considered in relation to his original editions.[1] The problem of why certain books were reprinted has not been given the attention it deserves, for a man's publishing policy embraces all the works he issued in their several editions. So in this article I would like to investigate this question. To start with it is necessary to review which books were reprinted. I shall exclude from the discussion the various indulgences he printed since we may assume that here he was acting as a printer rather than a publisher, and I shall also exclude the two texts, *History of Troy* and *Jason*, which appeared in French as well as in English versions. The French versions of these texts were printed in Bruges in 1474 or 1475 and may have been produced to keep the presses working while Caxton was making the arrangements to transfer his business from Bruges to Westminster. They were not intended for the English market (the English translation of the *History of Troy* having already appeared before the French edition was released), and so there can be no question of a reprint in the traditional sense in these cases.

Of the two English texts printed in Bruges one was reprinted. The *Game of Chess* first issued in 1474[2] was reprinted in 1483 with a new prologue and with illustrations. Several of the texts which appeared about 1477, shortly after Caxton's return to England, were reprinted almost immediately. *Churl and Bird* and *Horse, Sheep and Goose* each appeared in two editions, both dated to 1477; in either case the reprint reproduces the format of the original edition. *Cato* was also

1. See for example H.B. Lathrop, "The First English Printers and their Patrons," *The Library*, 4th Ser. 3 (1922-3), 69-96; D.B. Sands, "Caxton as a Literary Critic," *Papers of the Bibliographical Society of America*, 51 (1957), 312-18; and N.F. Blake, *Caxton and his World* (London: Deutsch, 1969), pp. 64-78.

2. For this dating see N.F. Blake, *Caxton's Own Prose* (London: Deutsch, 1973), pp. 11-19 ; and see above, chapter 6, pp. 75-87.

printed twice in 1477, but a third edition of his text appeared in 1481; this edition contains two woodcuts not found in the earlier ones. *Dicts or Sayings* was printed in 1477, and the John Rylands copy of this edition contains a colophon not found in the other copies. It is uncertain whether this colophon was made as a running correction or whether it should be regarded as forming a second edition. In addition *Dicts or Sayings* was reprinted in about 1479 and 1489. Another early text reprinted frequently was the *Horae*. The dates of the four editions are uncertain, though they have been assigned to 1477, 1480, 1489 and 1490. There are differences in illustration and type among these four editions and it is possible as some of them are known only from fragments that there were further editions printed by Caxton which have not survived. The other early text to be reprinted was Chaucer's *Canterbury Tales*. This was first issued in 1478 or even in 1477 and reprinted six years later. The reprint was issued with a new prologue explaining the reasons for its appearance and with woodcuts. Three texts printed in 1480 and 1481 were reprinted. These were the *Chronicles of England*, issued on 10 June 1480 and reissued on 8 October 1482; the *Mirror of the World*, printed first in 1481 and reprinted about 1490; and *Reynard the Fox*, printed first about 1481 and reissued about 1489. Apart from one or two minor changes the reprints reflect the pagination and layout of the original editions. From 1482 both the *Festial* and the *Quattuor Sermones* were reprinted, the former once (c.1491) and the latter twice (c.1485 and c.1491). The reprint of the *Festial* was based on a different text from Caxton's original edition, but the *Quattuor Sermones* reprints were essentially unchanged. In 1483 the *Golden Legend* was also printed for the first time. This text is difficult in that some gatherings seem to have been reset. Some copies have only the original gatherings while others contain some of the original and some of the reset gatherings. These reset gatherings have been interpreted as indicating a second edition, even though no copy survives which contains only reset gatherings. Those who accept a second edition date it to 1487; but this is a problem which will need further discussion. A similar difficulty exists with Caxton's edition of Lydgate's *Life of Our Lady*. This was printed about 1484. However, some leaves of this poem differing in considerable detail from those of the known edition were discovered in an old binding and it is possible that they are part of an otherwise lost second edition. But bibliographers have been unwilling to accord these leaves the status of a second edition and they have generally been dismissed as cancelled leaves of the first edition. Of the later books printed by Caxton the *Directorium Sacerdotum* and the *Speculum Vitae Christi* both appeared in two editions, and there are two different versions of the broadsheet, the *Image of Pity*.

The first thing to strike one about the above list of reprints is that none of Caxton's translations of chivalric works were reprinted. *Jason, History of Troy, Eneydos, Charles the Great, Blanchardin and Eglantine* and *Paris and Vienne* were printed only once each. This is surprising since the texts are those with which Caxton is particularly associated and with which he would have wished his name to be linked by his contemporaries. These are the ones normally given a prologue or epilogue. Why did Caxton not reprint them, for other publishers were not slow in reissuing them? The *Short Title Catalogue* lists eight editions of the *History of Troy,* and this list is incomplete.[3] A reason that some texts were not reprinted may have been their length, since a work like the *History of Troy* consists of 352 folio leaves. Clearly it would be financially hazardous to reprint a work of this length unless a good sale could be guaranteed. But as some of the chivalric works are much shorter than this, length cannot in itself have been the main reason why they were not reproduced. The most reasonable interpretation is that they were not reprinted for the same reason that they were originally printed. These texts were fashionable rather than practical and they would have been bought by those who wanted the latest fashionable reading matter. But this was a market which would soon be satisfied and naturally it had to be supplied with material that was new and up-to-date. Caxton in his prologues and epilogues frequently refers to the French original which had come "late" or "of newe" into his hands, thereby seeking to impress his readers with the novelty of the work. It would clearly be impossible for him to reprint works of this nature since there could be no element of newness or of up-to-date fashion in a reprint. This type of literature was hardly one where he could achieve a bestseller which could be constantly reprinted. By printing this type of work he was forced constantly to find and to translate new and different books. So it is a matter worth emphasizing that he did continue with this type of litera-ture right up to the end of his career even though he knew that he would not be able to reprint his translations. It shows that he deliber-ately chose to issue these books as part of a publishing policy; it was not something into which he just drifted.

Of the texts printed in 1477 and subsequently reprinted, those by Lydgate deserve attention. Caxton printed poems by Chaucer and by Lydgate in his early years at Westminster, but only the *Canterbury Tales* among Chaucer's poems was reprinted and there were special reasons for that. The Lydgate poems were printed individually

3. A.W. Pollard and G.R. Redgrave, *A Short-Title Catalogue of Books printed in England, Scotland & Ireland . . . 1475-1640* (London: Bibliographical Society, 1926), 15375-15382.

whereas the Chaucer ones were issued in composite volumes. In the latter case it is likely that Caxton simply reprinted the contents of the manuscripts available to him. Although we cannot tell whether he had manuscripts of individual Lydgate poems like the *Horse, Sheep and Goose,* it is unlikely since they were usually preserved in collections. It would seem as though the printer went out of his way to issue Lydgate's poems in separate editions, presumably because he considered them worthy of this individual attention. He reprinted these poems because his clients liked reading them and there was a sale for them. We today often praise Caxton for printing Chaucer's works, though it would seem that Lydgate was the more admired poet in the fifteenth century. As I have suggested elsewhere Caxton saw Chaucer through Lydgate's eyes and was perhaps uncertain how to react to Chaucer who was in so many ways less of a moral and didactic author than Lydgate.[4] Caxton could presumably have reprinted some of Chaucer's shorter poems individually, but he never did so. His printing of Chaucer was evidently more mechanical, for he showed greater editorial response to Lydgate. That he reprinted Lydgate poems shows that this policy of issuing individual poems by this poet was a successful one.

Even *Cato* by Benedict Burgh was reprinted and thus may also be regarded as a more successful poem than many by Chaucer. The third edition of this work is of interest, however, because it was issued with woodcuts. Although undated it must have appeared about 1481, immediately before or after the first edition of the *Mirror of the World.* These two texts are the first to be issued by Caxton with woodcuts. Evidently 1481 was the earliest time that he was able to recruit the services of a woodblock artist or that he felt it desirable to do so. The series of cuts in *Cato* and the *Mirror of the World* was certainly executed by the same hand and the reason *Cato* was reprinted in 1481 was probably that Caxton felt it was the most suitable of his works issued so far to be decorated with woodcuts. The position may have been something like this.

The English translation of the *Mirror of the World* was made by Caxton from the French text in British Library MS Royal 19 A ix, a manuscript made in Bruges in 1464. Since Caxton adds in his prologue to the translation details about the French manuscript which are not found in the manuscript itself, it is possible that Royal 19 A ix had been in his possession for some considerable time, perhaps even since it was finished in 1464. He may have thought of it as a potential work for translating long before he actually embarked on its translation in 1481, but was unable to accomplish the idea because the pictures were

4. See below, chapter 11, pp. 149-65.

an integral part of the work and he had no economic means of reproducing them. For to include hand-painted miniatures would be to increase the costs of production sharply. When he acquired the services of an artist in late 1480 or 1481, it is natural that he should think of producing this work with illustrations; and we may assume that if he had not acquired the services of the artist the *Mirror of the World* would never have been printed by Caxton. But the text was translated "at the request, desire, coste and dispense of the honourable and worshipful man Hugh Bryce, alderman and cytezeyn of London, entendyng to present the same unto the vertuous, noble and puissaunt lord, Wylliam Lord Hastynges."[5] In this case it is quite likely that Bryce asked Caxton to translate a text, rather than the *Mirror of the World* specifically, since it would be a coincidence if Bryce came along with a text worth illustrating exactly at the time when Caxton had acquired the services of an illustrator. It is more reasonable to assume that the manuscript was in Caxton's shop and that he suggested to Bryce that it would be a suitable text to present to Lord Hastings. The two woodcuts in the third edition of *Cato* are stylistically similar to the illustrations in Royal 19 A ix, though there are no originals for the two cuts in that manuscript. But the two cuts from the *Cato* edition are inserted at suitable places in *The Mirror of the World*. Either the artist produced two extra cuts for the *Mirror of the World* and these two cuts where chosen by Caxton to illustrate *Cato*; or the artist made the two cuts for *Cato* first, imitating the style of the illustrations in Royal 19 A ix. These two cuts were then included in the *Mirror of the World* since they were available. The latter solution seems the more probable and raises the fewest problems. In that case *Cato* might be regarded as a trial run to see how the workshop would cope with illustrations and how his public would respond to them. Caxton might have looked through his printed output up to this time to find a short text which was related to the *Mirror of the World* in style and approach so that his artist could try his hand out by producing a couple of cuts for that; *Cato* would have been a reasonable choice in the circumstances. Caxton chose a text already printed because it would be easier for the artist to read and because copies would be available in his shop.

While what I have written in the previous paragraph is largely speculation, it is clear that the availability of an artist or of illustrative material was an important factor in the choice of works to print or reprint, a factor which has not been taken into account before. That the *Mirror of the World* was itself one of the few translations by Caxton to be reprinted is attributable to the availability of the

5. The quotations from Caxton's prologues and epilogues are taken from *Caxton's Own Prose*.

woodcuts. For woodblocks were not thrown away after use; they represented a capital investment which could be employed again or which could be sold off to other printers. An important consideration in the reprinting of several texts in the period 1481-1484 is that Caxton could draw on the services of artists at that time. But even when choosing a work to be illustrated with woodcuts he preferred one with a moral or religious flavour to one with a chivalric nature. At least that would seem to be the reason a text like the *Game of Chess* was chosen for reprinting as against the *History of Troy*. After all the *Game of Chess* had to have a different prologue because the first edition had been addressed to George Duke of Clarence, who was now in disgrace. However, it is a text which can be illustrated quite simply, because it deals with certain classes represented by the chess pieces. The illustrations are bold and can readily be re-used elsewhere. The appearance of a reprint of the *Game of Chess* about 1483 is attributable to causes other than literary ones.

The appearance of the second edition of Chaucer's *Canterbury Tales* in 1484 or 1483 is interesting in the light of this discussion about the other reprints appearing about then. For Caxton's reprint of Chaucer was issued with woodcuts made by one of the artists available to him in the period 1481-4. At the same time Caxton informs us in his prologue that he had been asked to produce a second edition by a gentleman who promised to get hold of his father's manuscript copy which had a better text than his first edition. No mention of the illustrations is made in this new prologue, but this applies equally to his second edition of the *Game of Chess* and indeed to all his other reprints which have woodcuts. No doubt the illustrations would have been an important sales feature of the new edition, but they were perhaps so obvious that no comment was needed in the prologue; whereas that the text of the second edition was revised from a better manuscript would not be something apparent to the casual observer. The problem that we have to consider is whether he added the illustrations to the text he was reprinting simply because he happened to have an artist available at that time or whether the availability of the artist was an important element in his calculations as to whether to reprint. In the present state of our knowledge it is not possible to come to a decision, but I think that the availability of the woodcuts is an argument which should receive greater weight than it has done in the past. Dunn has shown that the revision of the text for the second edition is perfunctory and superficial,[6] and what we know

6. T.F. Dunn, *The Manuscript Source of Caxton's Second Edition of the Canterbury Tales* (Chicago: University of Chicago, 1940).

of fifteenth-century reading habits would lead us to suppose that few readers of fashionable literature would rush to buy the second edition of the *Canterbury Tales* simply because it had a revised text. The woodcuts, on the other hand, would have been an attraction for such clients and may have enticed them into purchasing the second edition as well. As it is the only one of Chaucer's poems to be reprinted we cannot assume that Chaucer was as popular a writer as Lydgate at this time or that his books would sell so well. It is worth noting that the other Chaucer poems printed for the first time when the second edition of the *Canterbury Tales* appeared do not have woodcuts—even though they appeared when the artists were still working for the press. This might be taken to mean that although one edition of a Chaucer work could be expected to sell without added attractions, further editions would need additional selling points, such as woodcuts or a revised text. The appearance of the woodcuts may also indicate that Caxton was trying to sell the second edition to the same people who bought the first edition, whereas there was sufficient extra demand for those texts reprinted without woodcuts.

This is an appropriate place to consider the case of Lydgate's *Life of Our Lady*, printed about 1484. Some leaves which are in the same type but which differ in spelling and minor details of layout are to be found in the Bodleian, the British Library and the University Library, Cambridge. It may be significant that the fragments in all these libraries consist of leaves 3 and 6, though the British Library fragments also include leaves 2 and 7, in that the recurrence of the same leaves has led bibliographers to assume that the fragments represent cancelled leaves rather than a new edition. That there are variant leaves in Caxton editions is shown by the occurrence in the Hague copy of the *Cordial* (29 March 1479) of two versions of folio 3, each of which differs in spelling and lineation from the other. But in this case also it is undecided whether we are dealing with a reprint or not, though in the case of texts like the *Horae* the discovery of new fragments has always been taken to indicate new editions. It may be that some times the printers ran off an incorrect number of leaves of a particular folio and that the mistake was only discovered when the book was being assembled. As the page of type would have been broken up by then, it would be necessary to reprint the missing leaves. On the other hand, it is clear that as long as the printing shop was using the same type new editions were set up in accordance with the pagination of the previous edition, though spelling and lineation might differ. It was only when woodcuts were included in a reprint that this system broke down and a new pagination became necessary. The advantages of working like this are obvious in that the text is already arranged into suitable pages and gatherings can be divided among the available compositors without the need for any further editorial work. The reprints of the Lydgatian poems about 1477 and the recently discovered second edition of the *Quattuor Sermones* have all been set up on the pattern of the first editions.[7] In these cases the absence of woodcuts and the similarity of pagination would mean that most readers would not realize that their copy was from the second edition. The text must have sold out and been reprinted to meet a demand which did not need further attractions. That *Quattuor Sermones* was reprinted fairly soon after its first appearance about 1483 shows that it was not only in 1477 that reprints appeared almost immediately after the first edition. As the *Life of Our Lady* is a poem by Lydgate and as his poems were the works most frequently reprinted, it would seem more likely that these extra leaves represent another edition rather than cancelled leaves. For the theory of cancelled leaves to be acceptable we would need to have some good reason for cancellation, and there are no glaring mistakes which would lead us to suppose that the printers went to all the trouble to reset these pages. While running corrections were made, we have as yet insufficient evidence to suppose that the press was so conscientious that it reset pages for aesthetic rather than textual considerations. It might lead to fewer difficulties if we accept that there were two editions of the *Life of Our Lady* about 1484.

The problem of what constitutes a reprint arises with several other texts. One is *Dicts or Sayings*, the first edition of which had the added colophon in the John Rylands copy. As the colophon is something that could have been added during printing without resetting any pages and as the various copies are otherwise identical, there is little need to assume that the first edition should be considered as two. This is the first text to be issued with a colophon by Caxton and it is quite likely that during the printing he decided to insert some indication as to the date of publication. We may note that he made a point of including details of printing in the various translations by Earl Rivers he printed, and this is something he may have hit on while the first edition of the *Dicts or Sayings* was printing. However, this work did appear in two other editions, about 1479 and 1489. But it is not a chivalric work; it has more the nature of a moral didactic book. As such this work reinforces the comment made earlier about the absence of reprints of chivalric works; moral and didactic works obviously

---

7.   C.A. Webb, "Caxton's *Quattuor Sermones:* A Newly Discovered Edition," *Essays in Honour of Victor Scholderer,* ed. D.A. Rhodes (Mainz: Pressler, 1970) 407-25; and N.F. Blake and L. Reffkin, "Caxton's First Edition of *Quattuor Sermones," Gutenberg Jahrbuch* (1974), pp. 77-82.

had wider appeal and sales that the books of chivalry normally printed by Caxton.

Another text which seems to have been reprinted, even though a complete second edition consisting of only reset pages is not known, is the *Golden Legend*. It has woodcuts which are the same in both editions, though the headings of the saints' lives are in different type in each. This text is one of a religious nature, and although issued under the patronage of the Earl of Arundel it would presumably have appealed as much, if not more, to a clerical audience. Indeed the size of the volume makes it suitable for reading from a lectern only, and this in turn may suggest it was intended for institutions rather than for homes. That the *Golden Legend* was reprinted brings it into line with the *Festial* and *Quattuor Sermones*, both of which are principally directed at clerics. Indeed these two texts, like the *Golden Legend* itself, were reprinted constantly after Caxton's death and the market for them was evidently considerable. The *Festial* overlaps considerably with the *Golden Legend*, for it contains saints' lives adapted from the Latin *Legenda Aurea*. The second edition of the *Festial* is not printed from the first, for it contains, at the beginning or end, material not found in the first edition. No reference to this extra material is made by Caxton. It has often been assumed that the reprint was made from the Oxford edition of Rood and Hunte, but it is equally possible that the reprint was made from a manuscript. It may be that Caxton had sold out of the first edition and simply printed the second edition from a manuscript available to him at that time. If so, he may not have been aware himself that the two editions differed. We should be cautious about attributing modern motives to him in his reprinting programme. In all these cases we can see that works suitable for a clerical audience and consisting of items of a practical religious nature were in constant demand and had to be reprinted. The same applies to the *Directorium Sacerdotum* which he printed twice, and thus it needs no further comment.

Other texts we need to consider are *Speculum Vitae Christi*, the *Horae* and the *Image of Pity*. All are religious texts and if we include the first two of the four editions of the *Horae*, all are illustrated. But whereas in the period 1481-4 Caxton had artists available at Westminster, later in his career he appears to have imported woodcuts from the Continent. This fact has never received the consideration it deserves in evaluating the books he chose to print. For example, it is often claimed that he printed more books of a religious nature late in his life because he became more devout as death approached. This view is improbable if only because he was translating and printing chivalric books like *Eneydos* shortly before his death. The reason for the religious books lies in the woodcuts. It was clearly much easier to buy sets of religious blocks from Continental suppliers than sets of other subjects; and such sets would be interchangeable in a vast range of books since so many works were of a religious nature. But once he had acquired sets like the one appearing in *Speculum Vitae Christi* he would naturally have to choose religious works if he was going to make use of them. The issue of *Speculum Vitae Christi* by Caxton is unusual in that it belongs to the native mystical tradition, for it was translated by Nicholas Love of Mountgrace Priory. It was the sort of book that Caxton seems otherwise to have avoided printing, for it is only reasonable to suppose that many books in this tradition passed through his hands. If he had acquired a set of cuts dealing with the life of Christ, his choice of a suitable text in English in which to use them would be limited; hence he chose *Speculum Vitae Christi*. Although he used individual cuts from this series in other of his translations, the existence of the series probably led him to issue a reprint when the first edition sold out. The same may apply to the third and fourth editions of the *Horae* which have a series of cuts similar in style to those in *Speculum Vitae Christi*. It is indeed possible that Caxton acquired both sets at the same time. A similar state of affairs applies equally to the *Image of Pity*.

A text not yet discussed is *Reynard the Fox*, printed in 1481 and again about 1489. In many lists of Caxton's printed works this is listed under "satire" and is the only book in that genre. But such a listing is unsuitable. This text is the only one of Caxton's own translations without woodcuts to be reprinted and one naturally wonders why. Later printers were not slow to embellish it with cuts and as Caxton had used an animal series in his *AEsop* he could easily have pressed some of these into service again in the second edition of *Reynard the Fox*. That he did not suggests it could sell well enough without them. It is likely that Caxton thought this book had more the nature of a moral or didactic work than of a satire, [8] and it was for this reason he reprinted it. It would then not be unlike *Dicts or Sayings* which was reprinted twice. If so, it would reinforce what we have noted so frequently already: that there was a much more established and reliable market for works of this kind rather than for books of chivalry.

The *Chronicles of England* should be considered within the framework of the historical works published by Caxton. It was evidently a popular text since manuscripts of the *Brut* are numerous and Caxton printed it twice within two years. He also used it to bring Trevisa's translation of Higden's *Polychronicon* up to date for it forms

---

8.   See N.F. Blake, *History of Reynard the Fox*, EETS 263 (London: Early English Text Society, 1970), pp. xlvii-lix.

the major source of the seventh book which was added by Caxton to that volume. The geographical section of that translation was itself issued separately as the *Description of Britain* so that one could say his edition of the *Polychronicon* is a reprint at its beginning and end. These works show that Caxton tried to capitalize on historical works, for one was reprinted and the other was first printed in extract and then expanded to bring it up to date. The whole shows a resourcefulness not exhibited in his other publications (there were no extracts of any chivalric works), and it was all confined to the years 1480-2. It is as though he realized there was a market for history and provided for it plentifully for two years before abandoning it. Like moral and didactic literature, history was a vein that could have been exploited more fully than it was. It was obviously too peripheral to his main interests to be developed further.

From what has been written it must be accepted that Caxton was aware of the profits which were available from certain lines in publication, for his reprints made this clear. Yet he steadfastly refused to develop those lines even though it would have been easier for him to do so. This attitude must influence our appreciation of him in that, although a merchant, he was not in the printing business simply to maximize his profits. He preferred, or thought others preferred, a particular type of literature and went out of his way to provide it, even possibly at some financial sacrifice to himself. Certainly he let himself in for more work and trouble than he needed to if he was simply going to keep his business solvent.

Prologue

Of eche of hem so as it semed me
And whyche they were and of what degre
And in what aray eke they weren ynne
And at a knyght thenne I wyl begynne

Knyght ther was a worthy man
That fro the tyme that he first began
To ryden out / he loued chyualrye
Trouthe & honour fredom and curtesye
Ful worthy he was in hys lordis werre
And therto hadde he ryden noman ferre
And as wel in crystendom as in hethenesse
And euer hadde honour for hys worthynesse
At alisaundre he was whan it was wonne
Ful ofte tyme he hadde the boord begonne
Abouen alle nacions in pruce
In lettowe hadde he reysed and in Ruse

Plate 1. The Knight, from the second impression (1484) of Caxton's edition of *The Canterbury Tales*.

9

Caxton and Courtly Style

IN this paper I should like to consider how Caxton reacted to contemporary trends in literary English and what information this yields us about the development of fifteenth-century English prose. Those who have commented on Caxton's attitude to the literary language have usually been content to review the opinions found in his prologue to *Eneydos*. But *Eneydos* was one of the last books he printed, and the prologue represents the culmination of his views about English which had been developing over the previous twenty years. Consequently a juster appreciation of Caxton's attitude towards English may be obtained by examining his prologues and epilogues in the order in which they were written, for not only are his final views of interest, but also the influences which caused his opinions to change in the way they did are important for an understanding of the fifteenth century. So I shall commence by tracing briefly the development of his opinions.

We must naturally start with the *History of Troy*, the first English book to be printed. In his various prologues to this work, Caxton claimed that he took pleasure in the 'fayr langage of Frenshe' (4),[1] for the original was written 'in prose so well and compendiously sette and wreton, whiche me thought I vnderstood the sentence and substance of euery mater' (4). When he had completed some of his translation he showed it to Margaret of Burgundy who found fault with his English. What criticism she made is not revealed, though it is more than likely she thought the style not sufficiently ornate. As it was, Caxton claimed that he followed the original as closely as he could, but nevertheless the

[1] The references in brackets after Caxtonian quotations are to pages in W. J. B. Crotch, *The Prologues and Epilogues of William Caxton*, EETS o.s. 176 (London, 1928). I have, however, modernized the punctuation.

result was a 'rude werk' (5) containing 'rude Englissh' (6). The impression one gets is that Caxton followed the French closely in order to share the merits of its style which was so 'compendious' and intelligible, but that unfortunately something was lost in the process of translation. No doubt some of this attitude is conventional for it was traditional to decry one's own merits by employing the humility formula. But both the praise of French style and the words used to express that praise are important. Caxton praises French prose, but mentions no English prose as being comparable. Yet the word 'compendious', which he uses to describe French prose style, was a favourite one with Lydgate, as a few examples will show:

> Undir a stile breeff & compendious (*Fall of Princes* I. 90)
> Compendiously this mateer for to declare (ibid. VIII. 2647)
> Withoute frute he was compendious (*Troy-Book* Prol. 351)
> Now must I ful besy ben a whyle . . .
> Myn auctor folwe & be compendious (ibid. V. 2315–19).

Conciseness was not in fact a virtue of the French original or Caxton's translation, or even indeed of Lydgate. But it was evidently considered a necessary virtue of style. The term was used by Lydgate to describe his own poetic style. It was adapted by Caxton to the French prose style of his original in order to show that it had the same stylistic features as English poetry. It was these features which he wished to give to his own prose by close translation. The quotations from Lydgate's *Troy-Book* are important for Caxton knew this work, to which he refers in his prologue. But he refers to it in tones of the greatest respect. His own translation, he writes, cannot in any way be compared with Lydgate's poem though it covers much of the same ground. Caxton completed his translation only because his own was in prose.

After his return to England Caxton printed the *Dicts of Philosophers* translated by Earl Rivers and his own translation of *Jason*. While the latter repeats that Caxton's translations have little in the way of elegant prose, in the prologue to the former Caxton wanted to pay Rivers a compliment on his translation. To us today there seems little difference stylistically between the two, though Caxton speaks of them in quite different ways. The one has no 'beaute or good endyting of our Englissh tonge' (34), the other is 'right wel & connyngly made & translated into right good and fayr Englissh' (20). The important thing to notice is the paucity of Caxton's critical vocabulary. He has neglected to use 'compendious' and there is no reference to rhetoric. He has not yet learned how to praise a work. This he was to do by printing Chaucer's *Boethius*, for through this work he became aware of the critical opinions about Chaucer common in the fifteenth century. There is a significant enlargement of Caxton's critical vocabulary in the prologue to this book. Chaucer was the 'first translatour of this sayde boke into Englissh & enbelissher in making the sayd langage ornate & fayr' (37). The 'langage' appears to mean English in general rather than the prose of the translation, for Chaucer is also called 'the worshipful fader & first foundeur & enbelissher of ornate eloquence in our Englissh' (37). It has been shown that Caxton took these phrases from other works about Chaucer which were known to him.[1] Caxton is absorbing the fashion current at the time, in which the two words 'ornate' and 'embellisher' appear constantly.[2] Nevertheless we should not forget that Chaucer is also praised for following the Latin 'as neygh as is possible to be vnderstande' (37). The same point is made in *Of Old Age*. The Latin text, in which matters are 'specyfyced compendiously' (42), is difficult, but 'this book, reduced in Englyssh tongue, is more ample expowned and more swetter to the reder, kepyng the iuste sentence of the Latyn' (42).

Trevisa's translation of Higden's *Polychronicon* was treated differently. Although made within ten years of Chaucer's *Boethius*, this translation was considered by Caxton to be outdated, though good. Consequently he has 'chaunged the rude and old Englyssh, that is to wete certayn wordes which in these dayes be neither vsyd ne vnderstanden' (68). Trevisa evidently did not have

---

[1] See below, chapter 11, pp. 149-65.

[2] C. F. E. Spurgeon, *Five Hundred Years of Chaucer Criticism and Allusion*, I. 1357–1800 (London, 1914).

quite the same stylistic reputation as Chaucer and therefore his language wanted modernization. As a close translation of Higden it was estimable, but it wanted some embellishment.

With his second edition of *Canterbury Tales* Caxton repeats many of the critical comments he had made about Chaucer in his prologue to *Boethius*. Chaucer embellished English and made it ornate. But Caxton now also mentions what had been characteristic of English prior to Chaucer. Then the English language was 'rude' and 'incongrue, as yet it appiereth by olde bookes' (90). Whether these old books were in poetry or prose is not revealed. But there is a clear indication that Chaucer polished English by making it rhetorical and ornate as one can see by comparing his writings with older books. Caxton goes on to praise Chaucer for his conciseness and his 'sugred eloquence' (90), the sentiments and the words being alike borrowed from Lydgate.[1] Caxton has become more deeply involved in the current critical fashions about Chaucer and court poetry.

At this stage his involvement begins to affect his descriptions of his own prose. He has become aware of what is expected in a good style. In *Charles the Great* he uses the critical vocabulary of rhetoric to comment on his own translation for the first time. He is still, as usual, apologetic for his style which he calls 'rude & symple reducyng' (96). But he goes a step further by commenting on the lack of rhetoric: 'though so be there be no gaye termes ne subtyl ne newe eloquence, yet I hope that it shal be vnderstonden' (96). His association with the court and his knowledge of Chaucerian criticism must have made him conscious of what was fashionable. Yet he still attaches importance to comprehension as well as to decoration, a point to which he returns: 'And yf in al thys book I haue mesprysed or spoken otherwyse than good langage substancyally ful of good vnderstondyng to al makers and clerkes, I demaunde correxyon and amendement' (98). It seems as though a good style and comprehensibility go hand in hand. From now on an apology for the absence of the gay terms of rhetoric 'as now be sayd in these dayes and vsed' (105) is a constant feature of his prologues. It is found particularly in *Feats of Arms* and

[1] See below, chapter 11, pp. 149-65.

Blanchardyn and Eglantine. Quotation from these hardly seems necessary. Yet he still goes on insisting that he has followed his French source closely and uttering the hope that his works are comprehensible.

The discussion of rhetoric in the prologue to *Eneydos* is the natural culmination of the other prologues. In some ways Caxton has not changed. He still translates because of the style of his French original: 'in whiche booke I had grete playsyr by cause of the fayr and honest termes & wordes in Frenshe, whyche I neuer sawe to fore lyke ne none so playsaunt ne so wel ordred' (107). The difference is now that he has a greater stock of words with which to express his pleasure. He admits, however, that there are some gentlemen who have taken objection to his translations because he used 'ouer curyous termes whiche coude not be vnderstande of comyn people' and they wanted him to use 'olde and homely termes' (108). This fact is interesting in showing that Caxton's opinions were influenced by the fashion of the court and also that there was an anti-rhetorical faction at court. Caxton goes on to say that he read an old book which he found difficult to understand because of its 'rude and brood' English. Similarly at the request of the Abbot of Westminster he looked at some old documents whose language was more like 'Dutch' (i.e. Low German) than English so that he was unable to understand it. This leads Caxton on to the everchanging nature of the English language, an opinion which he may well have picked up from the poets of the courtly tradition.[1] The implication of his argument is that those who wish for the old and homely terms are foolish, for English has progressed beyond that state whether they like it or not. He prefers modern terminology since his books are designed for a cultivated and educated audience. However, he will try to maintain a middle position between the extremes of old and homely terms and over-refinement. But significantly he refers those who fail to understand his language to Virgil and the *Epistles* of Ovid, from which one can assume that he was on the side of the educated, Latinate clientele and that he thought his rhetorical embellishments were based on Latin. Finally, Caxton

---

[1] Cf. *Confessio Amantis*, Prol. 142, *Troilus and Criseyde* II. 22–5.

praises the work of John Skelton extravagantly. Since Skelton was one of the most prominent aureate writers of the time, it confirms that Caxton was in favour of rhetoric and embellishment and it suggests that he wanted his own work to be judged by such standards.

Now that this survey of Caxton's views is complete, it is time to evaluate the points arising from it. The most important is the evidence that at the start of his publishing career he had little critical vocabulary, but that he enlarged this vocabulary over the years. The two major influences contributing to this increase were the critical opinions surrounding the works of Chaucer and the opinions of his fashionable clientele from the court. The greatest impetus within the former influence came undoubtedly from the works of Lydgate, since Lydgate followed what he thought was the Chaucerian poetic tradition and wrote many lines in his praise. Indeed there is much to suggest that Caxton looked at Chaucer through the works of Lydgate. But the Chaucerian criticism was directed more to the poetic language than to English in general. Caxton was forced to follow the poetic model even though he was writing in prose, because the new poetic style had such prestige and because there was no English prose in the courtly style which he could emulate. To some extent the absence of such a prose style was beginning to be rectified at the end of Caxton's life by the works of Skelton, and clearly a court which contained such an aureate writer as Skelton as tutor to the Prince of Wales could hardly avoid being concerned with rhetorical fashion. This in its turn would influence Caxton. But in general the absence of a native prose style was overcome by translating from Latin or French and by following the original style closely. This is why Caxton constantly refers us to the French and Latin originals. Their style has those features which English prose lacks, but which could be found in English poetry. At the same time there was in existence in English an older prose style, which was not considered a satisfactory model, just as there had been an older poetic style which had been outmoded by the Chaucerian revolution. That style could be seen in old books. Exactly what this style consisted of is not clear, since Caxton never discusses the matter in detail, though the general history of late medieval English literature leads me to accept that it was the alliterative style. For Caxton the disadvantages of this old style were its vocabulary and lack of rhetorical refinement. Old books used an obsolete vocabulary, they used words no longer fashionable. Presumably they were words of Anglo-Saxon or Norse origin instead of being modern words coined from French or Latin. Similarly the old books followed the native stylistic traditions instead of following the rhetoric found in French or Latin models.

So far I have been considering Caxton's developing attitude to style and rhetoric, and the influences which caused that attitude to change. Now it is necessary to consider to what extent Caxton's own style was influenced by the fashionable acceptance of rhetoric. Wendelstein,[1] for example, has pointed to some minor rhetorical flourishes in Caxton's *Charles the Great*. Thus he notes the repetition of the suffix *-ly* at the end of clauses: 'and dyd do paynte the hystoryes after somme poyntes of our crysten fayth moche ryche*ly* and repayred the places ryght delycyous*ly*. And on that other he dyd do ordeyne & founde chirches autentyk*ly*, & compose baptyzatoryes & frentes conuenab*ly*' (fol. a8ᵛ). He also singles out the pointing of clauses by the use of rhyming words: 'Whan thys was de*maunded*, it was com*maunded*' (fol. b6ᵛ). But Wendelstein omitted to mention that these rhetorical tricks are taken over directly from the French *Fierabras*, which Caxton was translating: (i) 'puys a paindre histoires selon aulcuns poins de nostre foy cristienne moult riche*ment* et les places reparer tres delicieuse-*ment*, et d'aultre part il fist ordonner et fonder esglises auctentique-*ment* et composer baptitoires conuenable*ment*' (fol. b1ʳ); (ii) 'Cecy estre de*mandé*, il fut com*mandé*' (fol. b8ʳ). Here we should recall that one of Caxton's major theses was that English prose style was at its best when it kept as close as possible to a French or Latin original. He insisted on this because it was intended that some of the fine French or Latin style would show through in the English translation. It should not, therefore, be a matter for surprise that this did in fact happen from time to time. It does not of course follow that Caxton was aware of all the places where this had

[1] L. Wendelstein, *Beitrag zur Vorgeschichte des Euphuismus* (Halle, 1902), p. 4.

taken place. And it is certainly true that his own original compositions cannot be shown to have been influenced by foreign models. No rhetorical flourishes have been pointed out in his own compositions, which are more notable for their clumsy style than for their balanced or rhythmical sentences.[1] His style becomes very loose when he has no guide. His appreciation of rhetoric is superficial: he was unable to practise what he preached. The one exception could be his use of doublets, which was a type of embellishment. This feature had been used by Chaucer, and is largely confined in Caxton to passages which demand a more elevated style. They allow Caxton to use French loanwords and thus to give his work a more fashionable appearance. The French content of Caxton's vocabulary depends likewise on whether the passage is translated or original. Original passages contain far fewer loanwords than translated ones, though they do not have words from the alliterative style. His own prose uses a limited vocabulary, though he does use words which were no doubt fashionable such as 'noble'.[2] Neither his style nor his vocabulary was particularly affected by French when he made an original composition. Furthermore we should realize that his policy of translating closely from Latin or French was one which he probably adopted because it was the fashion of the time to do so. He did it, he says, to transfer the elegances of French and Latin style to English. Yet he also translated closely when he translated from Flemish, as in *Reynard the Fox*, which meant he imported many Flemish loanwords. Yet since in his prologue to *Eneydos* he stated that the older English, which he was trying to avoid, and Low German had much in common, one might have supposed that he would have avoided imitating Flemish style and introducing Flemish loanwords. He did not; and once again we see that Caxton did not carry out in his own work what he claimed as desirable. This inability to carry out his own stated preferences is important in confirming that his opinions reflect contemporary ideas rather

[1] R. R. Aurner, 'Caxton and the English Sentence', *University of Wisconsin Studies in Language and Literature*, xviii (1923), 23–59.

[2] N. F. Blake, 'Caxton's Language', *Neuphilologische Mitteilungen,* lxvii (1966), 122–32; below, chapter 10, pp. 137-47.

than his own observations and practice. This is why his evidence is so valuable.

Even though Caxton may not have been able to provide much in the way of rhetorical embellishment in his individual compositions, one would expect contemporary prejudices to manifest themselves in his choice of texts for he would have to sell them to his fashionable clientele. Although my subject is prose rather than poetry, the evidence from the poetry is important and I shall deal briefly with that first. The major poets printed by Caxton are Chaucer, Gower and Lydgate, and these three represent the triumvirate of the courtly tradition. Their names were constantly linked by fifteenth-century and early sixteenth-century writers who commented on the new poetic fashion. All the other poetry printed by Caxton may be said to be part of this new tradition. Benedict Burgh was Lydgate's pupil and finished some of his work; the *Court of Sapience* was often attributed to Lydgate himself; and the poet of the *Book of Courtesy* looks back to Chaucer, Gower and Lydgate as the three great poets and thus reveals his allegiance. All the poems use stanza or couplet, a markedly French vocabulary and many rhetorical expedients. On the other hand, Caxton has often been blamed for not printing *Piers Plowman*. Since so many manuscripts of this poem circulated in the fifteenth century, and since some of them were connected with London, it seems likely that Caxton knew of its existence. We cannot be certain about this, but we can imagine that if he did know of the poem he would not have printed it, for it must have represented to him the older poetic tradition from which Chaucer had broken away. It uses the old alliterative metre with old words arranged in the traditional English manner. In terms of poetry Caxton must have meant the alliterative poems when he referred to 'old books'.

It would be natural to assume that Caxton and his contemporaries were affected by the current fashion towards poetry in their attitude to prose. As far as Caxton is concerned, this would mean that we would expect him to publish work in the courtly stylistic tradition and to avoid the alliterative or native prose. This assumption may be tested firstly by considering what type of prose work

Caxton chose to print and secondly by examining how he edited the books before printing them. The characteristic feature of the prose printed by Caxton is that it consists either of translation or of work based on foreign models. I must emphasize that I am not here concerned with Caxton's own translations, but only with those works which already existed in an English version before coming into Caxton's hands. Such works include Earl Rivers's two translations, *Dicts of Philosophers* and *Cordial*; Chaucer's translation of *Boethius*; Worcester's translations, *Declamation of Noblesse* and *Of Friendship*; the earlier English translation of *Of Old Age;* Trevisa's translation of Higden's *Polychronicon*, with which we may include the *Description of Britain*; and Malory's *Morte Darthur*. This book we today tend to think of as a re-creation rather than a translation, but to Caxton it was 'take oute of certayn bookes of Frensshe and reduced' (94) to English. The above list is in no way comprehensive, for it excludes many of the more specifically religious works, such as *Mirror of the Life of Christ* and *Pilgrimage of the Soul*. All these are translations as well, except for Mirk's *Festial* which is a re-telling of the *Legenda Aurea* rather than a straightforward translation. Of all the publications issuing from the press only one can properly be said not to be a translation, namely the *Chronicles of England*. And this work, which originated as a translation and for which there were foreign models, is closely associated with London and the court. It has no trace of the alliterative style. What is noticeable, therefore, about Caxton's choice of books is that he did not print anything by an Englishman written in what we may call the native tradition. Such authors as Rolle, Hilton and the author of the *Cloud of Unknowing* are completely passed over, even though their works were popular and many manuscripts survived. Though sometimes modelled on foreign sources, the works of these authors can hardly be thought of as translations. And more importantly they belong stylistically to the native prose tradition.[1] Furthermore,

[1] There has been some discussion as to whether there were several styles in Middle English prose, e.g. E. Zeeman, 'Continuity in Middle English Devotional Prose', *Journal of English and Germanic Philology*, lv (1956), 417–22. But as Caxton does not discriminate between varieties of the old style, I have regarded alliteration as the style he was referring to.

even such original English compositions as there were in the fifteenth century were not printed by Caxton. There can consequently be no doubt that Caxton favoured translated works and that this prejudice was shared by many members of the court. The most cultivated and respected men of the time, such as Rivers, Worcester, Skelton and later Berners—to name only a few—made translations rather than original compositions. It is significant that the only works by Skelton which Caxton referred to are all translations: 'For he hath late translated the Epystlys of Tulle, and the boke of Dyodorus Syculus, and diuerse other werkes oute of Latyn in to Englysshe' (109).

It is not difficult to understand how this prejudice came about. In the fifteenth century the distinction between poetry and prose was not so great as it is now. It was accepted that poetry had broken out of the old mould by using foreign models. Chaucer had modelled his poems on French or Italian ones, and Gower had made good use of Ovid. Lydgate had made many poetic 'translations', of which his *Troy-Book* is perhaps the outstanding example. Though we today tend to highlight Lydgate's statements that he was writing in the Chaucerian tradition, we should not forget that he also in the *Troy-Book* pays many fulsome tributes to Guido's style. It was natural that prose should follow the lead set by poetry; that it should emancipate itself from the native tradition by following foreign models. But there was one important difference. In poetry there had been Chaucer; in prose there was no English model of comparable stature. Therefore while Lydgate and other fifteenth-century poets could claim to be writing in the Chaucerian manner, although more often than not they were imitating foreign models, the prose writers could not claim to be following any English model. Hence they were thrown back on their sources which they tended to follow slavishly. It is of course easier to be more literal in prose, and we may notice that even poets such as Chaucer and Skelton made literal prose translations. But it is the great misfortune of late medieval English prose that neither Skelton nor Chaucer established himself as a model. This meant that there was no English model which could curb the worst excesses

of translation and make the translator lift his eyes from his
source.

We must now consider the other aspect of Caxton's publishing
activity, namely to what extent he altered the texts he had decided
to print. In many cases it is not possible to come to any decision
since his version is the only one that survives. But from what he
wrote in his prologues it would seem unlikely that he altered the
translations by, say, Rivers or Worcester. Similarly he did not
materially change Chaucer's *Boethius*. These translations were not
touched because Caxton had too much respect for the translators.
There are, however, two works which Caxton did alter considerably, Malory's *Morte Darthur* and Trevisa's translation of Higden.
The reasons which led Caxton to adapt these works differ; but it is
better first to discuss what the changes were before considering
what caused them.

From even a glance at Vinaver's edition of Malory,[1] it is
evident that Caxton altered Book Five most. This is the book
which is based upon the English alliterative poem, *Le Morte
Arthure*, and Malory took over much of the vocabulary and alliteration. Let us consider a short passage from this book together
with Caxton's adaptation:

Malory: Than the kynge yode up to the creste of the cragge, and
than he comforted hymself with the colde wynde; and than he
yode forth by two welle-stremys, and there he fyndys two
fyres flamand full hygh. And at that one fyre he founde a carefull
wydow wryngande hir handys syttande on a grave that was
new marked. Than Arthur salued hir and she hym agayne, and
asked hir why she sate sorowyng. 'Alas,' she seyde, 'carefull
knyght. Thou carpys over lowde! Yon is a werlow woll
destroy us bothe.'
Caxton: And soo he ascended up in to that hylle tyl he came to a
grete fyre, and there he fonde a careful wydowe wryngynge

---

[1] E. Vinaver, *The Works of Sir Thomas Malory* (Oxford, 1947). Both passages
quoted below are from this edition, p. 200. For a discussion of Malory's language
and Caxton's handling of it see Sally Shaw, 'Caxton and Malory' in *Essays on
Malory*, edited by J. A. W. Bennett (Oxford, 1963), pp. 114–45; and W.
Matthews, *The Ill-Framed Knight* (Berkeley and Los Angeles, 1966).

her handes and makyng grete sorowe, syttynge by a grave new made. And thenne kynge Arthur salewed her and demaunded of her wherefore she made such lamentacion. To whom she ansuerd and sayd: 'Syre knyghte, speke softe for yonder is a devyll; yf he here the speke, he wyll come and destroye the.'

In the Caxton passage we may note the avoidance of alliterative groups: *creste of the cragge, comforted . . . colde, fyres flamand, sate sorowyng, carefull knyght.* Some of the alliteration may have been eliminated incidentally through the attempt to modernize the vocabulary. It is interesting to see how often this modernization takes the form of introducing French words: *ascended (yode up), demaunded (asked), lamentacion (sorowyng)*; though in other cases it merely involves using a less specific word for the forceful older word: *devyll (werlow), speke (carpys).* Caxton also uses vague adjectives such as 'great' as in *'grete* fyre' and *'grete* sorowe'. The tone of the conversations has become more elevated in Caxton, for not only does the lady address Arthur as 'Syre knyghte', but her speech is also more subdued from the brusque tone it has in Malory. In general Caxton's version is more courtly and less specific. Finally we may note the use of repetition in 'wryngynge her handes and makyng grete sorowe', in which the latter phrase has been added by Caxton. The use of the doublet may have been an attempt by Caxton to heighten the pathos by using a rhetorical figure. The changes I have pointed to show how Caxton adapted the text. It is significant that the passage should be from the fifth book. The remaining books, which are for the most part based on French sources, are generally only modified rather than rewritten.

Trevisa's translation was different from Malory's. It was an older English translation of a standard Latin work by a man who had achieved some eminence as a translator. Caxton, for example, also mentions his translations of the Bible and *De Proprietatibus Rerum.* Nevertheless, Caxton felt that Trevisa's language should be modernized. As with Malory, these changes often involved the introduction of French words: *embelysshers (hizteres), encrece (eche), doctryne (lore), obedient (buxom), disposed (icast)*, though in many cases we find the replacement of one Germanic word by another: *calleth* (*clepeth*), *after* (*efte*), *dyches* (*meres*), *right* (*swiþe*).[1] Yet there is a difference in Caxton's attitude towards these two authors. Trevisa made use of alliteration in his translation, but more often than not the alliteration is confined within a doublet. Caxton has not altered these doublets as a general rule so that such expressions as *halkes and huyrenes* and *wayes and wrynclis* remain. The reason for this is twofold. Trevisa's alliteration is a stylistic ornament superimposed upon the basic sentence pattern, which is solidly based on Higden's Latin. In Malory's Book Five, on the other hand, the alliteration is an integral part of the sentence structure and any recasting of the sentence results in destroying the alliteration. But in Trevisa the alliteration, being decorative, occurs in doublets and the revision of any sentence would not necessarily lead to its elimination. And Caxton, as we have seen, was partial to doublets. Indeed one of the notable features of his adaptation of Trevisa is the increase in their number.[2] Furthermore, doublets had been used by Chaucer and other courtly writers, so that in Chaucer's *Boethius* we find such pairs as *commoevynge and chasynge*, *duskid and dirked*, *felonyes and fraudes*. Thus Trevisa must have had many stylistic virtues in Caxton's eyes, even though his vocabulary was not sufficiently modern. It would seem as though Caxton thought Trevisa, though an older writer, less old-fashioned than Malory.[3]

Certainly Caxton would also have considered Malory more old-fashioned than Chaucer. But how would he have regarded Trevisa in relation to Chaucer? Both men were translating at approximately the same time. Yet Caxton claimed that Trevisa's language was no longer up to date, whereas he has nothing but praise for Chaucer's. In so far as the matter has been studied, it would seem that Caxton made few alterations to Chaucer's

[1] Not much work on Caxton's treatment of Trevisa's language has been done, but see C. Babington, *Polychronicon Ranulphi Higden Monachi Cestrensis*, vol. I (London, 1865), pp. lxiii–lxviii, and B. L. Kinkade, *The English Translations of Higden's Polychronicon* (Urbana, 1932).

[2] Kinkade, op. cit., p. 20.

[3] We should not forget that Caxton thought so highly of Trevisa that he kept his own continuation apart from Trevisa's work; see Crotch, p. 68.

prose.[1] Caxton allows such words as *yclepid* and *apayed*, which he frequently altered for his printing of Trevisa, to remain in Chaucer's text. There are not, however, many such words in Chaucer, for his language is definitely more Latinate and his style more ornate than Trevisa's. This difference is attributable to the different areas in which they lived and possibly the tastes of their patrons. Chaucer's association with the court and London no doubt influenced his style. Trevisa wrote his work in the West Country which was less affected by courtly fashions. It would seem as though Caxton viewed Chaucer, Trevisa and Malory in that descending order of stylistic excellence. This order also represents the extent to which he modified their translations. Furthermore, he did recognize the differences between various styles, and he considered style sufficiently important to justify his rectifying what was not fashionable.

The preceding survey has necessarily been brief, but it has shown that Caxton attempted to print works written in what he considered to be the courtly style and that when a book was not written in that style, he altered it to make it conform. There can also be little doubt that he acted in this way because he was attempting to follow the fashion of the court. This conclusion leads to some further observations. Today we tend to think that modern prose style originated with Malory. To Caxton and the fifteenth century it must have seemed as though Malory was the culmination of the old, alliterative style: he represented the end of one style rather than the beginning of another. It is time now that we reconsidered the position of the fifteenth century in the history of English prose, for we have hitherto failed to recognize that the authors of the time were trying to break new ground. Consequently their achievement has been undervalued. They could see that poetry had made a new start and they wished to do the same for prose. But since they had no English model and were forced to rely on foreign ones, it is only to be expected that their attempts to fashion a new style should seem naïve to us. But this does not mean that the fifteenth-century translator 'had seldom any

---

[1] A start was made by L. Kellner, 'Zur Textkritik von Chaucer's Boethius', *Englische Studien*, xiv (1890), 1–52.

interest in English style'.[1] On the contrary, he was intensely conscious of it and tried to improve it. Naturally the first steps were uncertain, but the fifteenth-century translators paved the way for the achievements of the sixteenth century. And if Berners is the first to write modern English prose, it was only because many before him had shown him the way. But this does not mean that there was such a straight line of descent from early medieval English prose to Renaissance prose, as some writers on Middle English prose have suggested.[2] Of course, the translators were influenced by the alliterative tradition which they were trying to supersede. And we have seen that some alliteration was acceptable. But the fifteenth century was trying to make a definite break with the prose of the past, and they were to a large extent successful. Modern scholars have tended to minimize this break because insufficient attention has been paid to the works and aims of fifteenth-century translators.

Finally, I should like to consider whether the attitudes to prose I have traced in the fifteenth century might have any bearing upon our views of the Alliterative Revival, though here I can do no more than make one or two general suggestions. There is a tendency to link the revival with the north and west of the country, and even to suggest that it might have been fostered by baronial opposition to the central monarchy.[3] For Caxton and the fifteenth century the alliterative style in both prose and poetry represented the old English style for the whole country. Chaucer had broken away from it in poetry and many fifteenth-century disciples had followed in his footsteps. Similarly prose writers had tried to adapt his stylistic revolution to prose by basing their work on foreign models. The new style was associated with London and the court. Yet even there in the fifteenth century there were

---

[1] I. A. Gordon, *The Movement of English Prose* (London, 1966), p. 64.

[2] See, for example, R. W. Chambers, *On the Continuity of English Prose* (London, 1957) and M. W. Croll, 'The Sources of the Euphuistic Rhetoric', reprinted in *Style, Rhetoric, and Rhythm*, ed. by J. M. Patrick and R. O. Evans (Princeton, 1966), 241–95.

[3] J. R. Hulbert, 'A Hypothesis concerning the Alliterative Revival', *Modern Philology*, xxviii (1931), 405–22. But see more recently E. Salter, 'The Alliterative Revival', *Modern Philology*, lxiv (1966–7), 146–50; 233–7.

still people who favoured the old alliterative tradition and who wanted Caxton to follow that style. Wynkyn de Worde did in fact revert to the older style by publishing the works of such authors as Rolle. These two facts show that the old style was still popular in London and elsewhere, and that it was the Chaucerian style which was new and trying to break away. For many in London the alliterative style must still have been the accepted one. Chaucer and his followers were the innovators, not the alliterative writers. This, I suggest, is how the fifteenth century saw the relationship of the two styles. And if they saw it in this way, it could well be that this was what in fact had happened. Certainly it seems unlikely that, if the alliterative style was characteristic only of the North and West, there would have been sufficient adherents of the style in London to make Caxton give it serious attention.

I hope I have shown that Caxton can tell us a great deal about contemporary literary fashion. Caxton is important because he is one of the few people who discuss what they are trying to do. Too many other fifteenth-century authors have merely left translations without giving us any insight into their method of working. Caxton tells us why he produced certain works and at the same time, as he is not himself a literary innovator, he reveals what others were thinking as well. This evidence has been overlooked in the past, but I would venture to suggest that it is of crucial importance for an understanding of the development of fifteenth-century English prose.

10

Caxton's Language

It has been shown that some of Caxton's prologue to his version of the *Polychronicon* is based on the preface in the *Historical Library* by Diodorus Siculus. The Greek was translated into Latin by Poggio Bracciolini, though it has been suggested that Caxton used a French version of Poggio no longer extant.[1] The marked difference in sentence construction between the translated section and Caxton's original composition has been commented upon by scholars who have noted how the well-constructed and balanced sentences of the first part give way to the rambling, unorganised sentences of the second.[2] Differences in vocabulary have not been investigated. Yet Caxton himself in his prologues frequently refers to the difficulties facing him as translator. Some felt his language was too ornate, others that it was too simple.[3] Though it is possible that Caxton's critics were referring to his rhetorical techniques, it seems more likely that they had his choice of words particularly in

[1] S. K. Workman, "Versions by Skelton, Caxton, and Berners of a Prologue by Diodorus Siculus," *Modern Language Notes*, LVI (1941), 252—8.

[2] *Ibid.;* see also R. R. Aurner, "Caxton and the English Sentence," *Wisconsin Studies in Language and Literature*, XVIII (1923), 23—59.

[3] W. J. B. Crotch, *The Prologues and Epilogues of William Caxton* (London, 1928), particularly pp. 107—110.

mind. It seemed, therefore, that it might be useful to investigate the prologue to see how Caxton's language in a piece of his own composition differs from that of his translations. A quick survey, however, soon revealed that the two sections of the prologue would not form comparable samples. They are not the same length, their subject matter is different and Caxton could easily have carried over into the second section words which were still fresh in his mind through translating the first section.[1] I decided consequently to compare the translated section of his prologue to the *Polychronicon* with his epilogue to the *Order of Chivalry*. Both deal with comparable subjects: the benefits of history on the one hand and the advantages of chivalry on the other, both are about the same length (the epilogue is in fact a little shorter) and both were made at roughly the same time.

Even a cursory glance through the two texts is sufficient to reveal that there are differences. The vocabulary in the prologue to the *Polychronicon* is weightier and more Latinate. Consider, for example, the adjectives in both pieces, which are included in the following lists:[2]

> (a) *Polychronicon:* acceptable, aduerse, amyable, aourned, auncyent, brutyssh, conteynyng, contynuel, cotydyan, couragyous, cruel (2), delectable, desyryng, detestable, digne (3), distributed, dyffused, dyscrete, dyuerse, equale (2), eternal (2), excellent, excluded, famous, fayre, ferdful, feyned, fortunat, good, grete (6), hye, infynyte, inmortall (3), large, laudable, lerned, longe,

---

[1] The first or translated section ends in Crotch's edition with the words *ryghtful lif* (p. 66, four lines from bottom). The next sentence begins 'Thenne syth historye is so precious and also prouffytable. . .', both of which adjectives are used in the preceding section.

[2] I have used Crotch's edition as my text: the *Polychronicon* passage is on pp. 64—66 and the *Order of Chivalry* epilogue on pp. 82—84.

lower, lyteral,[1] moeuynge, mortal (3), noble (9), olde (2), passyd, permanente, perpetuel (2), polytyke, precious (2), presente, propre, prouffytable (4), pryncypal, pryaute, publyke (2), puyssaunt, representynge, reputed, requysyte, rude, ryall, ryghtful, same, sayd, semblable, short, sondry, spredd, straunge, syttynge, terryble (2), tryumphal, vnlerned, vnprouffytable, vnyuersal (2), variaunt, vecordyous, vycious, vyctoryous, vyrtuouse, whyteheeryd, wicked, worthy, wyse (2), yonge (2).

(b) *Order of Chivalry:* accordynge (3), almyghty, auncyent (2), best, broken, comprysed, comyn, dradde, due, dwellynge, everlastyng, exercysed, gentyl, good, grete (2), honest, honoured, incredyble, large, later (2), latter, long, lytyl (2), mete, naturel, noble (19), old, passed, prosperous, redy, redoubted, requysyte, round, sayd, short, souerayne (2), syttyng, transitory, vnyuersal vsed, vertuous (2), vyctoryous, yong.

It will be seen that the variety of the adjectives is more limited in the *Order of Chivalry*. *Noble*, always a popular word with Caxton, is used frequently, and there are other words similar in meaning such as *gentyl*, *good*, *redoubted* and *souerayne*. Without these words the selection of words in this passage tends to be Germanic and many of them are short. Words of Germanic stock are about 50 % of the total, though without the words mentioned above the proportion would be much higher. On the other hand, there is a very large selection of adjectives in the *Polychronicon* passage. This can partly be explained by Caxton's habit of including an English equivalent to an adjective taken over from his source to form a doublet: 'auncyent and whyteheeryd', 'digne and worthy' etc. This type of doublet occurs in the *Order of Chivalry* only in set phrases which had become clichés: 'my redoubted naturel and most dradde

[1] Caxton's text reads *lyberal*, but emendation seems preferable here; see further *infra*.

souerayne lord'. The doublets of all types are noticeably fewer in the *Order of Chivalry*. The adjectives in the *Polychronicon* are much heavier and contain more syllables because many of them are Latinate. The endings *-able/ -ible, -ian, -al, -ate* and *-ant* occur frequently. Many adjectives in this passage are not recorded in English in OED before the fifteenth century: *detestable, laudable, lyteral, permanente, puyssaunt* etc. The adjective *vecordyous* is not recorded at all in OED. and it must be doubtful whether it occurs elsewhere in English.[1] This word should not be interpreted as an attempt on Caxton's part to enrich the English vocabulary: it is just taken over direct from his source.[2] For in the *Order of Chivalry* although there are one or two words recorded first in the fifteenth century such as *incredyble* and *redoubted*, these words and the rest of the adjectives are fairly common in occurrence at that time. They are not so learned or esoteric as the adjectives in the *Polychronicon*. This difference is one which can best be explained by assuming that Caxton took most of the heavy words in the *Polychronicon* direct from his source and that his own language and unassisted composition tended to be fairly simple and unadorned. From this it can be inferred that the difficult or unusual words in Caxton's writings are normally taken over from a source and that Caxton himself made little attempt to enrich his own vocabulary.

A similar conclusion is arrived at from an investigation of the nouns, though there are too many of them for me to give a list of them here. In the *Order of Chivalry* we find once again a much smaller range of nouns and a heavy reliance on one or two words such as *knyghtes* (10 examples) and *chyualry* (12). Words of Germanic stock are frequent, though Caxton does include many French words. These generally had been long introduced

[1] OED records only *vecord* from 1788 and *vecordy* from 1656.

[2] On this see particularly N. F. Blake, "William Caxton's *Reynard the Fox* and his Dutch Original," *Bulletin of the John Rylands Library*, XLVI (1964), 298—325 ; see below, chapter 16, pp. 231-58.

into English, like *chyualry, curtosye, gentylnesse* and *noblesse*. It must be mentioned, however, that there are two words in the epilogue which are recorded by OED as occurring in English for the first time in Caxton's writings. They are *baynes*[1] and *excersytees*. But these words occur frequently according to OED in Caxton's translated works and we may perhaps assume that from frequent use in his translations they passed unconsciously into his stock of words. It is worthwhile to remark that both are concrete nouns. Though he does use one or two abstract nouns such as the ones quoted above, normally he uses more concrete words. It is this which gives this passage the atmosphere which is so completely different from that in the prologue to the *Polychronicon*. Whereas the latter is an abstract discussion of the merits of history, the former is a more practical survey of the decay of chivalry and what ought to be done about it. Caxton himself was prosaic and practical. Even his own continuation to the prologue of *Polychronicon* is an account of the previous versions of the *Polychronicon;* Caxton does not continue the abstract discussion. His vocabulary suits his outlook: the words he uses are prosaic, concrete, common and generally of not more than two syllables. The vocabulary of the translated section of the prologue of the *Polychronicon* is different. Here we find a great many heavy abstract words, many of which have entered the language fairly recently or indeed which are here making their first appearance in English. Words like *assertryce, inconuenytys* and *malefaytes* are not listed in OED. *Conservatryce* is listed only in the Latin form *conservatrix* from 1582. *Dyuulgacion* is not listed in OED before 1540, and *institutes* not before a.1520. The words *benewrte*[2] and *ocyosyte* are recorded as occurring for the first time in Caxton, the former according to OED occurs only

---

[1] MED *Bain, n.*(a) records two earlier examples from Malory. As MED is still incomplete, I have used OED though variations in MED are noted in the footnotes.

[2] MED *Beneurte, n.* records an example from c. 1475 in the *Book of Noblesse.*

in Caxton. Many other words were introduced in the fifteenth
century: *dyuturnyte, obprobrye, infamye, tuicion* etc. These few
words quoted should be sufficient to show how different the
stock of words is in the *Polychronicon*, and this list could easily
be extended. Not only is the choice of words much greater, but
also their abstract quality puts the passage on a completely
different level. It was because it was such an abstract discussion
that it was borrowed so easily by several different authors and
adapted to their own use. Caxton's epilogue could not have been
used by others in the same way: it is too much of its own
time.

It should not, I think, be necessary to investigate the other
classes of words in these two passages to prove my point. Even
though the passages are short, a sufficient number of Caxton's
works have now been edited in recent times to show that the
way he tackled the prologue of the *Polychronicon* can be parallel-
ed elsewhere in his translations. The validity of the results of
my investigation into the epilogue of the *Order of Chivalry* can
be tested by looking through an edition of Caxton's prologues
and epilogues. One does not find a nonce or even a rare word in
them. When not based on a source, the prologues and epilogues
tend to be factual, prosaic and often autobiographical. Subjects which could have given rise to a general discussion are
treated in a practical, almost anecdotal, way. The complaints
about his vocabulary made by his customers are merely reported at second hand and give rise to no real discussion on translation. In the prologue to *Eneydos*, for example, the complaints
lead on to an account of the abbot's lending Caxton some Old
English documents and the story of the merchant and the eggs.
Any consideration of general principles is not involved. As a
writer Caxton was practical and prosaic. Naturally his vocabulary grew as a result of his translation work, but this growth is
not significant. It was probably largely subconscious. At least
from our investigation it is difficult to think that Caxton made
any attempt to increase his vocabulary.

It may be suggested then that Caxton's personal vocabulary was limited and generally of a prosaic and practical nature, but that when he translates he carries over into English many words taken from his source. Apart from what this tells us about Caxton the man, this is a general rule which if remembered could be of help in solving many minor Caxtonian problems. Firstly, where a source cannot be directly identified, it might help us to establish what sort of source Caxton used. The prologue from the *Polychronicon* is a case in point. No French version of Poggio's Latin text survives, but Caxton's language proves that he must have used a French source. He would not have formed such words as *assertryce*, *conservatryce* and *malefaytes* from a Latin original. Furthermore where it is accepted that there is no source for something printed by Caxton, the application of this rule might help us to decide whether the piece was written by Caxton or not. For example, at the end of the *Moral Proverbs* of Christine de Pisan there are two verses in Caxton's text which have no parallel in Christine's work. Both verses are normally printed in collections of Caxton's prologues and epilogues, though some editors accept that the ascription of the first verse to Caxton is doubtful.[1] But the vocabulary of the two verses is strikingly different and the difference is exactly that which we found between the *Polychronicon* and the *Order of Chivalry*. It is sufficient to point to the rhymes to make this clear. The first verse has *aucteresse/maistresse*, *intelligence/experience/sentence* and *rehers/Ryuers*, whereas the second has *me/the*, *lorde/worde/recorde* and *daye/vraye* as rhymes. I think we should probably accept that the first verse was written by Earl Rivers, the translator of the work. On the other hand, there has been some discussion as to whether Caxton translated the poem attributed to Alain Chartier and printed by Caxton at the end of his trans-

---

[1] The verses are printed in Crotch, *op.cit,.* p. 32 and N.S. Aurner, *Caxton Mirrour of Fifteenth-Century Letters* (New York, 1926), pp. 236—7. Both treat Caxton's authorship of the first verse as a possibility.

lation of the *Curial*.[1] All that one can say is that it is done exactly as Caxton would have done it: it is virtually a word for word translation with many of the French words taken over directly into the English translation. It seems best, therefore, to attribute the English version to Caxton.

Secondly, the application of this rule might help editors of Caxton's texts. Recently Mrs. Offord, who is at present preparing an edition of *The Knight of the Tower*, showed me a textual difficulty in that text. Where Brussels MS. 9308, the manuscript which Mrs. Offord has proved to be the closest to Caxton's version but not his actual source, reads 'hault leué sur longues espingles d'argent', Caxton's text reads 'hyghe culewed. . .'. The passage in question refers to the elaborate head-dresses which women were accustomed to wear at that time. The word *culewed* must represent a translation of *leué*. It does not occur elsewhere and one therefore suspects a typographical mistake, though it would be natural for an editor to investigate whether it could be considered an actual word. As *culewed* did not seem to be a possible word, Mrs. Offord had considered the possibility of emendation and had toyed, as one does, with such possible emendations as *culewred* 'coloured', *culemed* or *culemned* 'columned' *cleued*, 'cleft' and *clewed* 'coiled'. But these possible emendations disregard the principle I am suggesting here. Caxton's language is fairly simple unless a word is lifted straight from his source. It is unlikely that he would have coined a nonce-word like *culewed* or that he would have changed *leué* into a relatively uncommon English word. Any emendation must take the actual word of the original into careful consideration. When one does this, one sees immediately that there is a close correspondence between *leué* and (*cu*)*lewe*(*d*), particularly as in Caxton texts a *v* (*u*) often appears as a *w*.[2] The *lewed* is the English past

---

[1] The French ballade and the English translation are edited with discussion by P. Meyer in F.J. Furnivall, *The Curial made by maystere Alain Charretier* (London, 1888), pp. 17—19.

[2] For example, H. Wiencke, *Die Sprache Caxtons* (Leipzig, 1931), p. 65 cites the spellings *ywell* and *ewill* for 'evil'.

participle based on the French *leué*. Consequently the best emendation is in my opinion to *enlewed*, for a typographical confusion of *cu-* with *en-* is quite understandable. In French *lever* and *enlever* have the same range of meanings. As we do not have Caxton's actual source it is not impossible that the manuscript that Caxton used had *enleué*.[1] Other emendations may be suggested through the same reasoning. Thus in the prologue to the *Polychronicon* I suggested earlier that Caxton's *lyberal* should be emended to *lyteral*, though this has not been introduced into editions of Caxton's prologues and epilogues. But Poggio's text has *litterarum*, and Skelton and Berners both follow this reading.[2]

Finally, this principle might be borne in mind in discussions of Caxton's language and dialect. J. Hammerschlag made an investigation into dialect influence on Caxton.[3] He discovered that there was only one word in Caxton's writings which showed any influence on the Kentish dialect. This was the word *flyndermows* 'a bat' (fol. k6ʳ). But this word is taken over directly from the Dutch prose *Reinaert* which reads *vledermuys*.[4] This word is typical of so many words in Caxton's *Reynard the Fox;* they are taken over direct from the Dutch.[5] They do not always have exactly the same form in Caxton's text as in the original. It is doubtful whether the word can be regarded as having any signi-

---

[1] There are some examples of confusion of words with or without the prefixes *en-* and *in-*, cf. *The Curial, ed. cit.* p. l, fn. 2. (I should like to take this opportunity of thanking Mrs Offord for her help with this paper.)

[2] The reading 'perpetuelly conseruyd by lyberal monumentis' makes little sense. For references to other versions of the preface see *Workman, op. cit.*

[3] *Dialekteinflüsse im frühneuenglischen Wortschatz nachgewiesen an Caxton und Fabian* (Bonn, 1937), pp. 109—113.

[4] W. Gs. Hellinga, *Van den Vos Reinaert* (Zwolle, 1952), P 5875.

[5] For a study of the Dutch loanwords in *Reynard the Fox* see, *The History of Reynard the Fox*, ed. N.F. Blake, EETS 263 (London, 1970), pp. xxi—xlvii.

ficance in Caxton studies. Caxton normally uses *batte* to translate *vledermuis; flyndermows* was merely suggested by the source on one occasion. It cannot be regarded in any way as a part of Caxton's regular vocabulary. Likewise it should not be regarded as conclusive evidence of dialect influence on early Modern English vocabulary. The whole basis of Hammerschlag's investigation as far as Caxton is concerned is somewhat suspect because he did not pay sufficient attention to Caxton's sources.

We may say then of Caxton that when he used a source he tended to follow this closely taking over many of the foreign words directly into his translation. When he composed on his own, not only was his sentence structure muddled, as others have shown, but also his vocabulary was limited. There is no evidence to show that he was consciously trying to enlarge his vocabulary through his translations, though naturally some words did go over into his ordinary stock of words. Admittedly the samples used in this investigation are small, but the general results seem to be borne out by other investigators. The conclusion is also interesting in furthering our knowledge of Caxton himself. Some scholars have claimed that Caxton was something of a scholar and man-of-letters.[1] If so, one might have expected him to polish and refine his style. There is no evidence that he did so. In his translations it has been pointed out by many that though Caxton had a good knowledge of both French and Dutch he often makes mistakes in translation or fails to find an English word for the foreign one. This has generally been interpreted to mean that Caxton worked in great haste. His interest lay not so much in the text and its quality, but in getting it translated and into print. This is an attitude not so much of a scholar as of a man of business. His own writing adds confirmation to this view. His vocabulary is straightforward and simple with few adornments or rhetorical flourishes. The way in which he

---

[1] See particularly H. R. Plomer, *William Caxton (1424—1491)* (Boston and London, 1925), *passim.*

approaches things is practical and prosaic. He was not worried by any philosophical or abstract questions; for him problems were practical matters to be solved, not to be mulled over as general principles.

11

Caxton and Chaucer

In order to build up that picture of Caxton as a man of letters which they have tried to foster, many writers have tended to highlight his various editions of Chaucerian works as an example of his literary taste. Although his editions of Lydgate and Gower have often been discounted as a mere pandering to the fashions of the time, his appreciations of Chaucer have been hailed as the mark of a man of refined sensibilities. This trend was initiated by Blades, who wrote: "The poetical reverence with which Caxton speaks of Chaucer, 'the first founder of *ornate* eloquence in our English,' and the pains he took to reprint the "Canterbury Tales" when a purer text than that of the first edition was offered to him, show his high appreciation of England's first great poet."[1] In this century, as a result of the controversy which has arisen over whether Caxton printed his works under patronage or on his own initiative, those who have sought to defend Caxton have relied even more on his Chaucerian editions to refute their opponents. Thus Professor Aurner asserted that "In the *Canterbury Tales* we have an *editio princeps* in every sense of the word. First in literary significance, in poetic rank and in date, it was one of the first fruits of England's earliest press, and the selection — apparently without the suggestion of any patron — of the first English printer and publisher."[2] Professor Aurner also attributed "high rank as judge and critic" to Caxton, not only because he printed Chaucer's works, but also because he did not link Chaucer's name with those of Gower and Lydgate, as was so common at that time. Even Professor Sands, who accepted that Caxton printed many volumes under patronage, has claimed that, when Caxton was free to print what he liked, he showed discrimination in his choice. Naturally his editions of Chaucerian works form one of the main planks in this argument. Sands does not, like Aurner, despise Caxton's editions of Gower and Lydgate, but he stresses that the English poets were produced on Caxton's own initiative and without patronage.[3] In view of statements like this it might be considered time to investigate Caxton's attitude to Chaucer in its entirety to see if these claims can be justified. Such an investigation might help to illuminate his general appreciation of English literature, and it should certainly enable us to decide how a typical late fifteenth-century man developed and expressed his literary tastes. One

[1] W Blades, *The Biography and Typography of William Caxton*, 2nd ed. (London and Strassburg, 1882), p.89.
[2] N. S. Aurner, *Caxton, Mirrour of Fifteenth-Century Letters* (London, 1926), p.163.
[3] D. B. Sands, "Caxton as a Literary Critic," *The Papers of the American Bibliographical Society*, LI (1957), 316.

way to tackle Caxton's attitude to Chaucer is to approach it on several different levels. Firstly, why did Caxton print Chaucer's works, and did he print them for any particular person? Secondly, what was Caxton's treatment of the text? How accurate are his editions? Thirdly, to what extent do the various appreciations that Caxton wrote of Chaucer's work represent his own views? This last point will naturally include a consideration of Caxton's printing of Surigone's eulogy to Chaucer.

Caxton printed a considerable number of Chaucer's works. In none of them is the date when he printed the work found, so that the datings have to be arrived at by a comparison with his other printed books. The following is a list of Chaucer's works printed by Caxton with the estimated dates of printing as found in Blades. *Canterbury Tales* (first edition c.1478); *Parliament of Fowls* and other pieces (*ante* 1479); *Anelida and the False Arcite* and *Chaucer's Complaint to His Purse* (*ante* 1479); the prose translation of the *De Consolatione Philosophiae* by Boethius (*ante* 1479); *Canterbury Tales* (second edition c. 1484); *House of Fame* (c.1484); *Troilus and Criseyde* (c.1484). One interesting point that emerges from this list is that there were two periods in which Caxton issued Chaucerian texts, one about 1478 and the other about 1484. The main work in each period was the *Canterbury Tales*. One might assume, therefore, that Caxton issued the the other texts at about the same time as the *Canterbury Tales* to reap the advantage of the interest in Chaucer which such an edition would create, just as it is common today for a publisher to follow up a success with other texts by the same author. The minor texts would support the *Canterbury Tales*, just as the *Tales* would help to sell them; the publisher was thus able to offer a more complete list of the poet's works. In this connection it is interesting to note that the minor texts printed were different ones in each of the two periods. In both periods it is the *Canterbury Tales* which were printed by request, though none of the other volumes with the exception of the Boethius was ordered by clients as far as we can tell. Whether a volume was actually requested or not, Caxton would almost certainly have assumed that Chaucerian texts were likely to sell well, because Chaucer was held in high esteem by Lydgate and other fifteenth-century writers, and because he must have known that Chaucer manuscripts had been, and perhaps were still being, produced by bookshops in London and the provinces.[4] When asked to produce an edition of the *Canterbury Tales*, he is not likely to have hesitated long; their known popularity would minimize the risk involved. After the *Tales* it would be a logical step to print the minor works, as I have already suggested.

I stated in the previous paragraph that Caxton produced both editions of the *Canterbury Tales* on request. This has not been accepted by all scholars, and it is necessary to review the evidence for this statement. The evidence comes entirely from Caxton's prologue to the second edition of the *Tales*. Here he tells us that his first edition, which had been set up six years earlier, was printed from a manuscript which had been brought to him.[5] The best way to interpret this statement is to assume that the manuscript had been brought to him by someone who was wealthy enough to own a manuscript of the *Tales*, with a request that the printer should print it.

4   See particularly J. M. Manly and E. Rickert, *The Text of the Canterbury Tales* (Chicago, 1940), I, 561-605.
5   Caxton's prologues and epilogues to his editions of Chaucer are to be found in W. J. B. Crotch, *The Prologues and Epilogues of William Caxton* (London, 1928). Page references in brackets throughout this article are to this work.

It is difficult to see who else would have brought a manuscript to Caxton. He naturally does not reveal who brought him the manuscript because he now claims that the manuscript of the first edition was not a good one. That Caxton did set up texts from manuscripts brought to him is well known; and the phrase in the prologue to the second edition of the *Canterbury Tales* echoes one in the prologue to *King Arthur* (1485). This latter text was set up "after a copye vnto me delyuerd" (p.94); and since Caxton had been urged to print *King Arthur* by various gentlemen, one may assume that it had been brought to him by one of these gentlemen. The same thing probably happened with the first edition of the *Canterbury Tales*. But if Caxton was indeed asked to print it by someone, it might well be asked why he did not notify us of this detail in the first edition. This question may not have a simple answer, but the following facts should be taken into consideration. Caxton's earliest texts which have prologue or epilogue are all dedicated to members of the royal family or are translations by Earl Rivers. The *History of Troy* is dedicated to Margaret of Burgundy, the *Game of Chess* to the Duke of Clarence, and *Jason* to the Prince of Wales; and the *Dicts of the Philosophers* and the *Moral Proverbs* were translated by Earl Rivers. It was about this time that the *Canterbury Tales* was produced, and Caxton may not yet have realized that there might be commercial advantages to be gained by mentioning the names of the gentlemen for whom he produced a book. In his Boethius edition, produced only a little later than the *Canterbury Tales*, we learn for the first time that a volume had been printed at the request of someone other than a member of the royal family or Earl Rivers. Significantly the name of this person, possibly the mercer William Pratt, is withheld. This "friend" receives little notice in the epilogue, which is used rather to glorify Caxton and Chaucer. The reasons for this oblique reference to the friend I have considered elsewhere;[6] clearly Caxton felt under some obligation to refer to him, though he did not think the friend's name would promote sales of the edition. It is only when we get to the first edition of the *Chronicles of England* (1480) that Caxton introduces a prologue to inform us that he had been requested to print the book by diverse gentlemen.[7] It is from then onwards that Caxton used the prologue more generally to give us information about the book, to underline its suitability for genteel readers, and to refer to or name the people who had been instrumental in getting it into print. This development might help to account for the use of the title in the edition of the *House of Fame*, which belongs to Caxton's second Chaucerian period. Although no extant manuscript has a title to the poem which attributes it to Chaucer, Caxton's edition has the title *The book of Fame made by Gefferey Chaucer*.[8] None of the poems in the first period is

---

[6] N. F. Blake, "Investigations into the Prologues and Epilogues of William Caxton," *Bulletin of the John Rylands Library*, XLIX (1966-7), 17-46.

[7] This prologue is not in Crotch; see Blades, p.247.

[8] The question of the ascription of the individual texts to Chaucer is a complicated matter which I cannot discuss in full here. I have assumed for the purpose of the article that Caxton knew all the works were by Chaucer. He mentions Chaucerian authorship of the *Canterbury Tales, House of Fame*, the Boethius and *Chaucer's Complaint to His Purse*. Since this last poem was printed with *Anelida and the False Arcite*, it is probable that he ascribed this poem to Chaucer as well. *Troilus and Criseyde* is such a major work that its Chaucerian authorship was probably widely accepted in the fifteenth century. Caxton would have known it was Chaucer's work from Lydgate's *Troy Book*, in which it is referred to in several places. Caxton could likewise have known that the *Parliament of Fowls* was written by Chaucer from the *Retracciouns* which he printed at the end of the *Canterbury Tales*.

issued with title or prologue. Yet in the second period not only is the *House of Fame* issued with a title, but the second edition of the *Canterbury Tales* is issued with a prologue. This opens pompously enough "Grete thankes laude and honour/ought to be gyuen vnto the clerkes/poetes/and historiographs that haue wreton many noble bokes of wysedom of the lyues/ passions/& myracles of holy sayntes of hystoryes/of noble and famous Actes/and faittes/And of the cronycles sith the begynnyng of the creacion of the world . . . "(p.90). The opening sentence is largely copied from his prologue to the *Polychronicon* (1482): "Grete thankynges lawde & honoure we merytoryously ben bounde to yelde and offre vnto wryters of hystoryes . . ." (p.64). This correspondence between the two prologues indicates that, although Caxton was beginning to appreciate the value of prologues, he had not enough literary ability to compose his own grand openings. His prologue to the *Polychronicon* is itself a translation of a prologue by Diodorus Siculus.[9] It is probable, therefore, that Caxton developed an awareness of the usefulness of the prologue and that this development was not far advanced at the time he issued his first edition of the *Canterbury Tales*.

In his second edition of the *Tales* Caxton tells us the familiar story of how a gentleman came to see him about the text of his first edition, an episode which naturally raises the question of how Caxton treated the text of the poem. But I shall defer my discussion of this problem in order to consider the identity of the two gentlemen who requested the separate editions. Unfortunately, I do not think it is possible for us today to identify either of the gentlemen. Manly and Rickert suggested that the manuscript used for the first edition may have belonged to William Earl of Arundel, but their grounds seem quite insufficient.[10] I myself have suggested that the name of the gentleman who requested the second edition was withheld for political reasons.[11] Although this fact suggests that he was in the Woodville sphere of influence, Caxton tells us too little about him for us to be able to name him. Regrettably neither gentleman can be identified. But although we cannot name them, there is no reason to belittle the part they played in getting Chaucer into print. We owe the two editions of the *Canterbury Tales* to them, as much as to Caxton.

What then was Caxton's attitude towards the text of the poems? As we have seen, it has been widely argued that Caxton was interested in producing a good text of the *Canterbury Tales*, and that it was for this reason he revised his first edition when it was pointed out to him that it was textually corrupt. Caxton says in the prologue to his second edition of the *Canterbury Tales* that six years earlier a text of the *Tales* had been brought to him, which he, assuming it to be a good text, had printed. But now another gentleman had come along, and had told him that his edition was imperfect and that his father had a copy of the *Tales* which was much better. This gentleman promised to try to get his father to lend his copy to the printer, if Caxton was willing to print a second edition. This Caxton agreed to do. When the manuscript came into his hands, he corrected his first edition, which he then reissued (pp. 90-91). Although others have viewed this prologue as an expression of Caxton's sense of responsibility as an editor, I am not convinced that this is the correct interpretation. One noteworthy omission on Caxton's

9   S. K. Workman, "Versions by Skelton, Caxton, and Berners of a Prologue by Diodorus Siculus," *MLN*, LVI (1941), 252-258.
10 Manly and Rickert, I, 81. In my paper referred to in footnote 6, I have tried to show that the Earl of Arundel took little interest in the press.
11 Blake, "Investigations into the Prologues and Epilogues of William Caxton."

part is the complete lack of any indication as to why he accepted that the second manuscript was better than that used for his first edition, or why he had originally accepted that the first manuscript brought to him was a good one. He does not give us any example of the textual inferiority of the first edition. He does note that some Chaucer manuscripts have verses omitted and added; but this is a general statement without particular reference to his own text. It seems most likely that, when the first manuscript was brought to him by his client, he assumed the text was accurate because it probably never crossed his mind that it might not be. When the second gentleman came along, he accepted that the manuscript belonging to the gentleman's father contained a better text because the gentleman said it did. Caxton apparently agreed to print a second corrected edition *before* he had seen the second manuscript. He can have had no idea as to the quality of this manuscript; he merely believed what he was told. His ideas as to what formed a good Chaucer text were not based on his own knowledge of the manuscripts; they were based on the observations of his visitors. The principal motive for the second edition must have been Caxton's desire to please a noble customer. He could naturally also claim that he did it "to satysfye thauctour" (p.91); but it must be regarded as doubtful whether he knew why the second manuscript was thought to be better than the first edition. Caxton was in no sense a textual critic. He was not sufficiently familiar with Chaucer's text to realize that what he printed in the first edition was not necessarily accurate; and he did not, as some printers did, employ scholars to produce an accurate text for him.[12] It was the gentleman and his father who knew their Chaucer so well that, when they read the printed edition, they realized it was different from their own text. Whatever credit there is for the second edition belongs to these two, not to Caxton. Furthermore, there were many manuscripts of the *Canterbury Tales* produced in the fifteenth century, and it should have easy enough for Caxton, living at Westminster, to acquire other manuscripts if he had wanted to make a collation. If he had wanted to produce as correct a version as possible for his first edition, he would no doubt have got others to do it for him. He did not, and the evidence shows that he merely printed what he was given and believed what he was told.

When the second manuscript was brought to him, he did not print the new edition from this manuscript. He corrected his first edition and then reissued it. Caxton may have adopted this method of procedure because it was easier for the compositor to work from a printed book than from a valuable, and no doubt bulky, manuscript. But it also meant that the original text would only be superficially altered; the first edition, which Caxton accepted had a bad text, still remained the basic text. The changes he made are of two kinds: minor adjustments to the order of the tales and small changes in the text itself. Caxton's first edition had been based on a manuscript of group *b*,[13] which was closely related to the New College and Trinity College, Cambridge, R.3.15 manuscripts. The order of the tales in the first edition is $AB^1F^1E^2DE^1F^2GCB^2HI$. This order is changed in the second edition in that F^1 and F^2 are united and placed after E^2. This means in effect that Caxton found the link between the Squire's Tale and the Franklin's Tale in the second manuscript; and he united these two tales

12   L. Febre and H. J. Martin, *L'Apparition du Livre* (Paris, 1958), pp. 217-222.
13   Useful charts of the groupings of the manuscripts of the *Canterbury Tales*, which I have used, are to be found in Manly and Rickert, II, 494-495.

through their link and put them in a slightly different position. The link between the Squire's Tale and the Franklin's Tale is found in most manuscripts of group *a*, and it does not occur in manuscripts of the other groups. It would be natural to assume from this fact that Caxton's second manuscript belonged to group *a* rather than to any other group. It is not possible, however, to equate his second manuscript with a single extant manuscript in this group, because all show further differences in the arrangement of the tales which do not reappear in the second printed edition. This does not mean, as some have assumed, that the second manuscript was of a completely different type from those in group *a*. The most likely explanation is that in the revision of his first edition Caxton took only certain features from the manuscript which he had borrowed. That is to say, the revision was a haphazard affair: Caxton making such changes as caught his attention or as he could manage without a far-reaching reorganization. One need not assume that he made a detailed collation of the two texts.

The changes in the text were probably made in a similarly haphazard way. These are all of a minor nature as will be seen by comparing the following lines from the Pardoner's Tale in both editions:

First edition.

> And who so fyndith hym out of suche blame
> Comyth vp and offir in goddis name
> And I assoyle hem by the auctorite
> Suche as by bull was grauntid me
> By this gaude haue I wonne many a yeer
> An hundrid mark syn I was pardoner
> I stonde lik a clerk in many a Pulpet
> And shewe lewd peple and doun they set
> I preche so as ye haue herd before
> And telle an hundrid false Iapis more   (97-106)

Second edition.

> And who so fyndeth hym out of suche blame
> Comyth vp and offyr in goddis name
> And I assoyle hem by the auctoryte
> Suche as by bull was grauntid to me
> By this gaude haue I wonne many a yeer
> An hundred mark syn I was pardoner
> I stonde lyke a clerke in my pulpet
> And whan lewd peple be doun y set
> I preche so as ye haue herd before
> And telle an hundred Iapis more.

I have chosen lines from this tale as an illustration because it was the one edited by Koch from eight different manuscripts, including the two earliest printed editions.[14] Koch concluded from his study of the Pardoner's Tale that Caxton's second manuscript belonged to group *a*, though there are places where his readings differ from any known manuscript; Koch was therefore unable to specify a particular manuscript within this group. Greg, who made a collation of the first 116 lines of the Knight's Tale, was unable to confirm Koch's suggestion, for the readings in the second edition did not

---

[14]   J. Koch, *The Pardoner's Prologue and Tale by Geoffrey Chaucer* (Heidelberg, 1902). For his discussion of Caxton's texts see pp.li-lii.

indicate a particular group of *Canterbury Tales* manuscripts sufficiently clearly. The manuscript could have belonged to any of groups *a*, *c* or *d*.[15] It is difficult to draw a firm conclusion from these investigations. But from the evidence of the arrangement of the tales in the various manuscripts and editions and from Koch's researches into the Pardoner's Tale, it may be suggested that Caxton's second manuscript probably belonged to group *a* of the *Canterbury Tales* manuscripts. Greg's work neither confirms nor refutes this suggestion, but we may note that he realized that the link between the Squire's Tale and the Franklin's Tale which is found in Caxton's second edition could only come from a manuscript of group *a*. Unless that manuscript was very different from any extant manuscript in group *a*, one can only conclude that Caxton's treatment of the text was somewhat cavalier. He made some changes, but not others, in the order of the tales which must almost certainly have been in his manuscript. He corrected some of the readings in the first edition. But these corrections were not carried out in any systematic way; some indeed may have been made by Caxton himself without the authority of the manuscript. It is because of this haphazard treatment by the editor, to say nothing of possible typographical mistakes, that the second manuscript is so difficult to identify. Such evidence as there is indicates, therefore, that Caxton did not produce his second edition with that care which some modern writers have attributed to him. It was, like so much else of his work, carried out in haste. Modern editors of his translations have all commented upon the haste with which Caxton carried out his translating work; it would be strange if this were not also the case with his editorial activities on the English poets.

In addition to his treatment of the *Canterbury Tales*, we can learn something of Caxton's attitude to Chaucer's text by examining his handling of the *House of Fame*. This text is interesting because Caxton had a manuscript which was less complete than the two best extant manuscripts. Where the poem in these manuscripts ends at line 2158, Caxton's manuscript ended at line 2094. No doubt the last sixty-four lines had been on the last folio which had become detached from the rest of the manuscript. When he issued the poem in 1484, Caxton added a brief poetic conclusion as well as an epilogue. From the epilogue it is clear that he accepted Chaucer had left the poem unfinished, although he evidently took no steps to discover whether what he had of the poem was all that was extant. Once again he just accepted the evidence of the manuscript he had. In the epilogue he wrote "This noble man Gefferey Chaucer fynysshyd at the sayd conclusion of the metyng of lesyng and sothsawe/ where as yet they ben chekked and may not departe" (p.69). The words he uses echo two lines near the end of the manuscript he possessed: *A lesynge and a soth sayd sawe* (2089) and *They were a chekked bothe two* (2093);[16] and they thus reveal that Caxton did not know of the existence of the other sixty-four lines of the poem. The former line is particularly illuminating. We do not have any of the manuscripts from which Caxton set up his Chaucerian texts, and so it is not possible for us to judge how accurately the printed versions reflect the manuscripts. Yet we may justly conclude that Caxton's line *A lesynge and a soth sayd sawe* contains a typographical error. The extant manuscripts read

---

[15]   W. W. Greg, "The Early Printed Editions of the *Canterbury Tales*," *PMLA*, XXXIX (1924), 737-761.

[16]   Caxton's text and the manuscript versions are printed in F. J. Furnivall, *A Parallel-Text Edition of Chaucer's Minor Poems* (London, 1871-9), pp. 179-241.

A lesynge and a sad sothe sawe here. The words *lesyng and sothsawe* in Caxton's epilogue reflect the order in the manuscripts, *a sad sothe sawe*, not that of his own edition, *soth sayd sawe*. Caxton's manuscript must have had a reading similar to that of the other manuscripts; in his edition *sad* has become *sayd* and been transposed after *soth*. This example shows that Caxton cannot have been so interested in the text of Chaucer's poems that he corrected what his compositor set up. Yet this would have been an easy and convincing way "to satysfye thauctour."

Because his text of the *House of Fame* was incomplete, Caxton assumed that Chaucer had left the poem unfinished. Although he stated this in his epilogue, he nevertheless took it upon himself to compose a twelve-line conclusion to the poem. He pointed this out to the reader by printing *Caxton* in the margin opposite the first line of this continuation. Since Caxton expresses a high opinion of Chaucer's poetic achievement and frequently confesses to a lack of literary ability on his own part, it is surprising that he should seek to emulate such a poet as Chaucer in this way. If the poem was incomplete, he could have let it remain so in his edition, particularly as his own conclusion is so unsatisfactory — though we may perhaps add that it was for a long time accepted as genuine. It reads:

> And wyth the noyse of them [t]wo   Caxton
> I Sodeynly awoke anon tho
> And remembryd what I had seen
> And how hye and ferre I had been
> In my ghoost/ and had grete wonder
> Of that the god of thonder
> Had lete me knowen/ and began to wryte
> Lyke as ye haue herd me endyte
> Wherfor the studye and rede alway
> I purpose to doo day by day
> Thus in dremyng and in game
> Endeth thys lytyl book of Fame.

We may note that Caxton was not inspired to write a continuation as such; we are not to learn what happened at the meeting of *lesyng* and *sothsawe*. His addition is merely a way of concluding the poem as quickly as possible. He made his own conclusion by modelling it on the last stanza of the *Parliament of Fowls*, which he had printed six years earlier. In his edition this last verse reads:

> And syth þe shoutyng/ whan þe song was do
> The fowles made at her flight away
> I woke/ and other bokes toke me to
> To rede vpon/ and yet I red alway
> I hope ywis to rede so somme day
> That I shal mete somme thinge for to fare
> The better/ and thus to rede I wil nat spare.[17]

Skeat has suggested that Caxton may have had the last lines of the *Book of the Duchess* in mind as well.[18] But since there is no evidence that Caxton had read this work and since the parallels are not very close, this

---

[17]   Furnivall, p.98.
[18]   W. W. Skeat, *The Complete Works of Geoffrey Chaucer* (Oxord, 1900), III, 287.

suggestion may be discounted. It seems that when Caxton noticed the *House of Fame* was incomplete, he used the *Parliament of Fowls* as a model and wrote a brief conclusion for the poem. Why he should have done so remains uncertain; perhaps it is merely an expression of that common medieval wish to have a complete work. He completed the *House of Fame* because he thought it wanted only a brief conclusion; he did not of course attempt a conclusion for the *Canterbury Tales*.

Let us turn now to a consideration of Caxton's opinions of Chaucer. Within his first group of Chaucerian editions only the Boethius volume contains an evaluation of Chaucer. Before discussing the Boethius epilogue in detail, we should note that in 1477 Caxton had published the *Book of Courtesy* which contains a fulsome eulogy of Chaucer and other English poets by an unknown poet. Caxton had by 1478 also become acquainted with Surigone's epitaph to Chaucer, which he printed as part of his epilogue to Boethius. I mention these two because they show that Caxton must have been aware that Chaucer was generally regarded as the greatest English poet. Furthermore, in his epilogue to Book II of the *History of Troy* (c. 1473) he mentions that Lydgate had written an account of the final siege and fall of Troy (p.6); and in Lydgate's *Troy Book* there are several passages in praise of Chaucer. It does not follow that Caxton had read Lydgate's poem merely because he referred to it, but as there is a verbal echo of Lydgate's poem in Caxton's epilogue it is likely that he had in fact done so. Caxton's "[I] am not worthy to bere his penner & ynke horne after hym" (p.6)[19] probably echoes Lydgate's remark that no-one "worþi was his ynkhorn for to holde" (V, 3530). We may, therefore, confidently assert that by 1478 Caxton was acquainted with at least three eulogies of Chaucer. It was in the shadow of these that he composed his own.

In his epilogue to the Boethius, Caxton opens his praise of Chaucer by describing him as "the worshipful fader & first foundeur & enbelissher of ornate eloquence in our englissh" (p.37). This is a direct imitation of a line in the *Book of Courtesy*: "O fader and founder of ornate eloquence."[20] Even Caxton's next phrase "I mene/ Maister Geffrey Chaucer" echoes a further line from this same stanza of the *Book of Courtesy*: "I mene fader chaucer/ maister galfryde." That Caxton should have modified *fader and founder* to *worshipful fader & first foundeur & enbelissher* may be attributed partly to Caxton's use of doublets and partly to the common application of these expressions to Chaucer. The phrase *first founder* had become a cliché applicable to Chaucer or, in the plural, to the triumvirate of Chaucer, Gower and Lydgate. Hoccleve was probably the author of it in his *Regement of Princes*, in which he describes Chaucer as "the first fyndere of our faire langage" (4978); though it later became a commonplace to write that Chaucer was the *first* to make the English language eloquent and ornate. This claim is found in Lydgate's *Troy Book* and it is echoed in Surigone's epitaph. On the other hand, the word *embellisher* is first recorded in the *Oxford English Dictionary* from this Caxtonian epilogue. But while there is no known earlier use of the noun, it was quite common to write that Chaucer had *embellished* the English language. John Shirley could about 1456 link in the same passage *first foundid* with *þemvelisshing of oure rude moders englisshe* when referring to Chaucer.

---

[19] The *ynkhorn* was probably transformed into *penner & ynke horne* because this was a common doublet, and as such was used elsewhere by Caxton.
[20] F. J. Furnivall, *Caxton's Book of Curtesye* (London, 1868), p.35.

Similarly George Ashby about 1470 wrote of Chaucer, Gower and Lydgate that they were

> Primier poetes of this nacion,
> Embelysshing oure englisshe tendure algate
> Firste finders to oure consolacion.[21]

So when Caxton wrote that Chaucer was "the worshipful fader & first foundeur & enbelissher of ornate eloquence in our englissh" he was merely filling out the line from the *Book of Courtesy* with critical commonplaces of the day. Caxton follows up this statement with the remark that for his translation "in myne óppynyon he [Chaucer] hath deseruid a perpetuell lawde and thanke of al this noble Royame of Englond." This is such a general statement that one would hardly seek to provide an exact parallel. It is sufficient to say that many before him had made similar remarks. Thus Lydgate in his *Troy Book* wrote:

> To whom honour, laude, & reuerence,
> þoruȝ-oute þis londe ȝoue be & songe. (IV, 4244-5)

The rest of the epilogue merely repeats what Caxton has already stated in praise of Chaucer earlier in his epilogue. It is unnecessary to look for further parallels, for nothing new is added.

The conclusion of the epilogue of the Boethius volume is of great interest as it raises another problem. Caxton mentions that Chaucer's body is buried at Westminster Abbey "by whos sepulture is wreton on a table hongyng on a pylere his Epitaphye maad by a poete laureat wherof the copye foloweth &c." (p.37). The epitaph, which is of some thirty lines in Latin, is preceded by three Latin lines, which one may assume were engraved on the *table* by the tomb and copied from there by Caxton. They read:

> Epitaphium Galfridi Chaucer. per
> poetam laureatum Stephanum Surigonum
> Mediolanensem in decretis licenciatum.

In the text the epitaph is also followed by four lines in Latin, which are generally attributed to Caxton himself:

> Post obitum Caxton voluit te viuere cura
> Willelmi. Chaucer clare poeta tuj
> Nam tua non solum compressit opuscula formis
> Has quoque suas laudes. iussit hic esse tuas.

Reading Caxton's epilogue, one would assume that on a pillar by Chaucer's tomb there was a tablet with Surigone's epitaph. This epitaph Caxton had copied down in order to print it at the end of his Boethius. However, this is not how Caxton's words are generally interpreted. Blades, who is responsible for the currently accepted interpretation, claimed that "not only did

---

[21]   For both these passages see C. F. E. Spurgeon, *Five Hundred Years of Chaucer Criticism and Allusion* 1357-1900 (London, 1914), I, 54.

Caxton perpetuate the memory of the great Poet by printing his works but
... also raised a public monument to his memory before St. Benet's Chapel,
in Westminster Abbey, in the shape of a pillar supporting a tablet upon
which the above "Epitaphye" was written."[22] If this were so, one might
well wonder why Caxton was so reticent in the English part of his epilogue
about his putting up the tablet. He was not usually slow to draw attention
to his own expenses;[23] and there is nothing in Caxton's remarks quoted
above to imply that he had actually set up the pillar or the tablet. As Blades
makes no reference to Leland's evidence (for which see *infra*), it must be
assumed that he based his hypothesis on the evidence of the last of Caxton's
four Latin lines. Presumably he interpreted *hic* to mean "here, i.e. on the
pillar." But it would be more natural to understand it to mean "here, i.e.
in this edition of Boethius"; that is, he has not only arranged for the publication of Chaucer's works, but has ordered the epitaph made by Surigone
to be printed in the edition of Boethius. It is only if we read the Latin in
this way that it can harmonise with the remarks in English which introduce
the epitaph.

It follows from what I have written that I do not think that Caxton's
Latin lines were engraved on the tablet. They were written for the edition.
Those who agree with Blades must accept that these four lines were
engraved on the tablet, if *hic* is to mean "here on the pillar." If this were
so it would mean that the tablet must have been set up in 1478, for Caxton
mentions printing Chaucerian works and no Chaucer edition is dated before
then, and the Boethius volume was itself printed *ante* 1479. If Caxton did
put up the tablet in 1478, we have to discover when and how he managed
to get hold of the epitaph by Surigone. Unfortunately not a great deal is
known of Stefano Surigone. Originally from Milan, he came to England
and taught at Oxford at some period between 1454 and 1464. He may
possibly have stayed till about 1471, when we know he was in Cologne,
for he matriculated then at that University. He is known to have taught also
at Strassburg and Louvain. Weiss has suggested that Caxton may have met
Surigone at Cologne in 1471. He has also suggested that Surigone returned
to England about 1478 when he seems to have established a connexion
with Caxton. "The learning of the Milanese obviously impressed Caxton,
who having then an edition of Chaucer's *Boethius* in the press, requested
him to compose a Latin elegy in praise of Chaucer to be included in the
book. The elegy was printed at the end of the *Boethius*, which Caxton
issued in 1478, and it is not to be excluded that he may have availed himself of Surigone's help in editorial activities, as he did later with Carmeliano."[24] These are large inferences to be drawn from such slender evidence
as is found in Caxton's epilogue. But Weiss also draws on the evidence of
Leland in his *De Scriptoribus Britannicis*, in which Leland says that
Surigone composed the Latin epitaph on Chaucer at Caxton's request and
that the last two lines from that epitaph were engraved on the tomb also at
Caxton's request.[25] But Weiss neglected the fact that Leland goes on to say
that all the verses were inscribed on a tablet (*tabella*) which Surigone had

---

22 W. Blades, *The Life and Typography of William Caxton* (London, 1863), II, 67.
23 For example, he says he set the *History of Troy* up in type at his own "grete
    charge and dispense" (p.7).
24 R. Weiss, *Humanism in England during the Fifteenth Century*, 2nd ed. (Oxford,
    197), p.139.
25 J. Leland, *De Scriptoribus Britannicis* (Oxford, 1709), pp. 425-6.

caused to be fixed to a pillar near Chaucer's tomb: " . . . elegos in nivea tabella depictos, quos Surigonus Visimonasterii columnæ, Chauceri sepulchro vicinæ, adfixit." Leland's account of the epitaph is therefore as follows. Caxton asked Surigone to make an epitaph for Chaucer. This epitaph Surigone had inscribed on a tablet which he affixed to a pillar by Chaucer's tomb. The two lines preceding Caxton's additional lines, which form the conclusion of the epitaph proper, were then inscribed at Caxton's request on Chaucer's tomb. This order does make sense, but it is sufficiently unusual for it to seem more likely that Leland merely inferred these facts from Caxton's epilogue. Furthermore, Leland in his transcription of the epitaph includes the four lines which are generally attributed to Caxton. Unless one is to think that Surigone had Caxton's four lines inscribed on the tablet with his own verses, one must accept that Leland got the verses from Caxton's edition of Boethius for which they were almost certainly written. Yet if it can be shown, as I think it can, that Leland knew Caxton's Boethius, then it is not improbable that what he wrote about Caxton and Surigone was merely what he had deduced from Caxton's epilogue and the Latin verses. Whether the tablet or the inscription on the tomb were still there in his day[26] (assuming that there ever had been an inscription on the tomb) is not clear; but I doubt whether we can give much weight to Leland's evidence.

Without Leland's comments, the most natural interpretation of the epitaph's history would be as follows. Surigone was in England for some time between 1454 and 1464, and may have stayed till about 1471. During his stay he gave lectures on Latin composition at Oxford and was clearly regarded as a man of learning and a poet of some accomplishment. While in England he either spontaneously or more probably by request composed an epitaph on Chaucer. This was then placed by some admirer or by Surigone himself on a pillar by Chaucer's tomb. Since many eulogies of Chaucer were written in the fifteenth century and since two gentlemen and one merchant asked Caxton for editions of Chaucerian works, it need not surprise us that someone wanted to put up an epitaph to Chaucer by his tomb. When Caxton came to Westminster, he saw and copied the inscription. This he subsequently printed in his edition of Boethius together with four of his own verses. As Caxton was willing to write Chaucerian verses at the end of the *House of Fame,* it is unlikely that he would hesitate to write Latin verses in imitation of Surigone. Caxton's verses were meant for his edition and were never added to the tablet. This interpretation would be straightforward enough without Leland's comments, for Caxton makes no mention of setting up the inscription or of meeting Surigone or of asking for the epitaph to be written. Leland's information, however, would be crucial if we could decide whether he used any sources other than Caxton's Boethius. Unfortunately, there is no proof as to whether Leland did have any other sources of information; but it seems very likely that he could have inferred what he wrote from Caxton's epilogue. As Blades interpreted Caxton's words in much the same way as Leland did, we need have no

---

[26] A new tomb for Chaucer was constructed by N. Brigham in 1555, so it is possible that Leland saw the old tomb, though it has not yet been proved that he did. Several of Leland's statements suggest he was merely filling out Caxton's words. Thus he says Surigone was a well-known poet and famous figure, though very little is known of him (cf. R. Weiss, "Humanism in Oxford," *TLS,* Jan. 9, 1937, p.28).

hesitation in thinking that the sort of information Leland gives us could have been taken from the Boethius epilogue. If we understand the tablet and epitaph in the way I have suggested there is no need to make Surigone return to England, a visit for which there is no evidence, and there is no reason to make Caxton act in an untypical manner. It would be unusual for Caxton not to state quite openly that he had paid for the inscription to be put up, if he had done so. He had little dealings with the humanists and it is unlikely that he would have commissioned an epitaph from one of them.[27] But if there was an epitaph already in situ, this would naturally by virtue of that very fact have had an authority which Caxton might well have wished to use to help to sell his edition. Furthermore, Caxton's opinions about Chaucer were largely second-hand. There is no evidence that by 1478 Caxton had a sufficiently independent appreciation of Chaucer to want to commission a Latin epitaph. There is, however, abundant evidence to show that he used material which was available to him. Caxton appropriated Surigone's epitaph, as he had done the eulogies in the *Book of Courtesy* and Lydgate's *Troy Book*. To conclude, I suggest that an interpretation along the lines I have indicated accounts best for the presence of four Caxtonian lines. One can hardly imagine that Surigone wrote these lines, for the epitaph is rounded off nicely by its last two lines:

> Galfridus Chaucer vates et fama poesis
> Materne hac sacra sum tumulatus humo.

The addition of another four lines by Caxton destroys the whole balance and elegance of the epitaph; and one cannot believe that the humanist Surigone would have written them or even consented to their appearance on the tablet. They are, however, a typical Caxtonian addition.

We saw that the words Caxton used in praise of Chaucer in the epilogue to the Boethius were for the most part borrowed from other fifteenth-century writers. There is little originality in his comments. It is time now to consider his remarks about Chaucer in the works in his second period of Chaucerian printings. We should note first that before this second period began he had printed further eulogies of Chaucer. These for the most part are to be found in works by Lydgate or attributed to him. Of these the most important is *De Cura Sapientiae*, printed about 1481, a poem which is no longer accepted by all scholars as part of the Lydgate canon. Also during the time he was engaged in his second series of Chaucerian poems he printed Lydgate's *Life of Our Lady* (c.1484), which likewise contains some extravagant praise of Chaucer. Only two of the Chaucerian works in this second period contain a prologue or epilogue by Caxton, the *House of Fame* and the second edition of the *Canterbury Tales*. As the latter is the major work, we may start by considering what Caxton had to say about Chaucer in that work. Caxton opens his remarks by repeating much of what he had written in his epilogue to Boethius. He writes "we ought to gyue a synguler laude vnto that noble & grete philosopher Gefferey chaucer the whiche for his ornate wrytyng in our tongue may wel haue the name of a laureate poete/ For to fore that he by hys labour enbelysshyd/

---

[27] The problem of Caxton and humanism is one that has not yet received sufficient attention. I have, however, discussed Caxton's attitude to John Tiptoft, Earl of Worcester, in my earlier article (note 6 above), 25-26.

ornated/ and made faire our englisshe" (p.90). Many of the words Caxton uses here are the same as those in the Boethius epilogue. The only new idea is that Chaucer ought to be called a "poet laureate." This idea was common in fifteenth-century criticism of Chaucer, though it was often expressed in various ways. It was more usual to write that Chaucer was worthy to have the laurel of poetry, as Lydgate did in his *Life of Our Lady*:

> The noble rethor Poete of breteine
> That worthy was the laurer to haue
> Of poetrie [*text:* peetrie].

This and similar expressions were widely used in the fifteenth century. But it is quite possible that Caxton got the expression "poet laureate" from the *De Cura Sapientiae*. In that work a passage in praise of Chaucer is followed by the poet's plea that those who think his writing dull should go to "Galfryde the poete laureate"[28] and others. By this *Galfryde* the poet probably meant Geoffrey of Vinsauf, but it is quite likely that Caxton, when he printed the text, understood it to mean Geoffrey Chaucer and adopted it as part of his critical ideas on Chaucer.

Caxton continues his passage by praising Chaucer for his contribution to the elevation of the English language. He writes: "in thys Royame was had rude speche & Incongrue/ as yet it appiereth by olde bookes/ whyche at thys day ought not to haue place ne be compared emong ne to hys beauteuous volumes/ and aournate writynges." That Chaucer made eloquent our rude language is another commonplace in fifteenth-century Chaucerian criticism and is found particularly frequently in Lydgate. Thus in his *Troy Book* Lydgate says the English language was

> Rude and boistous firste be olde dawes,
> þat was ful fer from al perfeccioun,
> And but of litel reputacioun
> Til þat he cam, &, þoru3 his poetrie,
> Gan oure tonge firste to magnifie,
> And adourne it with his elloquence.   (III, 4238-43)

Lydgate does not, as far as I can discover, use *incongrue* to describe the English language. It is, however, a word used in other contexts by Caxton and was no doubt introduced by him to form a doublet, a stylistic procedure which we have seen him adopt elsewhere. The reference to "olde bookes" was probably also added by Caxton himself following the hint found in Lydgate. Caxton had recently published Trevisa's translation of the *Polychronicon*, the language of which he modernized, and it may have been works of this sort which Caxton had principally in mind. Caxton's phrase "beauteuous volumes/and aournate writynges" may echo a line from Lydgate's *Serpent of Division*, in which mention is made of "the large writings and golden vollums of that woorthye Chaucer."[29] But as it cannot be shown that Caxton knew this work, and as Caxton's phrase is similar to one he had used frequently in his earlier prologues, it is more likely that it was modelled on them. For example, in the prologue to the *Polychronicon*, which served as a model for the prologue to the second

---

28 Spurgeon, p.17.
29 Spurgeon, p.14.

edition of the *Canterbury Tales*, he used the phrase "large and aourned volumes" (p.64). A similar phrase, "fair and Aourned volumes" (p.50), is found in the prologue to the *Mirror of the World* (1481) where it translates the French *beaulx & aournés volumes*. Caxton may well have taken a hint from Lydgate which he then expressed in his own way. Caxton concludes this section of his eulogy of Chaucer by noting that he had written many works in prose and rhyme. This statement, we may assume, reflects the fact that Caxton had already printed many prose and poetic works by Chaucer.

Caxton now launches into a discussion of the virtues of Chaucer's works. This discussion is based for the most part on Lydgate's *Siege of Thebes*. In the first place Chaucer's compositions are "craftyly made." This no doubt echoes Lydgate's phrase "crafty writinge" in his passage on Chaucer in the *Siege of Thebes* (l.57). Then Caxton goes on to write that Chaucer "comprehended hys maters in short/ quyck and hye sentences." This part of Caxton's eulogy is not from the *Siege of Thebes*. In his *Troy Book*, however, Lydgate does describe Chaucer's writing as being of "ful hiȝe sentence" (III, 4248) and Caxton may have taken his cue from this. But Caxton's expression is so similar to a line in the General Prologue that one may accept he took it from there, even if, as is not improbable, he quoted the line from memory. In the description of the Clerk of Oxenford we find the line:

> And short and quyk and ful of hy sentence.[30] (306)

Finally, the passage enumerating Chaucer's virtues ends "eschewyng prolyxyte/ castyng away the chaf of superfluyte/ and shewyng the pyked grayn of sentence/ vtteryd by crafty and sugred eloquence." This passage is probably based on two passages from the *Siege of Thebes*.[31] These are lines 52-7:

> Be rehersaile/ of his Sugrid mouth,
> Of eche thyng/ keping in substaunce
> The sentence hool/ with-oute variance,
> Voyding the Chaf/ sothly for to seyn,
> Enlumynyng/ þe trewe piked greyn
> Be crafty writinge/ of his sawes swete;

and lines 1907-8:

> In eschewyng of prolixite,
> And voyde away/ al superfluyte.

The first of these two passages is in praise of Chaucer, though the second is not. Since one may assume that Caxton had recently read this poem, one may accept that he conflated the two passages, though he could have done so unconsciously rather than deliberately. Certainly the manner in which the last words of the clauses rhyme, *prolyxyte/superfluyte* and *sentence/ eloquence*, reveals that Caxton was borrowing from some verse work. And the occurrence of the adjective *sugred*, so typical of Lydgate's works, and of the phrase *pyked grayn* confirms that this verse work must have been by

---

30 It is interesting to speculate whether Caxton thought there was any similarity between Chaucer and the Clerk of Oxenford.
31 This correspondence was noticed first by E. Ekwall in a review in *Anglia Beiblatt*, XLIII (1932), 302-304.

Lydgate. Caxton often borrowed from various sources and there is no difficulty in assuming that he may have used different passages from the same
work. The rest of the prologue consists of some general remarks about the
Canterbury Tales, which Caxton probably made up from his own reading
of the *Tales;* no parallel need be looked for.

The last Chaucerian work to which Caxton added an appreciation of
the poet was his edition of the *House of Fame.* After mentioning that
Chaucer had left the poem incomplete, Caxton goes on to give his reasons
for Chaucer's greatness as a poet. First, he gives a general statement about
Chaucer's excellence: "in alle hys werkys he excellyth in myn oppynyon
alle other wryters in our Englyssh" (p.69). This statement implies that
Caxton put Chaucer above even Gower and Lydgate. But he was not alone
in his opinion, for although Chaucer, Gower and Lydgate were the three
great English poets, Chaucer was regarded as pre-eminent among them.
Lydgate himself frequently gives expression to Chaucer's excellence and
pre-eminence. In his *Troy Book* he describes Chaucer as "þe noble Rethor
that alle dide excelle" (III, 553). Similarly in the *Siege of Thebes* Lydgate
wrote that Chaucer was

> Floure of Poetes/ thorghout al breteyne,
> Which sothly hadde/ most of excellence
> In rethorike/ and in eloquence.   (40-2)

As we have seen, Caxton knew the *Troy Book* by 1473 and he drew on
the *Siege of Troy* in the prologue to his second edition of the *Canterbury
Tales,* so he would have been quite familiar with both these passages.
Furthermore, Lydgate also referred to Chaucer's pre-eminence in his *Life
of Our Lady,* which Caxton printed in c.1484. In this poem the expression
of Chaucer's excellence is very different from that found in the epilogue
to the *House of Fame,* but I mention it as further proof that Caxton was
well acquainted with the current literary fashion which placed Chaucer
above all other English poets. After his statement on Chaucer's excellence,
Caxton justifies himself by telling us in what it consists: "For he wrytteth
no voyde wordes/ but alle hys mater is ful of hye and quycke sentence."
This claim repeats, with many of the same words, what he had written in
the prologue to the *Canterbury Tales.* It is almost as though he could recall
some, but not all, of what he had written and then used it again. But
he had not used the adjective *voyde* in his prologue, even though he uses

it here in the epilogue. This word does, however, occur in the passage from
the *Siege of Thebes* which he had used in the composition of the prologue.
In that passage the phrase "Voyding the Chaf" (l.55) had been used by
Lydgate. It seems as though Caxton's recollection of the passage from the
Siege of Thebes had become fused in his mind with the passage in his own
prologue; and from this fusion sprang the new expression in the epilogue to
the *House of Fame.*

We have now completed our investigation of Caxton's editions of
Chaucerian works and we may conclude by trying to summarize the results.
It is clear that Caxton's views of Chaucer are all second-hand. He followed
what authorities he could get hold of and used their words to compose his
own appreciations. The principal source Caxton used was Lydgate, and it
would hardly be an exaggeration to say that he saw Chaucer through Lydgate's eyes. It does not follow that, because the way in which he expressed
his praise of Chaucer was based on others' words, his feeling for Chaucer

was not genuine. But we may well imagine that it was not very profound and that it was largely inspired by the taste of those around him. Certainly the impetus for his printing of the major Chaucerian texts came from others, and it may well be that he printed the minor texts to build up a comprehensive list of the poet's works. Commercial gain rather than *pietas* may have been the principal motive behind those works which Caxton printed on his own initiative. Finally, it is impossible to accept the view that Caxton took care to publish as accurate a text as possible of Chaucer's works. He printed the manuscript he had available without worrying about its accuracy or completeness. Some of his readers were anxious about the accuracy of his texts, but even when they pointed out to him the faults in his editions, he did not do all he could have done to put those faults right. Even compositorial mistakes made when the text was set up were not corrected. Such evidence as there is suggests that Caxton treated Chaucer's works in the same way as all the other books he printed; there is nothing special about his Chaucerian editions. They show the same faults and virtues as his other printed books.[32]

[32] This paper was completed before any announcement of the discovery of the first part of Caxton's Ovid was issued. A facsimile of the complete manuscript is now being prepared. When this is ready and available to scholars, it is possible that one or two of the statements made here may have to be modified; but it is not thought that the contents of the manuscript are likely to affect the main conclusions arrived at. For provisional accounts of the manuscript see J. A. W. Bennett, "Caxton's Ovid," *Times Literary Supplement* (24 November, 1966), and *Catalogue of the Celebrated Collection of Manuscripts formed by Sir Thomas Phillipps, Bt.* (1792-1872) (Sotheby & Co., 27-28 June, 1966), pp. 12-16.

12

John Lydgate and William Caxton

It has been recognised for some time that Caxton made use of Lydgate's work in many ways: he may well, for example, have read Chaucer through Lydgate's eyes.[1] However, the primary influence upon Caxton has usually been understood to be his residence in the duchy of Burgundy, which led to his attempt to act as an intermediary for Burgundian culture in England. This attitude towards Caxton has prevented a detailed assessment of Lydgate's influence on him from being undertaken, presumably because it was assumed that there was not sufficient influence to make such a study worthwhile. Recent developments in Caxton scholarship indicate that it is now time to consider more fully what the relationship between these two literary figures was.

William Caxton was both mercer and merchant adventurer. In his latter capacity he participated in the cross-Channel trade and eventually spent considerable periods of his life in the Low Countries, particularly in Bruges. He dealt in various types of merchandise and probably had a hand in the importation into England of Flemish manuscripts, since Flanders was in the fifteenth century an imporant producer of elaborate illuminated manuscripts which were much valued in Northern Europe. Caxton prospered in his trading ventures and about 1462 he was elected to the position of Governor of the English Nation in Bruges. As governor he became involved in many of the diplomatic negotiations which were then taking place among England, Burgundy and France, and it is possible that he attended the marriage of Margaret, Edward IV's sister, to Duke Charles of Burgundy in 1468, since that was intended to cement the Anglo-Burgundian alliance against France. In 1471 Caxton went to Cologne to acquire a printing press. On his return to Bruges he started publishing and, of the six books he published there, two were his own translations. These two books, *The History of Troy* and *Jason* were translated from the French versions by Raoul Lefèvre who had been a secretary to Duke Philip of Burgundy. *Jason* had a particular connection

---

[1] See above, Chapter 11, pp. 161-65.

with Burgundy since its chivalric order was the Order of the Golden Fleece. The assumption naturally arises that Caxton knew of the ducal library and was imitating its contents in his choice of material to publish.[2] This view gains support from the fact that Margaret of Burgundy is mentioned by Caxton in his prologue to the *History of Troy* as the person who urged him to complete his translation: the finished book was dedicated to her. Furthermore, Burgundy had in the fifteenth century a dominating cultural influence in Northern Europe, and England was particularly susceptible to its lead in such matters as chivalry and pageantry.[3]

Lotte Hellinga has recently suggested that we need to be more circumspect in deciding what is Burgundian and in evaluating how far Caxton was trying to promote Burgundian culture and reading matter in England.[4] It has also been shown that many of the books he chose for translation came from France rather than from Burgundy, and that even those which do come from Burgundy already had a wide distribution by the time that Caxton translated or printed them.[5] There is little evidence that Caxton was interested in the Burgundian manifestations of chivalry for he certainly makes no reference to any of the major chivalric events of his time. For example, though Anthony Earl Rivers was one of his 'patrons', Caxton made no mention of his famous tournaments against the Bastard of Burgundy. He was clearly more concerned with history and with how the past could be exploited for moral commentary, as his editorial preface to Malory's *Morte Darthur* reveals. Furthermore, he was not employed by any member of the court as secretary or librarian, and he therefore occupied a different position from people like Raoul Lefèvre at the Burgundian court; he was not a courtier. He was a merchant whose business was to publish books, and in that business he made use of the names of prominent people (as is indeed still a method of promotion used by publishers).

Caxton started to translate the *History of Troy* in 1469, though after a few quires were completed he put it to one side. He took up the translation again two years later at the insistence, he says, of Margaret of Burgundy who gave him advice about improving his style. The translation was completed in 1471 and Caxton printed the book on his return to Bruges from Cologne; it appeared in late 1473 or early 1474. A feature of Caxton's translation is that it is divided into three books, as is Lefèvre's original

---

[2] N.F. Blake, 'William Caxton: His Choice of Texts', *Anglia* 83 (1965) pp. 289-307.

[3] G. Kipling, *The Triumph of Honour* (Leiden, 1977), and M. Kekewich, 'Edward IV, William Caxton, and Literary Patronage in Yorkist England', *Modern Language Review* 66 (1971) pp. 481-7.

[4] Lotte Hellinga, 'Caxton and the Bibliophiles', *Actes du XIᵉ Congrès International de Bibliophilie Bruxelles 1979* (Brussels, 1981) pp. 11-38.

[5] N.F. Blake, 'William Caxton Again in the Light of Recent Scholarship', *Dutch Quarterly Review* 12 (1982-3) pp. 162-82.

which he was using. At the end of the second book there is an epilogue which suggests that Caxton had not originally intended to translate the third book. Part of the epilogue reads: 'Whiche werke was begonne in Brugis and contynued in Gaunt and finysshid in Coleyn in the tyme of the troublous world . . . that is to wete the yere of Our Lord a thousand, four honderd lxxi' (p. 99).[6] The use of *finysshid* certainly implies that his translation was complete at this point. He goes on in the epilogue to indicate that there was no need to translate the third book since the story in it had been translated recently by John Lydgate, whose qualities as a writer are then praised. However, Caxton decided in the end to translate the third book because of Margaret's instructions to complete the translation, because Lydgate's translation was in verse, and because Lydgate may have used a different source (since his account differs from the one Caxton was following). Whether Caxton was going to limit his edition to the first two books is uncertain, but his association of the edition with Lydgate is important. Margaret may be the arbiter of his style, but Lydgate is the author with whom he associates his subject matter. Lydgate was the most famous English poet of the fifteenth century and not unnaturally Caxton would wish to harness his name to help the sales of his book in England. Caxton's edition could be presented as a complement to Lydgate's poem and this would naturally help to promote it in England. Although by choosing a work by Raoul Lefèvre to translate Caxton seems to be purveying Burgundian culture, it may well be that the influence of Lydgate on this choice is much greater than we have hitherto realised.

Although Caxton refers only in passing to Lydgate's *Troy-Book* there can be no doubt that he read it and that he knew it quite well. There are several verbal parallels between the two texts; although some of them represent the common themes of medieval literature, cumulatively they suggest considerable familiarity on Caxton's part with the *Troy-Book*. Caxton refers to Lydgate in much the same glowing terms that Lydgate had used of Chaucer. Where Lydgate writes:

> Was neuer noon to þis day alyue,
> To rekne alle, boþe ȝonge & olde,
> þat worþi was his ynkhorn for to holde   (V 3528-30),[7]

Caxton has 'after whos werke I fere to take upon me, that am not worthy to bere his penner and ynkehorne after hym' (p. 99). In the same epilogue to the *Troy-Book* Lydgate refers to his lack of poetic ability and to his general ignorance , but nonetheless he decides to try to make his version of the work:

[6]   References are to N.F. Blake, *Caxton's Own Prose* (London, 1973).
[7]   References are to H. Bergen, *Lydgate's Troy Book A.D. 1412-20*, EETS ES 97, 103 and 106 (London, 1906-10).

For to deme þer is noon so bolde,
As he þat is blent with vnkonnyng:
For blind Baiard cast pereil of no þing,
Til he stumble myddes of þe lake! (V 3504-7).

Lydgate frequently used the image of blind Bayard for a foolish writer (it occurs again in *Troy-Book* at II 4731), and Caxton imitated his use of this image to represent an ignorant translator who launches blithely onto his work when he wrote: 'And forthwith toke penne and ynke and began boldly to renne forth as blynde Bayard in thys presente werke' (p. 98). Lydgate also made frequent use of the humility formula by claiming to have no rhetorical expertise and by asking his readers to correct or augment what he has written, as at V 3476ff. He asks his readers' indulgence, he claims to be ignorant and rude, and he invites his readers to amend what he has written. His excuse is that he has followed what his author wrote. Caxton makes the same points in his prologue and epilogues to the *History of Troy*. He throws himself on Margaret's benevolence in the hope that she will take it in the spirit in which it is offered. He has followed the original closely and asks his readers 'to correcte hyt and to hold me excusid of the rude and symple translacion' (p. 99).

It is interesting to note that when Caxton refers to his completion of the translation in 1471, he identifies that time as 'the tyme of the troublous world and of the grete devysions beyng and reygnyng as well in the royames of Englond and Fraunce as in all other places unyversally thurgh the world' (p.99). The last phrase makes the passage seem general rather than specific, although England had just gone through the problems of the rebellion of Warwick the Kingmaker with the consequent flight of Edward IV to the Low Countries. France had not been wracked with the same problems, though there was constant trouble between Burgundy and France. Lydgate in his epilogue to book five of the *Troy-Book* refers to the long-standing wars between England and France and he prays that the two countries will find peace under a united throne, for Henry V will also become King of France on the death of Charles VI. Caxton seems to echo Lydgate here. Both writers also refer to earlier authors who had written on the Trojan War and to the different biases which they had held with the consequent problem of deciding what precisely was the truth. Caxton's reference is fairly brief: 'For dyverce men have made dyverce bookes whiche in all poyntes acorde not, as Dictes, Dares and Homerus. For Dictes and Homerus, as Grekes, sayn and wryten favorably for the Grekes and gyve to them more worship than to the Trojans. And Dares wryteth otherwyse than they doo' (pp. 100-1). Authors on both sides, however, agree on the essentials of the story. Lydgate frequently refers to these same three authorities, though he is critical of Homer whom he regarded as a liar. Lydgate also notes that both Dictes and Dares agree in essentials (V 3335-40). Finally it may be mentioned that Caxton adds that he undertook to finish the translation to avoid idleness and that everything is written, as St Paul said, for our benefit; and these two ideas, although commonplaces in medieval literature, are commonly found in Lydgates's writings.

In addition to the verbal parallels between the two texts, there are some more general points of similarity. Lefèvre's French which Caxton was translating contains a dedication and prologue. Caxton kept both of these, but he inserted his own prologue between them. This prologue recounts the genesis of his translation in a relatively informal manner. He mentions that he had decided to make a translation since he had some free time and since the French version of the story he was translating was not known in England, for it had only recently been made. He started on the translation, but when he remembered his lack of command of French and English, he fell into despair and put the work to one side. One day he mentioned the fragmentary translation to Margaret of Burgundy, who asked to see it. After looking at it, she suggested some improvements in style and commanded him to finish the translation. Since Margaret had showed Caxton many favours, he dared not refuse this command and so set about completing the translation. The idea of this prologue may have occurred to Caxton because of Lefèvre's prologue, though that seems unlikely since Lefèvre's prologue is formal and contains little more than a note of the command by Duke Philip to make the translation and an outline of the contents of the work. With later works Caxton did occasionally expand and modify the original author's prologue, though he did not do so in this case. He clearly had some model of an informal prologue, and it is likely that his model was Lydgate who frequently introduced accounts of the genesis of his poems (accounts which can be both lengthy and relatively informal). The *Troy-Book* is no exception. In its prologue Lydgate appeals first to Mars and other classical gods and goddesses to assist him in the task of translation. He has not embarked on the project because of pride, but because Prince Henry had commanded him to do it. Henry enjoyed reading old books to learn virtue and to avoid the sin of sloth. Lydgate commenced his translation in 1412. He saw in this book an example of historical writing, for without such books knowledge of the past would disappear and the glory of old heroes would vanish. Books tell the truth about men and so encourage people to live virtuously. Lydgate then goes on to mention those authors who have written on the Trojan War. He ends by pointing to his own insufficiency as a poet and asks for his readers' indulgence. Many of the same points are taken up again in Lydgate's epilogue following book five. There, however, we also learn that the translation was finished only in 1420. There the translator identifies himself as John Lydgate, monk of Bury. He emphasises his shortcomings and refers to his master Chaucer who acts as his model. History shows how fortune is fickle and encourages us to be virtuous on this pilgrimage through life. He concludes his epilogue with an envoy in which he dedicates the book to Henry V.

In addition to the *Troy-Book* Caxton was also familiar with Lydgate's *Siege of Thebes* to which he refers in his epilogue to *Jason*. In that epilogue he mentions that his source, i.e. the French original, did not contain everything about the story of Jason. There is more to be found in Boccaccio's *De genealogia deorum* and in Lydgate's *Siege of Thebes*. Since Lydgate referred to Boccaccio, it is possible that Caxton picked up the reference to him from there. At all events it is clear that he knew Lydgate's poems well and that he saw his own work as a complement to them. He tried to build on what Lydgate had done and the reputation he had acquired.

There are many other points of comparison between Lydgate and Caxton. Caxton's French sources tend to have a relatively formal prologue which contains a dedication, though that prologue may indicate the reason for the book's appearance. Thus Raoul Lefèvre wrote *Jason* because of a vision he had in which Jason appeared to him and commanded him to write his story to clear his name. Lydgate's prologues are more diffuse and he inserts interpolations and other remarks at various stages. His *Troy-Book* has a variety of prologues and epilogues, as well as numerous authorial interjections to add moralisings and other comments. The same is true of Caxton. Lydgate's prologues are informal and comment on the genesis of the work, even though the precise reasons for the work's appearance remain uncertain. He was asked to produce the *Troy-Book* by Prince Henry, but where and under what circumstances are not specified. There was also a long gap between its inception and completion, though how this affected his relations with his patron is not stated. Caxton also had a royal patron, but her part in the book's appearance remains ambiguous. Having received a command to complete the work, he went away to Cologne to acquire a press although one might suppose that this would interfere with the completion of the royal command. It took Caxton a long time to complete his *History of Troy*, though not as long as Lydgate had taken, and when finished it was dedicated to the patron though there is little to suggest that author and patron had had any contact in the meantime. Both are, however, long works, and Caxton may have found the courage to translate and print this book because of Lydgate's example. Lydgate's work is in verse and Caxton's in prose, but they do complement each other in most other respects.

What is particularly important about Lydgate's use of prologues to indicate the genesis of the works he was writing and the patronage he enjoyed is that it is a relatively new feature of English literature. Caxton could hardly have borrowed it from other English poets. Chaucer rarely mentions for whom he wrote a work and as infrequently dedicates it to anyone. It is widely assumed that the *Book of the Duchess* was written for John Duke of Gaunt, but there is nothing in the poem to indicate that the

Duke had any hand in the poem's genesis or even received a copy when it was finished. Other poems are often understood to be occasional ones, which may have been demanded by particular patrons. Many scholars interpret the *Legend of Good Women* as a court poem which was perhaps asked for by Richard II himself. Whether these claims are true or not, Caxton cannot have acquired his technique of prologue writing from them, for the only dedicatory prologue Chaucer has is that to little Lewis in his *Astrolabe*, one of Chaucer's works Caxton did not print. It is true that Gower in his *Confessio Amantis* has a prologue in which he claims he was asked to write the work by Richard when they met by chance on the River Thames one day, though this story is not found in all manuscripts and was not present in the manuscript from which Caxton printed his edition. Some other fifteenth-century writers do include prologues, but none do it with the consistency found in Lydgate. John Shirley who issued manuscripts with many of Lydgate's poems in them also wrote prologues to some of these works, and as he acted as a kind of publisher his example may have influenced Caxton as well.[8]

Two features of Lydgate's work in general and of the *Troy-Book* in particular may be mentioned, for they could easily have influenced Caxton. Lydgate composed many historical works, particularly those from classical antiquity, which are moralised. The idea of using the past as a guide to the present is very developed in the fifteenth century, though it finds particular expression in Lydgate. It has been accepted for some time that Caxton's prologue to the *Polychronicon* is based ultimately on that in the *Historical Library* of Diodorus Siculus. It is thought that Caxton may have taken his version from a French intermediary, but it is equally possible that he took it over from an English writer like Lydgate though no earlier English version has so far been discovered. Certainly the views expressed in that prologue reflect the attitude shared by both Caxton and Lydgate towards history. There are many points of contact between it and the prologues in *The Fall of Princes*. The second feature of the *Troy-Book* is that although it is in verse it is divided up into books and chapters. This division enables the work to be divided into sections which can easily be moralised, for each section has a particular point or message. This type of division grew in popularity during the fifteenth century, though its use by Lydgate not only in the *Troy-Book* but also in *The Fall of Princes* may have influenced Caxton in his division of Malory's *Morte Darthur* and in the way he set out his edition of Gower's *Confessio Amantis*. Many of the works published by Caxton are either histories or romances which have a historical bias in that they are not based on some classical source like *Eneydos*; they deal either with historical events like *The Siege and Conquest of*

---

[8] See A.I. Doyle, 'More Light on John Shirley', *Medium Ævum* 30 (1961) pp. 93-101, and E.P. Hammond, *English Verse Between Chaucer and Surrey* (Durham, N.C., 1927) pp. 191-7.

Jerusalem or with an ideal past like *Blanchardin and Eglantine*. All these works are divided into chapters and most have moralising comments.

Caxton published many of Lydgate's works as well as those which he probably attributed to Lydgate. The former include *The Churl and the Bird*, *The Horse, Sheep and Goose*, *Life of Our Lady*, *Stans Puer* and *The Temple of Glass*; the latter, *The Court of Sapience*, *Medicina Stomachi* and *The Pilgrimage of the Soul*. Some of these were among the very first works published by Caxton on his return to England and so form a natural continuation to his Lydgate-inspired translations of the *History of Troy* and *Jason*. Most of them are didactic. The same might also be said for verse in the Lydgatian tradition which Caxton published such as the *Book of Courtesy* and Burgh's *Cato*. While this represents a considerable achievement, it is very little when compared with Lydgate's total output. It is notable that Caxton printed none of Lydgate's major works, although he printed both the *Canterbury Tales* and *Confessio Amantis*. From this one might assume that although he was influenced by Lydgate's example, he did not particularly go out of his way to popularise Lydgate's own work. It was rather that he recognised the literary direction Lydgate represented and decided to follow it. This may perhaps be exemplified in Caxton's edition of *Reynard the Fox*.

This text has often been considered the odd man out among Caxton's publications because it was translated from Dutch rather than from French and because it is often described as a satire. Although the Dukes of Burgundy had copies of the French *Roman de Renart* in their library, there is no evidence that they were acquainted with the Dutch prose version. The prose version is made 'for nede and prouffyte of alle god folke',[9] for it teaches them how to avoid sin and the guiles of the wicked. In its rôle as a guide to behaviour it is similar to the allegorised animal fables. In addition to *Reynard the Fox* Caxton printed a version of *Æsop's Fables* and the two Lydgate pieces *The Churl and the Bird* and *The Horse, Sheep and Goose*. These three works have animals as their main participants and their behaviour is allegorised to make it applicable to humans. In *The Churl and the Bird* Lydgate refers to the assembly held by Noble the lion, which he may have taken from a version of *Reynard the Fox*. In addition Lydgate had translated a versified *Isopes Fabules* from French, though that was not printed by Caxton. At first sight there would appear to be little connection between *Reynard the Fox* and Lydgate, but closer investigation suggests that Caxton's translation and publication of this work may have been prompted by the interest in England for allegorised animal fable which was particularly popularised by Lydgate. The influence is not so much direct as by example.

So far in this paper I have concentrated on Lydgate's influence upon Caxton. But Caxton may be able to give us some insights into Lydgate and

---

[9] N.F. Blake, *The History of Reynard the Fox*, EETS OS 263 (London, 1970) p. 6.

his attitudes to literature and its promotion. Particularly important for both men as we have seen was the question of patronage: what was the relationship between a writer and the man for whom the work was ostensibly produced? and how did they get in touch with each other? These are questions that have been much debated about Caxton, partly because of the controversy as to whether he led or followed popular taste. It has not been given much attention in Lydgate studies, partly because of the paucity of scholarship in general, and partly because it has been assumed that as a 'creative writer' Lydgate gave a lead in poetic matters and was besieged by orders from patrons. What Lydgate says about the genesis of his works has usually been taken at face value as though he only included what was fact.

Characteristic of Caxton's relationship to patronage is that there are a lot of different names which occur in his works. He does not have a single patron to whom the majority of his works are dedicated. A large number of patrons occur only once. Some of these were unknown to him. The first edition of *The Game and Play of Chess* is dedicated to George Duke of Clarence and Caxton says specifically that he is a 'humble and unknowen servant' of the Duke. He may possibly have thought to dedicate the volume to him because he was the brother of Margaret of Burgundy, who was the dedicatee of the *History of Troy*. Caxton was still in Bruges when the book was published and Clarence was in England, and no communication is likely to have taken place between them before the book appeared. What may have been the next book to have a dedicatee, *Jason*, was dedicated to the Prince of Wales who was probably no more than six years old when the book appeared. Caxton writes in his prologue that he intends with the 'licence and congye' of the King and with the 'supportacion' of the Queen to present the book to the Prince. Although *Jason* was printed in Westminster, it need not follow that words like *licence, congye* and *supportacion* mean that the King and Queen had given their written or verbal permission directly to Caxton, or even at all. The Prince was still a boy and Caxton may have felt it politic to include the parents in the dedication, implying that he had their permission. Certainly the Prince did not know the work of the printer, and one may question whether the King and Queen were familiar with *Jason*, although Caxton says he is sure Edward IV has a copy in French. A later work, *Caton*, is dedicated to 'the noble, auncyent and renommed cyte, the Cyte of London in England' (p. 63). Although Caxton was himself a member of the Mercers Company in London, this dedication was not one which had to have permission from the Lord Mayor or anyone else in London. In many instances then Caxton used the names of people or places without asking their permission and without necessarily knowing them. The names were an attraction in selling the book, and Caxton may well have wished to imply that he was more acquainted with the aristocracy and other leaders of fashion than was in fact the case.

On other occasions he does not dedicate his translations to anyone but he refers to people from the past in much the same way as he refers to his patrons. *Of Old Age* was translated for Sir John Fastolf, whose exploits are recounted in some detail. These details were no doubt borrowed by Caxton from the manuscript he was using. He does not, however, give any details of the translator, and many might easily have got the impression that the book was translated by Caxton himself. Nevertheless, at the end of the prologue he says he is printing the book 'under the umbre and shadowe of the noble proteccion of our moost dradde soverayn' (p. 122), Edward IV, who is asked to forgive this presumption. Later in the same volume Caxton included *The Declamation of Noblesse* in the translation by John Tiptoft of Worcester. Once again considerable information is given about the Earl who has been executed in 1469. In both these cases what is important is that there should be a member of the aristocracy who is linked with the book rather than that he should be associated directly with Caxton or its printing. The name simply gives a certain dignity to the material.

Another feature of Caxton's patronage is that he used both general and anonymous patronage. By general I mean that the book is said to have been produced for gentlemen or for merchants or for some wide class of readers. By anonymous I mean that the book is apparently dedicated to a particular individual, though that individual is not named. This unnamed person may, of course, have been a fiction, though in some cases an identification is possible. General patronage is found in his first book, *The History of Troy*. Although in his prologue Caxton informs us that he was commanded to finish the book by Margaret of Burgundy, in the final epilogue he says 'I have promysid to dyverce gentilmen and to my frendes to adresse to hem as hastely as I myght this sayd book' (p. 100) and consequently he had printed the book. Since he had had to go to Cologne to acquire the press, if this statement were true it would mean that the translation and printing of this first book was caused more by these anonymous friends and gentlemen than by Margaret. It is more likely that in his first book Caxton wanted to have different sorts of advertising and so included both a named patron and the anonymous gentlemen and friends. It is probable that neither played an important role in the book's appearance. A similar position appertains in his edition of Malory's *Morte Darthur*. This had been printed, he claimed, from a copy presented to him. This copy is often linked by modern scholars with the gentleman who had been most vociferous in asking for a book about Arthur to be printed and in insisting that Arthur had been a historical person. Nevertheless, the book itself is directed in the prologue 'unto alle noble prynces, lordes and ladyes, gentylmen or gentylwymmen, that desyre to rede or here redde of the noble and joyous hystorye of the grete conquerour and excellent kyng, Kyng Arthur' (p. 109). There is apparently a single patron, this time anonymous, and a general dedication to all gentlemen and gentlewomen.

Frequently only one or the other is found. *The Chronicles of England* was printed 'atte requeste of dyverce gentilmen' (p. 69). On the other hand, *The Order of Chivalry* was translated 'at a requeste of a gentyl and noble esquyer' (p. 126), though as no further details are given about him he cannot be identified (if indeed he existed). Later in the epilogue the book is in fact formally presented to King Richard III so one suspects that the squire was no more than a convenient fiction.

One of the anonymous patrons is the 'noble lady which hath brought forth many noble and fayr doughters which ben vertuously nourisshed and lerned' (p. 111) who, according to Caxton, requested the translation of *The Book of the Knight of the Tower.* From various hints in the prologue it seems that this lady is Elizabeth Woodville, at that time Edward IV's widow and in sanctuary at Westminster.[10] As she was in Westminster she was of course a neighbour of Caxton's there, and he may well have seized the opportunity to make her patron of this volume. Whether she had actually asked for it to be translated is another matter.

Finally there are many named patrons who usually are connected with a single volume each. Margaret of Burgundy is the patron of the *History of Troy*; Margaret of Somerset of *Blanchardin and Eglantine*; William Daubeney of *Charles the Great*; Arthur Prince of Wales of *Eneydos*; Henry VII of *Feats of Arms*; William Earl of Arundel of *The Golden Legend*; and so on. Others we have referred to earlier. It seems unlikely that Caxton was known to many of these people personally. It is interesting that in *The Book of the Feats of Arms and Chivalry* he refers to his audience at the court when he was presented to Henry VII to receive the copy to be translated. This description suggests that his appearance at court was sufficiently rare for him to make much of it when it occurred. The idea that kings and other members of the aristocracy dropped into his workshop to discuss what should be published next is a romantic one which may be discounted. Caxton may well have wanted to give that impression, though that does not mean it is something which happened. In many cases there was contact between Caxton and his patron. He presumably did attend court to meet Henry VII. He says that William Earl of Arundel sent his servant John Stanney to him to convey the Earl's request. The patronage was therefore not always done without the knowledge or consent of the patron. But in view of the many patrons there are, it seems more likely that Caxton took the initiative in recruiting the patrons rather than that they sought out the printer with a commission. Arundel had risen to prominence under Richard III when he patronised a book; Henry VII had recently come to the throne when he patronised his book; Elizabeth Woodville was in sanctuary near Caxton when she patronised a book; and Margaret of Burgundy was domiciled in Flanders and Brabant near Caxton when she

[10] N.F. Blake, 'The Noble Lady in Caxton's *The Book of the Knyght of the Towre*', *Notes and Queries* 210 (1965) pp. 92-3.

patronised a book. The pattern suggests that it was the publisher who chose suitable patrons according to the opportunities of the moment. It is unlikely that people came to Caxton to patronise a book as soon as they came into prominence. In only one case was a patron used more than once. Anthony Earl Rivers patronised three books and he may be linked with a fourth. This is rather a special case since the three books were all translated by Rivers who therefore had some interest in seeing them in print. Even in this case Rivers seems to have dealt with the printer through his secretary, who is referred to in *The Moral Proverbs*. If Rivers did have a closer link with the publisher than any other patron, it is nevertheless significant that his name is not used in any other volume. He never became the publisher's principal patron or the arbiter of literary fashion at the time. Either his influence over Caxton was limited or the latter preferred to recruit a wider range of patrons.

What then can we deduce from these facts? Evidently Caxton felt a name was important in the promotion of his books and he preferred the name to be of someone in the public eye. He also preferred variety in his patrons, and he never established a particular relationship with one patron who lent his name to most volumes which were produced. It is likely that the initiative for involving a person, either directly or indirectly, remained with the publisher who nevertheless cast himself into the traditional role of the servant of the patron. He often invented an informal narrative to explain why a particular book was published and what the involvement of the patron was, though these occur more frequently with the anonymous patronage. It is probable that Caxton acquired many of his attitudes towards patronage from Lydgate, though these are likely to have been accentuated by his knowledge of books and manuscripts produced abroad in France and the Low Countries. In any case patronage was becoming less important in the fifteenth century, as has recently been pointed out: 'Caxton's public existed before Caxton came along, like the shrewd businessman he was, to exploit it. But the implications of this fact for patronage have not previously been noticed. Whereas in the fourteenth century a writer was often to a large extent dependent on an individual patron to help secure himself a public, this situation gradually changed. In terms of sheer volume English literary patronage reached a peak in the fifteenth century, but because of this volume of activity the whole system as it had previously existed was already showing signs of weakness when the new conditions brought about by the introduction of printing led to patrons becoming less essential'.[11]

The purpose of the patronage was to sell the books through the implicit recommendation provided by the patron. In this respect translation is no different from creative writing, though in the latter case the patron can

---

[11] P.J. Lucas, 'The Growth and Development of Patronage in the Later Middle Ages and Early Renaissance', *The Library* 6th ser. 4 (1982) pp. 243-4.

only ask for a work to commemorate some event or on some particular topic, he cannot request that a particular work be written as he can do with translation. It is interesting that Lydgate and Gower who both have patrons were interested in the production of manuscripts of their own works, presumably for noble readers. They had some incentive to look for patrons. But Chaucer seems to have been little concerned for the dissemination of his works and so was less worried about patronage. At least no poetic manuscripts date from before his death and it cannot be shown that he exercised any supervision over the publication of his works. The plethora of manuscripts of *The Canterbury Tales* and *Troilus and Criseyde* does not reflect any involvement by Chaucer in promoting these works. Yet neither Gower nor Lydgate was a secretary to a nobleman or even employed in a household. Lydgate was a monk and he must have experienced some of the same problems facing Caxton in the matter of patronage. Did the patrons seek out Lydgate or did he, like Caxton, take the initiative in recruiting them?

It is current thinking to accept that the fifteenth century was an age of court poetry which was set in motion through Chaucer's example. As long ago as 1914 Eleanor Hammond wrote 'The dependence of Hoccleve, of Lydgate, of Barclay, of Hawes, of Chaucer himself upon the generosity of the wealthy is more and more recognised as a factor in their choice of subjects, sometimes in their choice of words'.[12] Lydgate in particular has been regarded as the poet who was submerged by requests from patrons and who therefore wrote too much. Schirmer noted of him: 'Most of Lydgate's works owe their origin to a commission'.[13] More recently Green has commented that many of his poems 'might also be taken to imply that Lydgate often attended the court in person during the decade or so after Henry V's death'.[14] From the secondary literature one gets a picture of a poet who was more courtier than monk, who had frequent discussions with the aristocracy about literary matters, who was besieged by commissons from nobles and merchants, and who tried to live by his pen because he frequently complained about the financial rewards he received from his patrons. As we have noted, similar claims have also been made for Caxton. The more recent books by Pearsall and Renoir[15] do not controvert this picture (though, of course, their main concern is with the literary qualities of Lydgate's poetry).

The first point worth stressing is that not all Lydgate's poems have patrons or were commissioned. In general it is the longest works which

[12] E.P. Hammond, 'Poet and Patron in the *Fall of Princes*: Lydgate and Humphrey of Gloucester', *Anglia* 38 (1914) p. 121.

[13] W.F. Schirmer (trans. A.E. Keep), *John Lydgate: A Study in the Culture of the XVth Century* (London, 1961) p. 23.

[14] R.F. Green, *Poets and Princepleasers* (Toronto, 1980) p. 190.

[15] D. Pearsall *John Lydgate* (London, 1970) and A. Renoir, *The Poetry of John Lydgate* (London, 1967).

have the patrons, though there is one notable exception. The *Siege of Thebes* has no patron, although it does contain a lengthy prologue in which a patron could have figured. In that prologue Lydgate praises Chaucer who had told the *Canterbury Tales* to which the *Siege of Thebes* was appended as the tale of the monk Lydgate on the pilgrims' return journey from Canterbury. The prologue contains elaborate praise of Chaucer and the words of the host to Lydgate which imitate scenes found in the links of the *Canterbury Tales*. Since the *Siege of Thebes* is dated to 1421, Chaucer's reputation was well-established and many manuscripts of the *Canterbury Tales* were available. It may be that Lydgate felt a patron for this poem was unnecessary, because its links with Chaucer's poem would be sufficient to recommend it to potential readers. It was not precisely new and so did not need promotion; and we may recall that when Caxton produced the first printed edition of the *Canterbury Tales* he also introduced no patron and did not even bother to have a prologue. Other poems written by Lydgate in imitation of Chaucer likewise have no patrons. In view of this it may be that patronage was a means Lydgate used to promote those works which were unfamiliar, and this in turn would imply that it was the poet rather than the patron who took the initiative in linking a particular name with a book.

In Lydgate's *œuvre* there are two ways of indicating patronage. The first is when the poet includes a reference to his patron and the commissioning of the work in some prologue or epilogue. The second is a reference to the genesis of the work in a prose headnote in English or in Latin. These headnotes are not found in all manuscripts and may not have been included by Lydgate himself. So it is not always possible to tell whether what they include is genuine, for in some cases they may have resulted from intelligent guesses by fifteenth-century scribes or booksellers like John Shirley.

If we take all these examples of patronage to be genuine, we can note certain significant features about them. The patrons are not localised in the Suffolk area around Bury St Edmunds. Although there are signs of local families in East Anglia patronising local writers and translators,[16] Lydgate drew his patrons from a much wider area. In general each patron commissions only one work, though there are occasional examples of the same patron being linked with two works. The patrons are noblemen, high churchmen and London merchants; that is, they are people whose names carry weight with a potential readership. However, there is also both general and anonymous patronage. Finally, much of Lydgate's output consists of versified translations, usually from French, and it is these which are most likely to have a patron associated with them.

His first major work to have a patron was the *Troy-Book*, which he began

---

[16] S. Moore, 'Patrons of Letters in Norfolk and Suffolk', *PMLA* 27 (1912) pp. 188-207, and 28 (1913) pp. 78-105.

c. 1412 and finished c. 1420. In its prologue, as we have seen, Lydgate appeals to Mars for help, and then says he has undertaken the translation which he began in 1412 at the bidding of Henry Prince of Wales (the future Henry V). He comments next on the virtue of history and the accounts about Troy found in the extant sources and their reliability. He is fulsome in his praise of Guido of Colonna. There is an epilogue to the whole work which repeats many of the same points, but adds that the book was not completed till 1420. Lydgate does not add why he had taken so long to fulfil the King's commisson (Henry V having succeeded to the throne in 1413) or why he had turned out other poems in the meantime. He also gives little information about why the Prince had asked for the book, how he received it, or even what he knew about it. The details are very general. There is no formal dedication to the King. I think we do need to question whether this translation represents a formal commission from the then Prince. We ought to consider the possibility that it was Lydgate who proposed the translation to Henry rather than the other way round. After all Henry did not commission other works from Lydgate or from other poets, but Lydgate did have a variety of other patrons. For one's first long work it would be sensible to invoke the name and reputation of the heir to the throne, and in this Lydgate would have been following Gower's example in linking first Richard II and then Henry IV with *Confessio Amantis*. It would have been a fortunate coincidence for Lydgate if the first patron to approach him was the Prince of Wales.

Many of Lydgate's other patrons were important noblemen connected with the royal house or with the regency in England and France. As is natural with aristocratic families, some of these patrons had family ties but it need not be thought, as is sometimes suggested, that Lydgate was passed around from one patron to another as a poet who could turn out something for you. It is more likely, as with Caxton, that he chose to recruit people because of their family connections with others he had used as patrons. After Margaret of Burgundy, Caxton chose George Duke of Clarence, her brother, and then the Prince of Wales, her nephew. Similarly Lydgate may have taken Richard de Beauchamp Earl of Warwick as patron of *The Title and Pedigree of Henry VI* because he had earlier used his daughter Margaret Countess of Shrewsbury as patron of *Guy of Warwick*. Naturally, there may be instances where the patron took the initiative, as is true of some of the political material translated and written by Lydgate. The *Title and Pedigree of Henry VI* had been written in French by Laurence Calot at the request of John Duke of Bedford, the Regent in France. So there would be good reason why Warwick should know of it, though equally Lydgate may have spotted an opportunity to make himself useful and so suggested the translation himself.

Perhaps Lydgate's most famous patron was Humphrey Duke of Gloucester, who asked for the translation of Boccaccio's *De casibus virorum illustrium*. Lydgate made his translation from a French prose version.

Scholars have noted the paradox that Humphrey who was influenced by the new Italian humanism should have patronised a work which in its essential medieval quality seems quite untouched by the humanism.[17] This paradox could be mitigated if the translation was Lydgate's idea and if it was he who involved Humphrey rather than vice versa. In his prologue to book one Lydgate refers to the French original by Laurence Premierfait and to its source, Boccaccio's *De casibus*. The contents of the book and the moral it contains are then expanded upon. The role of Fortune is an important aspect of this life. Despite his ignorance of good style Lydgate will deal faithfully with his original, but his work will not equal that of Chaucer who refined the language. Many of Chaucer's writings are then listed. Poets were the favourites of kings in the past and Caesar used to listen to the teaching of Cicero. In England there is a Prince who is fond of learning and who upholds the Church by his actions against the Lollards. He knew of Boccaccio's book and asked Lydgate to make a translation of it, which he will do to the best of his ability. It can be appreciated that in this prologue Humphrey Duke of Gloucester plays a relatively minor role: Laurence Premierfait, Boccaccio and Chaucer all seem more important. Gloucester himself is as much praised for his fight against heretics as he is for his love of learning. Once more there is the simple notice of the command to make the translation, but there are no details of how or when this command was given. There is little indication that Gloucester had much personal involvement either with the original or with the translation. What there is comes in the prologue to the second book where Lydgate mentions that as the translation was progressing Gloucester asked him to add an envoy to every tragedy outlining its remedy for the benefit of other nobles. This Lydgate proceeded to do. While this certainly suggests a greater involvement by Gloucester, the provision of such moralisations is typical of the additions Lydgate makes to his translations and it is not impossible to think that the impetus for them came more from Lydgate than from Gloucester. In his prologue to book three Lydgate mentions his weariness at the task and how he keeps going only because he is doing the translation for a lord who recompenses his dependants handsomely. At the end of the work there is one envoy about the translation and the works of previous writers and another addressed specifically to Gloucester though it is addressed in very general terms of morality and virtue. Some final verses send the book on its way. Although there are some signs of involvement by Gloucester, in general Lydgate makes far more of the literary tradition in which he is writing than of the patronage which he has received. He could certainly have made Gloucester's rôle far more prominent than it is. Gloucester's name is introduced but not much else.

The same is true of Lydgate's translation of *The Pilgrimage of the Life of*

---

[17] Pearsall p. 224.

Man, made at the request of Thomas Montacute Earl of Salisbury. In the prologue Lydgate dilates on the need to remember that worldly possessions are here only for a short time with the corollary that one needs to be wise in this life. Man's life is a pilgrimage during which man should prepare for the next world. This is the theme of the French version which Thomas asked Lydgate to translate. Thomas was in Paris when the translation was begun in 1426. Lydgate urges the readers to pay more attention to the matter than to his style. Once again we see that little information is given about the patron, Thomas, or why he wanted a translation of this work. Because he was in Paris, it is assumed that Lydgate was too, though he does not say so. He could have been because he almost certainly made at least one visit to Paris, though documentary evidence to support it is not available. And since Caxton often dealt with patrons through their secretaries, the same could have been true of Thomas. Indeed, it is possible that the translation was Lydgate's idea rather than the Earl's.

In most of these cases all we get is the indication of a command by a nobleman to make the translation. No details of the occasion are given and in many instances there is little evidence that the nobleman was interested in or a patron of other literature. Lydgate tells us more about the book being translated, the moral to be drawn from it, and the great writers of the past than he does about his patrons. There are no formal dedications to the patron, as we find in some books written for the Dukes of Burgundy, for example. I think therefore that we do need to be a little careful in assuming that it was the noblemen who took the lead in having the translations made or even that they had much contact, if any, with Lydgate.

This view is perhaps supported by the frequency of anonymous patronage in Lydgate, since the introduction of anonymous readers or patrons suggests that he was trying to create the impression that there was a demand for his works which would make others want to have copies. For example, *The Serpent of Division* was made 'bi commaundemente of my moste worschipfull maistere & souereyne'.[18] MacCracken has identified this master as Humphrey Duke of Gloucester, though there is nothing to support this identification.[19] It is possible that the master is a fiction. According to its headnote, *Bycorne and Chychevache* was written 'at þe request of a werþy citeseyn of London'.[20] A similar headnote mentions that *A Ballade of Her that Hath all Virtues* was written 'at þe request of a squyer þat serued in· loves court'.[21] His *Complaint of a Black Knight* is

[18] See Schirmer pp. 82-8.

[19] H.N. MacCracken, *The Serpent of Division* (London and New Haven, 1911) p. 1.

[20] H.N. MacCracken, *The Minor Poems of John Lydgate*, EETS ES 107 and OS 192 (London, 1911-34) p. 433.

[21] *ibid.* p. 379.

addressed to an unnamed princess; unidentified French clerks drew his attention to the *danse macabre* painting in Paris which led to his translating the text, though it is not clear whether they sent him the words or whether he was in Paris and copied them down himself; his *Defence of Holy Church* is addressed to an unnamed member of the royal house; and the *Legend of Seynt Gyle* was written for an unnamed patron. Some of these notices about patrons occur in the headnotes and so may not be attributable to Lydgate, but this does not apply to all of them. In his *Legend of Seynt Gyle*, for example, he writes:

> Wher-vp-on my purpos to ffulfylle,
> By Goddis grace, fortune, or aventure,
> Ther was to me brouht a lytell bylle
> Of greet devossionn by a cryature,
> Requyryng me to do my besy Cure,
> Affter the tenour only ffor Gyles sake,
> Out of Latyn translate that scripture.
> Folwyng the copie, this labour vndertake.[22]

Similarly *A Defence of Holy Church* is addressed to a 'Most worthi prince' in its first line. In these instances there is clear evidence that Lydgate himself was responsible for the anonymous patronage. Since Schirmer suggested in the case of the *Legend of Seynt Gyle* that Lydgate was using the modesty topos he presumably thought the gentleman referred to was fictitious.[23] This may well be so, unless good reasons can be found for concealing the names.

In the past we have too readily assumed that fifteenth century poetry was part of a court culture and that most poems were produced for patrons.[24] Often this has meant that the poetry produced has been excused because the poets were trying to satisfy the whims of their patrons. We have therefore tended to believe everything that a poet told us about the genesis of his poem. Yet once patronage became a recognised way of promoting a poem or a poet, it could well be that poets searched out patrons rather than that patrons took the occasional book to a poet. Because with Caxton we have been so bemused by the influence of Burgundy upon him, we have not realised that he was influenced by conditions prevailing in England as much as or more than those abroad. And Caxton can tell us something about literary conditions which were operative earlier in the fifteenth century in England. There are so many parallels between Caxton's and Lydgate's use of patronage that it should make us more cautious about accepting much that has been written about

---

[22] *ibid.* p. 162.
[23] Schirmer p. 159.
[24] For a re-valuation of court culture see *English Court Culture in the Later Middle Ages*, ed. V.J. Scattergood and J.W. Sherborne (London, 1983).

Lydgate's attitudes towards his patrons. Lydgate was after all a monk, not a courtier. Although Henry VI and other nobles visited Bury, we do not need to assume that they came with books in their hands. No doubt Lydgate did receive some specific commissions for particular translations, but as he knew the literary scene well it is likely that in many cases he proposed a translation to a patron or even secured a patron after a translation was complete. He may even have used a patron's name without his knowledge. The literary and social pressures which produced this need for patronage are something which require further investigation.

13

Caxton's Copytext of Gower's Confessio Amantis

Although Gower may well have been one of Caxton's favourite authors, for we know he used *Confessio Amantis* in his translation of the *Ovide Moralisé*[1], Caxton's handling of Gower's text has never been investigated. Since Macaulay's edition of *Confessio Amantis* it has been accepted that Caxton had at least three manuscripts of the poem, of which one was probably Magdalen College, Oxford, 213. If this were so, it would make Caxton's edition of *Confessio Amantis* exceptional among his editions of the works of English poets, for there is no evidence that any of Chaucer's or Lydgate's poems were set up from more than one manuscript. It is time then that Caxton's edition of Gower's poem was reconsidered.

I would like to begin by considering Caxton's prologue to the poem. Since this is not included in Crotch's edition of the prologues[2], the evidence it contains has been neglected. Two interesting facts emerge from this prologue. Firstly, Caxton describes Gower as a "squyer borne in Walys". There is evidence enough to support Caxton's contention that Gower was an "esquire", but no scholar has seriously examined whether Gower was of Welsh birth[3]. It is generally held that Gower came from either Yorkshire or Kent. It is possible that the name Gower led Caxton to guess that the poet was born in Wales; it is possible, but not very likely. Caxton gives no information about Chaucer's or Lydgate's birthplace, and there was no need for him to make any guess at Gower's birthplace. He could

---

[1] J. A. W. Bennett, "Caxton and Gower", *Modern Language Review*, xlv (1950), 215–216.

[2] W. J. B. Crotch, *The Prologues and Epilogues of William Caxton*, EETS, o. s. 176 (London, 1928).

[3] The evidence for his birthplace is reviewed by J. H. Fisher, *John Gower, Moral Philosopher and Friend of Chaucer* (London, 1965), pp. 37 ff.

merely have omitted any reference to it, for the information is quite superfluous as far as the poem is concerned. It seems more reasonable to assume that he included it because it was accepted to be true at the end of the fifteenth century; his statement probably reflects contemporary opinion. Since Gower himself died only at the beginning of the fifteenth century, biographers of Gower should perhaps pay more attention to Caxton's claim in future, if only to explain why he made it. Secondly, we learn from the prologue that Caxton added a table of contents for the convenience of his readers. It is common in Caxtonian editions of prose works that the printer should add chapter headings and a table of contents, the most famous example being his edition of Malory's *Morte Darthur*. But it is unusual for him to include a table of contents for a poetic work, as he clearly felt himself less free to adapt poetry than prose. Why should he then have done it for his edition of *Confessio Amantis*? It is possible that he took the table of contents from the manuscript he was using. But only one extant manuscript, Magdalen 213, has a table of contents and that one is very much briefer than Caxton's. *Confessio Amantis* differs from the poetic works of Chaucer and Lydgate in being divided in most manuscripts into sections which are headed by a brief statement in Latin of what each section contains. It was consequently easy enough for Caxton to make a table of contents by translating the opening words or by giving the sense of these Latin headings in the text. This is what he proceeded to do, and the following may stand as an example of his practice:

Hic in principio declarat qualiter in anno Regis Ricardi secundi sexto decimo Johannes Gower presentem libellum composuit et finaliter complevit, quem strenuissimo domino suo domino Henrico de Lancastria tunc Derbeie Comiti cum omni reverencia specialiter destinavit.

Fyrst the prologue how Johan Gower in the xvj yere of Kyng Rychard the second began to make thys book and dyrected to Harry of Lancastre, thenne Erle of Derby.

Caxton's table of contents to *Confessio Amantis* is thus an example of his opportunism. He liked to add a table of contents and found that he could do it here easily enough without touching the text, for the division of the poem into sections had already been made. We may accept that Caxton made the table of contents as he tells us that he did[4]; and the table shows that hastiness of execution which is such a feature of much of his work.

Scholars accept that the approximately fifty manuscripts of *Confessio Amantis* can be reduced to three major recensions of the poem[5]. The first had a prologue and conclusion honouring Richard II, the conclusion also containing a short passage in praise of Chaucer. In the second recension the original prologue is replaced by a dedication to Henry IV, then Earl of Derby, and the conclusion together with the reference to Chaucer gives way to a generalized summing-up of the dream allegory and less specific references to the state of England. The third recension is an intermediate one which is characterized by changes in the text, particularly in books v and vii. Generally, but not invariably, manuscripts of this recension have the later prologue and conclusion. But it must be remembered that not all the manuscripts fall very easily into this somewhat rigid pattern. I shall refer to these three recensions as the first, second and intermediate, for although this is not the normal terminology, it seems in many ways more satisfactory. Although the second recension is clearly later than the first, the chronological position of the intermediate one is not easy to determine. From his examination of the manuscripts Macaulay suggested that Caxton had at least three manuscripts representing the three different recensions and that the manuscript he had of the second recension was either Magdalen 213 or one remarkably like it. The reason given for this claim is that Caxton's text contains parts of the text which come from the three different recensions and that therefore he must have had three manuscripts. No convincing reason was given by Ma-

---

[4] "I haue ordeyned a table here folowyng of al suche hystoryes and fables."

[5] See particularly G.C. Macaulay, *The Complete Works of John Gower* (Oxford, 1899–1902), II. cxxvii ff., and Fisher, *op. cit.*, pp. 116–127.

caulay as to why he had singled out the Magdalen manuscript as Caxton's copytext for the early part of the poem, though he pointed to a few readings which the two shared. Professor Gavin Bone went further when he stated that in a collation of the two versions up to book v. 4525, "I have often found only the minutest differences in a space of two or three hundred lines together"[6]. Nevertheless he also remarks that since Caxton's text contains lines not in the manuscript, the Magdalen manuscript cannot have been the only one Caxton had access to. Furthermore Gavin Bone noted that there are some marks in the manuscript which correspond to the beginnings of columns in Caxton's text, though these occur only sporadically in the manuscript. I cannot regard these marks as significant. If the compositor was setting up the text from the Magdalen manuscript, as this interpretation of the marks implies, he would have needed some indication as to when to include the lines missing in his copytext. For example, lines 1089–1098 of the Prologue and line 18 of book i are missing in the manuscript, though there is no indication to the compositor that he should include something else at these points. The absence of any such indication makes it very doubtful that the Magdalen manuscript was the copytext.

Furthermore, although Gavin Bone claimed that Caxton's edition and the Magdalen manuscript were almost identical in wording, a collation of the two shows many differences[7]. The following are a few examples I have collected from the prologue.

	Caxton	*Magdalen*
(i) Words not in Ms.:		
opening Latin 1.3 canit insula Bruti		*omit* Bruti
354 Than knowe al that the byble sayth		*omit* that

---

[6] "Extant Manuscripts printed from by W. de Worde, with Notes on the Owner, Roger Thorney", *The Library,* 4 th series, xii (1932), 285.

[7] I am indebted to the Librarian of Magdalen College for providing me with a microfilm of Magdalen 213.

(ii) Different readings:

211 Or curyd or without cure	Or curyd or whiche ought cure
311 But of the world is nought foryete	*read* worde
386 Is none of hem that vnderfongeth	Is now of hem that vnderfongeth
482 I here & wyl nought vnderstonde	I hiere it wel nought vnderstonde
727 Where Rome than wold assayle	The Rome than he wold assaill
966 Why this world is deuyded so	Whi this world deuide so

In all these cases (and indeed in many others) Caxton's text agrees with the better manuscripts and with the text printed by Macaulay; though it should also be stated that there are occasions where Caxton's text has a worse reading than that in the manuscript. We may therefore conclude that, since Caxton's text contains lines not in the Magdalen manuscript and disagrees with it in many readings, Caxton did not use that manuscript as a copytext. It is important to establish this fact first, for if he had used it then he would have had to have access to at least one other manuscript of *Confessio Amantis,* since the Magdalen manuscript does not contain all that is in Caxton's text.

We must now turn to a consideration of what evidence there is that Caxton had three manuscripts. As the theory was propounded by Macaulay, it might be best to quote his own words.

[Caxton's] text is a composite one, taken from at least three MSS. At first he follows a copy of the third [i. e. second] recension, either the Magdalen MS. itself or one remarkably like it, and he continues this for more than half the book, up to about v. 4500. Then for a time he seems to follow a second [intermediate] recension copy, either alone or in combination with the other, but from about v. 6400 to the end he prints from a manuscript of the unrevised first recension, inserting however the additional passages in the seventh book and the conclusion (after the Chaucer greeting) from one of his other MSS. The account of the books 'Quia vnusquisque' at the end is from a first recension MS. The principle, no doubt, was to include as much as possible, but two of the additional passages, v. 7015 *– 7036 * and 7086 *–7210 *, were omitted, probably by oversight, while a first recension copy was being followed. The later form of epilogue was perhaps printed rather than the other because it is longer. Caxton prints the lines at the end of the Prologue, which are given only by *Δ* [Sydney Sussex College, Cambridge, *Δ*. 4. 1], and there are some other indications that he had a MS. of this type; but he also had one of the AdBT group [other intermediate-recension manuscripts], which alone contain vii. 2329 *–2340 * and 3149 *– 3180 [8] *.

This is not in fact a very closely argued passage and it might seem that the conclusions were too sweeping to be drawn from such evidence. The evidence was marshalled a little more cogently by J. H. Fisher whose remarks can be summarized as follows. Caxton had three manuscripts because his text contains the second prologue and conclusion (recension II), the expanded passages in books vi and vii (intermediate recension) and the Chaucer allusion of the original prologue (recension I)[9]. These arguments are not by themselves conclusive. Since many manuscripts of the intermediate recension have the revised prologue and conclusion, there is no need to posit that Caxton had a manuscript of the second recension unless it can actually be shown from textual collation that he used a manuscript of this type. I hope I have proved that he did not use Magdalen 213. We may then accept that the evidence so far adduced is not sufficient to prove that Caxton had a second-recension manuscript. Similarly the fact that Caxton included the Chaucer allusion is not in itself convincing proof that he had a first-recension manuscript, since at least one manuscript of the intermediate recension contains the allusion worked into the revised conclusion. This is the Wollaton Hall MS., which however has the corruption of Chaucer's name to "Cuther". Despite this corruption, this manuscript confirms that the Chaucer allusion had been worked into the revised conclusion before Caxton's time. Macaulay's assertion that the account of the books at the end "Quia vnusquisque" was taken by Caxton from a first-recension manuscript is totally without founda-

---

[8] Macaulay, II. clxviii–clxix. A strict reading of this passage would mean that Caxton had four manuscripts, one each from the two first recensions as well as one from each of the sub-groups of the intermediate recension.

[9] *op. cit.*, p. 12.

tion, since it is found not only in that group, but also in one of the sub-groups of the intermediate recension and in the Fairfax manuscript of the second recension. The evidence that Caxton had a first-recension manuscript is no stronger than the evidence that he had a second-recension one.

We are left to accept that Caxton had a manuscript of the intermediate recension. At least we can say that it is a manuscript of this recension which contains the additional lines to the prologue (1089–1098) found also in Caxton[10]. It is the intermediate recension which contains the extra lines in books v and vii. In other words there are features in Caxton's text characteristic otherwise only of this recension, and in every case at least one manuscript of this recension also contains those other features found in Caxton's text which were thought to be characteristic of the other recensions. Unfortunately these features are not to be all found in the same manuscript. The Wollaton Hall MS. contains the Chaucer allusion and together with the manuscripts of its sub-group the extra lines vii. 2329–2340 and 3149–3180. But it is the other sub-group in the intermediate recension which contains the additional lines in the prologue. They are found in the Sydney Sussex MS. and may well have been in the Stafford MS., in which the relevant folio has been lost. This need not mean, as Macaulay seemed to imply, that Caxton had at least two manuscripts of this recension, for it is possible that he had a manuscript of the intermediate recension which combined these features, but which is no longer extant. A glance through Macaulay's description of the manuscripts should be sufficient to convince one that this is quite feasible, for many manuscripts have been revised or corrected against some other manuscript by their scribes. Similarly, and it is a point not mentioned by Macaulay or Fisher, there are some special readings in manuscripts of the second recension. These occur for the most part in the Latin headings and in the lines which introduce the stories in the prologue and book i. Second-recension manuscripts are generally a little fuller here. Some of these extra pieces are also found in individual manuscripts of the intermediate recension. Thus the opening

---

[10] It is also found in Hatton 51, which is said to be copied from Caxton's text.

Latin prose heading which I quoted earlier is found in the Keswick Hall, Harley 7184 and Magdalen 213 manuscripts of the second recension as well as in the Wollaton Hall MS. However, according to the textual notes of Macaulay's edition, not all of these extra lines are found in manuscripts of the intermediate recension; but I would not regard it as impossible that an intermediate-recension manuscript which included these extra lines did once exist.

Because of the position I have outlined in the preceding paragraph I do not think it can yet be disproved that Caxton had more than one manuscript. It can be shown that the theory that he had at least one manuscript of each recension lacks sufficient evidence to make it a viable one. It is certain that he had a manuscript of the intermediate recension, and it is conceivable that he had one of the second recension. Another, more thorough collation than Macaulay's might bring certainty; but this would be a mammoth undertaking quite beyond the scope of this article. For the time being those who can accept that there could have been a single manuscript which incorporated the different features mentioned may be satisfied by assuming that Caxton had only one manuscript. Those who feel that the boundaries established between the various recensions by Macaulay are immutable and that therefore passages found in one recension and not in another must necessarily mean that Caxton must have had access to a manuscript of that recension will no doubt still continue to hold that Caxton must have had at least two manuscripts. In that case they will have to take into account how Caxton would have handled more than one manuscript, which is a point we must now consider.

Macaulay and Fisher have suggested that Caxton, when faced with conflicting versions, picked the longest alternative. This is not, however, a principle that one can trace in Caxton's other editions. Normally when he knew variants of a story, he was unable to choose between them and usually ended up by including both. Thus in his own continuation (*Liber ultimus*) to Trevisa's translation of Higden's *Polychronicon* he gave two versions of Richard II's death, leaving the reader to choose the one he thinks most likely. And indeed it is characteristic of Caxton to pass on information without coming to any decision about it. In the same way when he used more than one source, he often conflated the wording of the two accounts. This can clearly be seen in his edition of the *Golden Legend*. Kurvinen has shown that he will often take the wording of two of his sources and amalgamate them to produce those doublets and involved sentences which are so characteristic of his style[11]. He acted in a similar manner when he produced his second edition of the *Canterbury Tales*. Dunn has shown that the second edition is a conflated text in which readings from the first edition and the new manuscript were incorporated side by side[12]. This evidence is particularly important since Caxton was here dealing with a poetic text and since he expressed a high opinion of Chaucer. If Caxton had a second-recension manuscript with the expanded introductions to the stories as well as an inter-mediate-recension one, such evidence as we have at the moment suggests that he would have conflated the two versions rather than that he would have just chosen the longer one. There is nothing in his text of *Confessio Amantis* to suggest that any lines are the result of conflation.

One aspect of Caxton's approach to texts which has received greater attention recently is the haste with which he tackled most of his editorial and translating activities. Many of the elementary mistakes he made are attributable to this haste. This is easily accounted for by the vast output of material from his press and by the considerable duties which Caxton would have had to perform as editor and translator. This haste can be traced in his table of contents to *Confessio Amantis*[13]. Yet the theory

---

[11] "Caxton's *Golden Legend* and the Manuscripts of the *Gilte Legende*", *Neuphilologische Mitteilungen*, lx (1959), 353–376.

[12] T. A. Dunn, *The Manuscript Source of Caxton's Second Edition of the Canterbury Tales* (Private edition distributed by the University of Chicago Libraries, 1940).

[13] For example, the story of the Gorgons in book i is given in the table of contents as "Of Phorceus and hys thre doughters whiche had but one eye, & how Phorceus slewe them", though the Latin has correctly that Perseus killed them. Similarly the next story of the snake and the carbuncle is given in the table as "How the serpente that bereth the charbuncle stoppeth his one ere wyth hys tayle and that other wyth the erthe whan he is enchaunted", though the Latin has "contra verba incantantis."

that Caxton had at least two manuscripts must also imply that
he made a careful collation of the texts. He must have noted
the differences between them and chosen the longest alter-
natives. He would have included all the extra Latin headings
and he would have remembered to use them all for his table of
contents, which is complete in this respect. It is of course possible that he did do this, but it is not probable. He certainly
did not act in this way when he produced his second edition
of the *Canterbury Tales*. Furthermore Caxton did not seem to
be aware till he was told that there were discrepancies in the
manuscripts of the *Canterbury Tales,* so that it is quite possible
that it would not cross his mind that there were differences in
the various manuscripts of *Confessio Amantis*. We should not
attribute modern textual concepts to him. Scribes and printers
of the fifteenth century were not as insistent upon textual accuracy as we are. We should also not forget that it would not
have been a simple task for the press to produce a collated edition. If Caxton had more than one manuscript and wanted to
produce a conflated text, three possibilities were open to him.
The compositor could have worked from more than one manuscript, collating as he went along. This would have been an
extremely tedious business, and as we have no evidence that
such a procedure was ever followed by Caxton's press, we may
dismiss it. Secondly, the editor could have marked in one manuscript where the compositor was to consult his other manu-
script(s), in which one would expect the lines to be included
to have been marked in some way. Although some manuscript
copytexts are marked[14], one must remember that the manuscripts of Gower were often lavishly produced. If Caxton had
borrowed manuscripts, he would not have wished to defile
them[15]. If he owned the manuscripts, he would almost cer-

---

[14] The only certain copytext used by Caxton which is extant is discussed by J. Ruysschaert, "Les manuscrits autographes de deux œuvres
de Lorenzo Guglielmo Traversagni imprimés chez Caxton", *Bulletin
of the John Rylands Library,* xxxvi (1953–1954), 191–197. As this
manuscript was Traversagni's autograph and as he may have been
present when it was set up, it is not a situation which is comparable
with the printing of a luxury manuscript.

[15] Borrowed manuscripts appear to have been carefully treated by

tainly have wished to sell them again afterwards. Excessive marking would tend to diminish their value; and one would have to consider whether Caxton would have taken his duties as editor so seriously that he would have taken a loss on two or three manuscripts. Moreover no marked manuscript of Gower which can be shown to have been used by Caxton has yet come to light. Although one can easily accept that one manuscript may have got lost, it becomes less probable that one of two or three such manuscripts would not have survived, when one considers that 49 manuscripts of *Confessio Amantis* are extant. It could be, furthermore, that a desire not to mark a manuscript was the reason the second edition of the *Canterbury Tales* was set up not from the manuscript, but from the first edition, which would in any case lose its value as soon as the second edition appeared. Finally, it is conceivable that Caxton could have had the text copied out again with the corrections before it was printed[16]. This would have involved so much extra work and expense that one may doubt that Caxton would have bothered to do it. He was not such a conscientious editor that he would go to such lengths.

When Caxton translated *Legenda Aurea,* he had three different versions, in Latin, French, and English, and modern scholars have proved that he made use of all versions. But the important point is that Caxton himself supplied us with this information in his prologue to the edition. Similarly when he reprinted the *Canterbury Tales* he wrote a prologue explaining how he had become aware of the differences between the various texts of the poem. One gets the impression that the printer is here seeking to impress his clients with his own industry and with the quality of the text. But in *Confessio Amantis,* which was issued at about the same time as these other two works, there is nothing in Caxton's prologue to tell us that he

---

fifteenth-century printers, cf. Gavin Bone, *op. cit.,* and R. W. Mitchener, "Wynkyn de Worde's Use of the Plimpton Manuscript *De Proprietatibus Rerum*", *The Library,* 5th series, vi (1951–1952), 7–18.

[16] Some have suggested that the manuscript of his translation of the *Ovide Moralisé* may have been used as a copytext. Even if this were likely, which it is not, it could hardly be used to support the hypothesis since it is a manuscript of a translation, not of an English poem.

had more than one manuscript of the poem. Since he did write a prologue to the edition, it seems probable that he would have informed his customers that he had used more than one manuscript if he had in fact done so, for this would have redounded to his own credit and to the value of the printed book. His silence suggests that he used only one manuscript.

It may be admitted that some of the above arguments taken individually are not entirely convincing, though together they make it seem more than likely that Caxton had only one manuscript. As I have mentioned earlier, certainty will probably be achieved only when all Gower manuscripts are submitted to another fullscale collation. Until then, I would merely suggest that the balance of probability favours the view that Caxton had only one manuscript.

14

Caxton Prepares his Edition of the Morte Darthur

According to the colophon Caxton completed his printing of Malory's *Le Morte Darthur* on 31 July 1485; to avoid confusion with Malory's text I shall refer to this edition as *King Arthur*. An incomplete manuscript of Malory's text, formerly at Winchester College, is now in the British Library. Caxton's edition retains its importance both as our only source for the beginning and end of Malory's work and as the version from which attitudes to the Arthurian story derived from the fifteenth to the twentieth century.[1] I have therefore thought it of interest to consider what the various stages were that led to the book's appearance: why it was chosen, how it was prepared for the printer, and how it was promoted by the publisher. This approach to one text has not been attempted previously for a Caxton edition because scholars have been more concerned with his total output than with the particular details of printing and publishing. I would, however, suggest that it is from detailed studies of individual texts that we can gain a more accurate picture of the way in which Caxton worked.

The first matter to consider is the collation of *King Arthur* since that may reveal the way in which the book was put together. It is (i-iiii)^8 (v-viii)^{10} a-z & A-Z aa-dd^8 ee^6. In other words the two initial gatherings do not have normal signatures. The text itself was set up in quaternions, and the compositor began with signature *a* and when he had gone through the alphabet he used the ampersand. Then he went on to capitals and, when they were exhausted, he used double lower-case letters. The book concludes with a ternion because there was not enough material to fill a quaternion. This arrangement from a^1 to ee^6 follows the

---

[1] E. Vinaver, *The Works of Sir Thomas Malory*, 3 vols., 2nd edn. (1967); the first edn. appeared in 1947. This year the Winchester manuscript is to be published in facsimile with an introduction by N. Ker by the Early English Text Society and Caxton's text with an introduction by R. Needham by the Scolar Press.

normal practice of the printing shop. The first two gatherings are unusual. Instead of letters they have Roman numerals as signatures; and although one gathering is a quaternion, the second is a quinternion. The difference in signature letters and the use of a quinternion can be explained only on the assumption that these two gatherings were printed after the rest of the book. While this need not mean that the contents of these two gatherings, Caxton's prologue and the table of contents, were written after the rest of the book was in type, this is the most natural explanation. If so, two points need stressing. The first is that the date given in the colophon, 31 July 1485, may not be the actual date of the book's completion since the initial gatherings had yet to be set up. The second is that Caxton's prologue contains information about the edition's genesis. If what he says is accurate, there is little reason why the composition of the prologue should have been delayed since the necessary information was available.[2] I shall therefore make the assumption that this material is largely fictitious—and I hope the rest of this paper will show that assumption to be well founded. Since Caxton has often been considered truthful and honest, we have in the past accepted all he wrote at face value. But this chain of reasoning is circular since all we know about him and his outlook comes from his writings.

In the prologue Caxton says that several gentlemen during the course of a conversation criticized him for printing the lives of foreign heroes and neglecting the one English hero, Arthur. One of these gentlemen was particularly ardent in his claims for Arthur. So Caxton decided to print Arthur's life from a manuscript which was delivered to him. It is notable that he uses very general terms to refer to his supposed customers: they are "many noble and dyvers gentylmen". Such vague descriptions occur elsewhere in his prologues and epilogues and are usually a sign that he hopes people of this sort will be interested in his productions. It is true that in *Caxton and his World* I suggested that he concealed the names of these gentlemen for political reasons, because the book was published in the troubled reign of Richard III. But this no longer seems an adequate explanation, and I think that, apart from the *Knight of the Tower*, none of the books published under anonymous patronage at this time had real patrons. This certainly applies to the second edition of *Canterbury Tales* and *Order of Chivalry*.[3] That Caxton's story in the prologue to *King Arthur* is fictitious is suggested also by his handling of the text for he made alterations to his copy-text. It is unlikely that he would have made these changes if the edition had been particularly requested by a noble patron who had lent him his manuscript for the purpose.

If what Caxton tells us in his prologue is a publisher's fiction, how did he come to print this particular text? The simple answer is that he acquired a manuscript version of it. That he should get hold of a manuscript is not surprising, even if

---

[2] This question is discussed further in chapter 2 above, pp. 19-35.

[3] For my original arguments see *Caxton and his world* (1969), pp. 92-5. The second edition of *Canterbury Tales* is treated in my article listed above.

there were few of them. Sir Thomas Malory wrote his version when he was a prisoner, and since the Malory of Newbold Revel (who is widely accepted to be the author)[4] had seen the inside of most London prisons including the Tower, it may be simplest to accept that it was written in London. He was buried in London near Newgate no more than a year after *Le Morte Darthur* was finished. How it was written remains uncertain, though such a long work would need the help of professional scribes, to say nothing of a large quantity of paper. These were readily available in London. It is indeed possible that the manuscript may have been copied outside the prison in some scrivener's shop. If so, Caxton would readily have heard about it. He had many friends in London and took an active part in the booktrade. He, no doubt, made it his business to acquire copies of likely books. Many texts must have passed through his hands which he did not print. Since Malory wrote his version only in 1469/70, it would still have been around in London when Caxton set up his shop at Westminster in 1476. This does not imply that Malory's version was popular. Since Caxton's copy-text was different from the Winchester manuscript, there were at least three manuscripts of it: these two and the original copy. It is not necessary to think that there were many, if any, other copies. It is noticeable that Caxton's edition was not copied in any manuscript version, whereas several of his courtly works were copied in manuscript form possibly for noblemen who preferred manuscripts to printed books. So it is quite likely that the work would have remained largely unknown if Caxton had not printed it. This makes his decision to print intriguing since he could definitely be said to be taking a gamble.

What appealed to him about the work? Perhaps the reason was simply that he liked it; he certainly knew it very well. He made extensive alterations to the section dealing with Arthur's campaign against Lucius (book 5) in that he amended Malory's alliterative vocabulary here. Since this book is well on in the work, it shows that Caxton had read the book sufficiently closely to detect a difference in style in one part of it. There is no question of his just knowing that it was a book about Arthur which he handed over to his workshop without knowing fully what was in it. His prologue suggests also that he was interested in Arthuriana since he could refer to some of its literary and archaeological manifestations. These may have been examples commonly mentioned in literary circles at the time, but that Caxton should note them down displays a certain level of interest. Then Malory's version is a translation from French—or at least the greater part of it was—and this would appeal to his interest in literature which was French-inspired. He is also aware that Arthurian stories are known on the Continent, though it is doubtful whether he had seen copies in all the languages that he mentions. Yet that Arthur was an important subject of romance may have been an important consideration, since the Englishness of Arthur could have been the

---

[4] For this Malory see Vinaver, *op. cit.* I. xiv–xxvi. The claims of this Malory have been attacked by W. Matthews, *The Ill-framed Knight* (1966), whose views have generally not found acceptance. See more recently P. J. C. Field, "Sir Thomas Malory M.P.," *Bulletin of the Institute of Historical Research* **47** (1974), 24–35.

greatest handicap to publishing the story, if one accepts that fifteenth-century Englishmen were convinced of the superiority of European culture. Finally Arthur was one of the Nine Worthies who represented the peak of chivalrous attainments. As such he would have appeal for the courtly and refined reader. It is uncertain which of these reasons was the predominant one; perhaps all played a part in the decision to print.

Once Caxton had decided to publish the work, he had to prepare the copy for the printer.[5] Here we are in some difficulties since he did not use the Winchester manuscript, but one which is a separate copy of the original. Although we must compare his version with that in the Winchester manuscript, it is not certain that the differences stem from Caxton rather than from the scribe of his own copy-text. That Caxton was responsible nevertheless remains the most likely explanation. It is also necessary to bear in mind that Caxton was using a manuscript which was probably as utilitarian as the Winchester one and that it was almost certainly one that belonged to him. This latter point is of some importance. We know that printers could treat borrowed manuscripts with the utmost care so that they were returned to their owners unblemished; but other manuscripts they scrawled over quite readily.[6] A utilitarian manuscript in the printer's possession is not likely to have been handled gently by editor or compositor. *Le Morte Darthur* is a long work and it seems improbable that Caxton would want to copy the whole text out again by hand simply to include his alterations; it is much more likely that he made running corrections to the manuscript as he went along. Only book 5 was copied out again before printing. The manuscript itself would become unusable as a result of this treatment; that may be why it has not survived.

The Winchester manuscript is divided into eight sections or tales. Whether these are considered independent works or not is not germane to our purpose. Caxton evidently considered them to form a complete work and his editorial activity made this unity more apparent. Instead of eight tales he divided the work into twenty-one books, each of which is further subdivided into chapters. The length of each book differs considerably and for the most part follows the lead given in the manuscript. The new arrangement does not reveal as much originality as might at first be imagined. The division itself into books and chapters was inserted by hand in the manuscript and this accounts for the form it took. The books have titles which reproduce, often in a modified form, the headings of the manuscript. The chapters have no headings, though these were

---

[5] For a more detailed consideration see N. F. Blake, *Caxton: England's first publisher* (1976), pp. 85 ff. The differences between Caxton and Malory are also investigated by Sally Shaw, "Caxton and Malory", in *Essays on Malory*, ed. J. A. W. Bennett (1963), 114–145.

[6] See, for example, R. W. Mitchner, "Wynkyn de Worde's Use of the Plumpton Manuscript of *De proprietatibus rerum*," *The Library*, 5th ser. **6** (1951–52), 7–18; and G. Bone, "Extant Manuscripts printed from by W. de Worde with Notes on the Owner, Roger Thorney," *The Library*, 4th ser. **12** (1931–32), 284–306.

later provided for the table of contents; they are simply introduced as "chapter one, chapter two" and so on. There was probably not room in the margins of his copy to introduce headings for the chapters; and to have done so might have caused confusion when the book was set up. The arrangement explains why many of the chapters begin at places which have a painted paragraph mark in the Winchester manuscript, since these appear to be natural divisions and allow a little more space to include a hand-written rubric. It also explain why some of the chapter divisions are illogical, occurring as they do in the middle of sentences and at other inconvenient places. These places may have corresponded with the end of the page or some other slight break in the copy-text where it would be easy for the adaptor to include a chapter division. A man going through a manuscript and adding in by hand where the breaks are to occur is likely to make more infelicitous divisions than one who is rewriting and revising the text.

As part of his reworking of the text Caxton cut out all explicits within *Le Morte Darthur* which make any reference to the author. Thus the explicits at the end of books 4 and 7 are deleted. Nothing replaces them. Here, again, we may think that when making running corrections in a book an adaptor can make deletions more readily than additions. It is, of course, possible that he felt some of the material in these explicits inappropriate and that he wanted to increase the unity of the story, though it is not necessary to accept either of these views. It may be simply that they did not fit in with the book divisions which he imposed on the text. Finally we must accept that a man who makes running corrections is not interested in any radical revision of the story as a whole. There was no attempt to abbreviate it, to make it more exciting or credible, or to reorganize the material. Only the style aroused his attention.

The changes made to the language have to be considered in two parts: those made in book 5 and the rest. The former may be attributed to Caxton; the others need not be. While it is possible that he may have altered individual words here and there, there is no need to assume this; indeed it is unlikely. Where it is possible to compare other English early printed books with their copy-texts, it is clear that the compositors took it upon themselves to modernize the language as they set up the type. Sometimes this was for the convenience of justifying the line and sometimes to eliminate archaisms. Where the copy-text is clean, changes are still numerous.[7] It is therefore best to assume that the changes in all books other than book 5 were the work of the compositors, though one could think that Caxton had issued a blanket directive to his compositors to modernize. Similarly differences in punctuation, the use of paragraph marks and other small linguistic details must be laid at the compositors' door. There may have been a house style, but there was no editorial policy for this work regarding these matters. The changes Caxton made to the vocabulary of book 5 have been discussed elsewhere and only a brief recapitulation is necessary here.[8] Malory had based this tale on

---

[7] See particularly Mitchner, *op. cit.*
[8] See above, chapter 9, pp. 119-35.

the English alliterative poem *Morte Arthure* and so took over into his prose many words and expressions associated with the more archaic alliterative style. These words were too uncouth for a courtly work and Caxton replaced them by the smoother, blander words of the romance style which was indebted to Chaucer and to French. The result is a loss of concreteness and particularity, for Caxton's rewording brings this book into line with the romance stereotype. As he was rewriting this book Caxton also made some changes to the length and arrangement of the story; but these were incidental results of his interest in style. They would not have been made if the style had not offended him. And 'offended' may well be the right word. The labour of revising this book can hardly have been necessary to help sell the volume as a whole. Since book 5 starts only at about page 150 and since he did not refer to the changes in his introduction, potential purchasers are unlikely to have been aware of the language of this book until long after they had bought the whole volume. A less scrupulous publisher would not have bothered with this extra work. Clearly the style touched a nerve in Caxton and he felt obliged to do something about it. Evidently he was himself fully convinced of the advantages of the French-based style; it was not a sales pose he assumed to help sell his books.

The editorial work consisted, then, of a total revision, involving the recopying, of book 5 and of the insertion of entries into the manuscript where the other books and their chapters began. A few deletions and the occasional alteration were also made. We need not think that the editorial work amounted to more than that. The only addition he made was the colophon—and that was easily done since it came at the end. Caxton included Malory's own explicit (or what we must take to be his since the end of the Winchester manuscript is missing) and then added his own. In it he gives a résumé of the book's contents which served to tell his customers what they could find in the book. This need to inform his customers explains why, although he gives the title *Le Morte Darthur*, he quickly goes on to say the book contains the whole life of Arthur and much else besides. He did not want to lose potential sales because customers thought the book too limited. In addition he referred to the author, Malory, and to his own contribution which consisted of dividing the work into books and chapters. The colophon contains all essential details about the book's contents and pedigree. To us it seems flat and unnecessary because we have read the prologue which lists the contents in great detail. But if we remember that the colophon was written before the prologue was contemplated, we can see why it appeared in the form it did.

Once the copy (apart from the prologue and table of contents) was ready, decisions had to be made as to the physical appearance of the book. There were questions of type, lay-out and decoration which had to be resolved, though this may have happened in the workshop rather than at the editorial desk. Some decisions reflect the particular stage the development of printing at Westminster had reached. The whole book is printed in type 4*, a *bâtarde* type. While the use of 4* among the various *bâtarde* type is explained by the date of the book's appearance, the use of a *bâtarde* type instead of a *lettre de forme* was a conscious decision arrived at because the text was intended for a courtly market. The latter was reserved for more ecclesiastical and educational works. What is interesting is that only one type is used in the book,[9] for it is common at this time to find books with two: one for the headings and quotations, the other for the text. Caxton could have emphasized his division of the work into books and chapters, out of which he made so much capital in his prologue, if he had printed the book and chapter numbers in a different type. But if the prologue was written after the book was in type, as I have suggested, it could be that this division grew in importance for him as time went on. Another indication that this may be so is the absence of pagination. This was already found in some texts like *Confessio Amantis* and *Golden Legend*, which in certain ways resemble *King Arthur* since they also contain short episodes within a larger framework—and the pagination allowed an index to be included. No doubt the inclusion of the pagination was time-consuming and avoided if possible. But if Caxton had attached as much importance to his editorial divisions early on as he did later, it is possible he might have wanted to include pagination to make an index based on those divisions. After all, a text like *Æsop* was provided with pagination, even though no index was ultimately included.

The size of folio page used was standard in the workshop, and only *Golden Legend* differs from the norm. But the decision to print in folio rather than in quarto was deliberate since folio was used for courtly works and quarto for the others. The lines of type ran across the page; the page is not divided into two columns. This arrangement was quite usual in Caxton though about this time the press was indulging in experiments. Thus *Confessio Amantis* and *Golden Legend* before and *Charles the Great* and *Paris and Vienne* after *King Arthur* all have double columns, and most could be considered as courtly as it. Since double columns were also quite usual in manuscripts at the time (the Caxton Ovid is written in this way), it is surprising that the press preferred to print across the page. The reason may be that it was easier for the compositor to justify the line, and so the choice may not be a significant one. The absence of woodcuts in *King Arthur* is attributable to two reasons. Since the Winchester manuscript has no illuminations, it is unlikely that Caxton's copy-text had any; it was a utilitarian manuscript. Caxton may therefore not have considered using woodcuts since he followed the lead of his originals in this matter. He did so because if the copy-text was without illustrations there would be no models for his artists to copy unless he could find a set of illustrations from some different volume which could be made to fit in with his text. Anyway after 1484 Caxton turned away from native artists and began to import sets of woodcuts from abroad. These were aesthetically more sophisticated than the English ones, but the subjects were all of a religious nature. So if he had already imported any by July 1485, they would have been of no use for this volume. It is surprising only that he did not acquire a set of woodcuts with chivalric themes because of his large output of courtly works. But the press

[9] In the supposedly diplomatic edition of Caxton's edition by H. O. Sommer (1889), two types are used and this may cause misunderstandings.

had recently imported a set of three-line and five-line initial capitals and these were used in *King Arthur*. They form its only decoration. The five-line initials are used at the beginning of each book; the three-line ones everywhere else. This plan was adhered to even though the compositor made mistakes in allowing a sufficient gap for these woodcut initials; often a five-line initial is squeezed into a four-line gap.

Once the decisions were made, the book was set up in type. This business was was left to the compositors, who imposed their own spelling conventions, punctuation and modernization. The text itself was set up without break and with no concern for the look of the page. Books and chapters start immediately after the end of the previous ones and not at the beginning of the next page. Paper was more valuable than looks. Certainly when it came to selling the books, their appearance was not an important consideration.

While the book was being set up, Caxton would turn his attention to its promotion. We must abandon the idea that, as long as he produced suitable literature, noble clients would simply drop into his shop and buy his books. Books were wares that had to be marketed—and this is precisely the function which he intended for his prologues. Many are the equivalent of the modern publisher's blurb. It is of course possible that individual books were further promoted by handbills such as his extant *Advertisement*. Indeed this handbill reveals how conscious Caxton was of the need for publicity and sales promotion. The inclusion of a prologue in a text is usually a sign that he was putting particular effort into its sale—and this in turn implies that there was no ready sale for it in Caxton's opinion. A demand had to be created—and this applies equally to *King Arthur* which we might think would be an automatic best-seller. That later editions were produced only shows that the book became popular; they do not prove that the version was already popular when it was first published. Probably Malory's translation was known only to a very limited audience—and Caxton was trying to sell hundreds of copies.

From other books he published we can see what avenues Caxton would explore. His first thought would be to look for a patron. That *King Arthur* does not have one may be because he could not find one or because he decided not to look for one. In either case the reason would be the political situation in 1485. *King Arthur* was finished on the last day of July; the Battle of Bosworth and the death of Richard III were only three weeks away. Although Caxton cannot have known what the outcome of the struggle between Richard and Henry Tudor would be, the crisis would keep men's minds on affairs other than patronising books and would possibly persuade Caxton that to have a named patron was folly. A named patron might become a dead patron before the book was available. By re-using the device of unnamed diverse gentlemen, he could sit on the fence: whoever was victorious could assume that these gentlemen were on his side rather than on the other. The same consideration would prevent Caxton from dedicating the book to the king, which was another solution he adopted when he could find no patron for a work.

His next line of approach would be to extol the literary elegance or the nobility of the translator. Antony Earl Rivers and John Tiptoft Earl of Worcester are given elaborate encomia in other prologues. Even Sir John Fastolfe, though only the patron of the original version of *Of Old Age,* has several lines devoted to him. Translators and non-courtly authors are similarly given extensive space in which their life or merits are extolled. Chaucer is the prime example. But details of John Trevisa's life and other translations are given in the *Polychronicon,* and details of Gower's life are included in *Confessio Amantis;* though in both there may be errors of detail. Even Benedict Burgh receives more than passing mention in *Cato.* Yet there is almost total silence about Malory. Since he was the translator of a version of the Arthur story and a nobleman, this is surprising and needs an explanation. Since Malory's translation was finished only fifteen years before it was printed, it seems improbable that Caxton, who was interested in literary affairs and the nobility, did not know more about him. After all, he is well informed on so many other authors. As Mr. Field has shown, Malory was both an important and a notorious man in the middle of the fifteenth-century whose name and reputation must have been quite widely known. Two explanations for Caxton's silence about Malory seem possible. The first is that contemporary literary opinion was so offended by Malory's alliterative style that emphasis on his name would be no help in selling the work. This view does not strike me as plausible. The second is that Caxton knew Malory's life had been somewhat disreputable—or at least unfortunate—and felt that to linger over it would detract from the chivalric tone of the book which he regarded as one of its main attractions. The discrepancy between the man's life and his work has often attracted attention, and it could be that Caxton was the first to react unfavourably against the man. We saw earlier that he deleted the explicits to some tales in which Malory is mentioned. All references to Malory as prisoner were consequently omitted; and this, rather than the creation of a literary unity, may have been the motivating force behind the deletions. Malory is simply referred to as "Sir Thomas Malory, knight" once each in prologue and colophon. The straightforward statement may have been intended not to attract too much attention.

Another possible approach was that of sources and the book's reputation among Continental writers. He resorted to this method frequently to encourage his readers to appreciate the courtly nature of his output, for Continental associations made a book more desirable to Englishmen. In his other prologues he refers to such writers as Roul Lefèvre, Jean Mielot, Laurence Premierfait and Jean de Vignay who had composed the version from which the English translation was made. But in *King Arthur* he says only that Malory had translated it "oute of certeyn bookes of Frensshe";[10] and this is presumably all he knew about the sources of the work. From this we can infer that Malory had not given any

---

[10] The prologue is reproduced in N. F. Blake's, *Caxton's own prose* (1973), 106–10.

precise information about the French books he had used in his own prologue or colophon, for it is certain that Caxton would have followed him in this matter if he had given him a lead. It also seems likely that Caxton knew little about the French or other Continental versions of the story. It is true that he claims he had read a French version when abroad, but he gives no details. Otherwise he includes rather general statements in his prologue, such as "there ben in Frensshe dyvers and many noble volumes of his actes" and "moo bookes made of his noble actes than there be in Englond, as wel in Duche, Ytalyen, Spaynysshe and Grekysshe as in Frensshe." But there is a notable lack of particularity in these remarks and the latter comment has almost a note of desperation in it because of the absence of any hard information from abroad. For Caxton's prologue in making Arthur historical necessarily makes him a very English figure, and he was anxious to show that he was a man of Continental importance. Similarly he could find no praise of the Arthur story by a Continental figure in the way that Poggio had praised *Caton*, which was duly recorded by Caxton. So he was forced to rely on the theme of the Nine Worthies for this lifted Arthur to European rank as he was the only Englishman among them. This theme also allowed him to mention his version of the exploits of Godfrey of Bouillon which he had dedicated to Edward IV, a reminder to his readers that he did have royal patrons. Since Edward was dead and his reputation growing, Caxton could afford to mention him here.

As none of his normal approaches was available for the promotion of *King Arthur*, he had to rely on more general arguments when he came to compose his prologue. This situation was not new to him and over the years he had invented a host of plausible reasons to persuade his customers to buy his books. What we may notice is that he confined himself to one particular attribute when promoting a text in this way. The message is designed to come across quite unmistakably. Thus the second edition of *Game of Chess* is recommended for its woodcuts, because the first edition was without any illustration. The second edition of *Canterbury Tales* is recommended because it contains a corrected text, for the first edition had been inadvertently printed from a corrupt manuscript. Although the second edition also differs from the first in having woodcuts, this information is not included because it is not part of his sales campaign. The promotion of Trevisa's translation of Higden's *Polychronicon* was based on the modernization of the text by Caxton. Though the changes made were those that any competent compositor would introduce on his own initiative, the clients had to be persuaded that they should have his version in modern English rather than some antiquated manuscript version. This argument has points of contact with that used to promote *Canterbury Tales*, but it is also strikingly different. It was not available to promote *King Arthur* for two reasons. It would throw too much emphasis on Malory the translator and it would be no recommendation to write that a merchant had been forced to correct a knight's style. The theme adopted was that Arthur is a historical English king who assembled the flower of chivalry at his court. Features present in the text, such as the modernized language, are not mentioned when they have no relevance to his theme.

So Caxton wrote his prologue on the historicity of Arthur and he deserves credit for hitting on such a provocative sales gambit. In its outline this prologue imitates that found in the second edition of *Canterbury Tales* in that in both Caxton pretends to respond to the pressing demands of his clients. The scene represented in *Canterbury Tales* is as fictitious as this one in *King Arthur*. Both prologues are built on the framework of a conversation between Caxton and his clients, and it is likely that its use in *Canterbury Tales* was instrumental in suggesting the same basic frame here. There are differences. In *Canterbury Tales* only one gentleman came to see Caxton, whereas in our text a whole crowd came along although one in particular appears to be the most vociferous. In the earlier prologue the story is told in the form of reported dialogue; in the later one the conversation is interspersed with arguments and statements which make the account diffuse and unconvincing.

The prologue opens by referring to many works that Caxton had already printed, though none are named. This is a common theme in his prologues, but is introduced here to fill the same role which the first edition had played in the prologue to the second edition of *Canterbury Tales*. These other books provide a convenient reason why his customers should complain that he had not printed the life of King Arthur. The motif is less convincing here, partly because of its generality and partly because few books published in the immediately preceding years had concerned chivalric heroes; only one had been devoted to one of the other Worthies. His visitors questioned why he had not printed an account of Arthur since he was an Englishman and one of the Nine Worthies. The nine are then detailed. The gentlemen then request that he print a version of Arthur, but Caxton replies that many believe him to be a fiction. Here the main theme of the prologue makes its appearance. The proofs of the historical Arthur are then paraded. Caxton does not say that his visitors outlined these proofs, but that is the impression he creates. In fact the information is quite diverse and shows that Caxton had a wide range of interests, even if most of it was picked up at second hand.

When he completed the proofs for the historicity of Arthur he mentioned versions known to him in French, Welsh and English. No details are given, and one may wonder whether he did know anything about these other versions. The statement is too vague to inspire much confidence. At this point he introduces Malory and his translation from French which he has used as the basis of the printed book. This is immediately followed by a brief review of the contents seen from an educational and literary viewpoint, which concludes "herein may be seen noble chyvalrye, curtosye, humanyte, frendlynesse, hardynesse, love, frend-shyp, cowardyse, murdre, hate, vertue and synne. Doo after the good and leve the evyl and it shal brynge you to good fame and renommee." This introduces a new theme in the prologue which stands in many ways in contrast with the first one. For Caxton continues "And for to passe the tyme thys book shal be plesaunte to rede in. But for to gyve fayth and byleve that al is trewe that is conteyned herin, ye be at your lyberte. But al is wryton for our doctryne and for to beware that we falle not to vyce ne synne, but t'excersyse and folowe vertu." This expression of doubt has been interpreted by many as a sign of Caxton's robust commonsense when presented with dubious evidence of Arthur's historicity by credulous nobles. I see it a little differently. His doubt here is a further indication of the fictitious nature of his whole prologue. If he knew that many gentlemen wanted an edition of the Arthurian story because they believed Arthur to be a historical person, he would probably have left it at that. If they had been convinced by their own arguments, Caxton would surely accept the historicity of Arthur as a sufficient promotional aid for he was only interested in selling the book. But he evidently felt that proof of the historicity of Arthur would not be enough to sell such a long work about Arthur and he consequently changed tack. Even if you do not believe in Arthur, he goes on to say, the book is courtly and full of wholesome instruction. For both points a historical Arthur is immaterial. The book is therefore dedicated to "alle noble prynces, lordes and ladyes, gentylmen or gentylwymmen, that desyre to rede or here redde of the noble and joyous hystorye of the grete conquerour and excellent kyng, Kyng Arthur". It is not dedicated to those who were supposed to have asked for it or, as we have seen, to the king. This general dedication may also reflect uncertainty in his mind whether these people will buy it and it, too, smacks of a little desperation on his part. The result is a lack of balance which is unusual in his prologues. But the book was long, the expense great, the times uncertain and the rewards doubtful.

It may be because he also wanted potential purchasers to be aware of the solid courtly fare in it that he decided to be so specific about the book's contents. For they occupy the rest of the prologue. When referring to Malory he gave one review of the book's contents. Now after his dedication he includes yet another general and brief account of the sort of things found in the volume. This concludes with a reference to his division of the story into twenty-one books. He then gives a complete list of each book, what its theme was and how many chapters it contained. This elaboration is not found in his other prologues and may suggest that the Arthur story was less well known than we like to think, which was why Caxton himself seemed so uncertain as to how the book would be received. The description of the contents of each book is modelled on the headings found in the body of the text, and it was a relatively simple job to collect the necessary information.

Caxton then set about making a table of contents. As we have seen, in the text itself the chapters were indicated simply by a number; no heading was provided. But for a table of contents more was needed. So the text had to be gone through to provide a suitable heading which was then entered into the table of contents. This labour was performed after the book was in print, for during its course various errors were discovered. These were chiefly a failure to include all numbers in the sequence of chapter numbering. Book 1 lacks chapters 4, 5 and 26, book 4 chapter 19, book 7 chapter 26, and so on. The compiler added the missing numbers to the previous one in his table so that we get entries like:

> How syr Marhaws justed with syr Gawayn & syr Ewayn and overthrewe them bothe. capitulo xviii and xix

He forgot, however, to do this for I.26. He also put the number 14 against what should have been chapter 13 in book 9, so there appears to be no chapter 13 in that book. That these errors which were discovered in the text during the compilation of the table were not corrected is itself sufficient proof that the text was already in print. The job of compiling the table was arduous and at first sight it seems unnecessary. But it was no doubt done because Caxton wished to stress the interesting nature of the contents.

When he had completed the prologue and table of contents, they were handed to the workshop to be set up. They were put in those two initial gatherings which were then joined to the rest of the book. The edition was now complete. We can only hope that Caxton's promotion was successful; later reprints suggest that it was. In the following century Ascham was able to claim that it had replaced the Bible in general popularity.

15

The Biblical Additions in Caxton's Golden Legend

Although we still lack a critical edition of Caxton's *Golden Legend* or any modern edition of the *Gilte Legende,* several scholars have contributed notable studies on the English versions of the *Legenda Aurea.*[1] As far as Caxton is concerned, these studies have been confined to assessing his personal contributions, to deciding which French and English versions he used, and to discussing how he may have adapted the French, English and Latin texts of the *Golden Legend* which he had in front of him. It has of course also been recognised that a large section of Caxton's printed edition (corresponding to pp. 105-244 of Ellis's edition [2]) was taken from a non-*Legenda* source and that much of this section is based ultimately on the Bible. But nothing has been done to examine this section in detail to determine where Caxton got his material and how he arranged it. This paper is devoted to an investigation of some of the problems involved in this part of the *Golden Legend* in order to provide a basis for further study and also to contribute to our understanding of Caxton's method as editor.

An essential first step is to outline the contents of this section of the *Golden Legend* and to decide what has been taken from the Vulgate and what may have come from elsewhere. In the following review I will give the heading of each section and then assess its relationship to the Vulgate by indicating to what extent Caxton's version differs from the Bible. I shall also quote the passages which appear to have been added by Caxton,[3] refer to non-Biblical material included, and list the non-Biblical sources.

---

[1] *Gilte Legende* is the name used to refer to the earlier English translation of *Legenda Aurea.* For work on *Gilte Legende* see A. Kurvinen, 'Caxton's *Golden Legend* and the Manuscripts of the *Gilte Legende,*' *Neuphilologische Mitteilungen* 60 (1959) 353-75. For work on the *Golden Legend,* see particularly Sister Mary Jeremy, 'Caxton's *Golden Legend* and De Vignai's *Légende Dorée,*' *Medieval Studies* 8 (1946) 97-106, and 'Caxton's *Golden Legend* and Varagine's *Legenda Aurea,*' *Speculum* 21 (1946) 212-21.

[2] F. S. Ellis, *The Golden Legend* (London 1892). Page numbers in parentheses throughout this paper refer to this edition.

[3] It is not always possible to be certain that Caxton added the interpolations ; the matter is discussed later in the paper.

> *Here folowen the storyes of the Byble.*[4]
>
> 1.   *The Lyf of Adam.*
>   *The Sonday of Septuagesme begynneth the storye of the Byble, in whiche is redde the legende and storye of Adam whiche foloweth.*

The account of Adam is based ultimately upon the Bible, but it is in no sense a direct translation. Occasional verses in Latin are given from the Vulgate. Non-Biblical features include:[5] (i) Adam is born in the field of Damask; (ii) the three sins of the serpent; (iii) Jubal is the father of singers who use harp or organ, but 'not of th'ynstrumentis for they were founde longe after' (p. 111); (iv) of Adam's children 'Somme hold opinyon xxx sones and xxx doughtres, and some l of that one and l of that other. We fynde no certeynte of them in the Bible' (p. 112); (v) Seth and the oil of mercy; the story is said to be 'of none auctoryte' (p. 112).

Authorities referred to: Bede (Satan chose a serpent with a woman's face); Methodius (Adam and Eve came from Paradise as virgins); Moses (Abel offered the fattest of his flock to God); Josephus (Jubal's pillar of marble survives; and Adam thought of procreation after Abel's death); and Strabo (Adam did not cohabit with Eve after Abel's death).

> *Here endeth the Lyf of Adam.*
>
> 2.   *Here begynneth the hystorye of Noe.*
>   *The first Sonday in Sexagesme.*

Like the Life of Adam, the account of Noah is based on the Bible but is not a direct translation. The account is shorter than that in the Bible, but it also includes some non-Biblical elements.

Non-Biblical features include: (i) the window of the ark 'whiche that the Hebrews saye was of crystall' (p. 114); (ii) 'And after his deth his sones deled alle the world bytwene hem: Sem had alle Asye, Cham Affryke, and Japhet all Europe. Thus was it departed. Asye is the best part & is as moche as the other two, and that is in the eest. Affryke is the south part & therin is Cartage and many ryche contre; therin ben blew and black men. Cham had that to his part Affrica. The thyrde parte is Europe whiche is in the north and weste; therin is Grece, Rome and Germanye. In Europe regneth now moste the crysten lawe and faith, wherin is many ryche royame. And so was the world departed to the iii sones of Noe' (p. 116).

---

[4] This information has been taken from Ellis's edition, but I have modernized the punctuation.

[5] Only a selection of these features is included, but I have tried to choose the more striking ones.

Authorities referred to: St. Jerome (Methuselah died the same year as the Flood); Jerome, the seventy interpreters, and Methodius (estimates of the length of the first age of man).

Thus endeth the Lyf of Noe.

3. *Here foloweth the Lyf of Abraham.*

The relation of this life to the Vulgate is the same as that of the previous two lives.

Non-Biblical features include: (i) of the Tower of Babel, 'The tour was grete: it was x myle aboute and v M lxxxiiii steppes of height. This Nembroth was the first man that founde mawmetryee and ydolatrye, whiche endured long and yet doth' (p. 117); (ii) 'Now I shal speke of Abram of whom Our Blessid Lady come' (p. 117); (iii) Abraham seeing three men worshipped only one of them, and 'That bytokeneth the Trynyte' (p. 121); (iv) the people of Sodom are denounced more forthrightly; (v) the statue of salt into which Lot's wife was changed survives to this day.

4. *Here begynneth the Lyf of Ysaac with th'istorye of Esau and of Jacob, whiche is redde in the chirche the second Sonday of Lente.*

The opening of this life is abbreviated from the Bible, but after that it tends to follow the Bible closely, though Caxton's text is sometimes a little more expansive.

Non-Biblical features include: (i) after the introduction of the main characters 'This aforsaid is for to brynge in my mater of th'ystorye that is redde, for now foloweth the legende as it is redde in the chirche' (p. 130); (ii) 'This is the tytle of the monumente of Rachel unto this present day' (p. 142); (iii) Isaac died 'in good mynde' (p. 142, cf. Gen. 35.29).

Authorities referred to: 'the mayster of historyes' (Isaac fell into a trance in which he realised that God intended Jacob to have his father's blessing).

Thus endeth th'ystorye of Ysaac and his two sones, Esau and Jacob.
5. *Hyer begynneth th'ystorye of Joseph & his brethern, whiche is red the thirde Sonday in Lente.*

The life follows the Biblical account closely, though several Vulgate chapters are omitted such as Gen. 38 and 48, the latter describing the blessings bestowed on each of Jacob's sons. Pharaoh's dream is not repeated, Caxton's text reading 'Thenne Pharao told to hym his dremes, like as is to fore wreton, of the vii fatte oxen and vii lene, and how the lene devoured the fatte, & in lyke wyse of the eeris' (p. 146).

Authorities referred to: Josephus, *Jewish Antiquities* (the reason which led Joseph to hide his cup in Benjamin's sack).

Thus endeth th'ystorye of Joseph & his brethern.

6. *Hyer next foloweth th'ystorye of Moyses, whiche is redde in the chirche on Myd-Lente Sonday.*

The story follows the order and words of the Biblical account relatively closely, though with abbreviation, additions and a few rearrangements. For example, Exodus 7 is rearranged in Caxton's text, the order of the plagues being more schematized. Thus Caxton's text reads 'This was the first plaghe and vengeance. The seconde was . . . ' (p. 167). Genealogical matter and the laws and customs of the Israelites are generally omitted. Thus Exodus 7 is paraphrased 'Thenne whan Moyses had said to the chyldren how they shold do er they departed, & ete theyr pask lambe & all other cerymonyes, as ben expressyd in the Byble' (p. 169). The Ten Commandments are not repeated, but are dismissed with an 'as fore be wreton' (p. 181). The psalm, *Cantemus Domino* (Ex. 15.1-19), is omitted.

Non-Biblical features include: (i) Moses tramples on crown; (ii) Moses eats burning coal; (iii) Israelites were not affected by the plagues God sent against the Egyptians; (iv) the locusts 'whiche is a maner grete flye, callyd in somme place an adder bolte' (p. 168); (vi) Moses's rod and a pot of manna are in the ark.

Authorities referred to: Josephus, *Jewish Antiquities* (Pharaoh's daughter, Termuthe, loved Moses; she saved him from Pharaoh); 'as doctours saye' (Moses received all preceding history with Ten Commandments).

Here endeth the Lyf and th'ystorye of Moyses.

6a. *Here folowen the Ten comandements of our lawe.*

Inserted in the Life of Moses there is an extended account of the Ten Commandments, quite different from the Biblical version. The Commandments are introduced in the Life of Moses by 'And [God] gaf hym the Comandementis first by spekyng and many cerymonyes as ben rehersed in the Byble, whiche is not requysyte to be wreton here. But the Ten Comandements every man is bounden to knowe' (p. 175).

7. *Th'ystorye of Josue.*

An extremely brief paraphrase of the Biblical account of Joshua. It ends : 'And dyverse dukes after hym juged and demed Israhel, of whom ben noble hystoryes as of Jepte, Gedeon & Sampson, whiche I passe over unto th'ystoryes of the kynges, whiche is redde in holy chyrche fro the fyrst Sonday after Trynyte Sonday unto the first Sonday of August. And in the moneth of August is redde the Book of Sapience, & in the moneth of Septembre ben redde th'ystoryes of Job, of Thobye, and of Judith, and in Octobre the hystorye of the Machabeis; and in Novembre the Book of Ezechiel and his visions; and in Decembre the hystorye of Advent; and the Book of Ysaye unto Crystemasse. And after the Fest of Epyphanye unto Septuagesme ben red th'epistles of Paule. And this is the rewle of the Temporal thurgh the yere &c' (p. 186).

8. *Th'ystorye of Saul.*
   The first Sonday after Trynyle Sonday unto the first Sonday of the moneth of August is redde the Book of Kynges.

The Biblical account is followed closely, though there are considerable omissions. The story opens 'This hystorye maketh mencion . . . ,' and then follows 1 Samuel. Alterations include changing much direct speech to indirect. Omissions include Anna's psalm (1 Sam. 1.28-2.10), which is dismissed with the words 'and ther made this psalme which is one of the Canticles *Exultavit cor meum in Domino et exaltatum est cornu meum in Deo meo,* and so forth all the remenaunt of that psalme' (p. 187). Twice it is added that Samuel served in the temple 'in a surplys' (pp. 187-8); it is also mentioned that the Philistines made seats of skin 'to sytte softe' (p. 189). The translator has conflated two verses of the Vulgate to give that Heli 'myght not see the lanterne of God til it was quenchyd and put out (p. 187, cf. 1 Sam. 3. 2-3).

> *Thus endeth the Lyf of Saul, whiche was first kynge upon Israhel, & for disobedyence of Godes comandement was slayn and his heyres never regned long after.*

9. *Th'ystorye of David.*
   Here foloweth how David regned after Saul & governed Israhel—shortly taken out of the Bible, the most historyal maters and but litil towched.

As the heading says, the account is taken from the Bible, though it is considerably shortened. There are two major additions: (i) the famous passage about David's penance;[6] (ii) at the end: 'This David was an holy man and made the holy psawter, whiche is an holy booke, and is conteyned therin the olde lawe and newe lawe. He was a grete prophete, for he prophecyed the comyng of Cryst, his natyvyte, his passyon and resurrection, and also his ascencion, and was grete with God. Yet God wold not suffre hym to bylde a temple for hym, for he had shedde mans blood. But God said to hym his sone that shold regne after hym shold be a man pesyble, and he shold bylde the temple to God. And whan David had regned xl yere kynge of Jherusalem over Juda & Israhel, he deyed in good mynde and was buryed with his faders in the cyte of David' (p. 210).

---

[6] Not given in full here because it is so well known ; see W. J. B. Crotch, *The Prologues and Epilogues of William Caxton* (EETS 176; London 1928) 74.

Thus endeth the Lyf of David, seconde kynge of Israhel.

10. Th'ystorye of Salomon.

A shortened version of the Biblical account. The opening is a paraphrase of some aspects of the Bible: 'After David regned Salomon, his sone, whiche was in the begynnyng a good man and walked in the wayes and lawes of God. And all the kynges aboute hym made pees with hym, & was kynge confermed, obeyed and pesible in his possession, and acordyng to hys faders comandement dyde justice' (p. 210).

Other additions to or adaptations of the Bible include: (i) About the temple: 'and for to wryte the curiosyte and werke of the temple, and the necessaryes, the tables & cost that was don in gold, sylver and laton, it passeth my connynge to exprese and englysshe them. Ye that ben clerkys may see it in the second Book of Kynges and the seconde Book of Paralipomenon. It is wondre to here the costes and expencis that was made in that temple, but I passe over' (p. 213); (ii) 'What shal I aldaye wryte of the rychesses, glorye and magnyfycence of kynge Salamon? It was so grete that it cannot be expressyd, for ther was never none lyke to fore hym ne never shal none come after hym lyke unto hym. He made the Book of Parables, conteynyng xxxi chapytres, the Booke of the Canticles, the Book of Ecclesiastes, conteynyng xii chapytres, and the Booke of Sapience, conteynyng xix chapytres' (p. 216); (iii) concerning Solomon's worship of heathen gods as a result of his marriage to non-Jewish wives: 'It is said, but I fynde it not in the Byble, that Salamon repentyd hym moche of thys synne of ydolatrye, and dyde moche penance therfor, for he lete hym be drawe thurgh Jherusalem and bete hym self wyth roddes and scorgys that the blood folowed in the syght of alle the peple' (p. 217).

Thus endeth the Lyf of Salamon.

11. Th'ystorye of Roboas.

A short account which opens by following the Bible literally, then goes over to paraphrase, and finally breaks off with: 'And here I leve alle th'ystorye and make an ende of Booke of Kynges for thys tyme &c. For ye that lyste to knowe how every kyng regned after other, ye may fynde it in the fyrst chapytre of Saynt Mathew, whyche is redde on Crystemas day in the mornyng to fore Te Deum, whyche is the genelagye of Our Lady' (p. 218).

12. Here foloweth th'ystorye of Job, red on the first Sonday of Septembre.

A literal translation of the beginning and end of the Book of Job. The central section (3-42.7), the discussion between Job and his three friends, is passed over by 'Thenne after that Job and they talked and spoken to gydre of hys sorowe & myserye, of whyche Seynt Gregory hath made a grete book, callyd the Morallys of Seynt Gregory, whiche is a noble book and a grete werk. But I passe over all tho maters and retorne unto the ende how God restored Job agayn to prosperyte' (p. 220).

> *Thus endeth the storye of Job.*

13. *Here foloweth th'ystorye of Tobye, whyche is red the thyrde Sondaye of Septembre.*

A literal and complete translation of this book. Two minor additions explain words: (i) 'irreprehensyble, that is to saye wythout repreef' (p. 230, cf. 10.13 *irreprehensibilem*); (ii) 'the sones of hys nevewis, that is the sones of the sones of hys sone, yonge Thobye' (p. 233, cf. 14.1 *nepotum suorum*). One verse (14.7) is misunderstood: the Latin says the desert will flower again, but Caxton's text reads 'All the londe therof shal be fulfyllid with deserte' (p. 233).

> *Thus endeth the hystorye of Thobye th'older and of hys sone, Thobye the yonger.*

14. *Here begynneth th'ystorye of Judith, whiche is redde the last Sonday of Octobre.*

A close, but abbreviated, translation. Judith's prayer (9.2-10.1) and the concluding psalm of triumph (16.3-21) are omitted. In this latter instance the opening verse is quoted in Latin and the rest is dismissed with '& so forth.'

There is no conclusion for either the Life of Judith or the group of Old Testament stories. The next passage starts immediately with the Life of St. Andrew.

In the interpolation in the Life of Rehoboam it is implied that this whole section of the *Golden Legend* is following the Temporale, that part of the breviary and missal which contains the daily offices in the order of the ecclesiastical year as distinct from those proper to saints' days in the Sanctorale. This perhaps provides us with a clue as to why Caxton included this additional section and why it is arranged in the way it is. The *Golden Legend* is a book which contains sermons suitable for reading on various days throughout the year. It is divided into three sections : (i) the episodes from the life of Christ; (ii) the early history of mankind; and (iii) the lives of the saints. The first two correspond to the New and the Old Testaments respectively; and it is quite possible that the second section was introduced to parallel the first, and that the two of them together formed a contrast as well as a parallel with the third section. Such an idea could easily have occurred to Caxton from a consideration of Mirk's *Festial* (as in MS Harley 2381) or any of the combined

Temporales and Sanctorales which were in existence at that time. If Caxton intended to complete the Temporale before going on to the Sanctorale, we can appreciate why he followed the French version of the *Legenda Aurea* instead of the Latin or early English ones. The French translation had the lives of the saints and the episodes from the life of Christ arranged in two different sections, whereas the Latin and English texts have the two sections combined so that the book follows the ecclesiastical year only once. By taking the French as his model, Caxton was able to include a third, comparable section. If he had followed the pattern in the other two versions, he would have had to put each story from the Old Testament in its appropriate place in the ecclesiastical calendar and the thread of the historical narrative would have been lost. But Caxton's arrangement did lead him into one difficulty. Sections (i) and (iii), whether arranged individually as in the French or combined as in the Latin and early English, start at the beginning of the ecclesiastical year with Advent and St. Andrew. If, however, one wants to preserve the narrative continuity, it is more sensible to begin the Old Testament stories with the Creation and to continue the chronological sequence. This meant commencing at Septuagesima with the result that this section does not fit in as comfortably as it might with the other two sections. Caxton was evidently not so worried about the general framework provided that the thematic relationship was clear enough, as indeed it is.

This disregard for the pattern set up in the main body of the *Legenda Aurea* can also be seen in the individual stories of this section, for they are hardly independent accounts which can be read in isolation. In some cases they have to be understood as part of a larger whole in order to be meaningful. The saints' lives in the *Legenda Aurea* follow a definite pattern, with the etymology of the name, the life and then the miracles forming the three major parts. This pattern is less clear in the episodes from the life of Christ, though even these remain completely independent sections which could be read aloud in church. But in the Caxtonian additions certain stories are unsuitable for reading aloud because they do not form a complete unit. The accounts of Joshua and Rehoboam are good examples. Furthermore, many of the stories, such as those of Saul and David, are so interconnected that they have to be read together in order to make the narrative meaningful. In fact these stories are much better suited to personal reading than to public declamation — and this may have been Caxton's intention. Nevertheless it does tend to undermine the original character of the *Legenda Aurea*. Instead of sermons which are to be read on certain days, we have a continuous narrative, parts of which are allocated to various days of the ecclesiastical year though this division has no bearing on the actual stories. We may note also that this central section contains those parts of the Old Testament which are narrative, to the detriment of those which are hortatory, admonitory, legal, etc. This has been carried out even within certain individual stories such as that of Job, in which the central discussion between Job and his three friends is omitted. We may assume that Caxton was interested in simple narrative rather than speculation; an interest which we can trace not only in the other sections of the *Golden Legend*, but also in his other translations. This question of the narrative content of Caxton's addition raises one further point, namely why Caxton stopped at Judith. In his summary of the Temporale he mentions that Maccabees is read in October, Ezekiel in November, the story of Advent and Isaiah in December, and the Epistles of Paul after that. The implication is that he was going to translate these books in order to complete the Temporale. Yet he failed to do this. Although we may accept that he may have thought that parts of the New Testament were unsuitable here, there seems to be no reason why he should not have included other Old Testament books. We could suppose that he perhaps thought Ezekiel and Isaiah lacking in narrative quality, but this is not a reason which would apply to Maccabees. After all, Judas Maccabeus was one of the Nine Worthies and the other two, Joshua and David, are both included in Caxton's additions (*supra*, Nos. 7 and 9), though Joshua is somewhat cursorily dismissed. Caxton in his prologues to the *Siege and Conquest of Jerusalem* and *King Arthur* speaks highly of all three of them and we know he was interested in heroic stories. It may be, then, that he got tired of his self-imposed task and so failed to get any further than Judith. The brevity of some of the later tales could indicate a slackening of determination, which may have resulted in the abandonment of the complete project. We know also that Caxton had some difficulties with the preparation of this edition.

There is one more general point I should like to mention before embarking on a more detailed investigation of the additions. It has become almost a cliché in Caxtonian scholarship that Caxton wanted to make a translation of the whole Bible, but was afraid to do so because of the controversy over the Lollards.[7] Thus he ended up by translating some of the Bible which he hid within the *Golden Legend*. This view is untenable in my opinion. We have already seen that Caxton took over the Old Testament stories to form a parallel to the New Testament ones, and that together they follow the readings in the Temporale. There is no question here of wanting to make a translation of the whole Bible, but merely completing a book by using the Bible as a source. And we know that the *Golden Legend* was a very popular book at the end of the Middle Ages, and if Caxton wanted to 'hide' his translation of the Bible, he certainly chose a very unsuitable place to hide it. Nor is there any evidence that Caxton attempted to hide the translation. Although it is true

---

[7] For example, C. C. Butterworth, *The Literary Lineage of the King James Bible* (Philadelphia 1941) 52.

that he does not mention the translations from the Bible in his prologue or epilogue, the heading of the Biblical section states quite baldly that the stories are drawn from the Bible and many of the individual headings make reference to their Biblical origins. It is surely unlikely that Caxton would have drawn attention to something he was trying to hide. Finally, there is no proof whatsoever that Caxton intended or even wanted to make a translation of the Bible in its entirety. Modern scholarship has shown that he produced books which were fashionable at the Burgundian and English courts or else books which were to be used in the services of the Church.[8] The English Bible falls into neither category, so that it is not a book which is likely to have appealed to Caxton. We may accept that Caxton never intended to translate the Bible and merely included a section of it in the *Golden Legend* in order to satisfy a particular need.

Let us now consider the text of the additions. The earlier stories can be distinguished from the later ones, those including and following that of Joshua, in that they all contain references to non-Biblical sources, such as Josephus, Jerome, Methodius, etc. For these stories there is thus a choice between assuming Caxton had access to the actual sources mentioned or that he took the references from some intermediate source. There can be no hesitation in affirming that the latter is the only acceptable hypothesis. Quite apart from the improbability of Caxton's having had access to all the named sources there is also the established fact that Caxton tended to borrow widely from the sources known to him. We would have expected him to use the original sources more completely if he had access to them. And when Caxton himself does refer to a book, as he does to St. Gregory's *Morals* in the later part, he merely mentions the title without quoting from the book or using it as an authority for a given statement. So Caxton must have had a non-Biblical source for the early tales, a source which he cannot be shown to have used for the later part of the Biblical additions. And when we compare the later with the earlier tales we may note further differences than this variation of source. It is the later section which contains tales which have been drastically abbreviated, such as those of Joshua and Rehoboam. It is here also that one finds those general references to Biblical composition or the Church's calendar. The composition of the Temporale is mentioned in the Life of Joshua, the authorship of Proverbs, Ecclesiastes, etc. in the Life of Solomon. Finally it is here that one finds the personal additions such as the remarks of Sir John Capons on David's penance, the inability of the author to describe the temple, and the suggestion that the genealogy of the Jewish kings can be found in St. Matthew. To my mind these factors set off the second part of the Biblical additions from the first part and suggest that Caxton had no other written

---

[8] See N. F. Blake, 'William Caxton: His Choice of Texts,' *Anglia* 83 (1965) 289-307.

source for this second part than the Bible. Nevertheless there are certain
similarities in phrasing and in the interpolations found in either part. Thus
the addition in the Life of Adam, 'Somme hold opinyon xxx sones and xxx
doughtres, and some l of that one and l of that other. We fynde no certeynte
of them in the Bible' echoes the addition in the Life of Solomon 'It is said,
but I fynde it not in the Byble, that Salamon repentyd hym moche of thys
synne of ydolatrye.' This similarity means, I think, that Caxton has also
added a few comments while arranging the first part for the press, which is no
more than he did throughout the rest of the *Golden Legend*. It may be suggested
then that Caxton had a source for the early Old Testament lives, which though
based on the Bible had made use of non-Biblical and apocryphal material.
He used this source with a few of his own modifications for those lives up to
and including that of Moses. When this source was finished, Caxton went
over to translating directly from the Bible. This meant that he tended to reduce those parts of it which were not fairly straightforward narrative and that
he included more personal asides. It is much more his own work than the
earlier tales. It is possible also, though we shall never be certain of this point,
that Caxton began to tire of his translation and brought it to a close earlier
than he had originally anticipated.

It is time now to consider the source that he used for the tales in the first
part of his Biblical additions. Caxton had three versions of the *Legenda Aurea*
when he made his translation, one each in Latin, French, and English. His
Latin text has not been identified, but his French version must have been
Vignai's translation as represented in MS British Museum Stowe 50-51 and
two printed books. For the English text he used a copy of the earlier English translation, the *Gilte Legende*. Of the extant manuscripts of the *Gilte
Legende*, MS British Museum Additional 35,298 is the closest to Caxton's
text and may indeed have been the one he used.[9] A review of the French versions has revealed that they do not contain any additional material which
Caxton could have used for these Biblical stories. But the *Gilte Legende* does
contain some non-*Legenda* material at the end of those manuscripts which
are intact. This material includes two stories which are called 'The Lives
of Adam and Eve' and 'The Five Wiles of Pharaoh.' It was suggested by
Wells that it was from the *Gilte Legende* that Caxton took the Biblical additions which form the second part of his *Golden Legend*.[10] However, a comparison of Caxton's text with that in Add. 35,298 shows that the two versions
are very different, though they cover much the same ground. A small example
should make this clear:

---

[9] See particularly the articles referred to in n. 1 above.

[10] J. E. Wells, *A Manual of the Writings in Middle English, 1050-1400* (New Haven 1916)
320.

Add. 35,298: After that many dayes whan Cayme shuld offre of the frutis of the erth and of his yeftis to the Lorde God, and Abel his brother offrid and vsid to offre the first begotyn thyng of his flok & of the fattist of them, & oure Lorde hym silfe behilde to Abelle and to his yeftis, and also vnto Cayme & to his yeftis he behilde not. And for this cause Cayme was wroth with his brother gretely [fol. 163ᵛ].

Caxton: Trouthe it is, after many dayes Cayn and Abel offrid sacrefyse and yeftes vnto God. . . . Cayn offrid fruytes, for he was a ploughman and teliar of erthe, & Abel offrid mylke & the first of the lambes, Moyses saith of the fattest of the flocke. And God behelde the yeftes of Abel, for he and his sacrefyses were acceptable to our Lord, and as to Cayn & his sacrefyses, God behelde hem not, for they were not to hym acceptable . . . [p. 110].

The difference is such that Caxton cannot have used Add. 35,298 as his source for the Biblical passages in his *Golden Legend*. All manuscripts of the *Gilte Legende* which are complete at the end have the same stories as those found in Add. 35,298. From this it can be assumed that, if Caxton did not actually use this manuscript of the *Gilte Legende*, the one he did use contained an identical account. One can of course never rule out the possibility that Caxton's manuscript may have had a different ending — but the balance of probability is certainly very much against it. In other words, it looks as though Caxton had certain apocryphal accounts of Adam and Eve and Moses available at the conclusion of his manuscript of the *Gilte Legende* and that he rejected these versions in favour of another. This conclusion is significant in that it confirms the view stated above that Caxton did have a non-Biblical source for the early Old Testament books. It is very unlikely that he would have rejected one source available to him in the *Gilte Legende* in order to compose his own account from various sources. That Caxton rejected the stories at the end of the *Gilte Legende* implies that he had another source available and that his preference for this other source may be accounted for by the fact that it was fuller. It contained more Old Testament stories than the *Gilte Legende* and therefore its adaptation would have caused Caxton less trouble.

The points raised at the end of the preceding paragraph seem to me also to refute those who think Caxton composed the Biblical additions from the Bible and Trevisa's translation of Higden's *Polychronicon*, which Caxton was working on at the same time as the *Golden Legend*. Thus Butler wrote: 'the great *Polycronicon* is chokefull of legendary matter, on which Caxton did not hesitate to draw.'[11] If we accepted Butler's hypothesis, we should have to explain why Caxton ignored the stories in the *Gilte Legende* in order to make his own composition. More importantly, there is no close verbal parallel between pieces in the *Polychronicon* and the *Golden Legend* dealing with the

---

[11] P. Butler, *Legenda Aurea, Légende dorée, Golden Legend* (Baltimore 1899) 80.

same episode,[12] and there are also a great many passages in the *Polychronicon* which Caxton could have used but he did not. Butler further suggested that in addition to using the *Polychronicon* Caxton may have had access to the Life of Adam found in Oxford MSS Douce 15, Rawlinson C 499 and Queen's College 213.[13] Again the similarity between Caxton's version and these manuscripts is not close; and if he had used this life from one of these manuscripts, we would still be left with the problem of where he got the material for the other lives in this group. The lives in the earlier part seem to be fairly uniform in tone and in their method of composition so that it is most likely that Caxton took them all from the same source.

This source that I have suggested Caxton used for the early Old Testament lives has not yet been identified, though this does not mean that it never existed. In the past most scholars have been content to think of this part of the *Golden Legend* as being principally drawn from the Bible and so the necessity for looking for a source has not generally been recognized. I have examined such material as has been available to me in England without result, but, since the possible sources could well be widely scattered, the material I have seen probably represents only a small part of the whole. However, there is one final point which I have not yet discussed and which might give us an additional clue about the nature of this source, namely in what language the source was written. This is a topic which is fraught with many difficulties; consequently my remarks here should be considered as preliminary. The source could have been an independent work or it could have been attached to one of the texts of the *Legenda Aurea* that Caxton was working from. As we have seen already, it did not form part of his English or French versions. But the Latin text he used has not been identified. Some Latin texts of the *Legenda Aurea*, such as Balliol College Oxford MS 228, have a version of the *vita* of Adam, so that it is possible that other Latin manuscripts had more Old Testament stories than this single *vita*. Unfortunately, there are so many Latin manuscripts and incunabula of the *Legenda Aurea* which have never been seriously studied that this suggestion must remain only a possibility. Until a full-scale investigation of the Latin manuscripts is made, we shall not be able to say with confidence whether Caxton used a Latin source attached to his text of the *Legenda Aurea* or not. There are, however, a few indications that the source Caxton used may not have been in Latin. Caxton was a very conservative translator, who tended, as was usual among fifteenth-century translators, to take over the words in the original he was translating and give them an English form. Thus his translations from French

---

[12] Cf. Caxton's account of Nembroth (p. 117) with that in the *Polychronicon* (ed. Babington, 1869, Vol. II, pp. 249-50).

[13] Butler 81.

have many French words and those from Dutch many Dutch ones. His own vocabulary was not particularly extensive.[14] Hence one would not expect to find many unusual French words in a Caxtonian translation from a Latin source. There are, however, a few words of French origin in the early stories which might be said to fit into this category. Thus *copulae* (Gen. 29.27) appears in Caxton's text as 'coplement and maryage' (p. 134). *Couplement* is a word not recorded in the *Oxford English Dictionary* before 1548 and it is not recorded in the *Middle English Dictionary* at all. Since Caxton is hardly likely to have introduced the word into English without the authority of a source, one could conclude that his source was not Latin. Similarly *foedus* (Gen. 31.44) appears as 'faste leghe and confedersy' (p. 138). The form of the word *confedersy* is somewhat unusual and is very rarely recorded, the more usual Middle English form being *confederacy*.[15] If this form has not arisen as a result of a typographical mistake, it must have come from Old French or Anglo-Norman. Another example is the word *commise* in the doublet 'doo ne commyse' (p. 122) translating *facere* (Gen. 19.7),[16] which is a word found only in the latter half of the fifteenth century. There are further examples of French words like this, but they are not numerous. They are certainly insufficient to provide proof that it was a French source that Caxton was using, though there are perhaps enough to make it unlikely that it was indeed a Latin source that he used for the early Old Testament stories. A suitable solution might be that Caxton was following an English source based on the Vulgate, the author of which was more prepared to use French loanwords on his own initiative than Caxton was. Such a deduction can at this stage be regarded as only speculative, since it is based on what is merely a preliminary investigation of the language. A complete investigation of the language of the Biblical additions in the *Golden Legend* is certainly a desideratum. For the time being it may be accepted as a working hypothesis that Caxton used an English source, as this helps to explain why he should have rejected the two Biblical stories at the end of the *Gilte Legende* and to account for one or two unusual English words such as *adderbolt*[17] which would be exceptional in a Caxtonian translation. If there was such an English source as I have suggested, it would have been independent of the *Gilte Legende*, since, as we have seen, Caxton's manuscript of that work contained 'The lives of Adam and Eve' and 'The Five Wiles

---

[14] See above, chapter 10, pp. 137-47.

[15] The form *confedersy* is not recorded at all in OED, which records only *confederacy* and *confederey*; but MED records it as an alternative spelling coming from Anglo-Norman.

[16] *Commise* is recorded in MED from 1450, and OED refers to some Caxtonian examples which occur in texts translated from French. The word entered English in the late fifteenth century as a result of translations from French, but it never became common.

[17] *Adderbolt*. The example from the *Golden Legend* is the earliest quoted in OED; no form is recorded in MED.

of Pharaoh.' It would be most probable that this source was part of a Temporale itself, many of which exist from the Middle English period either alone or together with a Sanctorale.

The preceding paragraphs have been designed to investigate how much of the Biblical additions Caxton took from another source and to indicate what the nature of that source may have been. Now we may turn to consider briefly the remaining stories which are based directly on the Bible. This other group of stories consists of direct translations from the Bible and some interpolations which can almost certainly be attributed to Caxton. There is nothing here to suggest the use of another source. As far as the Bible translation itself is concerned, it could be thought that it came about in one of three ways: (i) Caxton made the translation from the Vulgate; (ii) Caxton adapted an existing translation of the Bible; or (iii) the translation was part of the same source which Caxton used for the earlier Old Testament stories. The third possibility can be ruled out because the two groups are so different: the first containing references to a variety of sources, the second being a straight translation of the Vulgate. The two methods of composition are very different. The second possibility is that Caxton took his translation from one which was already in existence. The Wycliffite translations were available, but a comparison of these with Caxton's text reveals that their language differs so much that one may dismiss this possibility. Their similarities arise from their both translating the same work, the Vulgate, but their choice of words is often quite divergent.[18] Other English translations of the Bible may have been available in the fifteenth century. Caxton himself mentions a translation by Trevisa in his preface to the *Polychronicon*, and since this book was being prepared for the press at the same time as the *Golden Legend*, it could be imagined that he had access to Trevisa's translation at this time. Unfortunately, we no longer have an extant translation by Trevisa, and scholars have varied in their interpretations of Caxton's evidence. The latest investigator has suggested that Trevisa was involved in the production of the Wycliffite Bible rather than an independent translation.[19] If so, there could be no question of Caxton's having used it here. Although Professor Fowler's arguments are not entirely convincing, we may agree that there is little proof that there were separate translations of the Bible available in the fifteenth century other than the Wycliffite one. Consequently, we may accept it that Caxton made the translation of the later Old Testament stories himself, at least until such time as we acquire more evidence about Trevisa's translation. This may also be considered the most likely solution in the light of an argu-

---

[18] For an example see Butterworth (*cit. supra* n. 7) 255-68.

[19] D. C. Fowler, 'New Light on John Trevisa,' *Traditio* 18 (1962) 289-317, and 'John Trevisa and the English Bible,' *Modern Philology* 58 (1960-61) 81-98.

ment put forward earlier. There are signs that the later stories have been hurriedly done and curtailed in extent as though Caxton was tiring of his translating activities. But if he was using an English translation, there would have been less need for him to reduce some of the stories so drastically.

The conclusions of this study of the Biblical additions in Caxton's *Golden Legend* should be regarded as preliminary, because so much work remains to be done on the *Legenda Aurea*. This article has tried to point out the problems and how they might be answered without being able to provide the complete answers. In brief, it looks as though Caxton had access to a collection of apocryphal stories about the early Old Testament personages up to and including Moses. This collection of stories, probably part of an existing Temporale, which may have been in English and which was ultimately based on the Vulgate, has not yet been identified. While adapting it for inclusion in the *Golden Legend*, Caxton decided to add other Old Testament stories, which he translated from the Vulgate himself, by simply following the historical narrative of the Bible. Although some of our conclusions must remain tentative, the investigation nevertheless has given us some further information on Caxton and his method of editing. In his prologue he mentioned that he had ordered the contents of the *Golden Legend* differently from his English version, though he gives no reason for this change.[20] It is now clear that the major reason must have been the desire to include the additional stories with least trouble to himself. Furthermore, the inclusion of the Biblical narrative has raised the question of Caxton's tact as editor, because the additions, particularly those in the later group, are very different in tone and approach from the saints' lives which form the major part of the *Golden Legend*. The book has been transformed under Caxton's editorship, and although it has become more inclusive, it is also less homogeneous. The change was not necessarily one for the better. Finally, this investigation has added one more source to the list of texts Caxton had available when he prepared the *Golden Legend* for the press. In his prologue Caxton refers to the three versions of the *Legenda Aurea* he had. But he also had a Latin life of St. Rocke as well as the Vulgate and the unidentified source which he used for the early Old Testament stories. This number of sources is probably only equalled by the 'Liber Ultimus' of his *Polychronicon* among his printed books. It can only increase our respect for Caxton's industry and perseverance. At the same time, we may note that although the task was arduous, it was also self-imposed. He could merely have printed the *Gilte Legende* without worrying about the foreign versions; and this is clearly what his contemporaries expected him to do, as

---

[20] Crotch (*supra*, n. 6) 72-3: 'which I have ordryd otherwyse than the sayd Englysshe legende is, which was so to fore made.'

Caxton says in his prologue.[21] The difficulties about which he informs us in the prologue were to some extent of his own making, though, as I have suggested elsewhere, they may have been aggravated by the political conditions of the time.[22] There is evidence which suggests that Caxton was spurred on by a desire for inclusiveness. He did not like to pass over material which was available to him, even if it meant conflating the various texts he had.[23] The result was often that he included conflicting accounts of various events.[24] This wish to make use of all the accessible material was no doubt the driving force behind that fusion of the various sources which form his edition of the *Golden Legend*. The result is not a structurally satisfying whole, for the joints are still visible, but it enables us to get a glimpse of the working habits of a fifteenth-century editor: and it is this which makes the *Golden Legend* one of the most important texts which Caxton issued from his press.

---

[21] Crotch 72: 'ageynst me here myght somme persones saye that thys legende hath be translated tofore, and trouthe it is.'

[22] N. F. Blake, 'Investigations into the Prologues and Epilogues by William Caxton,' *Bulletin of the John Rylands Library* 49 (1966-67) 36 ff.

[23] Kurvinen (*cit. supra* n. 1), and T. F. Dunn, *The Manuscript Study of Caxton's Second Edition of the Canterbury Tales* (Chicago 1940).

[24] As for example in his account of the death of Richard II in the 'Liber Ultimus' of the *Polychronicon.*

16

William Caxton's Reynard the Fox and his
Dutch Orginal

IT is natural that the bulk of research on *Van den Vos Reynaert*
should be carried out in Holland and among the most prominent of the Dutch scholars in this field for many years was
Professor J. W. Muller. His critical editions and commentaries
are still standard reading for all who are interested in the development of the Reynard story, although the Dutch versions are now
available in a diplomatic edition with parallel texts edited by
W. Gs. Hellinga.[1] Yet the results of this research have an important
bearing on English literature, for, as is well known, Caxton translated a version of *Reynaert* into English which he printed in 1481.
Consequently Caxton's translation has been seized upon by
Dutch scholars as an important witness in their attempt to elucidate the textual history of *Van den Vos Reynaert*. The results so
achieved, which have important bearings on such problems as
when Caxton started translating and how he went about his translations, have perhaps been accepted too readily by other scholars
both in England and elsewhere. In my opinion the reasoning
behind Muller's arguments has not always been fully appreciated
and it is time that the whole problem of Caxton's source was re-
examined.

But before a start is made on a discussion of this sort, it is
well to be clear about the relationship and probable dates of the
various manuscript and printed versions of the Reynard story in
the Low Countries.[2] The earliest extant Flemish text is a poem of

[1] W. Gs. Hellinga, *Van den Vos Reynaerde : I Teksten* (Zwolle, 1952).
[2] Somewhat fuller accounts in English can be found in D. B. Sands, *The History
of Reynard the Fox* (Harvard and London, 1960), pp. 14-30, and W. T. H. Jackson,
The Literature of the Middle Ages (New York, 1960), pp. 328-53.

about 4,000 lines known as *Reynaert I* (RI).   This poem which
is largely based on the first branche of the French *Roman de
Renart* was composed in East Flanders about 1250.   The manuscripts mention two poets, Willem and Arnout, as the authors.   In
one manuscript it states that Willem continued the work of Arnout,
so that some scholars have suggested that Arnout should be
identified with Pierre of St. Cloud, one of the authors of the
Roman de Renart.   In the second half of the fourteenth century
a second poem, known as *Reynaert II* (RII), was written in West
Flanders.   This poem is based on RI, but it is almost twice the
length, for the poet has added a great deal of material not necessarily connected with the Reynard story as well as didactic and satiric
elements.   Then a prose version of the story was printed by
Gerard Leeu at Gouda in 1479 (P) and this version was reprinted
with one or two minor alterations at Delft in 1485.   Subsequent
versions, all different, were printed at Amsterdam (1487), Lübeck
(1498) and Antwerp (1564).

Caxton's edition of *Reynard the Fox* (RF), a prose version,
was printed in 1481.   As Caxton himself says that he translated
it from the Dutch, it follows that he must have used a Dutch text
extant and available in 1481.   He must, therefore, have translated the Gouda edition, one of the poetic versions such as RII or
a version no longer extant.   But even a cursory comparison of
RF with the Dutch texts shows that he must have been using
P or a version closely related to it.   It will be sufficient to mention
one point.   The table of contents in the Dutch versions appears
for the first time in P and was clearly composed for the prose
version of the story.   This table is translated fairly closely by
Caxton at the beginning of RF.   No one can any longer doubt
that he must have been following either a copy of P itself or
the manuscript version, no longer extant, used by Leeu in the preparation of his edition.[1]   Scholars are not agreed as to whether
there was in fact a prose version earlier than P.   Martin was of
the opinion that Leeu probably wrote the prose version himself or

[1] An earlier suggestion that Caxton might have used another source was convincingly disproved by D. B. Sands, " William Blades' Comment on Caxton's
' Reynard the Fox ' : The Genealogy of an Error ", *Notes and Queries*, cxcix
(1954), 50-51.

had it written for him shortly before he printed it and for that specific purpose.[1] Muller,[2] however, contended that RII was turned into prose by a clerk in the earlier part of the fifteenth century and that this version was probably copied many times during the course of the century. Finally a copy of it came into Leeu's hands, which he then used as a basis for his printed version of 1479. It is even possible, Muller thought, that there was a printed version earlier than Leeu's which has since completely disappeared without leaving any trace.[3] Muller goes on to argue that Caxton did not use Leeu's version of 1479, but that he translated the story from a manuscript of the prose version or from the earlier printed book.[4]

Muller's reasons, which we shall have to discuss fully, can be briefly stated as follows : (i) There are isolated instances where RF and RII agree against P.   (ii) There are many examples in RF which show that Caxton did not understand the Dutch text completely. As he spent thirty years in the Low Countries he must have become fluent in Dutch by the time he returned to England. Therefore these mistakes indicate that the bulk of the translation must have been completed when he was still a young man, towards the beginning of his long stay in Holland, i.e. before 1450. (iii) It would be much easier for Caxton to obtain a Dutch manuscript in Bruges during his long stay there than it would be for him to obtain a copy of a Dutch book in London between 1479 and 1481. As a result of Muller's work later

[1] E. Martin, *Reinaert, Willems Gedicht Van den Vos Reinaerde und die Umarbeitung und Fortsetzung Reinaerts Historie* (Paderborn, 1874), p. xxii.

[2] J. W. Muller and H. Logeman, *Die Hystorie van Reynaert die Vos, naar den druk van 1479, vergeleken met William Caxton's Engelsche vertaling* (Zwolle, 1892), pp. xi ff. It is not clear how much of this work was contributed by each of the authors, but as Muller reaffirmed the views expressed in this edition in his *Van den Vos Reinaerde* (Leiden, 1939), p. 49, I have for the sake of convenience attributed the views expressed to him alone. It will be understood that by Muller I mean the work edited jointly by Muller and Logeman.

[3] As almost happened, for example, to the assumed edition of *Reynard the Fox* printed by Wynkyn de Worde in the fifteenth or early sixteenth century. See E. Gordon Duff, *Fifteenth Century English Books* (London : Bibliographical Society, 1917), p. 100.

[4] Op. cit. p. xv. This view was reaffirmed by Muller in his *Van den Vos Reinaerde*, p. 49.

scholars who have written on Caxton or the Reynard story have been unable to agree on what source Caxton used. Some have favoured the Gouda edition, others a manuscript version ; and several have been content not to come to any conclusion in the matter.[1] But since his time nobody has bothered to examine his arguments, so let us now proceed to a detailed discussion of them.

Muller lists nine passages where he thinks RF shows a marked similarity with RII against P.[2] A few of these are so obviously doubtful cases that it hardly seems worthwhile to discuss them in detail here.[3] There are, however, four examples to which Muller attaches particular importance. Two of these concern omissions in P which are filled in RF. Muller claims that the words or phrases in RF not found in P are identical with those in

---

[1] For example H. R. Plomer, *William Caxton* (London and Boston, 1925), p. 120, F. S. Ellis, *The History of Reynard the Fox* (London, 1897), p. viii, and W. Foerste, " Von Reinaerts Historie zum Reinke de Vos ", *Münstersche Beiträge zur niederdeutschen Philologie*, vi (1960), 107-8, definitely accept the view that Caxton used an earlier manuscript ; but Sands in both " William Blades' Comment on ' Reynard the Fox ': The Genealogy of an Error ", op. cit. pp. 50-51, and *The History of Reynard the Fox*, p. 4 and *passim*, accepts that Caxton used the Gouda edition. S. K. Workman, *Fifteenth Century Translation as an Influence on English Prose* (Princeton, 1940), p. 190, does not seem to have come to any decision in this matter.

[2] In this paper references to RI, RII and P are to line references in Hellinga's diplomatic edition (RI, RII and P = Hellinga's A, B and P respectively). References to RF are to the foliation of the original 1481 edition, as there is as yet no suitable modern edition. The hypothetical text said to be the common source of P and RF is referred to as*PE in accordance with Foerste's abbreviation system (op. cit. p. 107).

[3] As an example compare the following readings:
P= " ende segget wt minnen den coninc die waerhede " (1962-3).
RF= " and telle my lorde the kynge here the trouthe " (d5^v)
RII= " En segt mynen heer den coninc waer " (2663).
RF and RII agree in having " heer "/" lorde ", which has been omitted in P. But the phrase " my lorde the kynge " occurs three times and " our lord the kyng " once within the first few pages of RF. But these examples are not translations of " min heer die coninc ", but usually of " heer coninc " (P 47, 79, 113). RII has a similar reading in all cases. It seems more than probable that Caxton used " my lorde the kynge " as an appropriate means of address for the lion no matter what the Dutch had, and so I cannot accept the above example of Muller's as being in any way conclusive. The other examples quoted by Muller and not discussed in the article are (i) RII 1520-1 ; P 1091-2 ; RF c2 ; (ii) RII 1635-7; P 1175 ; RF c3 ; (iii) RII 2190-1 ; P 1594-6 : RF d1 ; (iv) RII 4498-9 ; P 3384 ; RF f8^v.

RII. But a closer examination of the two passages reveals that this is not in fact the case.

(*a*) When the wolf, the bear and the cat are ready to lead Reynard to the gallows, the wolf says in RF : " hadde we an halter whiche were mete for his necke and stronge ynough/*we shold sone make an ende/* reynert the foxe whiche longe had not spoken/" (c6ᵛ). The italicized words which form the apodosis are not found in P, which has the reading : " Hadden wi een strop die na sinen crop te passe waer. ende starc ghenoech Reynert die langhe ghesweghen hadde " (1420-23). RII, on the other hand, does include an apodosis, which shows that its omission in P was a mistake which arose when the prose version was printed. RII reads :

> Her tybert hadden wi een strop
> Het wist lange reynaerts crop
> Wat sijn lijff mochte wegen
> Reynaert die lange had geswegen   (1959-62)

(" Sir Tybert, if we had a rope Reynard's neck would know for a long time what his body weighs. Reynard who had been quiet for a long time . . ."). The other manuscript of RII reads *achter*, " at the bottom " (line 1923), for *lijff*, " body ". But in either case the apodosis in RF is in no way a translation of that in RII.[1] It is possible that Muller here confused the reading in RI which includes the word " (h)ende " with that in RII. The reading of RI is :

> Langhe heden wist zijn crop
> Wat zijn achter hende mochte weghen   (1931-2)

But even this has little similarity with RF except for the inclusion of " ende " in both texts, though it means very different things in each case. Furthermore Muller claimed that RF was descended from a text *PE which is a prose version based on RII and which was the source for P. So even if there were a resemblance between RI and RF, it would hardly help to prove his theory. Consequently it is not possible to use this passage as proof that

---

[1] It is true that Caxton sometimes alters the Dutch text, but this is beside the point here. In order to prove his theory Muller must show that RF is an exact translation of RII or a translation that can be explained *only* by assuming that RII was Caxton's source.

Caxton's source was *PE. It seems more reasonable to suppose that on reading his Dutch text he realized that it made no sense. So he inserted a clause of his own making to restore the sense of the passage. As we shall see later, there are many examples which show that Caxton did make additions to the Dutch text in order to render it more intelligible to English readers.

(*b*) The second passage comes towards the end of the story when the fox and the wolf are about to engage in single combat. Each has to swear on the Bible that the other is a murderer and a traitor. When the wolf is to swear, RF has: " the rulers and kepars of the felde was the lupaert and the losse/they brought forth the booke/*on whiche sware the wulf* that the foxe was a traytour " (k1). The words in italics are not found in P which has : " Die crijt waerders waren die lupert ende die los die brochten daer die heylighen voert dat die vos een moerdernaer ..." (5436-8). This example is somewhat different from the previous one in that the words in RF and RII are almost identical, for RII reads :

> Die krijt wachters brochten die heiligen voort
> Dat was die lupert en die oss
> Die wolf die zwoer voor dattie voss
> Een morder was ende een verrader   (6908-11)

Yet it should be noted that the word order and phrasing is rather different in RF than it is in RII ; and in this context it is interesting to compare an almost identical passage a few lines later when the fox is to swear on the book. Here RF has " Reynart the foxe sware " (k1), P has " Reynert die vos swoer " (5442), and RII has " reynart die voss die swoer " (6914). In this example the words and word order are identical in the three texts. If Caxton's original had had a prose version of " Die wolf die zwoer " found in RII, it seems probable that he would have translated it as " The wulf sware ", just as a few lines later he translates " Reynert die vos swoer " as " Reynart the foxe sware ". But as there was nothing there he inserted something which he thought would make sense, i.e. " on whiche sware the wulf ". In my opinion in order to accept Muller's theory one has to assume a considerable lack of intelligence on Caxton's part. Caxton's command of

Dutch was not perhaps perfect, but it was certainly good
enough to know when the Dutch did not make sense.   It is well
known that he sometimes inserted little phrases or sentences to
make his story more intelligible.[1]   That he used the words he did
may be attributed to two reasons : firstly the parallel " Reynart
the foxe sware " a few lines later ; and secondly the lack of any
other suitable alternative with which to fill the lacuna.   It is
obvious that it is going to be the " wolf " who is going to call the
fox a murderer and traitor and that the book was brought in order
that he might " swear " to it " on it ", as was usual in such cases.
Consequently I do not think that this example can be used as
proof that Caxton was using *PE.

   (c) The third passage noted by Muller is one in which the
reading in RF is said to be closer to RII than P.   This, he argues,
can only be explained by assuming that Caxton was using *PE,
for otherwise it would be too great a coincidence to assume that
he happened to alter P in such a way that it resembled RII.
But let us look a little more closely at the texts.   RF has " or yf
ony man be seke in his body of venym/or ylle mete in his
stomack/of colyk/" (hl^v), which corresponds to P's " ende enich
ongesonde inden lichame die van enich versumene comen
mochten van vuylre spisen van quaden wine van vergiffenisse . . ."
(4132-5).   RII, on the other hand, reads :

> Off inden lichaem enich ongesond
> Die van versumentheit comen cond
> Van vergiffenisse ende venijn   (5384-6)

Muller thought that RF's " venym " corresponded to P's
" quaden wine " (" bad wine ") and he asks " Hoe kon hij bij
quaden wiue [sic] gissen, dat er in R. II *venine* [sic] stond, en daar-
naar vertalen?" (p. xiv). The question is superfluous, for
" venym " in RF does not translate " quaden wine ", but " ver-
giffenisse " which means " poison ".   The passage has been somewhat rearranged by Caxton and one must assume that during this
rearrangement the " van quaden wine " was omitted,[2] though of

----

[1] Muller and Logeman, op. cit. pp. xlv-xlvii, list plenty of examples and the
conclusion is : " Al deze uitbreidingen doen Caxton kennen als bewust er naar
strevende zijne vertaling zoo duidelijk mogelijk te maken " (p. xlvii).
[2] Also a common occurrence in RF, ibid. pp. xliv-xlv.

course we cannot tèll whether this was intentional or not. It is true that "venym", the word he uses to translate "ver-giffenisse", is found in RII which has "vergiffenisse ende venijn". But little can be proved from that. When translating "ver-giffenisse" Caxton could either anglicize the Dutch word or use one of the two English words then current, "poison" and "venom". I do not think that any theory can be built up on the fact that he happened to choose "venom", especially as this word is used elsewhere in RF.

(*d*) In the last passage listed by Muller the reading in RF makes sense whereas that in P is corrupt. Muller claimed that RF was here very similar to RII and that, since it is impossible that Caxton could by himself have emended P to agree with RII, he must here have been using *PE. RF has " that I thenne lose alle my good thoughtis and purpoos " (f4^v-5), which translates P's " Alsoe dat ic dan den goede sijn al verlien " (3108). Muller describes P's text as " onzin " here and it must be agreed that it is corrupt. The word " verlien " makes no sense as it stands and should presumably be either the infinitive " verliesen ", " to lose ", plus an auxiliary, or the first person singular of the present indicative of " verliesen ". In the Delft edition of 1485 it is emended to " verliesen ", but no auxiliary is added. Similarly the word " sijn " is corrupt because it contains a long vowel. RF has therefore a more intelligible reading than P, but that does not mean that it is similar to RII, which reads :

> Dat ic die vriheit heb verloren
> End dat leuen dair ic eerst in was   (4164-5)

(" That I have lost the freedom and that way of life I previously enjoyed. ") It is hardly credible to accept that RF is supposed to be a translation of this. RF's reading is to be explained in this way. Caxton used P and he understood " sijn " to be " sin ", Modern Dutch " zin ", " thought ", " mind ", etc.,[1] which he translated with the doublet " thoughtis and purpoos ". He then understood " verlien " to be a part of " verliesen " and

---

[1] It is interesting to note in this connection that although the Delft edition emends " verlien " tọ " verliesen " it does not change " sijn ". Professor W. E. Collinson has suggested to me that " sijn " may be a misprint for " syn ", a variant spelling of " sin ".

translated it as " lose ". There are three possible explanations of how Caxton read P in this way. The first is that his knowledge of Dutch was so sketchy, as Muller himself has claimed, that he did not realize that the text was corrupt. The second is that his knowledge of Dutch was so good that he emended P's reading to make sense. The third, which I think is the most probable, is that his translations were all carried out at top speed. In his haste he may well have overlooked that P read " sijn " and not " sin " and he may not have bothered too much about grammatical concordance, as in the case of " verlien ", as long as he understood the general meaning of the passage. At all events it is clear that the reading in RF is much closer to and can be explained more readily from that in P than that in RII.

When the relevant passages from the individual texts are juxtaposed, I hope it becomes evident that they do *not* prove that Caxton was using the hypothetical text *PE rather than P. The variations which RF shows against P can be convincingly explained without reference to *PE. But in order to make this quite clear it will be necessary to investigate the nature of his translation. In doing so we shall also go a long way towards answering Muller's second argument outlined above. In general it can be said that Caxton's work is a fairly close translation of the Dutch with occasional words, phrases and clauses inserted or omitted to make the story more acceptable to an English audience. This attempt to help his English audience is sometimes vitiated by mistakes which seem to have arisen principally on account of the haste with which the translation was produced. That the mistakes are caused by the speed at which he worked rather than his ignorance of the Dutch language is suggested by the petty nature of many of them, though one must of course accept that some of the mistranslations may be the result of an insufficient command of Dutch. Sometimes Dutch inflexions are carried over to English so that we find " lossem " (k5ᵛ) for " losse " and " dassen " (d3ᵛ) for " dasses ". Another simple mistake is when Caxton translates the Dutch " reynerts sijn broeder soen " (P 973) as the " foxes suster sone " (b8ᵛ), a mistake we cannot possibly attribute to his faulty Dutch. This type of mistake happens several times when Caxton is adding to or altering the Dutch. Thus he changes " lieue grymbart " (P 1210) to " dere eme " (c3ᵛ), though Grimbert was Reynard's nephew and not his uncle. Similarly in a passage where he adds such phrases as " the fox said, the cat said ", he makes a mistake and wrongly writes "quod the foxe" (b7) for " quod the catte ". On another occasion he translates "Segt ons bellijn " (P 2468, i.e. " Tell us Bellin ") as " saye on bellyn " (e4). In none of the above cases is it credible that he did not understand the Dutch or the passage in question. They are slips which have arisen from a too hasty translation and lack of revision. The many omissions, such as the omission of chapter 42 in the table of contents with the result that there are two chapters numbered 43 in the text, point the same way. There are, however, examples where he has made a mistake which could be attributed to his incomplete command of Dutch. Thus, when the bear, the wolf and the cat are leading the fox to the gallows, Bruin is told to guard the fox. He replies in P that " ick sal hem wel bewaren " (1506-7, i.e. " I shall guard him well "), which is translate in RF as " I shal helpe hym wel " (c7ᵛ). At another point in RF Bruin is described as " the mooste gentyl and richest of leeuys " (b1). The Dutch has " die edelste ende die meeste van loue " (P 423), where " loue " means " praise ". Caxton must have confused the word " loue ", " praise ", with " loueren ", " leaves ", which when it occurs at 2263 is correctly translated " leeuis " (e1ᵛ).[1] But these examples surely confirm what I have been suggesting. For in each case his reading is nonsense as it stands so that only a moment's reflection would have told him that he had made a mistake. If he could not understand the text, it is more likely that he would have left the phrase out or emended it to something more sensible. In his haste, however, he thought he understood the passage and did not bother to stop to think whether the sentence as a whole made sense.

On the other hand, we do find phrases and clauses which have been inserted by Caxton in RF in order to make his text more intelligible. In none of these additions is the reading suggested

---

[1] Muller, op. cit. p. xlvii, suggested that Caxton had confused the word with *geloue*, " faith, belief ".

by RII or any other text of *Reynaert* known to us. Thus, where
P has " Soe wie scade ende ongeual heeft elck wil daer mede ouer
wesen " (585-6) Caxton translates " who hath harme and scathe/
euery man wil be ther at *and put more to* " (b3ᵛ) ; P 689-90 " Ic
wil daer lieuer die bode of wesen " becomes RF " I wyl rather be
the messager my self *for to goo and paye hym* " (b4ᵛ) ; P 906-7
" die paep nam locken sinen wiue een offer kaerse " becomes RF
" the preest toke to locken his wyf an offryng candel *and bad her* "
(b7ᵛ) ; and P 1252-3 " so dat hem die plumen om die oren
stouen " becomes RF " that the fethers flewh aboute his eeris *but
the capone escaped* " (c4). The additions made by Caxton mentioned in this paragraph are no different in kind from those
singled out by Muller, and the weakness of Muller's theory is
surely that it does not provide a comprehensive reason for all the
additions in RF. As I have tried to show, there is no reason to
accept that any of Caxton's readings are nearer to RII than P, and
it is therefore logical to assume that all the additions in RF were
carried out on the same principle, i.e. to make the story more
acceptable to English readers.

We have noted above that Muller's second argument was that
RF contained so many mistakes it must have been completed by
Caxton when he was still a young man in the Low Countries. It
was then kept on one side until it was printed in 1481. But we
have just seen that Muller's interpretation of Caxton's translation
is incorrect. RF does contain mistakes, but these are more
readily explained by the speed at which he was working than
by an incomplete knowledge of the language. That he worked
at a furious tempo is accepted by all editors of his works and
is abundantly proved by the sheer bulk of his printed work.
A comment on one of his translations from the French is typical:
" On the whole, he understands his French, although there are
incorrect renderings here and there, owing more to hasty reading,
it seems, than to actual ignorance."[1] That Caxton was busy in
1481 is clear not only from the number of books printed but also
from three major translations carried out in that year, viz.
Reynard the Fox, *The Mirror of the World* and *The History of*

---

[1] M. N. Colvin, *Godeffroy of Boloyne* (E.E.T.S., Extra Series 64, 1893), p. viii.

Godfrey of Boloyne. We can perhaps excuse him then for the mistakes which arose on account of his consequent haste.

Muller's suggestion that Caxton translated the Dutch *Reynaert* while he was still a young man in Bruges loses its point if we attribute the mistakes in RF to his haste in translation rather than to his faulty Dutch. There are, however, some further reasons which make this hypothesis untenable. Caxton himself says that he translated RF from the Dutch and that he finished the translation on 6 June 1481. There is no indication that he had been working on the translation at a much earlier date and there is no reason to believe, as Muller suggested,[1] that he meant he *printed* RF in 1481, not that he *translated* it then. The words Caxton uses in the epilogue to RF echo those used in the epilogue to *The History of Godfrey of Boloyne* which was also translated in 1481. If he had meant printed rather than translated, he would no doubt have said so, as he does in so many of his other works. Furthermore, we have no evidence that Caxton did any translation before beginning *The Receyuell of the Historyes of Troye* in 1469,[2] and indeed we would have expected some reference to any previous efforts at translation in his prologue to that work in which he discusses his difficulties in translation. Finally, it should be noted that there are some reminiscences of Chaucer's *Nun's Priest's Tale* in RF. In the list of those who would complain of Reynard we find " Chantecler the cock. pertelot wyth alle theyr children " (c5ᵛ). But all the Dutch texts mention only Chantecler and his children, cf. P 1365-6 : " cantecleer ende sijn kinder ". Pertelot is not mentioned at all in the Dutch versions of *Reynaert* and her name was probably taken by Caxton from Chaucer. But towards the end of RF there is a distinct verbal echo of the *Nun's Priest's Tale.* Where P reads " Mer die alle dinck berechten wil die en is gheen dinck te wille te maken Ende soe wie dit verscrijft die wil dit

---

[1] Op. cit. p. lvii.

[2] It is true that H. Bradley, *Dialogues in French and English by W. Caxton* (E.E.T.S., E.S. 79, 1900), p. vi, suggests that the dialogues may have been translated in Bruges, though the reasons given are somewhat doubtful. There is no justification for the remark in Plomer, *William Caxton*, that " Translating was more or less a hobby with him, and he seems to have begun at a fairly early age " (p. 175).

doch laten alsoe hijt vijnt " (6256-60),[1] RF reads " And yf ony thyng be said or wreton herin/that may greue or dysplease ony man/blame not me/but the foxe/for they be his wordes and not myne/" (15ᵛ), which must be based on Chaucer's : " Thise been the cokkes wordes, and nat myne " (VII, 3265).[2] Caxton printed the *Canterbury Tales* in 1478 and it is more plausible to accept that his translation of RF was made after that date than before it, for it would be rash to assume that he had a copy of the *Canterbury Tales* with him in Bruges.

We come now to Muller's third point which is that it would be much easier for Caxton to obtain a manuscript of *Reynaert* in Bruges in the fourteen-forties than it would be for him to acquire a copy of the Gouda edition in London between 1479 and 1481. But modern scholarship has disproved this argument. An investigation into the fifteenth-century London Customs Accounts has shown that books were imported in quantity into England at least as early as 1477.[3] It is possible that they were imported earlier and before this date merely classified in the accounts as general merchandise. Not only were books imported in large numbers, but also Caxton was himself engaged in the book trade and was probably one of the most important importers. In 1488 alone, for example, he imported well over a thousand volumes to the total value of £42 1s. 8d. In view of this extensive trade in books, it is quite credible that the Gouda edition found its way to London shortly after publication. We may assume that

---

[1] W. J. B. Crotch, *The Prologues and Epilogues of William Caxton* (E.E.T.S., Original Series 176, 1928), p. 62, is wrong in claiming that the Dutch text has no epilogue. Caxton's epilogue is based on the Dutch one.

[2] A possible echo from the *Canterbury Tales* is to be found in the story of the wolf and the mare. This example differs from those already cited in that RF follows the Dutch text fairly closely, but yet Caxton's actual phrasing may well have been inspired by Chaucer's text. The Dutch " dat die beste clercken dicke die wijste niet en sijn " (P 3059-60) appears in RF as " that the beste clerkes ben not the wysest men " (f4), a translation which might well have been influenced by a line in the *Reeve's Tale* : " The gretteste clerkes been noght wisest men " (I, 4054).

[3] N. J. M. Kerling, " Caxton and the Trade in Printed Books ", *The Book Collector*, iv (1955), 190-9. Cf. also H. R. Plomer, " The Importation of Books into England in the Fifteenth and Sixteenth Centuries ", *The Library*, Fourth Series, vol. iv (1923-4), pp. 146-50, and " The Importation of Low Country and French books into England, 1480 and 1502-1503 ", ibid. ix (1929), 164-8.

Caxton noticed it and realizing that it was likely to become a good seller decided to translate it.   Numerous subsequent editions of *Reynard* proved him right.

It is possible to conclude, therefore, that none of Muller's arguments in support of the theory that Caxton used *PE as his source for RF when he was a young man in Bruges is tenable. We must accept that Caxton's source was P and that the existence of *PE cannot be proved from RF.   It is not, of course, part of my thesis to suggest that *PE never existed.   A final decision on this matter must be left to scholars of Middle Dutch literature who are more competent to decide it than I am.   All I wish to suggest is that its existence cannot be proved from Caxton's *Reynard the Fox*, which is a translation of the Gouda edition of 1479 with certain omissions and additions by him.

II

In the first half of this article I have tried to show which Dutch text Caxton used for his translation.   During the course of that discussion I had occasion to draw attention to some of the peculiarities of his translation.   In the second half of the article I wish to investigate these features in greater detail in order to discover how Caxton approached his source, whether he had any coherent system of translation and whether he tried to re-fashion his source or not.   He himself wrote at the conclusion of *Reynard the Fox* : " Prayeng alle them that shal see this lytyl treatis/to correcte and amende/Where they shal fynde faute/For I haue not added ne mynusshed but haue folowed as nyghe as I can my copye whiche was in dutche/and by me william Caxton translated in to this rude and symple englyssh " (15ᵛ).   But we need not assume that this is strictly true, for statements of this sort are part of the translator's stock-in-trade.   Caxton often claimed that he had followed his sources as accurately as possible[1];

[1] For example, cf. " I entende to translate the sayd boke of thistories of Iason. folowyng myn auctor as nygh as I can or may not chaungyng the sentence.   ne presumyng to adde ne mynusshe ony thing otherwyse than myne auctor hath made in Frensshe " (*Jason*), and " For I haue but folowed my copye in frenshe as nygh as me is possyble "(*Eneydos*).   Quoted from Crotch, op. cit. pp. 33, 110.

and other fifteenth- and sixteenth-century translators also stress their fidelity to their source.[1]

A comparison between the English and Dutch texts reveals that Caxton became more proficient as a translator as the translation proceeded. At first he follows his source fairly closely, but later on he becomes bolder and often changes his source considerably. In some ways this is surprising, for by 1481 he already had several translations to his credit ; and it is now accepted that, though his first attempts at translation were rather fumbling, he soon developed a considerable fluency as a translator.[2] But it should not be forgotten that RF is his first translation from Dutch and thus he was faced with problems somewhat different from those which he had met in his translations from French. In order to show his development as a translator it will be necessary to quote from RF with the corresponding passages from P : one from the beginning and one from the end of the work.

(*a*) In welcken historie bi parabolen bescreuen sijn veel schoen leren ende merckelike punten. bi welke punten men mach leren kennen die subtile cloecheden die dagelics gehantiert ende gebruyct worden onder den raet der heren ende prelaten gheestelic ende waerlic ende onder die coopluden. ende oec onder den gemeenen volc Ende dit boec is gemaect tot nutscap ende tot profijt alre goeder menschen op dat si daer in lesende sellen mogen verstaen ende begripen die voernoemde subtile scalcheden die dagelics in der werelt gebruijct worden. niet om datmense gebruyken sal . . . (2-15).[3]

In this historye ben wreton the parables/goode lerynge/and dyuerse poyntes to be merkyd/ by whiche poyntes men maye lerne to come to the subtyl knoweleche of suche thynges as dayly ben vsed and had in the counseyllys of lordes and prelates gostly and worldly/ and/also emonge marchantes and other comone people/And this booke is maad for nede and prouffyte of alle god folke/ As fer as they in redynge or heeryng of it shal mowe vnderstande and fele the forsayd subtyl deceytes that dayly ben vsed in the worlde/not to thentente that men shold vse them. . . (a3ᵛ).

---

[1] See H. S. Bennett, *English Books and Readers 1475 to 1557* (Cambridge, 1952), pp. 166 ff.; Workman, op. cit. pp. 69 ff.; F. R. Amos, *Early Theories of Translation* (New York, 1920) ; and H. B. Lathrop, *Translations from the Classics into English from Caxton to Chapman 1477-1620* (Madison, 1933).

[2] *The Book of the Ordre of Chyualry*, ed. A. T. P. Byles (E.E.T.S., O.S. 168, 1926), pp. xlii-xlvi.

[3] All references in the second half to the Dutch text are to P.

(b) Siet here dese lose scalc verriet mijn wijf eens alte leliken Ende hi deedse ouer enen dijck ende yn slijke doer dat water zere diep waden. ende hi maecte hoer wijs dat hij sinen sert int water steken soude daer soude cortel-iken veel vissche an comen. ya also veele dat sise nauwe met hem vierden eten en souden Die arme dwaesegghe waende oeck waers Ende ghinc ten buke toe in dat slijc eer sis in dat water quam daer si doe mitten sterte inne swam als si alre diepste conde Dit was eens wijnters dat hoor reynaert alsoe bedroech. want si hielt den stert alsoe langhe in dat water dat si daer ynne beuroes. So wat si ten lesten toech si en mocht daer niet wten ijse

(4862-77).

My lord I pray you to take hede/ this false theef betraied my wyf ones fowle and dishonestly/ hit was so that in a wynters day that they wente to gyder thurgh a grete water/and he bare/ my wyf an honde that he wold teche her take fysshe wyth her tayl/and that she shold late it hange in the water a good while and ther shold so moche fysshe cleue on it that foure of them shold not conne ete it. The fool my wyf supposed he had said trouthe/ And she wente in the myre to the bely to er she cam in to the water/And whan she was in the deppest of the water. he bad her holde her tayl stylle. til that the fysshe were comen. she helde her tayl so longe that it was frorn harde in the yse and coude not plucke it out (il^v-i2).

In the extract from the prologue, passage (a), Caxton follows the Dutch closely. Although he omits or adds a word now and again, there is nothing in his translation which does not have its counterpart in the Dutch, there is no attempt at reorganization or rewriting, and even the syntax is unchanged. For instance, he twice takes over unchanged the Dutch construction of " men " followed by an active verb to express the passive : " men maye learne " and " men shold vse ". This use of " men " cor-responds to the Old English and Middle English use of the in-definite pronoun " man ", " men ", " me ", though it appears to have died out of the language in the fifteenth century.[1] But Caxton soon learns to express this Dutch construction in a more English way either by using the passive or by rewriting the sen-tence. Thus " Tis recht datmen qualike quijt wort dat men qualiken gewint " (183-4) becomes " hit is ryght that it be euil loste/that is euil wonne " (a6) ; and " pleechmen te houe alsoe te doen " (890) becomes " is that the guyse of the court " (b7^v). In the translation as a whole Caxton shows an overwhelming

---

[1] In the *Oxford English Dictionary* s.v. Man, Me, Men *indef. pron.* the last quotation of " man " is dated to about 1375 ; of " me " to about 1483 ; and of " men " to 1484.

preference for the passive in his renderings of this Dutch syntactical usage.

Similarly in passage (*a*) he uses " mowe " to translate Dutch " mogen ".   " Mowe " is a perfectly good Middle English word coming from Old English " mugan ".   Kellner found in *Blanchardyn and Eglantine*, which was printed about 1489, that Caxton used " mowe " more frequently than " may ".[1]   But the evidence from RF is in direct opposition to this.   It is only in this one instance that he uses " mowe " ; elsewhere he uses instead " conne " (425 :   b1), " can " (507 :   b2) or " may " (628 :   b4).   This is striking because the Dutch word could easily have been anglicized to " mowe ".   But Caxton does not use " mowe " again and the evidence from RF rather suggests that he no longer felt " mowe " to be a living form.[2]   It is as though at the beginning of the translation he was not too sure of himself and tended to follow the Dutch text closely.   Yet even later in the text it frequently happens that he at first transfers a Dutch word into English and only when the word makes its second or third appearance does he try to find an English equivalent.   One of the most interesting of these words is the Dutch " iammerde " (2206), which on its first appearance is rendered " yamerde " (e1). When the word occurs a second time Caxton tried the English word " ermed " as a more suitable translation (e1^v).   But this word was probably already obsolete, for this is the last occurrence of it noted in the *Oxford English Dictionary* and before then the last person to use it was Chaucer, from whose work Caxton may well have borrowed it.   Whenever the Dutch " iammer " occurs again Caxton translates it as " haue pite " (f4, f8^v, g4^v, i1, i4 and i5), except that towards the end he feels so sure of himself that he is able to vary this phrase by using " haue compassion " (i5^v).   In much the same way he translates the Dutch " banne " (2013) as " banne " (d6) on its first occurrence.   But on the three later occasions on which " banne " is found in the Dutch, he uses " curse " (d8^v, g1, g1^v).   Although this use of " banne " as a substantive is new in English, it cannot have

---

[1] *Caxton's Blanchardyn and Eglantine c.* 1489, ed. L. Kellner (E.E.T.S., E.S. 58, 1890), pp. liii-liv.

[2] The last quotation for " mowe " given in *O.E.D. s.v.* May *v*[1] A1 is dated 1533.

appeared strange to his readers, for the verb " to ban " was not uncommon in Middle English, particularly in the North of England.
However, it does not invariably happen that when Caxton found
an English word that he stuck to it.   Thus he translates Dutch
" brueken " (2068) as " brokes " (d7) ; but when " broeken "
occurs at 2547 he translates it in a more English way as " ony
forfayte " (e5ᵛ).   Yet when the adjective " brokich " turns up
at 3302, he translates it as " gylty in ony feat or broke " (f7ᵛ).
Similarly the Dutch phrase " onder his eghen " is sometimes
translated as " vnder his eyen " (c1, k2ᵛ) ; and sometimes the
more English phrase " in his eyen " (k2, k2ᵛ) is used.   From
this evidence I think one can suggest that Caxton was always
casting around for the more usual English word to translate the
Dutch words ; but that often he did not stop long enough to find
it and so was content merely to use an anglicized form of the
Dutch.   It was not that he did not know what the word was, but
merely that he did not give himself enough time to find it.   Consequently I do not think it is possible to agree with those critics
who have suggested that Caxton was trying to enrich the language
by introducing new words.[1]

Let us now turn back to consider the second extract quoted
above, passage (*b*).   As a translation this passage shows far
greater freedom and ease in manipulation of the Dutch source.
Although many of the changes are of a trifling character, Caxton
has managed to reorganize the passage so that it is more coherent
and dramàtic.   He makes minor rearrangements such as moving
" in a wynters day " from near the end of the paragraph to the
beginning, where it more logically belongs.   He increases the rôle
played by Reynard by adding such phrases as " he wold teche ",
" he had said trouthe " and " he bad her ".   This makes the
interchange far more dramatic, for our attention keeps on turning
from the fox to the wolf's wife and back again.   In the Dutch,
however, the whole episode is related in a much flatter style.   It
is also noteworthy in passage (*b*) that Caxton does not follow his

[1] *Paris and Vienne*, ed. MacEdward Leach (E.E.T.S., No. 234, 1957), p.
xxvii : " like Lydgate too [Caxton] was concerned with introducing new words
into English ".   See also *The Book of Fayttes of Armes and of Chyualrye*, ed.
A. T. P. Byles (E.E.T.S., O.S. 189, 1932), p. liii.

source literally. He finds English equivalents for the typically Dutch expressions ; he does not attempt to anglicize the Dutch. Thus " hi maecte hoer wijs " is translated as " he bare my wyf an honde ". This freedom is characteristic of RF, particularly the second half. Yet even at lines 360-1 in the Dutch text he translates the Dutch proverb " Ic en salten soe verghelden dat hij wel tcortste eynde trecken sal " as " I trowe he shal come to late to mocque me " (a8^v). Sometimes Caxton adds to the Dutch by including concepts not found in it. Thus he translates the Dutch " diet al wel gaet " (5895) as " who that is riche and hye on the wheel " (k6), which introduces the wheel of fortune so favoured by moral writers. It is, of course, true that Caxton does not always manage to improve upon or even to retain the sense of his original. But so many critics have dwelt upon his slavish reliance on his sources, that it is worth stressing this is not true of RF.

In passage (*b*) it should also be noted that Caxton does not translate " dijck ", " a dike ", at all ; and a few lines later when Isegrim appears on the " dijck ", he translates it as " banke " (i2). He does not attempt in this case to keep the Dutch scene by using the word " dike ", even though it would perhaps have made the story a little clearer. On several occasions he eliminates the more particularly Dutch references. The Dutch " gulden " (844) becomes a " noble " (b7) ; when Grimbert tells Reynard not to speak in Latin but in Dutch (1077), the Dutch is changed to English (c2) ; and similarly when Isegrim makes a parade of all the languages he knows English is added in RF, though Dutch is not in this case deleted (f3^v). The place where Isegrim learned all these languages is no longer Erfurt (3009) but Oxford (f3^v). On another occasion when the lion says he has heard of " Parijs Aken Colen. ende Zyricxzee " though not of Kryekenpyt (1947), Zyricxzee gives way to London in the English translation (d5^v). But these are only minor concessions which Caxton made to his English audience, for he makes no attempt at localizing the story in England. Most of the place and personal names retain their Dutch forms. As far as the personal names are concerned this is not of great importance, for some of them, like Reynard, were already well-known in England. And occasionally a name is anglicized : " scerpenebbe " appears as " sharpebek " (e6ᵛ) and Isegrim's two children " ydelbalch " and " nymmer sat " (3764) become " empty bely " and " neuer full " (g5ᵛ). But the English readers must often have been puzzled by the many Dutch place names which occur in the story such as Hulsterloo and Kryekenpyt. Caxton makes no attempt to set the story in England. Although he was quite prepared to make one or two minor alterations in the story as he went along, he was clearly unwilling to recast the whole of the story in an English setting. To do this he would have had to spend more time and trouble over the translation than he was prepared to.

Although in passage (*b*) Caxton has made several additions and alterations, the English text is not noticeably longer than the Dutch one because in his rearrangement he has managed to leave out bits here and there. Sometimes he even reduces the verbosity of the Dutch ; thus " daer soude corteliken veel vissche an comen. ya also veele dat . . ." becomes " ther shold so moche fysshe cleue on it that . . ." with the repetition of the " veel . . . ja also veele " omitted. Kellner in his investigation of *Blanchardyn and Eglantine* found that " there are very few passages in which Caxton is less verbose than the original ".[1] This remark, how-ever, does not apply to RF for here Caxton not only omits short sentences but he also cuts down lengthy passages in the Dutch. The larger omissions often arise because he rearranged the text. The first of these passages occurs in the Dutch text at lines 1243-8 where Reynard leads his nephew Grimbert past the home of the black nuns. The Dutch text makes it clear that Reynard knew there were hens there. Consequently he speaks to Grim-bert and says that there is a short cut down that way. It is by talk like this that Reynard is able to persuade his nephew to go past the hens walking outside the nunnery. But Caxton merely has " and as they wente talkynge the foxe brought grymberte out of the right waye thyder and wythout the walles by the barne wente the polayle " (c4). He leaves out the direct speech which makes the scene less colourful. We are not shown Reynard's overt duplicity. He has only just finished recounting

[1] Kellner, op. cit. p. cxiv.

his sins to Grimbert and immediately afterwards he lies to Grimbert that the road beside the nunnery is the quickest way to the court. This is not made so explicit in the English version. Otherwise the major omissions in RF occur in passages which are not central to the story. When Reynard calls Cuwart before the lion to verify his story about Kryekenpyt, there are a few lines in the Dutch text devoted to the activities of Cuwart and Ryn the hound (1980-85.) But Caxton omits these neatly with " as he coude wel telle yf he were here "(d6). The further he gets in his translation the more he cuts down, so that towards the end he makes considerable reductions. The largest one is the description of Rukenawe the she-ape's children (3903-54). In the Dutch the habits and idiosyncracies of each child are described in some detail, whereas in the English translation they are each dismissed with a few words (g7-g7^v). No doubt Caxton found this passage too long and too far removed from the general action of the story, for the three children play only a small part in it. Similarly he shortens such episodic material as the account of Master Abrion, the story of Paris and the golden apple and the example of the ass and the hound.

It is worth recording that all the omissions of a fairly extensive character appear in the latter part of the story. There are probably two reasons for this. Firstly, Caxton perhaps became more critical as he progressed with his translation and cut down more liberally. Secondly, the second part of the tale, the continuation made by the poet of RII, tends to be more episodic with frequent digressions and moral examples and thus lends itself more readily to curtailment without any effect on the main narrative. Yet in the first half he misses such obvious chances to shorten as the double refutation of Courtoys's complaint, which is first rejected by Tibert and then by Grimbert. Yet the first one could well have been omitted, for it is brief and this is the only time that Tibert is on Reynard's side. Otherwise he is one of his implacable enemies. Nowhere in fact does Caxton go so far as to omit any scene or episode altogether : his shortenings and omissions are in that way largely superficial. The progression of the story is the same in the English as in the Dutch version. Nor has the shortening been carried out with any consistency. The story of the serpent and the man, which is merely introduced as an example of one of Reynard's past services to the crown, has not been cut down even though it is surely too long for the story as it stands. Such omissions and shortenings as occur support the suggestion that I have already made that Caxton was prepared to make re-arrangements to his story as he went along, but he would not look at it from a distance to rewrite it. This of course is even more true of the host of minor omissions which he carried out. These, unlike the major omissions, are found right from the start and in general they are sensible in that they make the English less repetitive than the Dutch. In the Dutch table of contents, for example, the title of chapter 39 repeats part of that in chapter 38 :

> Hoe reynaert ten cride quam ende hoe si ghinghen vechten
> Hoe reynert ende ysegrym begonnen te campen.

Caxton improves on this by cutting down the title of chapter 38 :

> How the foxe cam in to the feld
> How the foxe and the wulf foughten to gydre.

Apart from these many sensible intentional reductions, there are several examples when a phrase has been omitted accidentally. When Chaunteclere comes with his dead daughter before the lion P has " ende die hiet coppe " (224, " and she was called Coppe "). Unfortunately this clause is omitted in RF so that when a little later two hens are described as " coppens susters " (a6ᵛ) it is not altogether clear who this Coppen is. On another occasion Corbant the rook made his complaint against Reynard to the king. He and his wife had found Reynard lying seemingly dead in a field and consequently the rook says in P " wi bedreuen beyde vele rouwen om sinen doot " (2643-4, " We were both very upset at his death "). This clause, however, is not included in RF, which thereby fails to capture the rook's insincerity and duplicity (e6ᵛ). For we can be quite sure that had Reynard in fact been dead they would not have hesitated to eat him. Reynard is indeed a scoun-drel, but in the Dutch the other animals are as false and hypo-critical as he is. Reynard succeeds only because he is the cleverer. But this is not made so clear in RF.

The reverse side of the many omissions in RF is the large number of additions. These may be divided into two groups :

(i) stylistic and (ii) those included to make the story more acceptable to English readers. Several examples of the second type have already been quoted in the earlier half of this article and little more need be said about them. But it should be said of this latter group that they are all very short and are rarely longer than one clause; Caxton made no far-reaching additions to RF. A typical addition is the inclusion of a " the fox said ", " the wulf said " at the beginning of individual speeches. This prevents the indirect and direct speech from remaining somewhat confused as they sometimes are in the Dutch, and it is of course an invaluable help to the reader when a conversation is being held. When Tibert and Reynard are talking to each other before going off to catch mice (b6ᵛ-b7) Caxton adds five of these expressions. Nevertheless even this type of addition is not carried through systematically. The other additions which fall within the second group defined above are not essential to the story, but often add interesting pieces of information which tell us more about Caxton himself than they contribute to our appreciation of the story. When the fox's wife must swear " by the holy thre kynges of coleyne " (d2), the " of coleyne " has been added by Caxton. Although he might have got this information from books or travellers, we know that he visited the city in 1471[1] and it is surely not improbable that he had seen the relics himself. Other additions reveal to us Caxton's knowledge and his interests. For example, in the story of Pallas and the golden apple he includes facts not found in the Dutch and we realize that not only did he know the story well already, but that he also thought the account in his source needed some further elaboration.

The other group of additions in RF I have termed " stylistic ". By this I mean those additions which are included as a rhetorical adornment to the work. For the most part they consist of the doublets about which so much has been written. A doublet is the repetition of a word by another which has the same or almost the same significance. In RF Caxton frequently creates doublets where they did not exist in the Dutch. But these doublets are not uniformly distributed throughout the work; they are found

[1] See particularly H. Thomas, *Wilh. Caxton uyss Engelant : Evidence that the first English printer learned his trade at Cologne* (Cologne, 1928).

particularly in passages of description and instruction and also in passages of introductory and concluding matter. Thus, at the very end of RF in the short extract quoted right at the beginning of this half of the article we find two doublets introduced by Caxton : " correcte and amende ", and " rude and symple ". Similarly in the opening description of the Spring season at Whitsun Caxton makes the passage more elaborate by the inclusion of a string of doublets : " that the wodes comynly be lusty and gladsom/And the trees clad with leuys and blossoms and the ground with herbes and flowris swete smellyng and also the fowles and byrdes syngen melodyously " (a4). But these are all occasions which demand the high style and Caxton responds by introducing doublets. Yet in passages of narration he is far more restrained in his use of these doublets and in passage (*b*) above there is only one doublet in the whole paragraph. But interestingly enough this comes right at the opening of the paragraph and this is a point which has been overlooked by previous critics. In RF it frequently happens that in a passage of narration doublets occur only either at the end or at the beginning of each section. For example, the translation of P lines 1844-1942 is divided into two paragraphs in RF. In the body of each there is no doublet in the English version which does not have its counterpart in the Dutch ; and there are but few of these. But at the end of each paragraph there are several doublets introduced by Caxton. The first ends : " *And pardoned* and forgaf the foxe alle his mysdedes *and trespaces* of his fader and of hym also/yf the foxe was tho mery and glad it was no wonder/For he was quyte of his deth and *was alle free and franke* of alle his enemyes " (d4ᵛ) ; and the second : " that with thy subtyl wytte daluyst *and hyddest* here/this grete tresour/god gyue the *good happe and* welfare where euer thou bee " (d5). This can hardly be fortuitous, although it is by no means carried out regularly in RF. It does suggest though that he tried to finish his paragraphs off with a flourish. This concentration of doublets in passages which demand a slightly more elevated style is a fact of some importance. Most readers of Caxton never get beyond his prologues and epilogues, for these are works of his own composition. Yet because they necessarily come at the beginning and end of his books and are intended to recommend the book to a possible buyer, they had to be written in a slightly more ornate manner than the rest of the book. But it is not correct to regard this style as Caxton's only or even his usual style. For he can write in an easy-flowing and logical style, as witness passage (*b*) ; and those who confine themselves to his prologues and epilogues will never appreciate him to the full.

It would in any case be wrong to say that RF contains an excessive number of new doublets. The majority of those that do occur are taken over directly from the Dutch. Thus of all the doublets found in passage (a) only one, " in redynge or heeryng ", is introduced by Caxton. In all I have counted approximately 279 examples of new doublets in RF. A satisfactory total is difficult to obtain because not all scholars would necessarily agree whether all those I have included are new formations. Thus, where the Dutch has two adjectives Caxton often introduces an " and " to turn the adjectival phrase into a doublet : " Mit eenre geueynsder rouweliker spraec " (4077) becomes " Wyth a dissymylyd and sorouful speche " (h1). Similarly I have included in the total of 279 a group of examples which are not strictly doublets. These are examples in which a phrase or a clause is varied by the introduction of a parallel. This is a common feature of RF and has so far received little attention. Doubtless it is to be regarded as part of the same stylistic device by which the same thing is repeated in different words. Yet the variation in these cases is more artistic and less automatic than that in which a single word is echoed. In the following example Caxton has added the initial clause as a parallel to the latter one translated from the Dutch : " how myght ye do a more reprouable trespaas/how were ye so hardy to dore to me doo suche a shame " (g2^v). This is one of the more elegant examples in RF, but in few of these parallels does the one phrase or clause repeat exactly the sense of the other, though the following examples come much closer to the ordinary doublets than that quoted above : " wherfore I *stonde a cursed* and am in the popes banne . . . for to be assoyled *and take pardon* " (d6). Critics do Caxton no great service by not looking beyond the doublets, for I would suggest they are but a stage in his progress towards a more developed kind of parallelism which often adds balance and variety to his style. The more we are mesmerized by the doublets, the more we are in danger of thinking that his translation was far more mechanical than it in fact was.

Finally, one should bear in mind that there are many occasions when the Dutch text contains a doublet which has been simplified in RF. Caxton merely uses " spedde " (a2) as a translation of " geexpediert ende wt gherecht wort " in the title of chapter seven ; and " beschermen of bewaren " (301) becomes " kepe " (a7ᵛ). Altogether I have counted sixty-eight examples of simplification of a doublet in RF. So I think that, as far as this translation at least is concerned, Caxton's use of doublets was by no means excessive.

In the consideration of passage (a) I pointed out that Caxton did not alter the Dutch construction of " men " followed by a verb to express the passive, though he does frequently on other occasions. The question of his syntax is too complicated to go into here,[1] but I should like to indicate one or two ways in which he altered the syntax of his source. His Dutch original contains many constructions which are more reminiscent of Old English than fifteenth-century English and it is instructive to note that in general the Dutch constructions are replaced by the more typically modern English ones. Because constructions similar to the Dutch ones had at one time existed in English and because remnants of them were still to be found in the fifteenth century, it is very important to notice that Caxton does not take over the Dutch constructions into his translation, as he no doubt would have done if he had been a slavish translator. In Dutch, as in Old English,[2] subject and verb are often inverted, particularly when an adverb is the headword of a sentence. But throughout the Old and Middle English period this inversion decreases in frequency so that by the fifteenth century it had become

[1] For a thorough investigation of Caxton's syntax see Kellner, op. cit. pp. v-cx ; for a study of the syntax in RF see Paul de Reul, *The Language of Caxton's Reynard the Fox. A Study in Historical English Syntax.* (Université de Gand : Recueil de Travaux publiés par la Faculté de Philosophie et Lettres, fasc. 26e., Gand/London, 1901.)

[2] For this and other points of Old English syntax see S. O. Andrew, *Syntax and Style in Old English* (Cambridge, 1940).

relatively uncommon.[1]   Caxton frequently replaces inversion in
the Dutch and thus for " Also lange als ic leue soe sal ic v een
ghetrouwe vrient bliuen " (443-4) he writes " as longe as I lyue I
shal be to you a tryew friende " (b1^v).   It is when he fails to
change the inversion that his language seems strange to us, as in
" Ryght as the cony had made an ende of his complaynt/cam in
corbant the roek " (e6^v).   Another feature of the Dutch is that
the verb often comes at the end of a clause.   In main clauses this
happens only with verbal phrases when the past participle comes
at the end.   Usually Caxton gives these constructions a more
modern English appearance by bringing the past participle forward : " Ic hadde doch morghen te houe gecomen " (417)
becomes " I had neuertheles comen to court to morowe " (b1),
though sometimes it is left at the end : " what haue I by this pees
loste " (c5).   In subordinate clauses in the Dutch the verb
always comes at the end of the clause.   Yet Caxton, in step with
the general tendency of the language, replaces this by placing the
verb between subject and object or complement : " als hi noot
hadde " (376) is translated as " whan he had nede " (a8^v) and "dat
ic mine siel gaerne soude bedencken " (285) as " That I wolde
fayn remembre my sowle " (a7^v).   Finally, although a condi-
tional clause can be expressed in the Dutch by the use of the con-
junction " of ", it is normally expressed by inversion of the subject and verb.   This type of inversion is found in all stages of
English and can of course still be used today.   But even in
Caxton's time it was more common to use " if " to express condition and Caxton usually replaces the inversion in the Dutch by
an " if ".   Thus " soe suldi al geweldich wesen wil di mi hout
ende behulpelic sijn teghen mijn viande in des conincs houe Doe
ghelouede hem bruijn. woude hi hem hoenichs sat maken. hij
woude hem in goeden trouwen bouen alle een ghetrouwe vrient
wesen " (462-8) is translated by Caxton " whiche ye shal haue in
your holde. yf ye wille be to me friendly and helpyng ayenst

---

[1] For a graph showing this decrease in Old and Middle English see W.
Świeczkowski, *Word Order Patterning in Middle English* (The Hague, 1962), p.
106.   See also A. Reszkiewicz, *Main Sentence Elements in The Book of Margery
Kempe* (Wroclaw, Warsaw and Krakow, 1962), for further information on this and
other fifteenth-century syntactic phenomena.

myn enemyes in the kynges court/thenne promysed bruyn the
bere to hym.   that yf he myght haue his bely full˙ he wold truly
be to hym to fore alle other a faythful frende " (b1ᵛ-b2).

Although it is hardly possible within the compass of this
article to make a complete investigation of Caxton's methods as
translator, certain general trends have been revealed.   He
wanted to give his English readers a copy of a Dutch work and he
was consequently prepared to make certain alterations as he translated.   These alterations are of a somewhat superficial character,
though they become more extensive as the book progresses,
because he was not willing to spend time and trouble on
rewriting the story ; he was not himself an author.   But he did
try to translate the Dutch into current fifteenth-century English.
Sometimes he fails to achieve this and takes over the Dutch constructions literally.   These lapses, it has been suggested, arose
from the haste with which he executed the work.   He can, however, write in an easy flowing style, particularly in passages of
narration.   He makes mistakes and he fails sometimes to appreciate the subtleties of the Dutch, but this was because he translated
too quickly and failed to revise what he had written.   If he had
only taken a little more time over his translation, he could have
given us a minor masterpiece of some polish.   As it is, although
RF contains many exasperating small flaws, it is one of the best
and liveliest translations that Caxton made.

17

English Versions of Reynard the Fox in the Fifteenth and Sixteenth Centuries

All writers on the history of the English language agree that the introduction of the printing press was an important landmark in the development of the language. McKnight, for example, writes: " The printing press introduced by Caxton was one of the most important factors in fixing the English language in permanent form." [1] But although Caxton's language has been investigated,[2] few scholars have made any study of the language of the other printers of the late fifteenth and early sixteenth centuries to determine how this trend to conformity developed or how quickly the establishment of English in permanent form was achieved. Yet several books were constantly reprinted in the fifteenth and sixteenth centuries and by investigating the changes in orthography made in the printed versions of one of these minor best-sellers, it should be possible to make a contribution to the study of " the process and progress of the move towards conformity." [3] A study of this sort might help to show how the individual master-printers approached the language in which they were printing, the sort of changes they made and whether they attempted to standardize it.

One of the popular books of this period was William Caxton's *Reynard the Fox,* which he himself translated and then printed in 1481 (WC). This book was evidently so successful that Caxton reprinted it in 1489 (PL). This version is extant only in one copy now in the Pepys Library, Magdalene College, Cambridge; it lacks a couple of leaves at the end. Another reprint was issued about 1500 by Richard Pynson (RP). This version also survives only in one copy, which forms part of the Douce bequest to the

[1] G. H. McKnight, *Modern English in the Making* (New York, 1928), p. 68.

[2] H. Wiencke, *Die Sprache Caxtons,* Kölner Anglistiche Arbeiten No. 11 (Leipzig, 1930).

[3] The phrase is that of Professor N. Davis in his " Scribal Variation in Late Fifteenth-Century English," *Mélanges de linguistique et de philologie: Fernand Mossé in memoriam* (Paris, 1959), p. 95. Professor Davis stresses the need for investigations of this process.

Bodleian Library, Oxford. It likewise lacks several leaves at the end. A further edition, this one by Wynkyn de Worde, appeared about 1515 (WW). Only two leaves of this edition are known to exist and they are now in the University Library, Cambridge. The last edition I shall deal with was printed by Thomas Gaultier in 1550 (TG). This edition survives in several complete copies, one of which is in the Bodleian Library and another in the British Museum.[4] I shall confine my attention to the editions so far listed, for all subsequent editions, and there were many of them,[5] contain such extensive alterations that it is hardly possible to compare the language of these later versions with that of the earlier ones satisfactorily. Nevertheless between the first and the fifth edition there is a span of eighty years which should be sufficient to show whether there was any trend to conformity. Unfortunately only a small part of WW is extant so I have not always been able to use it in tracing the development of certain written forms because WW does not contain sufficient examples.

Before any discussion of the language can be attempted, it is necessary to elucidate the relationship of the various reprints. It is normally assumed that a reprint would be reprinted from the latest printed version.[6] This is not the case with *Reynard the Fox*, for although all the texts are closely related to one another, there is not a straightforward chronological progression in their printing history. PL is naturally a reprint of WC, for WC was the only English version available when PL was printed. RP is not, however, a reprint of PL, but it also is a reprint of WC. WW is likewise not a reprint of RP, but a reprint of PL. TG, on the other hand, is a reprint of WW. Thus RP might be said to stand outside the main line of descent of *Reynard the Fox*. This fact may be readily proved because the changes which are made in PL do not appear in RP, though they are found in the two later reprints. Consider, for example, the following passages:

---

[4] *A Short-Title Catalogue 1425-1640* (London, 1946), No. 20919-20925a and E. G. Duff, *Fifteenth-Century English Books* (London, 1917), pp. 99-100.

[5] C. C. Mish, "*Reynard the Fox* in the Seventeenth Century," *The Huntington Library Quarterly*, XVII (1953-1954), 327-344.

[6] See R. B. McKerrow's postscript to C. Bühler's article on *The Dictes or Sayengis of the Philosophres* in *The Library*, 4th series, XV (1934), 326-9.

```
WC  he that shoef your crowne
PL  he that shoere your crowne
RP  he that shoef your crowne
TG  he that shore your crowne

WC  but now he sorowed that
PL  but now he trowed that
RP  but nowe he sorowd that
TG  he trowed his iourney
```

Examples like these could be multiplied. Unfortunately the corresponding passages from WW are not extant for comparison, for the leaves of WW which survive correspond to a part of RP which is missing. Yet it is possible to show from the surviving leaves of WW that it reproduces a mistake made in PL and that therefore it must be a reprint of PL:

```
WC  I wyl al otherwyse on yow yet / abyde I shal brynge
PL  I wyl al otherwyse oon you yet byte I shal brynge
WW  I wyll yet al otherwyse byte you I shal brynge
TG  I wyll yet all otherwyse by you I shall brynge
```

From the above examples it can be accepted that there is a straightforward sequence of printing for four of the versions, *viz.* WC—PL—WW—TG, and that RP stands outside this sequence and is a reprint of WC.[7]

Throughout the eighty years covered by the survey there is no noticeable change in the haphazard use of *i* and *y*. PL differs considerably from WC in its use of these graphemes, but the changes made are purely random. Thus when the compositor was setting from WC a4[r], which includes all chapter 1 and some of chapter 2, he changed *i* to *y* eight times and *y* to *i* four times. In addition *e* is once changed to *y* and *i* once to *e*.[8] If anything *y* is used somewhat more frequently than *i* in PL, especially in such words as *wyth* etc., but both letters are used indiscriminately. There is certainly no attempt at standardization. The same state of affairs is to be found in all the later versions. Individual words are not necessarily spelt in the same way as in the copy-text, but no version shows a

---

[7] It is difficult to think of any satisfactory reason why RP is an isolated text, but it might be a fruitful matter for further investigation.

[8] The examples are as follows, the forms being given from WC: (i) *i* is changed to *y*: with, beestis (3), assemblid, his (2), first; (ii) *y* is changed to *i*: leuys, thys, thyder, wylle; (iii) *i* is changed to *e*: flowris; (iv) *e* is changed to *y*: wete.

particular preference for one letter or the other. In the endings
of the preterite of weak verbs and the plurals of nouns, however, *e*
did become the standard spelling by the end of the period. In
WC, PL and RP *-yd/-id/-ed* and *-ys/-is/-es* interchange freely,
though spellings with *e* are not common. In WW *e* spellings are
introduced a little more frequently; and in TG they become regular.
The *-yd/-id* and *-ys/-is* forms do not survive in TG. Similarly in
TG in the preterite of weak verbs the ending *-ed* is extended to
words which in the earlier versions formed their preterites by adding
-d or *-de*: *sauourd* and *prayde* appear as *sauoured* and *prayed*.[9]
The spellings with *-ed* are not found with any regularity before
TG. Although conformity was established in this case, WC's
standardized spellings were not always respected in later editions.
In WC *-y* is always used at the end of a word. There is only one
exception to this in the whole text: *herbi*. In PL, however, this
final *y* is often changed to *i*, so that words can be spelt ending in
i or *y*. The latest three versions also use either spelling. The
development of spelling in this period was not always towards
conformity.

It is well known that a final *e* was added or omitted indiscriminately in early printed books. The five versions of *Reynard the
Fox* are no exception. From WC through TG there is no discernible
reason for the omission or addition of the *e* in most instances, and,
as in the case of *i* and *y*, no version agrees with its copy-text as
to when final *e* is found or not. On the other hand, WC rarely
includes a medial *e* before the adverbial ending *-ly*. PL often adds
e in this position, especially after dentals and stops, so that WC's
sharply, *frendly* and *goostly* appear as *sharpeli*, *frendely* and
goostely. RP likewise frequently adds an *e*, and WW and TG
reflect the orthography of PL.

In WC *a* and *o* when followed by a nasal interchange freely. This
confusion is retained in PL where even the preposition *on* and the
article *an* are spelt indifferently with *a* or *o*. PL often changes
the spellings found in WC: *songe* (*sange*), *domage* (*damage*), and
stande (*stonde*),[10] but not systematically. In RP there is a marked

---

[9] But this change does not refer to *saide/sayde*.

[10] When examples are given with a similar form immediately following
in parentheses, it is to be understood that the first form is from the text
under discussion (in this case PL) and the form in parentheses is from
its copy-text (in this case WC).

preference for the *o* spellings: *vnderstonde, londe, stondyng*, except in the preposition and the article where *a* is common. There are insufficient examples in WW upon which to base any conclusions, but in TG an *a* is generally found where the copy-text has an *o*: *stande, lande, any, husbande*. Regularity is not achieved in TG, though the *a* spellings are dominant. The preposition, however, is spelt *on*. In all texts whether they use *a* or *o*, a *u* is frequently inserted between the *a/o* and the nasal when it is followed by another consonant. This change is found particularly in words of Romance origin: *penaunce, commaunde, condiciouns*. In PL and RP reverse spellings when the *aun/oun* is simplified to *an/on* do occur, thus PL has *danger* for WC's *daunger*. But these examples are few in comparison with those which show the change *an/on* to *aun/oun*. In TG there are examples only of a *u* being added; there are no words which drop a *u* which was found in the copy-text. The spelling *aun/oun* is not regular yet in TG in words of Romance origin, but this development is one of the few regular trends towards conformity which is found consistently in all the texts.

In WC words like *do* and *see* can be spelt with a final single or double vowel. PL does not differ much from WC, though some changes which are made in PL tend towards simplification of the final double vowel: *doo* and *see* appear as *do* and *se*; but *go* becomes *goo*. In RP, however, there is a very strong tendency to double all final single vowels: thus WC's *be, se, go, to, do, so, nothyng* appear as *bee, see, goo, too, doo, soo* and *noo thyng* respectively. The limited evidence from WW suggests that in that text whereas final *oo* was simplified, final *ee* was retained; this is the trend found also in TG. In neither WW nor TG are these spellings carried through consistently.

There is no uniformity in the use of *ou* or *ow* and *au* or *aw* in WC. In PL one can glimpse the beginnings of a tendency to use *au* and *ou* internally, as in *hauthorn* (*hawthorn*) and *coude*, and *aw* and *ow* finally, as in *yow* and *now*. Nevertheless there are many exceptions. RP still uses the spellings indiscriminately. WW develops the trend found in PL: it uses *ou* and *au* internally, except in the word *downe*, which is almost invariably spelt *doun(e)* in PL, and *ow* and *aw* finally, except in *you* where the *ou* spelling is regular. TG follows WW, though regularity is not achieved. But whereas in PL there are times when an internal *ou* or *au* in

WC is changed to *ow* or *aw* respectively, there are no occurrences of this reverse spelling in TG so that one may perhaps suggest that a preference had evolved. The spellings *ei, ey, ai, ay* vary freely among themselves in all texts, except that in TG a slight preference for *ay* may be noted. The variation between *er* and *ar* in such words as *merchant* and *Reynard* is decided finally in favour of *ar*. In WC and PL either spelling is used; in RP *ar* is found more commonly in common nouns: *marchauntes*, but *er* is used regularly in the names of the animals: *Grimberd, Reynerd*; and in WW and TG *ar* is the regular form in all words which had previously exhibited variation. One of the most remarkable features of this study of the five versions of *Reynard the Fox* is how the grapheme *ea* appears suddenly and becomes accepted as the standard spelling in some words in such a short time. It is rarely found in the three earliest versions which use *e* or *ee* instead: *grete, heed* etc. In WW *ea* makes its first regular appearance in the word *great*, though it is also found sporadically in other words in WW. Otherwise WW prefers to represent this long vowel sound by an internal and a final *e*: it changes PL's *breed, leep* and *feet* to *brede, lepe* and *fete*. In TG the spelling *ea* has become almost regular in such words as *teache, head, heade* (" heed "), *great* and *beast*.

As for the spelling of consonants and consonant groups a tendency to conformity can be noticed in the spelling of such words as *enough* and *through*. In WC *enough*, for example, is spelt as *inowh* and *inough*. The beginnings of the spread of spellings in *-ough* is found in PL, where, although many *-wh* spellings are retained and isolated examples are changed to *-uh*: *ineuh* (*inewh*), there are frequent occasions when the *-wh* is altered to *-ugh*: *thaugh, inough* etc. It is noteworthy that there are no examples of the reverse spelling *-ugh* to *-wh* in PL. RP, however, shows no particular advance over WC. But in the short passage from WW extant there are several examples where PL's *-wh* has been changed to *-ugh,* and in TG *-ugh* has become regular. A similar trend to standardization is apparent in the use of the graphemes *-tch* and *-dg-*. These spellings are already found in WC, but they are not as common as *ch* and *g(g)*: *cache, juge* etc. Already in PL many of the *ch* and *g(g)* forms give way to *-tch* and *-dg-* respectively: *fetche* (*feche*), *pledge* (*plegge*) etc., though reverse spellings also occur so that one cannot assume that *-tch* and *-dg-* were yet the dominant forms. RP tampers little with WC's spellings of these consonant groups, but in WW and TG *-tch* and *-dg-* become the most frequent forms, although they have not yet become the only ones.

It is not possible to trace such a consistent trend to standardization in the other consonant spellings. For example, both *k* and *ck* are used in WC. But many of the examples which have *k* in WC appear with *ck* in PL: *spack* (*spak*), *dranck* (*drank*) and *stomack* (*stomak*), whereas in RP many of WC's *ck* spellings are simplified to *k*: *spak* (*spack*) and *cok* (*cock*). In WW there is no sign of consistency: sometimes a *ck* is changed to *k* and sometimes a *k* to a *ck*: *spake* (*spack*) and *ducke* (*doke*). This variety is also characteristic of TG so that at the end of the period there is as much freedom in the use of *ck* and *k* as there had been at the beginning. Standardization did, however, begin to make itself felt in the question of whether a consonant should be doubled or not, either internally or finally. PL differs considerably from WC in its use of single and double consonants, but it does not reveal a decisive preference one way or the other. Sometimes a double consonant is simplified: *vylonye* (*vyllonye*) and *april* (*appryl*); and sometimes a single consonant is doubled: *ballock* (*balock*) and *fell* (*fel*). When a word ends in a double consonant followed by an *e* in WC, there is a tendency to reduce this group to the single consonant in PL: *at* (*atte*), *al* (*alle*) and *had* (*hadde*); though there are exceptions: *ranne* (*ran*). RP, on the other hand, exhibits the opposite tendency. Although internally consonants are not regularly doubled, a single final consonant is, particularly if the word is a monosyllable ending in *f, off, yff, wyff, selff, att, shall* etc. In certain words the final consonant is doubled and an *e* is added: *hadde* (*had*), *ferre* (*fer*) and *uppe* (*up*). WW has a different spelling system. In this text final *l* is usually doubled: *shall, lytell, all, tyll* and *well*. Other single final consonants are either retained or else they are doubled and an *e* is added, so that both *bad* and *badde* are found. Internally a few double consonants are simplified, but there is otherwise little change. TG follows the pattern of WW: its only consistent trend is to double final *l*, though there are examples where this has not been carried out. Otherwise single and double consonants occur side by side.

In WC the personal names often retain a Dutch form, many of them ending in *-aert*, e. g. *Reynaert*. In PL these Dutch forms are eliminated by the omission of the *a* or the *e* of *-aert*. Similarly the names which had been spelt with a final *-ard/-erd* in WC are changed to *-art/-ert* in PL: *Grimbart* (*Grimbard*). This preference for a final *t* is not found in the later versions which generally change it to a *d*. In RP this change of *t* and *d* when final is particularly marked and it may have influenced the forms of such words as WC's *market* which appears in RP as *marked*. The change of final *t* to *d* in the beast names is also found in WW and TG, in which such spellings as *Raynard* had become the standard ones. In WC and PL initial *w* and *wh* are interchangeable: *what/wat, where/were*. This confusion does not appear in RP or TG which both use initial *w* and *wh* in conformity with modern orthographic practice. The position in WW cannot be reliably checked, but it appears to approximate to the earlier confusion rather than the later regularity.

A few final minor points may also be recorded. WC and PL use *c* and *s*(*s*) interchangeably for the voiceless dental spirant *s* in the neighbourhood of front vowels, though the latter spelling is commoner. In RP there is an increase of the *c* spellings: *counceillys* (*counseyllys*), *Iustice* (*Iustyse*) and *seruyce* (*seruyse*). This preference also occurs in WW and TG, although in neither text does the *c* spelling predominate. Final *-re* in WC is changed occasionally to *-er* in PL: *Flaunders, togyder* and *lengher*. The trend to *-er* spellings does not manifest itself at all in RP, but it reappears again in WW and TG. A conflict in the expression of the initial palatal *g* is evident between some of the versions. In WC and PL it is represented by a *y* or a *g*; in RP many of the forms with *g* in WC are changed to *y*: *yates* (*gates*), *foryeue* (*forgyue*) and *foryeuenes* (*forgyuenes*); and in TG the *y* of its copy-text is changed to *g*: *gate* (*yate*) and *giue* (*yeue*). Finally mention should be made of the variation between *d* and *th*. Internally in words the variation appears first in RP which changes WC's *fader* and *vnther* to *father* and *vnder*. In TG this change is common: *murtherer* (*murderar*), *thyther* (*thyder*) and *wether* (*weder*). The variation between *d* and *th* occurs also in a final position. This variation appears not to have been remarked upon before, for it would often be impossible to detect were it not that each version can be checked against its copy-text. *Had* often makes as good sense as *hath* in individual contexts. The confusion occurs sporadically in all texts, but it is most frequent in RP where such examples as *hath byldeth* for WC's *hath bylded* occur. But even in PL we find that WC's *complayneth, sklaundryth* and *thanked* appear as *complayned, sklaundryed* and *thanketh* respectively.

In PL and RP there is little change from WC in the relative frequency of such pairs as *here/there, hem/them, fro/from* and *tho/then(ne)*. Changes are made occasionally, but they appear to be fortuitous. It is first in WW that one can notice a marked change in the spellings of these words. Although the extant passage of WW is little more than a thousand words long, *hem* is changed twice to *them*, and *tho* to *than* seven times. *Fro* is altered to *from* twice and remains only once. These changes do not eliminate all the *hem, tho* and *fro* forms, but they do indicate a marked preference for the more modern forms. In the passage in TG which corresponds to the extant part of WW all the older forms which had survived in WW are changed. *There, them, from* and *than* were standard in TG.

It has naturally not been possible to record all the variations in orthography in the individual versions: only the more significant forms have been dealt with. In each individual spelling treated one of three possible developments may be noted. (i) There is no appreciable difference in spelling habits: the letters *i* and *y* are used interchangeably throughout the period. (ii) There are definite and marked changes in orthography, but these do not show any consistent pattern: PL favours the spelling *ck*, RP favours *k* and the two later versions use either. Individual compositors had their own spelling habits, which were not always uniform among all compositors. (iii) There is a definite trend to consistency. Although in WC -*wh* and -*ugh* are found finally in such words as *though* and *enough*, by the time of TG only -*ugh* is found and most versions show a gradual spread of -*ugh* forms over -*wh* ones. Naturally all trends do not emerge at the same time. The preference for the spellings *aun/oun* in Romance words can be traced back to PL, whereas that for *ea* as against *e/ee* in such words as *great* is not manifest until WW. Consequently it will be appreciated that such general statements as that by McKnight with which I opened this paper demand so much qualification as to be virtually valueless. The printing press *can* be an important agency for the spread of uniformity, but it does not follow that it *was* at the end of the fifteenth and the beginning of the sixteenth century. Uniformity did not materialize overnight and the history of each separate grapheme has to be investigated, for consistency was achieved in some fields long before any trend to consistency can be noted in others. Before we can even begin to appreciate how uniformity developed, full studies of individual graphemes are essential. How else will we be able to tell why the grapheme *ea* makes such a forceful appearance in *Reynard the Fox* at the beginning of the sixteenth century and quickly becomes the standard spelling in some words. Ultimately the printing press will help the spread of conformity, but only when the printers themselves achieved a standardized orthography. This was not accomplished quickly and it may even be suggested that the initial result of the introduction of the printing press was to provoke variety in spelling rather than to promote uniformity. There were after all many printers and an enormous number of books was issued, the majority of which may have differed in orthography among themselves as much as the five texts examined here do. Even if there were trends to conformity which we can spot today, they might not have been apparent to contemporary readers, because in 1500 people were still buying and reading books printed years earlier. Furthermore although the scribes in the fifteenth century were generally fairly educated and probably went through some training,[11] the compositor was perhaps little more than a workman and even the master-printers were not necessarily very educated. For them a standard orthography may not have appeared so important as it did to the scribes.

The changes in the versions of *Reynard the Fox* are not confined to orthography. There are also many variations in vocabulary and syntax. As these offer some interesting sidelights on the attitude of the printer to his copy-text and to the language, a short account of these other changes will be given. In WC Caxton had introduced a great many Dutch words from his original some of which are replaced by English words in PL: thus *dasse* becomes *brocke* or occasionally *gray, hammes* becomes *buttockes,* and *rore* becomes *styre.* Even English words are occasionally altered in PL: *cryde* is replaced by *sayde, lerynge* by *lernynge,* and *that leep becam yl to the preest* by *that leep becam euyl to the preest.*[12] PL frequently changes phrases with a *many a* plus a substantive by omitting the *a* and putting the substantive in the plural: *many shrewd strokes*

---

[11] See particularly C. F. Bühler, *The Fifteenth-Century Book: the Scribes, the Printers, the Decorators* (Philadelphia, 1960).

[12] Some apparent changes in vocabulary, such as *truantyse* (*truantrye*), may be purely typographic, for *truantyse* is not recorded in *OED*.

(*many a shrewd stroke*), and *many yeopardys* (*many a iepardy*). In RP, however, changes in vocabulary are kept to a minimum. It differs from the other versions in making virtually no changes in WC's many Dutch loanwords: *dasse* remains unaltered. RP does contain a type of addition not found in the other texts: a word is added to form a doublet for a word already in the text. Thus *shame* (WC) becomes *shame and rebuke*, and *synnes* (WC) becomes *synnes and trespaces*. The changes made in the vocabulary of WW are extensive. Here is a selection: (a) Dutch loanwords replaced: *voyded* (*romed*), *scrapynge* (*skrabbyng*); (b) older English words replaced: *thought* (*wende*), *vauntage* (*fordele*); (c) older phrases replaced by more up-to-date idiomatic expressions: *on fote* (*to fote*), *she bad hym take hede* (*she said se wel to*), *it flewe in the wolues eyen* (*it flewe the wulfis eyen ful*).[13] In TG changes in vocabulary are also common, but since most of WW is missing it is not always possible to tell whether the changes were introduced in TG or in WW. TG's changes are similar to those in WW, except that in TG a latinizing tendency appears for the first time: *set* is replaced by *appointed*, *full* by *sacyate*, and *see* twice by *perceiue*. Such words as *auyse* and *auenture* are given a Latinate spelling: *aduise* and *aduenture*.

Changes in word order are found in all the texts. PL contains many instances of such changes, some of which were certainly caused by the compositor's carelessness for the sense of the resulting passage is clumsier than that of the original. Thus WC's *beware that reynart goo not away* becomes *beware that reynart not goo away*. On other occasions it would not always be obvious that a change had been made, were it not that we can compare PL with WC: thus WC's *I muste kepe it in secrete* appears as *I muste it kepe in secrete* in PL. This type of change is found in all versions, but they are especially common in RP. It is not always clear whether individual changes were made to modernize the language or whether they were dictated by some typographical reason. Some changes appear to be attempts at correction by the compositor. Not infrequently in RP, and occasionally in the other texts, the phrase *Noble the king* is changed to *the noble king*. It may be assumed that to a compositor with only a page of text in front of him the phrase *Noble the king* appeared to be a mistake, for he did not

---

[13] As so little of WW survives it is not possible to tell whether these changes were carried out consistently.

realise that Noble was the king's name. This is presumably why it is changed sporadically in all texts. There are a few changes in WW all of which modernize the language. For example the group *to . . . ward* is replaced by *toward*. In TG changes do occur, but they are not frequent.

All the changes that are made between a text and its copy can be classified in three groups which I shall call (1) editorial, (2) compositorial and (3) typographical. By a typographical change I mean a mistake which occurs because one piece of type has been incorrectly inserted into the composing stick in place of another. This mistake can arise through the compositor actually picking up the wrong piece of type and inserting it or through the compositor misreading a certain letter because its shape resembles that of another. I have not discussed this group of changes in the paper, because they have no relevance to the history of the language: they are mechanical errors. In these texts pairs of letters interchange: *f* and *s* (*fighte* WC: *sight* PL), *th* and *w* (*that* WC: *wat* PL), and *th* and *t* (*Thise, tho* WC: *Tise, to* PL). It is only necessary to recognize that this group occurs in early printed books and that all changes in it are mistakes which ought to be corrected in modern editions. This has not always been done.[14] Similarly by tabulating these confusions it is possible for an editor of a first edition of a Caxton translation, who is naturally unable to make a comparison with an English copy-text, to recognize what are typographical mistakes in the text.[15] A compositorial change (group 2), on the other hand, is a change made in the spelling or

[14] Despite the typographical variation between initial *t* and *th*, E. Arber, *The History of Reynard the Fox* (London, 1878) does not emend *thybert* (p. 31), *thibert* (p. 32), *thoucheth* (p. 68) and *thybert* (p. 116), although forms with *t* are otherwise regular and in the Dutch text *Tibert* is never spelt with a *th-*.

[15] In the discussion on orthography above I did mention that final *d* and final *th* interchange in all texts. But it seems probable that this variation is a typographical change, because such spellings as *byldeth* (for *bylded*) do not occur in manuscripts of this period. Mrs. Offord, who is at present editing Caxton's *The Knight of the Tower*, has kindly pointed out to me several examples of this mistake in that work: e. g. "**And yf** god gyue yow youre husbondes/ soo that soone after ye be wydowes/ *wedded* yow not ageyne for playsaunce ne for loue/" (ch. 113). (I am greatly indebted to Mrs. Offord for this quotation and for other help with this article.) G. Legman, "A Word on Caxton's *Dictes*," *The Library*, 5th series, III (1948), 172, suggests that *departeth* in the first edition has been

word order of the text by which one variant spelling or syntactical usage is replaced by another. These changes are not mistakes and should therefore never be emended in a modern edition. Until a standard spelling emerges it is just as "correct" to spell *with* as *with* or *wyth*. The changes may be considered compositorial, for they are haphazard in their occurrence: sometimes the copy's *with* will appear as *wyth*, and sometimes the copy's *wyth* will be changed to *with*. It is hardly credible to think that Caxton or any other master-printer went through a text changing some spellings one way and other spellings the opposite way.[16] Most changes between one fifteenth-century text and the next probably fall into this group. Even changes in word order were no doubt generally made by the compositor, probably to justify his line. It has already been noted that RP contains a considerable number of these changes. RP differs from the other texts in that it was set up in two columns per page and therefore the problem of justifying the line was more acute. This is probably why the compositor had to tamper with the word order more frequently. Changes in group (1) I have entitled "editorial" because they are made consistently through-out a text. They reveal an attempt to eliminate a certain spelling, word or syntactical usage from a text. The changes are therefore different from those in group (2). It is not always easy to decide whether editorial changes were made by an editor such as Caxton or by the compositor or even in individual cases by both of them. It may be that in the earlier texts the editorial changes, which are few, were made by the editors and that in the later texts both compositor and printer had a hand in them. It is perhaps more important to recognize that the only changes that a master-printer would have made are those in group (1), and consequently it is from an examination of them that we may gain some idea of his attitude to the text. PL shows that Caxton, for example, made very few changes in his second edition: only a few Dutch loanwords

corrected to *departed* in the second edition of the *Dictes* and that this helps to prove that the editions were issued in this order. But this evidence is inconclusive in itself, because the interchange of final *d* and final *th* is a frequent typographical change. It is conceivable that a first edition had *departed* which was incorrectly set up as *departeth* in the next one, just as RP has *byldeth* incorrectly for WC's *bylded*.

[16] It is, of course, theoretically possible that the master-printer had the text embodying his changes copied out by a scribe before it was passed on to the compositor and that changes in orthography could have been introduced by the scribe. But this is somewhat improbable.

are altered. There is no attempt to improve the style or language of *Reynard the Fox* and those scholars who think of Caxton as a man of letters would have to explain why he failed to improve his work.[17] The explanation may well be that Caxton was more of a businessman than a scholar and that he was more interested in producing a great number of printed works than in their merit as works of art. Certainly everything he translated seems to have been completed at great speed.[18] The changes made by Pynson in group (1) are likewise minimal. On the other hand, the changes from this group in WW are extensive. This is surprising for the attitude of modern scholars to de Worde is that he was an unimaginative printer who had not the same scholarly ability and interest as his former master Caxton.[19] Yet the changes indicate that there was an attempt to modernize the language in WW. It must be admitted that it cannot be proved that de Worde was responsible for the changes, for his compositor might have made most of them. It is, however, a matter that deserves further investigation, for it may be that we have been unjust in our estimation of de Worde in the past.

Some scholars, especially those working in the Renaissance field, may think that I have laboured the difference between the various groups of changes in early printed books which has revealed how large a part a compositor played in the final make-up of the language of a text. I have done so because scholars who have worked on Caxton and other fifteenth-century printers have often been specialists in the medieval field who appear not to have appreciated many of the difficulties connected with early printed texts. Wiencke made a thorough study of Caxton's language based on a survey of four of his printed books.[20] Yet nowhere in his study does he even mention the problem of how accurately the printed books

[17] H. R. Plomer, *William Caxton (1424-1491)* (London, 1925), *passim*.

[18] Most editors of Caxton editions comment upon the hastiness of his translation, see for example M. N. Colvin, *Godeffroy of Boloyne*, EETS extra series 64 (London, 1893), p. viii.

[19] " He was in no sense a scholar, and knew little about the literary value of books . . . no reason to believe he had any literary talent. . . . He had no high ideals, and his printing was solely a commercial undertaking for profit." H. R. Plomer, *Wynkyn de Worde and his Contemporaries* (London, 1925), p. 44 *et passim*.

[20] H. Wiencke, *Die Sprache Caxtons* (Leipzig, 1930). The four texts were *The Histories of Troy, Jason, Æsop's Fables* and *Eneydos*.

represent the copy-texts that were being set up. Nevertheless general conclusions are drawn about the language of London in Caxton's own day. Individual forms interpreted as having philological significance might have arisen as typographical changes; [21] and a book which shows marked variations in its forms might have been set up by two compositors.[22] Similarly it has been pointed out that in all the versions of *Reynard the Fox* investigated there are many examples of changes in the word order. Though some of these changes might have been made to modernize the word order, many of them were made by the compositor either to justify the lines or through sheer carelessness. In Šimko's recent investigation of word order in Caxton's printed version of Malory's *Le Morte Darthur* it is assumed that the printed text represents Caxton's own word order accurately.[23] If this investigation into *Reynard the Fox* is any guide, this assumption is at the best only very doubtful. The number of examples that Šimko produces for some of his changes in the word order is so small that one is tempted to think that they might be compositorial rather than editorial changes. In any investigation of this sort the nature of the compositorial changes in the text must be examined before an evaluation of the editorial changes can be attempted.

The study of the development of a standard orthography and of the attitude of the early master-printers to language is fraught with difficulties which have not always been taken into consideration. An enormous amount of work remains to be done in this field, but I hope that this brief survey of a minute part of the material available has shown what directions future investigations into the relationship of early printing to the English language could take and what difficulties will have to be overcome.

---

[21] Wiencke, *op. cit.*, p. 74, suggests that the only occurrence of *hondreth* in *Eneydos* for otherwise regular *honderd/hunderd* exhibits Scandinavian influence. Although this is possible, it could be that this is another example of the confusion by a compositor of final *d* and final *th*.

[22] Wiencke points out that the orthography in the first 160 pages of *The Histories of Troy* differs from that in the rest of the text. For example in the first 160 pages the proportion of *from* to *fro* forms is 94 : 41. In the text as a whole, however, the number of *from* forms amounts to only 29% of all occurrences of both *from* and *fro* forms, because *from* occurs so rarely in the latter part (p. 67).

[23] J. Šimko, *Word-Order in the Winchester Manuscript and William Caxton's edition of Thomas Malory's Morte Darthur (1485)—A Comparison* (Halle, 1957).

18

Manuscript to Print

I$_T$ IS COMMON PRACTICE in major libraries today for manuscripts and printed books to be housed in different collections and to be catalogued separately. This division encourages users of either to think that they form disparate entities. While it is true that the development of the technology of printing may have had an important influence on our methods of thinking and organising intellectual and scholarly activity,[1] there are many points of contact between the two ways of committing language to paper. The continuity between the two media is often stressed in modern scholarship.[2] To those who were alive at the time, the two processes must have seemed similar; both could be referred to as *ars artificialiter scribendi* by contemporaries.[3] A not dissimilar situation in new technology exists today with the development of copying machines. A book made up of xerox sheets will not to the average reader seem very different except perhaps aesthetically from one made of printed or photo-offset pages. We should always bear in mind then that the beginning of printing was seen only as a different way of writing, and although it affected the number of copies that could be produced, it did not at first influence the way one wrote or made books.

It is now accepted that Johannes Gensfleisch zum Gutenberg invented printing in Mainz and that his first book appeared about 1455.[4] From Mainz, printing spread up and down the Rhine, and Ulrich Zell brought it to Cologne about 1464. Several printers were established in Cologne by 1471 when William Caxton arrived there to acquire a printing press and assistants.

---

1 E.L. Eisenstein, *The Printing Press as an Agent of Change. Communications and Cultural Transformations in Early-Modern Europe*, 2 vols. (Cambridge, 1979) emphasises how printing changed our attitudes and ways of thinking.

2 See, for example, Bühler, *The Fifteenth-Century Book*, and R. Hirsch, *Printing, Selling and Reading 1450–1550* (Wiesbaden, 1967).

3 A. Swierk, 'Was bedeutet "ars artificialiter scribendi"', *Der gegenwärtige Stand der Gutenberg-Forschung*, ed. H. Widmann, (Stuttgart, 1972), pp. 243–51, gives examples of the phrase being used by manuscript writers and masters.

4 For a brief introduction see V. Scholderer, *Johann Gutenberg, The Inventor of Printing* (London, 1963).

He joined forces with Johannes Veldener, and together they were responsible for publication of at least two books. With Veldener's help Caxton established a press at Bruges at the end of 1472 or beginning of 1473, where he published his translation of *History of Troy* (*STC* 15375) in 1473, the first book in English to be printed. In 1476, or possibly even in late 1475, he returned to England and set up a press at Westminster. There he continued operating his printing and publishing business until his death, probably in 1492.[5] In the meantime other printers started to operate presses in Oxford, St Albans and London, though most of these operations were shortlived.[6] Since this book is concerned with England I shall confine my remarks to what happened there in the fifteenth century, though parallels from other European countries may supplement the evidence available. In England I will concentrate on William Caxton, the first English printer and publisher, since his output spans most of the English incunable period.

The invention of printing did not change people's reading habits overnight. The texts which were printed in the fifteenth century were those which were also copied in manuscripts. Printing did bring with it greater commercial pressures, for the possibility of overextending oneself financially was much greater for a printer than for a scribe. Although commercial scriptoria which produced manuscript books speculatively were found in the fifteenth century, the manuscript trade was largely a bespoke trade. With printing the problem is one of disposing of multiple copies of the same text. This encouraged new methods of selling and distribution, and as a mass market developed it would lead to intervention by the state in the control of published work.[7] The printers, as is true of publishers still, looked for new texts which fell into established patterns. Caxton translated many French romances into English because he wanted to produce new reading matter in a familiar genre.[8] It is doubtful whether he would have translated those texts if printing had not been invented; and to that extent printing encouraged a great increase in the production of texts. On the other hand, in presenting his texts Caxton imitated the presentation and letter forms of manuscripts. For example, his

---

5 For Caxton see N.F. Blake, *Caxton and his World* (London, 1969); G.D. Painter, *William Caxton, a Quincentenary Biography of England's First Printer* (London, 1976); and H.M. Nixon, 'Caxton, his Contemporaries and Successors in the Book Trade from Westminster Documents', *The Library*, 5th series 31 (1976), 305–26.

6 A complete list of books is included in E.G. Duff, *Fifteenth Century English Books*, Bibliographical Society Illustrated Monographs 18 (London, 1917). For a general bibliography, though it is far from complete, see W.L. Heilbronner, *Printing and the Book in Fifteenth-Century England* (Charlottesville, 1967).

7 See W.M. Clyde, *The Struggle for the Freedom of the Press from Caxton to Cromwell* (London, 1934), and, more generally, Eisenstein, *The Printing Press as an Agent of Change*.

8 See N.F. Blake, 'William Caxton: his Choice of Texts', *Anglia*, 83 (1965), 289–307.

vernacular texts are printed in a Flemish *bâtarde* type, while his liturgical and religious works are in a Gothic type; he did not employ title pages and only rarely did he include foliation; and his books were made up of quires marked with signature letters to ensure a correct binding sequence. It would be surprising if the technology used in the making of the manuscript book had not been taken over into the printed one, since manuscripts were the only models printers had available and they were still being produced side by side with printed books.

Books and manuscripts were not kept distinct in the fifteenth century in the way they are today. Libraries would shelve books and manuscripts together, as late fifteenth-century catalogues show.[9] Printed books were also bound together with manuscripts, as two examples of Caxton's books indicate. One of the three extant copies of his edition of *Saint Winifred* (*STC* 25853) is bound with manuscript religious and historical material in Lambeth Palace Library MS 306. The text has been provided with head-lines and marginalia by one of the manuscript's annotators. It occupies fols. 188–201v of the manuscript. One of the three extant copies of the *Propositio Johannis Russell* (*STC* 21458) is bound with mostly Latin religious material in an Ebesham manuscript, now Latin MS 395 in the John Rylands Library.[10] This behaviour is not surprising. Many manuscripts were little more than booklets, which were often grouped together in larger manuscript compilations. The inclusion of some printed books in this material, after printing was invented, is perfectly natural.

Printed books, particularly incunabula, often resemble manuscripts fairly closely. At first printing meant that only the text proper was produced by mechanical means. The technology to produce capitals or illumination mechanically did not exist. When a book was printed, it would be handed over to the rubricator and illuminator to be finished off, as had been the case with manuscripts. The printer would provide guide letters in the large initial gaps he left at the beginning of books and chapters so that the rubricator would know what letter to insert. The printer would also leave gaps to allow the rubricator to add paragraph marks where appropriate. In English printed books these were usually executed in red and blue ink alternately. It is much less common to find English incunabula which have been decorated by hand. It is often claimed that Caxton's edition of Gower's *Confessio Amantis* (*STC* 12142) has a space left for an illumination. On the folio which has the signature i 2, in the first gathering, there is at the top of the leaf the heading

---

9 For example, Mary Bateson, *Catalogue of the Library of Syon Monastery, Isleworth* (Cambridge, 1898).

10 See C. Horstmann, 'Prosalegenden i. Caxton's Ausgabe der h. Wenefrida', *Anglia*, 3 (1880), 293–319, and M.R. James, *A Descriptive Catalogue of the Manuscripts in the Library of Lambeth Palace* (Cambridge, 1932), No. 306 for Lambeth Palace Library, MS 306; and Doyle, 'William Ebesham', pp. 308–12, for a description of Rylands Latin MS 395.

Prologus and its number *Folio 2*. After that there is a gap and the prologue begins only halfway down the page and occupies the rest of the page. The top of the page appears to have been left deliberately blank as though it was going to contain some form of illumination. This is possible, though in this case it may have been a woodcut which was to fill the blank.[11] In one copy of Caxton's *History of Troy*, now at the Huntington Library, there is a frontispiece depicting the presentation of the book to its 'patron', Margaret of Burgundy. This frontispiece is a copper-plate engraving, and it was probably executed by the artist who is referred to as the Master of Mary of Burgundy, for its style resembles that found in manuscripts which he made for both Mary and Margaret of Burgundy.[12] However, as the frontispiece is found in only one copy, it may have been added specially to that copy. If so, it helps to make that copy like a manuscript, for one characteristic of manuscripts is that they are all different.

It is not common to find elaborate illustration in English incunabula. One copy of *Reynard the Fox* (*STC* 20919), Eton College MS 2.3.12, has initials painted floridly in gold, red and blue as far as fol. b1r, but it is possible that this ornamentation was executed only in the nineteenth century.[13] A more interesting example of decoration is the Cambridge University Library copy of the Oxford edition of *Expositio Symboli* of Rufinus printed in 1478 (*STC* 21433).[14] This copy contains the Goldwell arms, which probably belonged to James Goldwell, bishop of Norwich from 1472–1499. More importantly, the decoration in this copy, which consists of ornamentation and a miniature, is based on that found in British Library MS Sloane 1579, the manuscript which acted as copy-text for the printer, probably Theodoric Rood. The other ten extant copies of this edition are not decorated, and it may be that James Goldwell was the patron of the edition and was presented with a copy which was particularly elaborate. Sloane 1579 is an Italian manuscript which belonged at one time to Vespasiano da Bisticci, and its Italianate decoration may have been executed in Florence in the 1440s. Its use as a model in England is exceptional. The Pierpont Morgan copy of Caxton's first edition of the *Sarum Hours* (*STC* 15867), printed between 1476 and 1478, lacks the final eight folios. The rest that survives is printed on vellum and contains illumination which is modelled on that found in contemporary manuscript Books of Hours. The illumination is similar in style to that executed in Flanders in the second half of the fifteenth century. The edition is usually

---

11 W. Blades, *The Life and Typography of William Caxton* (London, 1861–3), I, pp. 140–1: 'This is the Author's prologue, which commences half-way down the page, the upper half being left blank for the insertion of an illuminator, as in several books printed by Colard Mansion.'

12 O. Pächt, *The Master of Mary of Burgundy* (London, 1948).

13 N.F. Blake, *The History of Reynard the Fox*, EETS 263 (London, 1970), pp. lxi–lxii.

14 For a full description see A.C. de la Mare and L. Hellinga, 'The First Book Printed in Oxford: the *Expositio Symboli* of Rufinus', *TCBS*, 8 (2) (1978), 184–244.

attributed to Caxton's Westminster period, though the illumination in this copy suggests that it may in fact belong to his Bruges period. The illumination of printed Books of Hours was not uncommon on the continent, though this is the only known example in a book published by an English printer.[15]

The illumination of printed books occurs most frequently in Latin texts, and a number of continental examples were catalogued by Olschki in 1914.[16] He noted the similarity between manuscripts and printed books, for the latter at first used the same letter forms, abbreviations, ligatures, punctuation and general disposition of the text. The signatures and capitals were introduced by hand, as was the decoration. As printed books at first had no title pages and could be printed on vellum, their similarity to manuscripts was considerable. After 1470 this similarity decreased as more of the printed book's layout, such as signatures and folio numbers, was executed in print. The illumination was the last feature added by hand to remain in printed books, and this included not only miniatures, but also decorations in the margins and elaborate initials. This type of illuminations was continued even after the use of woodcuts in printed books. Olschki was of the opinion that the addition of illuminations was designed to make printed books resemble manuscripts and perhaps even to deceive the buyers or owners; in some examples he noted that the printed colophon had been erased so that the evidence of printing was eradicated. Although there may have been isolated instances where printed books were passed off as manuscripts, it seems improbable that this was done on any regular basis. Illumination may have been added to make a book more valuable, and naturally this would apply to printed books as much as to manuscripts. Caxton himself adopted woodcuts for some of his texts, but even so they still in some cases had to be completed by hand. The woodcut illustrations in *Mirror of the World* (*STC* 24762) had to have the explanation of the symbols written in by hand.[17] Naturally, some texts like the *Indulgence* were more in the nature of modern forms, and these were completed in hand by the issuing officer.[18] In the case of the *Mirror of the World* the manuscript which Caxton made his translation from has been identified as BL MS Royal 19.A.IX.[19] The woodcuts in his edition were made

15 See *William Caxton: An Exhibition to Commemorate the Quincentenary of the Introduction of Printing into England* (London, 1976), p. 42.

16 L.S. Olschki, *Incunables illustrés imitant les manuscrits. Le passage du manuscrit au livre imprimé* (Florence, 1914), contains 49 examples of printed books made to resemble manuscripts: they are all Latin texts.

17 The text is edited and the woodcuts reproduced in Oliver H. Prior, *Caxton's Mirrour of the World*, EETS, ES, 110 (London, 1913). For a discussion of Caxton woodcuts see Edward Hodnett, *English Woodcuts 1480–1535*, Bibliographical Society Illustrated Monographs 22 and 22a, rev. edn (Oxford, 1973).

18 For the earliest indulgence which has handwritten entries see A.W. Pollard, 'The New Caxton Indulgence', *The Library*, 4th series, 9 (1929), 87–9.

19 N.F. Blake, 'The "Mirror of the World" and M.S. Royal 19.A.IX', *NQ*, 212 (1967), 205–7.

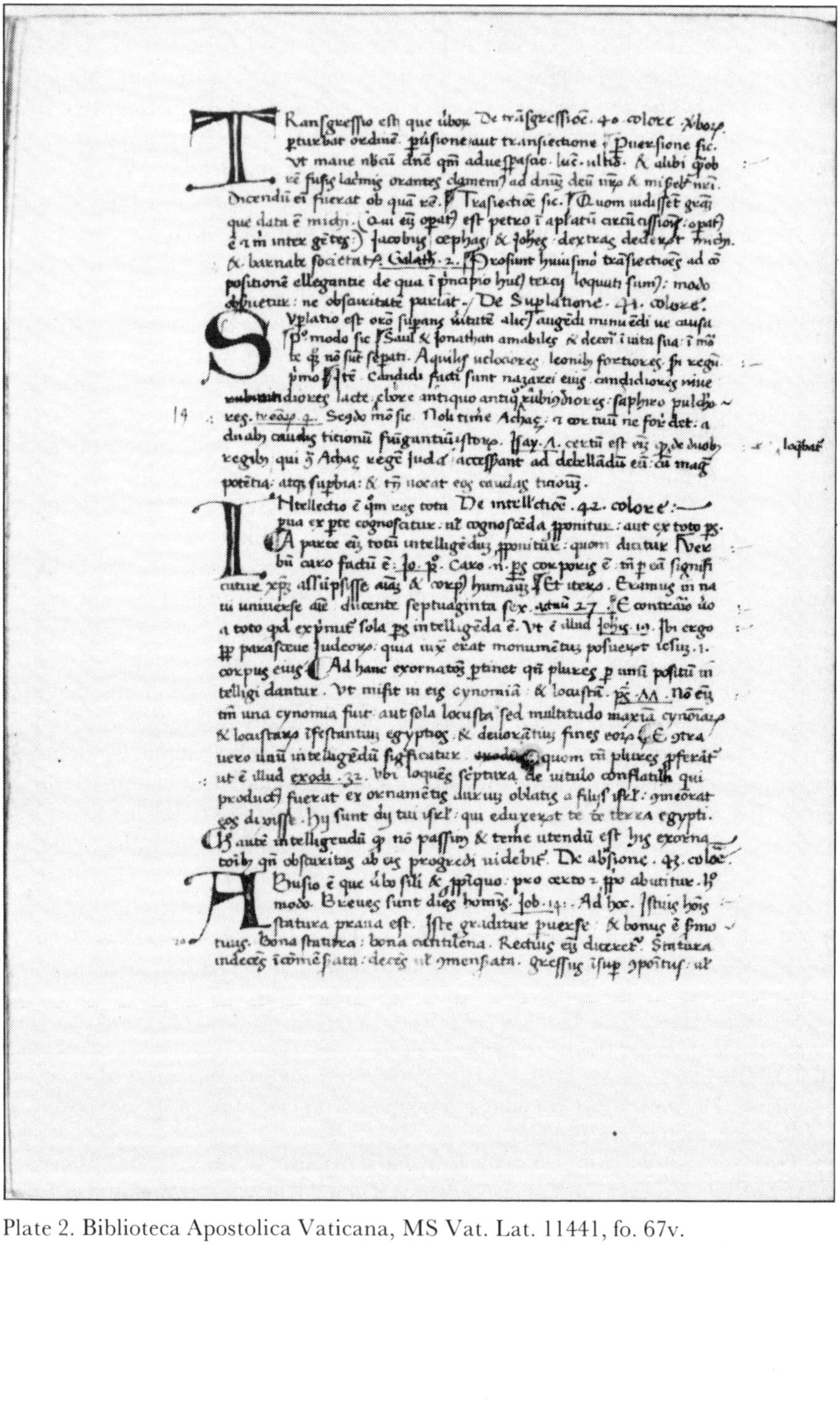

Plate 2. Biblioteca Apostolica Vaticana, MS Vat. Lat. 11441, fo. 67v.

Secundo modo sic. Noli time Achas: et cor tuu ne formidet
a duabus caudis ticionu fumigatiu istoꝝ. Isa. A. ctu e et
ꝗ loquelat de duobus regibus q gtra Achas regé Juda ac
cesserant ad debellandum eum cum magna potentia atq3 su
perbia: et tamen uocat eos caudas ticionu

Intellectio est quom res tota pua ꝓ parte ognoscitur
uel cognosceda ꝓponit: aut ꝓ toto pars Vl parte et
totu itelligendu ꝓponit: quom dicitur. Verbu caro factu e
Jo. 1. Caro eni pars corporis est: tame per eam sigficat
xpm assumpsisse aîam et corpus humanu. Et itep. Eru
mus in naui uniuerse anime ducente septuaginta sex
E contrario uo a toto quod exprimit sola pars intelligenda e
Vt est illud. Jo. 19. Ibi ergo ꝓ parasceue Judeoꝛ: quia
iuxp erat monumetu posuerut ihm id e corpus eius Ad hanc
exornacoz pertinet qn plures per unu positu intelligi dantur
Vt misit in eis cynomia et locustã, pš Non eni tan
tum una cynomia fuit: aut sola locusta / sed multitudo ma
xima cynomiaꝛ et locustaꝛ infestantiu egipcios: et deuo
rantiu fines eoꝛ. E contra uo unu itelligedu significat
quom tame plures ꝓferantur. Vt est illud exodi 32. ubi
loquens scriptura de uitulo conflatili qui productus fuerat
ꝓ ornamentis aurium oblatis a filijs israhel: commemo
rat eos dixisse. Hij sunt dij tui israhel: qui eduxerunt te
de terra egipti. Hec aute intelligendum ꝗ non passim et
temere utendum est hijs exornatiombus quando obscuritas
ab eis ꝓgredi uidebitur

Abusio e ꝗ ubo sili e ꝓplꝗ° ꝗ certo ꝓ ꝓprio abutit hoc
mõ. Breues st dies hois. Job. 14. Ad hoc Istius
hois statiu pua e. Iste igitur peruerse: et bonus est sermo

Plate 3. *Rhetorica nova*, printed by William Caxton, *c*.1479, fo. 98r. (*Corpus Christi College, Cambridge*)

wole and byseche the that thou reygne and haue the lord-
ship vpon vs durynge thy lyf . We hope that ther is none
that hath so wele deſeruid to be our kyng / And thus
they chees him to ther kyng and to their lord and corowned
him ʒ yaf him their bleſſinges / and praid to god that he
wold bleſſe ʒ maynteene him / To whom he said J haue
herde the prayer that ye haue made for me / beſeching to god
that he wol ſtedefaſte the loue of me in your hertes ʒ cora-
ges And that by no maner of the delectacio he ſuffre me to
do thing apon your proffites ne to my diſworſhip / ʒ ſone af
ter he ſent lettres to alle the prynces and goode toWnes of
his royaume / And Whan he had ſent his lettres One
daire kyng of perce ʒ of mede ſent to Alexandre for tribu
te like as he had of his fader. And he ſent him word that
the henne that leyd that egge was dede And after this
Alexander made grete conqueſtis . and Whan he had con-
quewd Jnde he Went to acontre callid bragman / the Whiche
Whan they Wiſte his compnyg / they ſente many Wyſe men to
him / Whiche ſale Wo him ʒ ſaide / ſir Alexauder thou haſt no
cauſe to Werre vpon vs / ne to be euil Willyg / for We ben both
pure ʒ meke / ʒ We haue no thing but only ſapiece / the Whiche if thou Wolt haue / pray god that he Wol yeue her the / for
by batayll thou ſhalt neuer haue her / And Whan alexander
herd hem ſaye ſo / he made al his Ooſte to tarye ʒ With felce
of his knyghtes Wente Withyn the ſaid contre for tenquere
further of the trouth / And Whan he entred Wyth in the
ſame ground / he fond many puer foolkes Women ʒ children al naked gadering herbes in the feldes And he aried
of them many queſtions ⹌ to Whiche they anſWerd right

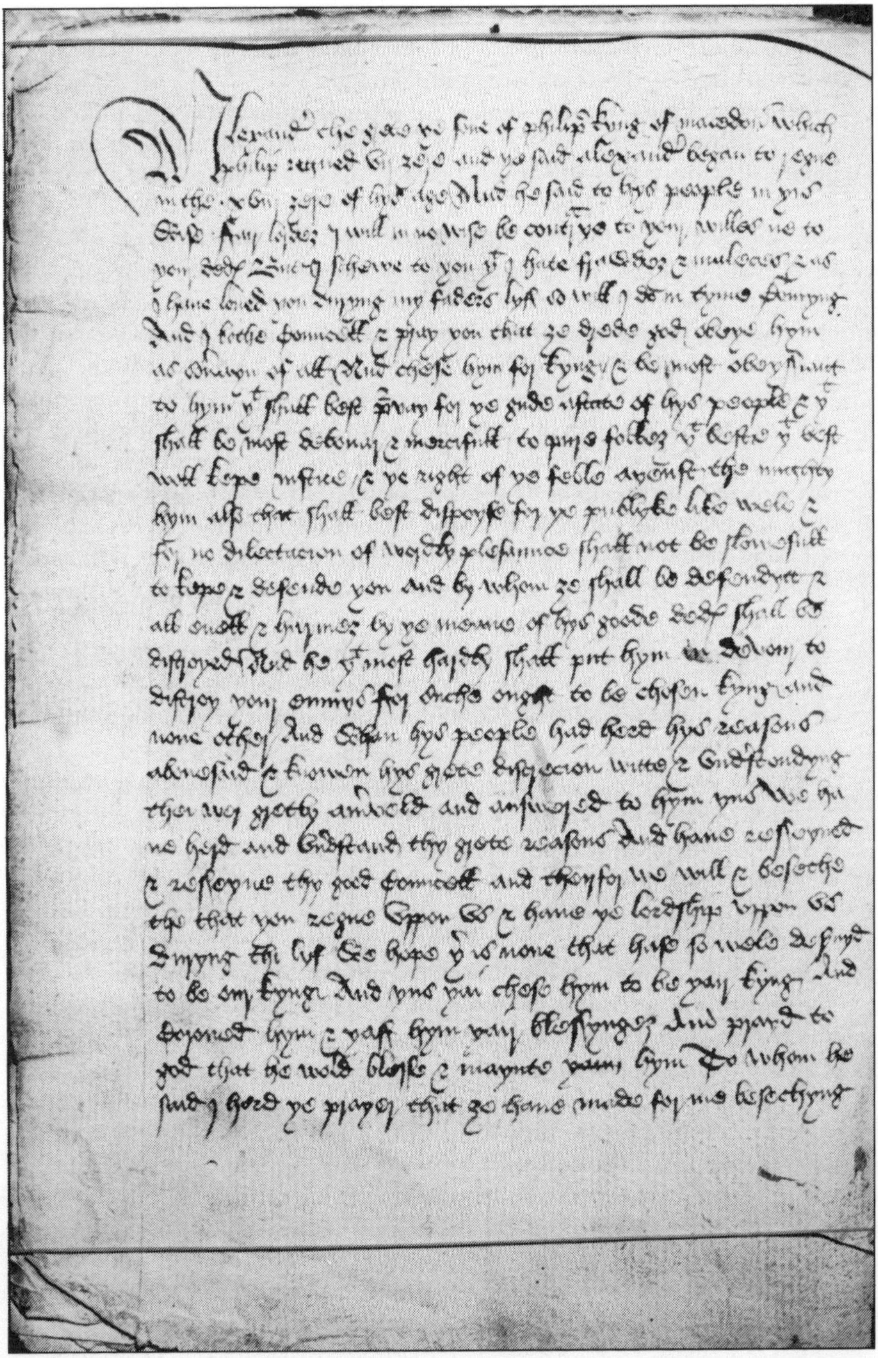

Plate 5. Trinity College, Dublin, MS 213, fo. 70v.

by an English artist on the model of the illuminations in this manuscript. The edition illustrates how in printed books illumination by hand gave way to woodcuts modelled on manuscript illumination.

Although a number of exemplars for incunables have been identified, it is hardly surprising that only one of Caxton's exemplars has so far been identified with certainty: Vatican Library MS Latin 11441 acted as copy for his edition of *Nova Rhetorica* (*STC* 24188.5).[20] Many of Caxton's publications were his own translations of French originals. Presumably his translations were made on loose sheets and then used as copy-text by the compositor. When the printing was finished, it is likely that the sheets would be disposed of as waste. Second editions were more usually set up from printed copies than from manuscripts.[21] When Caxton issued his second edition of the *Canterbury Tales* (*STC* 5083), he claimed to have used a better manuscript to improve the text found in the first edition. Instead of printing direct from this manuscript, he made alterations in a copy of his own first edition, and that was then used as exemplar by the compositor.[22] When a book was printed, it is not likely that all sheets were bound up for sale immediately. Probably the publisher kept many sets of sheets in his office. When sales went well and he decided on a second edition, he probably took one of these sets of sheets to mark up for the compositor. When the new edition was finished, these sheets would again be disposed of as waste. Since the early printers seem to have co-operated quite extensively, it is possible that something similar happened when one printer re-issued a text that had been published first by a different one.

Vatican MS Latin 11441 is a large folio manuscript, mostly made up of paper, consisting of 538 folios. It consists of eighteen booklets, containing works written either by Lorenzo Guglielmo Traversagni (1425–1503), the author of *Nova Rhetorica*, or by his brother Giovanni Antonio. Lorenzo was a Franciscan from Saona who studied and taught at various places in Europe. Among other places, he stayed at Vienne, Toulouse, Cambridge, London and Paris. While he was in the university of Cambridge he wrote the *Nova Rhetorica*, and according to the colophon it was completed on 26 July 1478. It was a text book suitable for university use, and it is not surprising that someone thought it should be printed. The *Nova Rhetorica* occurs on folios 1 to 88 of Latin 11441. Although the printed version has no indication of printer or date or place of publication, the paper sorts and the type prove that it was issued by Caxton. The compositor copied the colophon found in the manuscript, except that by mistake he reproduced the scribe's 26 July 1478 as 6 July 1478. Recently a study of the paper used in Caxton's books has indicated

20 For information about exemplars in English books see the appendices; for other exemplars see references in de la Mare and Hellinga, 'The First Book', p. 217.

21 See N.F. Blake, *Caxton: England's First Publisher* (London, 1976), pp. 85–119.

22 T.F. Dunn, *The Manuscript Source of Caxton's Second Edition of the Canterbury Tales* (Chicago, 1940).

that *Nova Rhetorica* was produced before the *Cordial* (*STC* 5758), which is dated 24 March 1479.[23] Hence the book was set up in print shortly after it was completed, and it is possible that Traversagni had Latin 11441 written to serve as exemplar for the compositors. The printed book consists of 124 leaves, so there is less on each of its pages than on those of the manuscript.

When a manuscript was copied it was possible for it to be written simultaneously by several scribes. To do this the manuscript was broken down into sections, usually of a quire each, and individual scribes were given their own

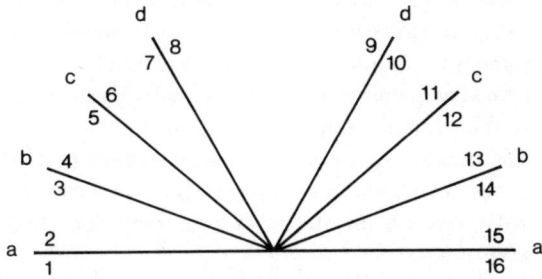

Fig. 1 Diagram showing the position of sheets in a gathering.

stint to complete. In such cases it was incumbent upon them to finish their stint at the end of a folio or quire so that it could be joined without any blank space to the stints written by other scribes.[24] In universities, texts were similarly broken down into smaller portions so that separate parts could be loaned out to students to make their own copies.[25] The technique of breaking up a text for simultaneous copying was well understood in the medieval period. The setting of printed books demanded a different method of organisation of the work, because it was usually neither economic nor technically feasible to print a book in the sequence in which it was written or read. If a printed book was made up of folio sheets of paper, each sheet would be folded once to obtain four pages of text. As the sheets were collected into gatherings, consisting usually of four sheets, the text which appeared as the four pages on any one sheet would not be consecutive passages. As may be seen from the diagram, the outer sheet of a gathering would have the first and second pages on the recto and verso of one half, and then the penultimate and last pages of the gathering on the recto and verso of the other half. If the gathering was a quaternion, that is a gathering of four sheets, the pages on the outer sheet would be 1, 2, 15 and 16. As the sheet was printed as a unit, it meant that

23 L. Hellinga, *Caxton in Focus* (London, 1982), p. 82.
24 A.I. Doyle and M.B. Parkes, 'The Production of Copies of the *Canterbury Tales* and *Confessio Amantis* in the early Fifteenth Century', in *Medieval Scribes, Manuscripts and Libraries*, ed. M.B. Parkes and A.G. Watson (London, 1978), pp. 163-210.
25 G. Pollard, 'The *pecia* System in the Medieval Universities', *ibid* 145-61.

pages 1 and 16 would lie side by side in the forme and be printed at the same time. The same applied to pages 2 and 15.

Most printers had only a limited supply of type and could not leave pages 1 and 2 set up in type until the compositor came round by natural sequence to pages 15 and 16. It was necessary to be able to set up page 16 immediately after page 1. Furthermore, it was usual for more than one compositor to work on a text, because the pressman could pull off the required number of printed sheets more quickly than a compositor could set up a sheet. Hence in order to keep the press working continuously, it was necessary to have sufficient compositors to keep the pressmen occupied. It was therefore essential to mark off the text in some way so that the compositor would be able to set up page 16 before he had tackled pages 2 to 15. It is these signs of casting off which usually provide the evidence that a manuscript has been used as a printer's examplar.[26] This method of compositorial casting off may have been taken over from practices developed in scriptoria, since there is evidence that many manuscripts were written on sheets before they were folded and cut to produce the extant pages.[27]

Different printers had their own methods of working, and in the fifteenth century one cannot assume that what is true of one text applies to all others. In many cases the nature of the text or manuscript may have determined the way in which a compositor worked. A poetic text was likely to cause few problems in casting off, but a prose text was different, particularly if it had glosses or marginal notes. In such texts compositors tend to cast off each page with approximately the same number of lines rather than with the identical number. In Latin 11441 the usual number was twenty-eight lines of manuscript at first, though that seems to have been reduced later to about twenty-four lines. The number allowed for on page 19 of that quinternion is 25. It is difficult to account for this variation precisely, but the following points should be borne in mind. Handwriting may vary in size from page to page, even if it is all the work of one man. There were also numerous ways in which a scribe could reduce or expand his language, and many of these ways were available to the compositor as well. The most common was to use or alternatively to expand abbreviations. Another was simply to crowd letters in more closely or alternatively to spread them out very widely. Gaps between words could also be reduced or expanded. It was possible to vary the spelling of words in many languages so that they become longer or shorter. In English the addition or omission of final -*e* and the spelling of words ending in a single

---

26 L. Hellinga, 'Notes on the Order of Setting a Fifteenth-Century Book', *Quaerendo*, 4 (1974), 64–9.

27 For a study of the way in which medieval manuscripts were written before their sheets were folded and cut see L. Güssen, *Prolégomènes à la codicologie. Recherches sur la construction des cahiers et la mise en page des manuscrits médiévaux* (Ghent, 1977). This work contains a bibliography.

consonant with a double consonant with *e* to give the variants *ship: shippe* are well known. Finally it was always possible to adjust the language by adding or deleting words. This could be done either by simple addition or by substituting a phrase for a word. Hence the texts of early printed books are liable to be less accurate at the end of pages than they are elsewhere.[28] The text was not sacrosanct, and the compositor had no qualms about making minor adjustments to the language to accommodate the text on a given page. As a last resort it would always be possible for the compositor to have an extra line or part of a line of type at the bottom of his page, though that expedient was not often employed.

In Sloane 1579 the text is cast off in pages and the beginning of each page is indicated by a pattern or three or four small dots at the beginning of the marked-off page. This method is not common and it may have been used to make as little disfigurement of the manuscript as possible, for the illuminated manuscript was valuable and may not have belonged to the printer. In Vatican 11441 the casting off is much bolder. The printed book was set up in quinternions, that is, there were five folio sheets each folded once to give ten leaves and twenty pages in each gathering. The general rule the compositor followed was to mark the beginning of each page by its number in the quinternion, so that a series of numbers from 1 to 20 runs through the manuscript. This marking off commences with a series which runs only from 5 to 20, because there were some blanks at the beginning of the manuscript which were taken over as blanks in the printed edition as well. In fact in the Cambridge copy of the edition the blanks are missing, if there were any, and the first sixteen pages are divided up into a ternion (three folios folded once each to give twelve pages) and a single folio page folded once to give four sides. In the copies of the edition preserved at Uppsala and Turin there is an initial quinternion consisting of four blank and sixteen printed pages. It may be that the Cambridge system was adopted later to save paper. The manuscript finishes with a series of numbers that runs from 1 to 12, because the text finishes at that point. The copies all have a ternion at the end with no blank pages. To cast off the page the compositor must have either counted (not always accurately) a certain number of lines, or simply judged from the look of the text how much was to be included on the page. He then put the appropriate page number of that quinternion in either the left- or right-hand margin. Each page was normally expected to begin at the start of a line, though this did not happen when a word was divided between lines. Then the page commenced with the first complete word of that line. Occasionally, when there was a quotation of some other textual feature at the beginning of the line, this could also be placed on the previous page. When that happened

---

28 See L. Hellinga, 'Manuscripts in the Hands of Printers', *Manuscripts in the Fifty Years after the Invention of Printing*, ed. J.B. Trapp (London, 1983), pp. 3–11.

there is usually some indication to this effect. The compositor when casting off also paid attention to new chapters or paragraphs which could be used as places to begin a new page. At the end of each cast-off page on the manuscript there is a little sign which resembles a tick. This is always placed in the right-hand margin. There are corrections in the manuscript, and these are incorporated in the text, such as the addition of *loquebat*.

An interesting feature of Latin 11441 is that it also contains immediately after the *Nova Rhetorica* a text of the *Epitome*, an abridged version of the earlier text (fols. 89–108). The colophon to the text notes that it was completed on 24 January 1480 under the protection of King Louis of France. The abridgement must have been composed during Traversagni's visit to Paris. Caxton also published an edition of this text, which, although undated, has been assigned to the period 1480–1 (*STC* 24190.3).[29] It must have been printed very shortly after it was completed, but Latin 11441 was not in this case used as the printer's exemplar. Presumably Traversagni had a copy made in Paris which he sent over to Westminster to be printed. It is interesting to think that he wanted the same printer to issue this second text, even though there were by 1480 enough printers in Paris to undertake this task. It may be that both texts were printed through the offices of Traversagni's Cambridge friends rather than because of his own efforts.

Other examples of manuscripts used as printer's copy have been identified and these are listed in the appendix. Although Wynkyn de Worde used a system similar to that found in Latin 11441, Pynson's method was somethat different. Of particular interest is a manuscript found in St John's College, Oxford (MS 266).[30] It occurs in a volume which is made up of printed texts and a manuscript text, and it is clear that these texts were meant to go together. The volume contains Caxton's *Troilus and Criseyde* (c. 1482; *STC* 5094), his second edition of the *Canterbury Tales* (c. 1482; *STC* 5083), his first edition of *Quattuor Sermones* (c. 1483; *STC* 17957 pt 2), and a manuscript version of Lydgate's *Siege of Thebes*. The Lydgate poem is written on paper, and the watermark evidence indicates that the paper was current from about 1476. The poem cannot have been copied until after 1482, because it was designed to fit in with the other texts. Each printed item in this collection is ruled by hand in red; and every page has full line and column ruling. The marginal lines are ruled right to the edges of the page so that they cross at the corners of the text. This ruling, which is uniform throughout, was obviously carried out after the pieces were collected together. But the ruling is continued on the pages which contain the text of the *Siege of Thebes*, although in this case it was

29 For a full description and edition see R.H. Martin, 'The *Epitome Margaritae Eloquentiae* of Laurentius Gulielmus de Saona', *Proceedings of the Leeds Philosophical and Literary Society: Literary and Historial Section*, 14 (4) (1971), 99–187.

30 G. Bone, 'Extant Manuscripts Printed from by W. de Worde with Notes on the Owner, Roger Thorney', *The Library*, 4th series, 12 (1931–2), 284–306.

executed before the text was copied since it continues beyond the end of the text for six leaves. There has been a conscious effort to unify the volume, even though it contains printed books and a manuscript text.[31] Gavin Bone, who published these details, also noted that the manuscript copy had been used as exemplar for Wynkyn de Worde's edition of *Siege of Thebes* (c. 1500; *STC* 17031), which survives only in an imperfect copy in the British Library. The two texts agree together against other manuscripts, and the St John's manuscript has the characteristic marks of compositorial casting off. Gavin Bone wondered whether the manuscript could have been copied from the printed text, but dismissed this possibility because of the compositor's marks and the date of the watermarks.

It may be that Gavin Bone dismissed the possibility that the St John's manuscript is a copy of a printed book too quickly; but if it is a copy, it is likely to be of a lost edition by Caxton rather than of the c. 1500 edition by de Worde. The *Siege of Thebes* is a continuation of the *Canterbury Tales* by Lydgate, for it contains the story that Lydgate the monk tells on the return journey from Canterbury. It would be a natural text for Caxton to publish at about the same time as the *Canterbury Tales*, which he re-issued c. 1482. In the prologue to that second edition he includes lavish praise of Chaucer. The language which Caxton uses for this eulogy is borrowed in part from the *Siege of Thebes*, which was evidently very familiar to Caxton at this period, since the passages from the poem he borrowed are taken from its middle and not from the beginning or end, which might indicate a superficial knowledge. It is also known that Caxton was very influenced by Lydgate, to whom he refers in his *History of Troy*, the first book he translated and printed.[32] Since the printed books in the St John's volume were issued by Caxton about 1482, it is possible to assume that he also printed an edition of *Siege of Thebes* at that time or a little earlier. It may well be that Roger Thorney, who owned this manuscript, could not acquire a copy of the printed version and so had a manuscript copy of it made for him to complete his volume. Attractive as this possibility is, for it has long puzzled Caxton scholars why he did not print any of Lydgate's longer poems, it is not possible to say that the evidence is strong enough to prove it. It should, however, be kept in mind as a distinct possibility. As we shall see, it was common to make manuscript copies of printed books, and there would be nothing untoward in Thorney having a copy made to complete a particular collection.

It may seem strange to modern readers that people would make manuscript copies of printed books, since it might easily be thought that the

---

31 For a similar instance in a Latin text see R.B. Haselden, 'A Scribe and Printer in the Fifteenth Century', *Huntington Library Quarterly*, 2 (1939), 205-11.

32 See above, chapter 11, pp. 149-65.

invention of printing would put an immediate end to copying.[33] A little reflection will suggest how improbable this is. Even in modern times, before the invention of the copying machine, a student at university, for example, who wanted a copy of an article had the option of buying the journal or copying out the article in full or in part. If the journal was no longer in print then the ways of getting one's own copy were restricted to the second-hand market or copying. As students often did not want the whole text, copying represented the quickest and cheapest method to use. The same would apply in the fifteenth century to all classes of reader. If you wanted a copy of a book, then you could have a copy made if you could not acquire a printed text. In the days when the book-trade was not so well developed throughout the country, it may well have been simpler and cheaper to have your own copy written out. Since this was what people had been accustomed to, it would be natural for them to continue employing this method even though the exemplar was a printed book. We do not know how the book distribution network operated or how effective it was, but if you lived in a small town in the Midlands you might have difficulty acquiring printed copies of texts. It is true that there is evidence that Caxton editions found their way to Scotland in the fifteenth century, where they were used by Henryson and other writers.[34] But it is not possible to tell how exceptional this was.

Another difficulty with printed books is that all copies of a given edition are virtually identical. The language in which they were written could not be adjusted for different parts of the country. Several of the copies of printed books that survive are in fact written in various northern dialects, and it may be that the owners preferred books in their own variety of English, though it may also be that it was more difficult to acquire the originals in these parts. Many people then as now made collections of writings which interested them and formed commonplace books. These more often contain matter copied from manuscripts or from oral sources. Inevitably some of the matter was also taken from printed books, for in scrap books of this kind there is no restriction on the source used. The rationale for the collection is usually the interest of the compiler. Inevitably with some books the printed version may have been

---

33 Attention has been given increasingly to this phenomenon. C.F. Bühler, 'The *Fasciculus Temporum* and Morgan Manuscript 801', *Speculum*, 27 (1952), 182–3, n. 29, provided a list of manuscript copies of Caxton prints which he supplemented in *The Fifteenth Century Book*, p. 34. Bühler has also written on copies of Latin manuscripts in that book and in 'An Unusual Fifteenth-Century Manuscript', *La Bibliofilia*, 42 (1940), 65–71. See also C.E. Lutz, 'Manuscripts copied from Printed Books', *Yale University Library Gazette*, 49 (1975), 261–7; S. Hindman and J.D. Farquhar, *Pen to Press. Illustrated Manuscripts and Printed Books in the First Century of Printing* (College Park, Md, and Baltimore, 1977), pp. 101ff.; and J.B. Trapp, *Manuscripts in the Fifty Years after the Invention of Printing* (London, 1983).

34 The evidence is disputed: for a discussion see D. Fox, 'Henryson and Caxton', *JEGP*, 67 (1968), 586–93.

the only source available to the person who wanted a copy. Even so it may seem surprising that some texts which were frequently printed, like the *Canterbury Tales*, were copied in whole or in part.

It is a common belief, though it is not supported by the evidence, that most collectors and many ordinary users preferred manuscripts to printed books, because the latter were more utilitarian. It is true that there are many manuscripts which are lavishly illuminated, but these form only a small proportion of the total manuscript output. The majority of manuscripts were as utilitarian as the average printed book. Even so, the belief that people appreciated manuscripts more has led many to assume that if a manuscript was made from a printed book it was to produce a de luxe version of the text, presumably for presentation to some patron. As we have seen, that was not strictly necessary, because a printed book could be illuminated to produce the same effect. With Caxton's output there is only one certain example of a de luxe manuscript produced from a printed book, though there is also one possible example.

The certain example is Lambeth Palace Library, MS 265, which is a copy of Caxton's *Dicts or Sayings* dated 1477. This is a manuscript made of vellum containing 109 folios. The verso of the first folio contains a presentation illumination. This illumination shows a well-dressed courtier, presumably Anthony Wydeville, Earl Rivers, presenting a book, which is bound in green with a single clasp, to Edward IV sitting on his throne and surrounded by his court, including the queen, Anthony Wydeville's sister, and the future Edward V. Next to Rivers there is another figure, also kneeling, who is dressed in black and has a tonsure. Although this figure has sometimes been interpreted as Caxton, it is more likely to be the scribe Haywarde, who signed the volume at the end of the epilogue. The illumination is frequently reproduced in modern books.[35] Underneath the picture is the rubric.:

> This boke late translate here in syght
> By Antony Erle   (*blank*)   the vertueux knyght

Although the name is either erased or not entered here and in other places in the book, the reference is clearly to Anthony Wydeville who translated the work from French into English and who, according to Caxton, requested that his translation should be printed. If this is so, then it is probable that Rivers also ordered the manuscript version of the translation to present to Edward IV. Why his name is erased is not clear, though he was beheaded by Richard III shortly after Edward's death.

Since the translation was made shortly before it was printed, and exists otherwise only in printed versions, this manuscript must have been made either from a printed version or from the copy-text which the compositor also

35 For the most recent discussion of this manuscript with plates see Hellinga, *Caxton in Focus*, pp. 77–83.

used. The similarities in the text confirm this hypothesis. However, Haywarde's copy contains the passages added to the text by Caxton and Haywarde's colophon is modelled directly upon that found in some printed copy rather than from the manuscript copy-text.

The position is, however, rather more complicated than this because of the textual and printing history of the translation. The *Dicts or Sayings* was printed three times by Caxton. The first edition is dated to 1477, but it exists in two forms. The copy of the first edition in the John Rylands Library has a colophon which contains the words 'sette in forme and emprynted in this manere as ye maye here in this booke see Whiche was fynisshed the .xviij. day of the moneth of Novembre, the sevententh yere of the regne of kyng Edward the fourth' (i.e. 1477). The ten other extant copies do not have this colophon, though some lack the final folio. It has recently been suggested that this colophon was added to the Rylands copy after the book had been printed and that it consequently provides no evidence for the date of its printing; or rather it provides simply a *terminus ante quem*.[36] The second edition printed by Caxton contains this same colophon unchanged, although this edition must have been printed after 1477. The type of the second edition suggests a printing date after 1478 and the watermarks suggest a date of 1480. The second edition contains a corrected text, and many of these corrections have been entered in Lambeth 265 though in a way which does not call attention to them. In other words, the manuscript was copied from the first edition, but the scribe had access to the colophon added to one or more copies of that edition, and he also had access to the corrections incorporated in the second edition. The colophon of the manuscript echoes the words of the printed colophon quoted above as follows: 'sette in fourme & enprinted in right substanciale maner. And this boke was ffinisshed the xxiiij day of Decembre the xvij^th yere of our liege lord king Edward þe iiij^th'.

It is not easy to interpret this evidence. We may conclude that the copying of the manuscript was completed on 24 December 1477, but the illumination and corrections would probably have been inserted later, though we cannot say. Although the first printed edition was produced before 18 November 1477, its precise date of publication cannot be established. It is probable that the scribe of Lambeth 265 had more than a month to complete his copying; it was not a job that was rushed through. It is not clear whether the corrections in the manuscript or the second edition were made first. It is possible that a copy of the first edition was corrected and that this served as copy for both the manuscript corrections and the second edition. At all events what is clear is that there was considerable liaison between the scribe and the printing press. The scribe may have been a Benedictine at Westminster Abbey and so a near neighbour of Caxton, though we know little about Haywarde. What is even more difficult to assess is what role Earl Rivers played in all this.

---

36 *Ibid.*

Another manuscript which also has a close connection with Caxton's press is the Magdalene College, Cambridge, manuscript of his translation of Ovid's *Metamorphoses*. The translation, which is in fifteen books, became split up. The last six books were bequeathed to the college by Pepys in his will, dated 1703. The first nine books, which were thought to be lost, turned up in 1964 among the papers of Sir Thomas Phillipps and were ultimately reunited with the other half in the Pepys collection. The colophon of the manuscript reads:

Thus endeth Ouyde hys booke of Methamorphose translated & fynysshed by me William Caxton at Westmestre the xxij. day of Apryll. the yere of oure lord m^l.iiij^c.iiij^{xx}. And the xx yere of the Regne of kynge Edwarde the fourthe.

The work has been translated by Caxton, and several insertions in it show that he had taken some interest in the work. The manuscript was probably written shortly after 22 April 1480, for it is copied in a late fifteenth-century Flemish hand. The book itself contains a prologue which has been translated from the French version which Caxton used as his source, which was printed by Colard Mansion in Bruges in 1484. The prologue gives us no information about the translation or its possible printing. The manuscript contains illuminations at the beginning of each book, or rather provision is made for illuminations there. But the artist has completed only the first four illuminations, and the blanks still remain at the beginning of the last eleven books.[37] The completion of the manuscript was interrupted, though whether this was because the buyer was no longer willing to finance the venture or because the artist died we cannot tell. Since Earl Rivers is connected with the other illuminated manuscript copied from a Caxton print and since he was beheaded in 1483, at a time when the manuscript could have been written, it is tempting to think that he also had some link with the Magdalene manuscript. There is, however, no evidence to link him directly with it. The reasons for the copying of the manuscript and for the absence of some of the illuminations will never be known.

The more interesting question is whether the manuscript was copied from a printed edition or not, although no copy of a printed edition survives. Since Caxton made the translation, he must have made it for a printed edition, since there is otherwise no evidence that he made translations for scribal copying. Since the translation was completed in 1480 and since there is no known reason at that period which might have prevented him from printing the text, it is likely that it was printed. In his *Golden Legend*, which was finished on 20 November 1483, Caxton refers to several works which he had already 'parfourmed and accomplisshed'. This list includes 'the xv bookes of *Metamorphoseos* in whyche been conteyned the fables of Ovyde'. The other five works which are named had all been printed by Caxton, and so it would be reasonable to assume that the Ovid had also been printed by that time. The question whether Caxton had printed the text is of some importance, for if he

37 For the illumination see K.L. Scott, *The Caxton Master* (Cambridge, 1976).

did not then he must have taken an active hand in the organisation of the production of the manuscript, for it would have to be copied from his papers. If the book was printed, it remains possible that someone had the manuscript made without the printer's consent or knowledge, though how likely that is remains uncertain. The only way that this difficulty could be resolved is if there is something in the text which could indicate a printed exemplar such as the scribal copying of what is clearly a printing mistake. So far nothing has been found that is significant, though the whole manuscript has not yet been edited. Nevertheless, it is on balance reasonable to suppose that the manuscript is a copy of a printed book, and that Caxton did indeed issue a printed edition of the *Metamorphoses*.

When a manuscript has been used as copy for a printed book it usually contains tell-tale marks of casting off. When a manuscript is copied from a printed book, there are no such signs to help determine whether the exemplar was a printed book or a manuscript similar to the printed book. In those case where the translation was made to be printed, there is naturally an assumption that any surviving manuscript was made from a printed version, since the printed copies would form the only copies of the text available – apart that is from the papers used by the compositor himself. At times it can be shown that a manuscript was in a printing office, though in itself this would not prove that the manuscript had been used as a copy or was indeed a copy of a printed book. The Winchester Malory, now BL Add. MS 59678, has offsets of printed characters on some leaves, and these offsets have been identified as types used in combination in Caxton's workshop between 1480 and 1483.[38] There are no signs of casting off in the manuscript, and so it would seem that it was not used as the exemplar; in theory it is possible to think that it may have been copied from the printed text. However, the two copies vary so much textually that this is not a likely hypothesis. Bodleian Library, MS Fairfax 16, a collection of Chaucerian and other poetry, contains smudges which can be interpreted as printer's ink, probably from the fingers of a compositor. Again there is no sign of casting off in this manuscript, so it was probably not used as exemplar. Furthermore, the smudges cannot be dated. As it is known that John Stowe, the sixteenth-century antiquarian, owned the manuscript, it is likely that the smudges got on to it at that time rather than in the fifteenth century.[39] Sometimes layout and particular aspects of a text can give some evidence that a manuscript was copied from a printed book, though that evidence will not usually be foolproof. The best evidence probably comes from misprints which are taken over into the manuscript. The type of misprint which a compositor makes is different from the one a scribe will make, because the compositor may put his hand into the wrong compartment

38 L. Hellinga, 'The Malory Manuscript and Caxton', *Aspects of Malory*, edited by T. Takamiya and D. Brewer (Cambridge, 1981), pp. 127–41.

39 For a description of the manuscript see *Bodleian Library MS Fairfax 16*, with an introduction by J. Norton-Smith (London, 1979).

of characters whereas a scribe will confuse similar letter forms. In Bodleian Library, MS Hatton 51, which is a copy of Gower's *Confessio Amantis*, there is a reading which reflects a compositorial misprint. On fol. 131rb the last line but one reads 'Or otherwkse yf it stode'. In Caxton's printed edition of 1483 (*STC* 12142) there is the identical misprint in the line which reads 'Or otherwkse yf it so stode'. The misprint arises either from faulty distribution of type or because the *i* and *k* compartments of type were side by side and the compositor put his hand in the wrong one. It is unlikely that if the scribe was copying from a manuscript he would have confused *k* with *i* or *y*. In the case of this manuscript, the scribe has also tried to keep the pagination of the printed book, with its two columns per page. He wrote the text first in black ink leaving gaps for the Latin quotations, headings, and capitals so that they could be filled with red ink afterwards. Not all the gaps were subsequently filled. Either to save space or through carelessness, he did not always leave a gap for the Latin prose glosses, so the text of the manuscript differs from that of the printed edition considerably in some places. Nevertheless, even without the misprints which point to a printed exemplar it is beyond reasonable doubt that this manuscript was copied from Caxton's edition, for it includes his prologue but not his colophon.

The difficulty of deciding whether a manuscript comes from a printed edition may be illustrated by Cambridge, Trinity College, MS R.3.15, a copy of the *Canterbury Tales*. Apart from sixteenth-century additions, this is a paper manuscript of 306 folios made at the end of the fifteenth century. Some of the watermarks are said to be identical with those in Caxton's paper. In the Manly–Rickert account of manuscript affiliations this text was allocated to their group *b*, to which Caxton's first edition (*STC* 5082) also belongs. In fact these two texts form a small sub-group within group *b*. The manuscripts in group *b* descend vertically, rather than radially, from the archetype of the group, and R.3.15 was placed lower down the stemma than Caxton's edition.[40] It would, therefore, seem that textually it could be a copy of the printed version. It is unlikely that the printed copy comes from the manuscript because the former was issued c. 1476 and the latter is dated from c. 1480 to 1500, though the watermarks suggest a date c. 1485. Manly and Rickert describe R.3.15 as a twin of Caxton's edition, though the order of the tales has been disturbed somewhat in the manuscript.[41] This is because, they feel, the common ancestor used by both became distorted after the printed edition had been set up. But this variation in the tale order could have come about through the disruption of the printed sheets rather than through the disturbance of a manuscript. It will only be possible to tell what the relationship of these two texts is if they are subjected to closer study; at present one may accept the possibility that R.3.15 is a copy of Caxton's first edition.

40 J.M. Manly and E. Rickert, *The Text of the Canterbury Tales* (Chicago, 1940), II, 57-59.
41 *Ibid.*, I, p. 530.

An interesting manuscript copy of printed texts is BL MS Sloane 779. This is a paper manuscript of 155 folios written in 1484 by 'Dominus Grace' for 'Dame Margaret Wodward'; presumably the former is a cleric and the latter may have been a pious lady or semi-recluse. The manuscript contains copies of Caxton's first edition of *Game of Chess* (*STC* 4920), which was printed on 31 March 1474 in Bruges, and of his *Cordial* (*STC* 5758), printed on 14 March 1479 at Westminster. The *Game of Chess* was issued in a second edition with woodcuts about 1482 at Westminster. The manuscript copy of the *Game of Chess* omits Caxton's entire prologue, which referred to George, duke of Clarence, and it begins with the main text proper. Caxton's epilogue is included, and although this refers to a lord, he is not named. The *Cordial* has no prologue in the printed version; it had a lengthy epilogue. This was substantially abbreviated by the scribe in Sloane 779, and all references to the translator, Anthony Wydeville, Earl Rivers, and the printer are omitted. The scribe very carefully copied parts of the epilogue but referred to Earl Rivers as 'the translatoure'. That the shortening was done by the scribe is suggested by various corrections. Where Caxton's edition reads 'Whiche werke present I begann', Sloane 779 has 'Whiche werke present [I *subsequently erased*] was begonne' (fol. 151r). The omission of all names would suggest that the scribe had no connection with Caxton or with the noblemen like Rivers. The names were omitted as irrelevant. Caxton may have included them to make the book appear more popular and fashionable, but that was of little interest to the scribe. Dame Margaret was presumably merely interested in the contents of the books, in their didactic material, and not in who else was reading it. The printed edition was simply a source for the text. Since the copy of the *Game of Chess* is from the first edition rather than the second, which being printed in 1482 was available in 1484, it is possible that the scribe was working outside London, where the printed text of the first edition, if not the second, would be easily obtainable. It does show that the edition printed in Bruges had made its way into many parts of England within a relatively short time. It also indicates how sensible Caxton was to concentrate on didactic works of this nature.

This last point is borne out by the number of manuscript copies made of the *Dicts or Sayings*. Caxton himself produced three editions of this work, but even so it was often copied out by hand. Its attraction lay not only in its message, but also in its composite nature. It was easy to extract shorter or longer passages from it to include in a different volume. Dublin, Trinity College, MS 213, contains the Alexander section only on folios 70v–72r. BL Add. MS 60577 (the Winchester Anthology) has a different extract. Even those texts which apparently contain the full text have sometimes shortened it, as is true of the Chicago copy. Although there was much didactic literature copied in manuscripts in the fifteenth century, the flood of printed texts must have made printed editions particularly popular both for reading and as source material for copying.

Not all scribes were averse to referring to Caxton as the source of their material, and some may have found his editions convenient to make copies from. This probably applies to Cambridge, Peterhouse MS 190 which contains a copy of Warkworth's Chronicle detailing events in the late fifteenth century. This chronicle follows on from a copy of the *Brut*. In fact this earlier material (fols. 1–214v) is copied from Caxton, which is clearly indicated by the scribe who on fol. 214v wrote 'ffinysched and ended after the Copey of Caxton then in Westmynster'. The material copied from Caxton has turned out to consist partly of the first edition of the *Chronicles of England* (*STC* 9991) printed in 1480 (fols. 1–202r) and partly of the end of his edition of Higden's *Polychronicon* (*STC* 13438), printed in 1482 (fols. 202r–214v). The reasons for this mixture of printed editions are not known, though it is possible that the amalgamation of parts of two printed books occurred in the publisher's office. It is also possible that the scribe's copy of the first book was incomplete, and so he turned to the second one to finish off his preliminary matter. In this instance Warkworth was acting much like other scribes of the *Brut*, which had had a series of additions tacked onto it as the events it described receded further into the past. Many felt the need to bring it up to date. That Warkworth used a printed copy rather than a manuscript may be purely fortuitous, although he may well have felt that a printed history was more authentic and wider known than any manuscript copy would be.[42]

The transition to printed books was a gradual one, and the expertise that accumulated in scribal techniques over the centuries was not abandoned quickly. The presses could satisfy only some of the demand for written material which to an extent it helped to generate; and so scribes continued to supply the rest of the market. There was no conflict between the two means of production, for they complemented each other.

42 See T. Takamiya, 'Print to Manuscript, or the Exemplars of Peterhouse MS 190', *TCBS* (forthcoming).

CAXTON PRINTS FOR WHICH A COPY-TEXT SURVIVES OR WHICH WERE USED AS COPY

1. CANTERBURY TALES, First Edition (*STC* 5082)

(i) Manly and Rickert, I, p. 530 describe Cambridge, Trinity College, MS R.3.15 as a 'twin' of Caxton's print. They suggest that the two texts share a common exemplar, but the MS may be a copy of the print. It uses paper, dated c. 1485, also found in Caxton prints.

(ii) Manly and Rickert claim that in Cambridge, Trinity College, MS R.3.19 part of the General Prologue and all of the Monk's Tale (which is included in a book described as Lydgate's 'Bochas') were 'copied from the printed Caxton of c. 1478 rather than from the MS used by Caxton' (I, p. 533). The text is a composite of the *Fall of Princes* and the *Canterbury Tales*. The booklets are of various dates from late fifteenth to sixteenth centuries.

(iii) Bodleian Library, MS Laud 739 contains a late copy of the *Canterbury Tales*, c. 1470–90. Manly and Rickert think that 'in the first part of the text there are corrections in an early 16 C hand, which seem to come from a Caxton' (I, p. 319).

2. CANTERBURY TALES, Second Edition (*STC* 5083)

Manchester, Chetham's Library, MS 6709 is a collection of saints' lives and miracles copied by William Cotson in March 1490. It contains two tales from the *Canterbury Tales*: The Nun's Tale and the Prioress's Tale (fols. 157–75v). Manly and Rickert say 'Almost certainly copied from Caxton's second edition' (I, p. 83). See LIFE OF OUR LADY.

3. CHAUCERIAN MINOR POEMS

In his introduction to the facsimile of Cambridge, Magdalene College, MS Pepys 2006 (Norman, Oklahoma, 1985) A.S.G. Edwards suggests that the texts in the second part of the manuscript were possibly 'copied from a printed source, whether Caxton or Caxton derived' (p. xxix).

4. CHRONICLES OF ENGLAND, First Edition (*STC* 9991)

(i) Lambeth Palace Library, MS 264, fols. 143–69, dated from late fifteenth/early sixteenth century, contains a copy of Caxton's print: see Bühler, *Speculum*, 27 (1952), 178–83. M.R. James, *A Descriptive Catalogue of the Manuscripts in the Library of Lambeth Palace* (Cambridge, 1932), p. 411, writes: 'This last section is very likely from Caxton's printed edition' [i.e. the final continuation]. Other manuscripts in which the continuation was probably copied from Caxton's edition are Huntington HM 136 and Glasgow, MSS Hunterian 74 and 228, in which the continuation was never completed, and BL Cotton Claudius A. VIII and Bodleian Library, MS Rawlinson poet. 32; see L. Matheson, *Speculum*, 60 (1985), 595–6. Matheson suggests that BL Add. 10099 may be a copy of Caxton's exemplar, which was completed as a presentation copy; and also that Caxton was the compiler of the continuation. See also POLYCHRONICON.

(ii) G. Raynaud, *Catalogue des manuscrits anglais de la Bibliothèque nationale* (Paris, 1884), no. 30, is a MS of the *Brut* which is described as 'Redaction incomplète de la *Chronique* dite de Caxton, dont la première édition est de 1480' (p. 11). The paper MS is of the fifteenth century, and it may contain a copy of Caxton's edition.

5. CONFESSIO AMANTIS (*STC* 12142)

Bühler, *Speculum*, 27 (1952), 178–83, notes that Bodleian Library, MS Hatton 51 (S.C. 4099) contains a copy of Caxton's print. The MS which contains the single work is dated c. 1500. It is written on parchment and contains 202 folios.

6. CORDIAL (*STC* 5758)

 (i) Bühler, *Speculum*, 27 (1952), 178–83, notes that BL MS Sloane 779, fols. 76v–151r contain a copy of Caxton's print made by Dominus Grace for Dame Margaret Woodward in 1484; see also GAME OF CHESS.
(ii) CUL MS Nn.3.10, a quarto MS of paper from c. 1500 containing *Cordial* and Mirk's *Festial*. The former, on fols. 1–27, is imperfect at beginning and end. Bühler, *Speculum*, 27 (1952), 178–83, and *A Catalogue of the Manuscripts preserved in the Library of the University of Cambridge*, IV (Cambridge, 1861), p. 479.
(iii) Edinburgh, Scottish Record Office, MS GD 112/71/1 (1) is a manuscript consisting of two parts (i) a prose life of Edward II, and (ii) a copy of Rivers' *Cordial*. The latter text occurs on fols. 14r–79v. It is a copy of Caxton's edition with anglicised spellings which contain some Scottish variants. The watermarks, according to Dr Lyall, suggest a date of 1479 and certainly not later than 1485. Since Caxton's edition appeared in 1479, this copy, which was probably made in Scotland, must have been written shortly afterwards. On the final folio there is a note 'Iste liber pertinet Iohannes Cambell' in what is probably a fifteenth-century hand.

7. COURT OF SAPIENCE (*STC* 17015)

Bühler, *Speculum*, 27 (1952), 183 claims the BL Add. MS 29729 contains a copy of Caxton, though without saying which text. The MS contains a collection of English poems mostly by Lydgate, many of which were written by or for John Stowe from a Shirley manuscript. The most likely item to be a copy of a Caxton print is the *Court of Sapience* on fols. 87–122, though the British Library catalogue makes no reference to the possibility.

8. DICTS OR SAYINGS, First Edition (*STC* 6826, 6827)

 (i) Lambeth Palace Library, MS 265, an illuminated MS on vellum written by Haywarde on 29 December 1477, was apparently intended for presentation to Edward IV. There are numerous references to it; see most recently L. Hellinga, *Caxton in Focus* (London, 1982), pp. 77–80. For a description of the MS see M.R. James, *A Descriptive Catalogue of Manuscripts in the Library of Lambeth Palace* (Cambridge, 1932), No. 264. See also C.F. Bühler, 'The Dictes and Sayings of the Philosophers', *The Library*, 4th series, 15 (1934–5), 316–29.
(ii) Chicago, Newberry Library, MS f.36 Ry 20, fols. 208–41 contains a shortened

copy of the printed edition made by a North English scribe; C.F. Bühler, 'The Newberry Library Manuscripts of the *Dictes and Sayings of the Philosophers*', *Anglia*, 74 (1956), 281–91.

(iii) Columbia University Library, MS Plimpton 259 contains a shortened version of one of Caxton's editions, though certain identification of edition is impossible. C.F. Bühler, 'New Manuscripts of *The Dicts and Sayings of the Philosophers*', *MLN*, 63 (1948), 26–30.

(iv) BL Add. MS 60577 (Winchester Anthology), fols. 38–44v (written in Winchester after 1487) has an acephalous extract of Caxton's print containing some of the sayings attributed to Hermes. See *The Winchester Anthology. A Facsimile of British Library Additional Manuscript 60577*, with an Introduction by Edward Wilson (Cambridge, 1981).

9. DICTS OR SAYINGS, Second Edition (*STC* 6828)

(i) BL Add. MS 22718, a vellum MS in folio from late fifteenth/early sixteenth century which contains a text of the *Dicts or Sayings* including the colophon. The first folio is missing. See Bühler, *Speculum*, 27 (1952), 178–83 and Scott, *The Caxton Master*, p. xi. For a full account, see Bühler, 'The Dictes and Sayings of the Philosophers'.

(ii) Dublin, Trinity College, MS 213, fols. 70v–72r, contains the Alexander extract from Caxton's print; the rest of the MS contains the *Wars of Alexander* and an A text of *Piers Plowman*. The MS is dated 1475–1500 and is associated with Durham Priory c. 1500. See T.K. Abbott, *Catalogue of the Manuscripts in the Library of Trinity College, Dublin* (London, 1900), No. 213; and Doyle, 'The Manuscripts', pp. 99–100.

(iii) Curt Bühler (New York) MS 11: see C.F. Bühler, 'New Manuscripts of *The Dicts and Sayings of the Philosophers*', *MLN*, 63 (1948), 26–30. This MS is in a fifteenth-century English hand.

10. ENEYDOS (*STC* 24796)

Princeton University Library, MS 128 contains a copy of Caxton's edition. The paper MS may be dated c. 1600. The copy has been given the title 'Caxton's translation of the Æneids out of French Dedicated to Prince Arthure Eldest sonne to King Henry the 7th'. It opens with Caxton's prologue. The colophon reads: 'Here finisheth the booke of Æneids, compiled by Virgill, wch hath beene translated out of Latine into French and out of French reduced into Englishe by mee William Caxton the xxij daie of June in the yeare of our Lord 1490 and in the fift yeare of kinge Henry the 7th.'

11. GAME OF CHESS, First Edition (*STC* 4920)

BL MS Sloane 779, fols. 1–76r, contains a copy of Caxton's print without prologue copied by Dominus Grace for Dame Margaret Woodward in 1484; see CORDIAL.

12. GOLDEN LEGEND (*STC* 24873)

(i) Bodleian Library, MS Bodley 952 contains a copy of the *Golden Legend* which is incomplete, but which was copied from Caxton's edition. The life of St Rock has the note 'The ffeste off saynt Rocke ys alwey holdyn on the morne after the day of Thassumpcion off owre lady whych lyff is traunslated owte off latyn in to englesche by me William Caxton' (fol. 219v). See M. Görlach, *The South English Legendary, Gilt Legende and Golden Legend* (Braunschweig, 1972), pp. 26–7, and C. Bühler, 'A New Middle English Life of Saint Winifred?' *Medieval Studies for Lillian Herlands Hornstein*, ed. J.B. Bessinger and R.R. Raymo (New York, 1976), p. 95. The MS is of the late fifteenth century and is incomplete at beginning and end.

(ii) New York, PML MS Bühler 26 contains *inter alia* a *Lyfe of St Weneffryde* written in the last quarter of the sixteenth century. Its colophon states that it is 'drawen out of an ould pryntinge boocke word by word'. Although it is not an exact copy of Caxton's version of the life in the *Golden Legend*, Bühler suggests that 'the most probable explanation' is that it is 'a free copy of the Caxton version, thus denying the very positive statement by the scribe and giving a fine example of the liberties which copyists were prepared to take with their exemplars'; see Bühler, *ibid.*, pp. 87–97.

13. HORSE, SHEEP AND GOOSE, Second Edition (*STC* 17018)

Huntington Library, MS HM 144, fols. 140v–144r, contains the second part of the poem copied from this edition: see C.F. Bühler's 'Lydgate's *Horse, Sheep and Goose* and Huntington MS. HM 144', *MLN*, 55 (1940), 563–9.

14. INDULGENCE 1476 (*STC* 14077 c. 106)

Queen's University Library, Belfast, has two MS copies of this indulgence, though both are a little damaged. They are included in a miscellaneous manuscript which may be dated to the end of the fifteenth century; the MS is Brett MS B50. See K. Povey, 'The Caxton Indulgence of 1476', *The Library*, 4th series, 19 (1938–9), 462–4.

15. JASON (*STC* 15383)

(i) Glasgow University Library, MS Hunterian 410, a paper MS of late fifteenth/ early sixteenth century of 125 folios written in Flemish hand on same paper sorts as found in Caxton's prints. See Bühler, *Speculum*, 27 (1952), 178–83; and J. Young and P.H. Aitken, *A Catalogue of the Manuscripts in the Library of the Hunterian Museum in the University of Glasgow* (Glasgow, 1908), No. 410.

(ii) CUL MS Dd.3.45, partly paper and partly vellum, written in a slovenly hand of late fifteenth century, contains only *Jason* in its 102 fols. It is imperfect at beginning and end. See *A Catalogue of the Manuscripts preserved in the Library of the University of Cambridge*, 1 (Cambridge, 1856), pp. 101–2.

16. LIFE OF OUR LADY, First Edition (*STC* 17023)

(i) Manchester, Chetham's Library, MS 6709, a collection of saints' lives and miracles, copied by William Cotson in March 1490, contains on fols. 6v–156r a copy of Caxton's print: see R.A. Klinefelter, 'Lydgate's *Life of Our Lady* and the Chetham MS. 6709', *Publications of the Bibliographical Society of America*, 46 (1952), 396–7. See CANTERBURY TALES, second edition.

(ii) According to *Bibliotheca Anglo-Poetica; or, a descriptive catalogue of a rare and rich collection of early English Poetry: in the possession of Longman, Hurst, Rees, Orme and Brown* (London, 1815), No. 414, pp. 187–8, there is a paper MS made in 1602 which is 'a transcript from the edition by Caxton'. The MS opens: 'This booke was compiled by dan John Lydgate monke of Burye, at the excitacion and stirynge of the noble and victoryous Prince king Hary the fifthe in honour glory and reverence of the berth of our most Blessed Lady mayde wyf and Moder of our lord Jhesu, Chryst.' The *Life of our Lady* is followed by 'other metrical lines entitled "Lydgats testament and last will"'. The MS is now Liverpool Cathedral Library, MS Radcliffe 16.

17. NOVA RHETORICA (*STC* 24188.5, 24189)

This edition was set up from Vatican Library, MS Latin 11441 fols. 1–88: see J. Ruysschaert, 'Les manuscrits autographes de deux oeuvres de Lorenzo Guglielmo Traversagni imprimées chez Caxton', *BJRL*, 36 (1953–4), 191–7.

18. ORDER OF CHIVALRY (*STC* 3356.7)

BL MS Harley 6149, a paper MS of 174 folios, is a composite MS containing mainly matters of heraldry. It was compiled by Adam Loutfut, Kintyr Pursuivant, a Scottish scribe in the service of Sir William Cummyn, in 1494. It contains the *Order of Chivalry* copied from Caxton's print on fols. 83–109, probably after 29 September 1494. Loutfut's copy is in the Scots dialect and is edited in A.T.P. Byles, *The Book of Ordre of Chyualry*, EETS, os, 168 (1929). Loutfut's version was itself copied three times: (i) by M.R. Anderson at the end of the fifteenth century in Oxford, Queen's College, MS 161 fols. 65–82v; (ii) by John Scrymgeour about 1530 in Edinburgh, Advocates' Library MS 31.5.2; and (iii) by Sir David Lindsay in 1586 in Edinburgh, Advocates' Library MS 31.3.20.

19. OVID'S METAMORPHOSES

Caxton translated this book on 22 April 1480. It survives as MS 2124 in the Pepys Library, Magdalene College, Cambridge. It may be a copy of a printed edition, though no trace of such an edition has been discovered. See S. Gaselee and H.F.B. Brett-Smith, *Ovyde hys Booke of Methamorphose* (Oxford, 1924); and *The Metamorphoses of Ovid translated by William Caxton*, 2 vols. (New York, 1968).

20. POLYCHRONICON (*STC* 13438)

(i) It has been accepted that Cambridge, Peterhouse, MS 190 contained a copy of some Caxton material since the publication of J.O. Halliwell, *A Chronicle of the First Thirteen Years of the Reign of King Edward the Fourth by John Warkworth*. Camden Society, os, 10 (London, 1839). L.M. Matheson, *Speculum*, 60 (1985), 593–614, has now shown that Glasgow Hunterian 83 (T.3.21) and BL Harley 3730 are linked with Peterhouse 190. After a version of the *Brut* which in Peterhouse 190 may be copied from the St Albans *Chronicles of England* ending in 1419, there is a continuation from 1419 to 1461 consisting of sections of text copied at first from a Caxton edition of *Chronicles of England* and then from Caxton's *Polychronicon*. This compilation is followed by *Warkworth's Chronicle*. Hunterian 83 seems to be the original manuscript and Harley 3730 is a copy of it. For the period 1419 to 1461 Peterhouse 190 is probably a copy of Harley 3730. Three manuscripts were probably made for the fellows of Peterhouse about 1484, and may have been made in the College itself. See also CHRONICLES OF ENGLAND. Professor Matheson is compiling a book about these manuscripts; his article contains references to some previous discussions.

(ii) Two MSS have used Caxton's edition as the basis for a composite history from Adam to Hannibal, which makes use of a wide variety of sources; they are Oxford, Trinity College D 29 and Huntington MS HM 144. See K. Harris, 'John Gower's "Confessio Amantis" and the Virtues of Bad Texts', in Pearsall, *Manuscripts and Readers*, pp. 31ff, and C.W. Marx and J.F. Drennan (eds.), *The Middle English Prose Complaint of Our Lady and Gospel of Nicodemus* (Heidelberg, 1988), p. 13.

21. SIEGE OF JERUSALEM (*STC* 13175)

BL MS Royal 18.B.xxvi, a paper MS of 256 folios dated to the middle of the sixteenth century, contains *The History of Holy Ware*, part 2 of which is 'a condensation of Caxton's translation': see M.N. Colvin, *Godeffroy of Boloyne*, EETS, ES, 64 (1893), p. xvii.

22. STANS PUER (*STC* 17030)

A copy of Caxton's print is included in Richard Hill's commonplace book, now Oxford, Balliol College, MS 354, fols. 158v–6ov, a paper MS of 248 fols. dating from the early sixteenth century. See R.A.B. Mynors, *Catalogue of the Manuscripts of Balliol College Oxford* (Oxford, 1963), pp. 352–4. R. Dyboski, *Songs, Carols and other Miscellaneous Pieces from the Balliol MS.354*, EETS, ES, 101 (1907), p. xxx, writes of *Stans Puer* that 'the Balliol text seems to be copied from Caxton's print'. On p. 179 Dyboski writes that *Salve Regina* and the rhyming rules which follow *Stans Puer* in the Balliol MS are also identical with Caxton 'so that we arrive at the conclusion, that the whole group of pieces, No. 60–3 in our catalogue table, were probably *transcribed in bulk from Caxton's quarto*'. The text of the *Book of Courtesy* in Balliol 354 is similar to that in Caxton's print, but it has not been identified as a copy of it. Balliol 354 also contains pieces copied from *Arnold's Chronicle* printed at Antwerp c. 1502–3 and at Southwark in c. 1521.

APPENDIX B
REJECTED CAXTON EXAMPLES

1. BOOK OF COURTESY (*STC* 3303)

Oriel College, MS 79 is listed by Bühler, *Speculum*, 27 (1952), 183, as a copy of Caxton's edition. The Caxton text and the Oriel MS were printed in F.J. Furnivall, *Caxton's Book of Courtesye*, EETS, ES, 3 (1868). It is clear that the Oriel text is different from Caxton's and cannot be copied from it.

2. BOOK OF GOOD MANNERS (*STC* 15394)

Bühler, *Speculum*, 27 (1952), 173–83, following Blades and the *Cambridge Bibliography of English Literature* I, p. 262, indicates that BL MS Harley 149 is a copy of Caxton's print. This is rejected by R.H. Wilson, in *A Manual of the Writings in Middle English*, II, edited by A.E. Hartung (New Haven, 1972), p. 943.

3. CONFESSIO AMANTIS (*STC* 12142)

G.C. Macaulay, *The English Works of John Gower*, EETS, ES, 81 (1900), p. clxiii, claimed that Oxford, Magdalen College, MS 213 was one of the three MSS used by Caxton as copy-text or else he used one so like Magd. 213 as to be indistinguishable from it. This position was supported by G. Bone, 'Extant Manuscripts Printed from by W. de Worde with Notes on the Owner, Roger Thorney', *The Library*, 4th series, 12 (1931–2), 285–6. He noted the similarity of the two texts and the occurrence in Magd. 213 of some indistinct crosses or circles which corresponded to the pages in Caxton's print. Bone did not think the proof for Magd. 213 as examplar for Caxton's edition conclusive, though he accepted it was very strong. This view was rejected by N.F. Blake, 'Caxton's Copytext and Gower's *Confessio Amantis*', *Anglia*, 85 (1967), 282–93, mainly on the grounds that the texts of the two were so different. Blake also claims that Caxton had only one MS of the poem.

4. CURIAL (*STC* 5057)

E.J. Hoffman, *Alain Chartier: His Work and Reputation* (New York, 1942), p. 162, indicates that there is a MS copy of Caxton's print in Bodley Rawlinson A338; and this information is repeated by R.H. Wilson in *A Manual of the Writings in Middle English 1050–1500* (New Haven, 1972) III, p. 938. Although this MS contains English translations of works by Chartier, it does not contain a copy of the *Curial*; for a description see M.S. Blayney, *Fifteenth-Century Translations of Alain Chartier's 'Le Traite de l'Esperance' and 'Le Quadrilogue Invectif'*, EETS, 281 (1980), II, pp. 4–9.

5. DICTS OR SAYINGS (*STC* 6826, 6827)

First Report of The Royal Commission on Historical Manuscripts (London, 1874), p. 60, col. 2, suggests that Lord Tollemache's MS (Helmingham Hall) is 'the same probably as that printed by Caxton'. C.F. Bühler, *The Dicts and Sayings of the Philosophers*, EETS, OS, 211 (1941), p. xxxix, dates the MS 'not after 1460' and so the text cannot be a copy of Caxton's. Bühler's book contains an edition of the text in this MS.

6. HOUSE OF FAME (*STC* 5087)

Bodleian Library, MS Fairfax 16 contains additional material to Chaucer's poems, including the *House of Fame*, which were added in Caxton's editions. These have been inserted in a seventeenth-century hand. The MS was listed by Bühler, *Speculum*, 27 (1952), 178–83 as a copy of a Caxton print. This extra material should be regarded as coming from a sixteenth-century edition of Chaucer rather than from Caxton.

APPENDIX C

OTHER INCUNABULA COPIED INTO MANUSCRIPTS OR FOR WHICH MANUSCRIPT COPYTEXTS EXIST IN ENGLAND

1. ASSEMBLY OF GODS (*STC* 17005, 17007)

According to G. Bone, 'Extant Manuscripts Printed from by W. de Worde with Notes on the Owner, Roger Thorney', *The Library*, 4th series, 12 (1931–2), 284–306, Wynkyn de Worde's c. 1498 edition of the *Assembly of Gods* (*STC* 17005), wrongly attributed to Lydgate, was printed from Cambridge, Trinity College, R.3.19, fols. 68r–98r; this MS text is edited in O.L. Triggs, *The Assembly of Gods*, EETS, ES, 69 (1896). In B.Y. Fletcher, 'The Textual Tradition of *The Assembly of Gods*', *PBSA*, 71 (1977), 191–4, it is claimed that this edition is later than *STC* 17007, traditionally dated c. 1500. The edition in *STC* 17007 was both copied in BL MS Royal 18.D.II, fols. 167a–180b (a manuscript made before 1520 which also includes a copy of Pynson's ?1515 edition of Lydgate's *Testament* (*STC* 17035)), and also served as the probable copytext of the c. 1498 edition, *STC* 17005.

2. BOKE OF ST ALBANS (*STC* 3308)

BL MS Lansdowne 762, fols. 16r–v contains various short items such as the properties of a horse, proverbs and various short verses which may have been copied from the *Boke of St Albans*; see C. Meale, 'The Social and Literary Contexts of a late Medieval Manuscript', D.Phil. diss., University of York, 1984, pp. 234–5.

3. CANTERBURY TALES (*STC* 5085)

Manly and Rickert, I, p. 416, say MS Phillipps 6570 was 'Probably used by Wynkyn de Worde to supplement his principal MS.' They do not offer any reasons for this statement. The MS is now Newberry Library, Silver MS 1, and a similar statement about its use by de Worde is made in C.O. Faye and W.H. Bond, *Supplement to the Census of Medieval and Renaissance Manuscripts in the United States and Canada* (New York, 1962), p. 176.

4. CHRONICLES OF ENGLAND (*STC* 9995)

According to L.M. Matheson, 'Historical Prose' in Edwards, *Middle English Prose*, pp. 224–5, Glasgow University Hunterian 83 contains at first a copy of the St Albans *Chronicles of England*: see also Appendix A.20 (i).

5. CONSOLATORIUM TIMORATE CONSCIENTIE

The Paris edition of 1478 of Johannes Nider's *Consolatorium Timorate Conscientie* (Hain–Copinger 11809) is copied in Dublin, Trinity College, MS 343, fols. 1–134: see T.K. Abbott, *Catalogue of the Manuscripts in the Library of Trinity College, Dublin* (London, 1900), No. 343.

6. DE PROPRIETATIBUS RERUM (*STC* 1536)

De Worde's edition c. 1495 used Columbia University Library, Plimpton MS 263 as copy-text; see Mitchner, 'Wynkyn de Worde's Use of the Plimpton Manuscript of *De Proprietatibus Rerum*', *The Library*, 5th series, 6 (1951–2), 7–18.

7. DIVES AND PAUPER (*STC* 19212)

Pynson's edition c. 1493 used Bodleian Library, MS Eng.th.d.36 as copy-text; see M.M. Morgan, 'Pynson's Manuscript of *Dives and Pauper*', *The Library*, 5th series, 8 (1953), 217–28.

8. FALL OF PRINCES (*STC* 3175)

The copy-text for Pynson's 1494 edition of this text has been identified as John Rylands Library MS English 2; see 'A Specimen of Early Printer's Copy: Rylands English 2', *BJRL*, 33 (1950–1), 194–6.

9. FESTIAL

Cambridge, St John's College, MS 187 (G 19) is a copy of Mirk's *Festial* and *Quattuor Sermones* printed at Rouen in 1499; the copy must have been made shortly after the book was printed. See Bühler, *The Fifteenth-Century Book*, p. 34; and M.R. James, *A Descriptive Catalogue of the Manuscripts in the Library of St John's College, Cambridge* (Cambridge, 1913), p. 224, no. 187.

10. LIFE OF ST EDITH

The extant copy of this work, BL Cotton Faustina B.iii fols. 199r–263r, contains marks probably from the late fifteenth century which may be interpreted as marking up for a printed edition; see J. Ayto, 'Marginalia in the Manuscript of the *Life of St Edith*: New Light on Early Printing', *The Library*, 5th series, 32 (1977), 28–36. No printed edition survives, if one was ever executed.

11. POLYCHRONICON (*STC* 13439)

Yale University Library, Beinecke Osborne Shelves MS 1.20 is a sixteenth-century paper manuscript contains an incomplete text of Wynkyn de Worde's 1495 edition of the *Polychronicon*. The MS contains only the prohemye, index to the whole work and an incomplete part of the first book. There are 25 paper leaves of text.

12. SIEGE OF THEBES (*STC* 17031)

A composite volume in St John's College, Oxford (MS 266), consisting of copies of Caxton editions and a manuscript version of Lydgate's *Siege of Thebes* was used as copy-text for de Worde's c. 1497 edition of *Siege of Thebes*; see G. Bone, 'Extant Manuscripts Printed from by W. de Worde with Notes on the Owner, Roger Thorney', *The Library*, 4th series, 12 (1931–2), 284–306.

13. SPECULUM AUREUM DECEM PRECEPTORUM DEI

A MS of this work in Latin by Henricus Harpius consisting of 320 vellum leaves was sold at Sotheby's on 6 December 1983 and is described in the sale catalogue. This MS was made in England, probably in London or Westminster, before 1492, when the donor William Morland, prebend of St Paul's, died. He bequeathed the MS to St Stephen's Chapel, Westminster Palace. The MS is copied from the first edition printed by Peter Schoeffer in Mainz in September 1474 (*Catalogue of Books Printed in the XVth Century now in the British Museum*, I, p. 30).

14. VITAS PATRUM (*STC* 14507)

BL Harley 2252, a commonplace book compiled by John Colyns, contains a section on the treachery of the English which was taken 'owte of A boke', and this is most likely to be de Worde's edition of *Vitas Patrum*, 1495.

15. THEODORIC WERKEN

This scribe copied Latin texts of Latin fathers for Christ Church, Canterbury, in 1477 and 1478 from editions printed in Italy; see R.A.B. Mynors, 'A Fifteenth-Century Scribe: T. Werken', *TCBS*, 1 (2) (1950), 97–104; and A.C. de la Mare, 'A Fragment of Augustine in the Hand of Theodoricus Werken', *TCBS*, 6 (1972–6), 285–90.

16. JOHN WHETHAM

John Whetham, monk of the Carthusian House at Sheen, copied in 1496 Chrysostom's *Homiliæ in evangelium S. Iohannis* for the Prior, Ralph Tracy, at the suggestion of the former Prior, J. Yngilby, then bishop of Llandaff. This MS, formerly in the possession of Mr W.L. Wood of Chandler's Cross, Hampshire, was sold at Sotheby's on 10 December 1969, lot 80. It appeared in the November 1974 catalogue of Charles Traylen, but its present owner is untraced. It was apparently copied from the 1470 or 1486 printed edition (Hain–Copinger 5036 and 5037). See N.R. Ker, *Medieval Libraries*, pp. 178, 305; and E.M. Thompson, *The Carthusian Order in England* (London, 1930), pp. 331–4.

APPENDIX D
REJECTED EXAMPLE

1. BOOK OF HUNTING (*STC* 3308)

Bühler, *The Fifteenth-Century Book*, p. 117, suggests that the *Book of Hunting* in the St Albans Printer's *Book of St Albans* may have been copied in Bodleian Library, MS Rawlinson poet.143 from the edition printed by de Worde in 1496. But Rachel Hands, *English Hawking and Hunting in the Boke of St Albans* (London, 1975), p. xxxiii, shows that the MS preserves an independent text from that of St Albans. Since de Worde's print was set up from the St Albans one, Rawl. poet.143 cannot be a copy-text of de Worde.

Index of Manuscripts

BELFAST, Queen's University

Brett M50   297

BRUSSELS, Bibliothèque Royale

9308   144

DUBLIN, Trinity College

213   292, 296
343   301

CAMBRIDGE

Corpus Christi 61   9
Magdalene, Pepys 2006   294
                       2124   289, 298
Peterhouse 190   293, 298-9
St John's 187 (G 19)   320
Sidney Sussex 4.1   192-3
Trinity R.3.15   153, 291, 294
      R.3.19   294, 301
University Library Dd 3.45   297
                Nn 3.10   295

CHICAGO, Newberry Library

f.36 Ry 20   295-6
Silver 1   301

EDINBURGH

Advocates 31.3.20   298
          31.5.2   298
Scottish Record Office
      GD 112/71/1 (1)   295

GLASGOW, University

Hunter   74   294
         83   298-9, 301
        228   294
        410   297

HELMINGHAM HALL   300

KESWICK HALL   194

LIVERPOOL, Cathedral

Radcliffe 16   298

LONDON

Lambeth Palace 264   294
               265   9, 287-8, 295
               306   277
British Library:
      Additional 10099   294
                 29729   295
                 35298   223-4
                 59678   16-17, 199-211, 290
                 60577   292, 296
      Cotton, Claudius A VIII   294
              Faustina B III   302
      Harley 149   300
             2252   303
             2381   219
             3730   298-9
             6149   298
             7184   194
      Lansdown 762   301
      Royal 18 B xxvi   299
            18 D ii   301
            19 A ix   2, 26, 33-4, 103,
                       110-111, 279
      Sloane   779   292, 295-6
              1579   58, 278, 283
      Stowe 50-51   223

MANCHESTER

Chethams 6709   294, 297
Rylands English 2   302
         Latin 395   277

NEW HAVEN, Yale University

Beinecke Osborne Shelves I.20   302

NEW YORK

Columbia, Plimpton 259   296
            Plimpton 263   302
Pierpont Morgan, Bühler 11   296
                Bühler 26   297

OXFORD

Balliol 228   225
       354   299
Bodleian:
    Bodley 952   296
    Douce 15   225
    Eng.th.d.36   302
    Fairfax 3   193
            16   290, 300
    Hatton 51   193n, 291, 295
    Laud 739   294
    Rawlinson A 338   300

C 499   225
poet. 32   294
poet. 143   303
Magdalen 213   187-92, 300
Oriel 79   299
Queen's 161   298
        213   225
St. John's 266   284-5, 302
Trinity D 29   299

PARIS, Bibliothèque Nationale

30   295

PRINCETON, University

128   296

ROME, Vatican

Latin 11441   7, 280-4, 298

SAN MARINO, Huntington Library

HM 136   294
HM 144   297, 299

STAFFORD   193

WOLLATON HALL   192-4

Index of Names

Aachen 249
Abbott, T.K. 296, 301
Abel 214, 224
Abraham 215
Abrion, Master 251
Adam and Eve 214, 223-5, 299
Advent 217, 220-1
Advertisement 73, 206
Aegidius de Columna 59
Aesop 27, 103, 126, 174, 205, 272n
Afer, Publius Terentius 59
Africa 214
Aitken, P.H. 297
Alcock, John, Bishop of Ely 70
Alliterative Revival 134
American Typophiles 53
Amos, F.R. 245n
Amsterdam 232
Anderson, M.R. 298
Andrew, S.O. 256n
Anelida and the False Arcite 150-1n
Anglo-Saxon 125
Anonymiana 5n
Antwerp 72, 232, 299
Anwykyll, John 59-60
Arber, E. 270n
Aretinus, Franciscus 59
Aristotle 59
Arnold's Chronicle 299
Arnout 232
Arthur, King 33, 131, 176, 200-4, 207-10
Arundel, William Earl of 10, 32, 105, 115, 152, 177
Ascham, Roger 211
Ashby, George 158
Asia 214
Assembly of Gods 301
Astrolabe 173
Aurner, N.S. 143n, 149
Aurner, R.R. 126n, 137n

Ayto, J. 302

Babel 215
Babington, C. 132n
Ballade of Her that Hath all Virtues 183
Barclay, Alexander 179
Barnes, Dame Iulyans 62
Bartholomaeus Anglicus 3, 65, 80
Bateson, M. 277n
Bayard 64, 170
Bede 214
Bedford, John Duke of 181
Belgium 2
Benjamin 215
Bennett, H.S. 245n
Bennett, J.A.W. 130n, 165n, 187n, 202n
Bergen, H. 169n
Berkeley, Thomas Lord 16, 68
Berners, Lord 129, 134, 137n, 145, 152n
Bible 16, 67, 71, 131, 211, 213-29, 236
Biographia Britannica 37
Blades, William 19-20, 23, 25, 37-8, 42n, 44-9, 76-7, 149-51, 158-60, 232n, 278n, 300
Blake, N.F. 11n, 19n, 21n, 23n, 27n, 32n, 60n, 64n, 69n, 75-6n, 89-90n, 96n, 105n, 107n, 114n, 116n, 121n, 140n, 151n, 167-9n, 174n, 177n, 202n, 207n, 222n, 226n, 229n, 276n, 278-80n, 300
Blanchardin and Eglantine 2, 109, 122, 174, 177, 247, 250
Blanche, wife of John of Gaunt 9
Blayney, M.S. 300
Boccaccio 96, 98, 172, 181-2
Bodleian Library 113, 260
Boethius 16, 99, 101-2, 121-2, 128-32, 150-1, 157-62
Bond, W.H. 301
Bone, Gavin 190, 197n, 202n, 284n, 285, 300-2

Bonifaunt, Richard 42
Book of Canticles 218
Book of Courtesy 127, 157-8, 161, 174, 299
Book of the Duchess 9, 156, 172
Book of Ecclesiastes 218, 222
Book of Good Manners 15, 300
Book of Hours 61, 278-9; see also *Horae*
Book of Hunting 303
Book of Kings 218
Book of Noblesse 141n
Book of Parables 218, 222
Book of Paralipomenon 218
Book of St Albans 62-3, 301, 303
Book of Sapience 216, 218
Bosworth, Battle of 206
Brabant 177
Bradley, H. 242n
Brett-Smith, H.F.B. 298
Brigettine Order 71
Brigham, N. 160n
British Library 2, 76, 113, 260, 285
Brothers of the Common Life 76, 82
Bruges 2-4, 11-14, 20-2, 27, 33-4, 38, 46-8,
    53-6, 64-6, 72, 75-87, 89-100, 107, 110,
    167-9, 175, 233, 242-4, 276, 279, 289, 292
Bruno, Leonardo 59
Brussels 76, 82
Brut 62, 116, 293
Bryce, Hugh 103, 111
Bryce, Thomas 49
Bühler, C. 260n, 268n, 275n, 286n, 294-7,
    299-303
Burgh, Benedict 26, 110, 127, 174
Burgh, Richard 46-9, 207
Burgundy 2-4, 14-15, 64, 67-9, 167-70,
    174, 183-4, 222
Burgundy, Bastard of 168
Burgundy, Charles Duke of 4, 64, 67, 167
Burgundy, Philip Duke of 4, 15, 64, 86,
    90-3, 97, 167, 171
Burley 80
Bury St Edmunds, Abbey of 10, 171, 180,
    185, 298
Butler, P. 224
Butterworth, C.C. 221n, 227n
Bycorne and Chychevache 183
Byles, A.T.P. 245n, 248n, 298

Caesar, Julius 182
Cain 224
Calot, Laurence 181
Cambridge 7-8, 60, 63, 69, 280, 283-4;
    University Library 58, 113, 260

Campbell, Iohannes 295
Canterbury 180, 303
Canterbury Tales 11, 13, 25-9, 73, 101, 104,
    108-9, 112-13, 122, 150-7, 161-4, 174,
    179-80, 195-7, 200, 208-9, 243, 280,
    284-7, 291, 294, 301
Capons, Sir John 222
Carmeliano, Pietro 8, 59, 159
Carter, H. 58n
Carthusian Order 71
Cato 26-7, 107, 110-11, 174, 207
Caton 175, 208
Caxton and his World 30-1, 200
Caxton International Congress 76, 80
Caxton, William, *passim*
Cham 214
Chambers, R.W. 134n
Charles the Great 13, 105, 109, 122, 125, 177,
    205
Charles VI (of France) 170
Chartier, Alain 143-4, 300
Chastising of God's Children 70
Chaucer, Geoffrey 5, 9, 16, 22, 26, 66, 101,
    108-13, 121-35, 149-65, 167, 169, 171-2,
    180-2, 187-91, 195, 204, 207, 242-3, 247,
    285
Chaucer, Lewis 173
Chaucer's Complaint to his Purse 150, 151n
Chaumpaigne, Cecilia 22n
Christine de Pisan 143
Chronicles of England 62, 73, 101-2, 108, 116,
    128, 151, 177, 293-5, 298-9, 301
Churl and the Bird 29, 107, 174
Cicero, Marcus Tullius 16, 59, 129, 182
Clarence, George Duke of 4, 12, 27, 78-9,
    96, 112, 151, 175, 181, 292
Cloud of Unknowing 128
Clyde, W.M. 276n
Collinson, W.E. 238n
Cologne 3-4, 6, 10, 23, 54-9, 65, 75-6,
    79-85, 93-4, 159, 167-9, 172, 176, 249,
    253, 275; Register of Aliens 23, 56, 75, 93
Colvin, M.N. 241n, 272n, 299
Colyns, John 303
Complaint of a Black Night 183
Complaint of Our Lady 299
Confessio Amantis 32, 89, 91, 122n, 173-4,
    181, 187-98, 205, 207, 277, 291, 295,
    299-300
Consolatorium timorate conscientie 301
Continent 60-2, 66, 69, 85, 115-16, 201
Copland, Robert 86-7
Cordial 78, 99-100, 113, 128, 281, 292, 295

Corsten, S. 65n, 75n, 80, 83
Cotson, William 297
Court of Sapience 127, 174, 295; see also
 De cura sapientiae
Croll, M.W. 134n
Crotch, W.J.B. 20, 37-8n, 43-4n, 46n, 49,
 119n, 137-8n, 143n, 150-1n, 187, 217n,
 228-9n, 243-4n
Crow, M.M. 22n
Cummyn, Sir William 298
Curial 99, 144-5n, 300

Dares 170
Datus, Augustinus 62
Daubeney, William 13, 105-6, 177
David 217-18, 220-2
Davis, N. 259n
De amicitia 16
De casibus virorum illustrium 181-2
Declamation of Noblesse 103, 128, 176
De consolatione philosophiae 16, 99, 150
De cura sapientiae 161-2; see also *Court of
 Sapience*
Dedes, Robert 43
De duobus amantibus 80
Defence of Holy Church 184
De genealogia deorum 96, 172
de la Mare, A.C. 57, 278n, 280n, 303
Delft 232, 238
De officiis 56
De proprietatibus rerum 3, 6, 16, 65, 80, 83-4,
 131, 302
Description of Britain 78, 102, 117, 128
De scriptoribus Britannicis 159
De senectute 16
D'Evelyn, C. 24
De vita philosophorum 80
de Worde, Wynkyn 3-4, 23, 57, 61-2,
 68-73, 80, 84-6, 135, 197n, 202n, 233n,
 260-73, 284-5, 300-3
Dibdin, T.F. 37
Dictes Cretensis 170
Dicts of Philosophres s.v. *Dicts or Sayings*
Dicts or Sayings 9, 75, 99-101, 108, 114, 116,
 120, 128, 151, 270-1, 287-8, 292, 295-6,
 300
Diodorus Siculus 104, 129, 137, 152, 173
Directorium sacerdotum 108, 115
Dives and Pauper 302
Doctrinal of Sapience 15
Doyle, A.I. 173n, 177n, 281n
Drennan, J.F. 299
Duff, E.G. 57-8n, 61n, 72-3, 75n, 233n,

 260n, 276n
Dukmanton, Henry 42
Dunn, T.F. 112, 195, 229n, 280n
Durham Priory 296
Dutch 68, 123, 145-6, 174, 208, 226,
 231-58, 265, 266-7
Dyboski, R. 299

East Anglia 53, 180
Ebesham, William 277
Edward IV 2, 4, 9, 12, 21, 30-1, 51, 64, 78,
 91, 96-7, 105-6, 167-70, 175-7, 208,
 287-8, 295
Edward V 31, 287; see also Prince of Wales
 (Edward)
Edwards, A.S.G. 60n, 294, 301
Eisenstein, E.L. 275-6n
Ellis, F.S. 213, 234n
Eneydos 15, 109, 115, 119, 122, 126, 142,
 173, 177, 244n, 272-3n, 296
England 1-5, 7-9, 14-16, 19, 23, 34-5, 39,
 48-9, 57-8, 60, 62, 64-73, 78, 84-6, 92, 96,
 99-100, 120, 149, 159-60, 167-8, 170-1,
 174-5, 181, 184, 189, 208, 225, 233,
 248-50, 276, 278, 292, 303
English 5, 60-73, 77, 84-7, 90-3, 99-102,
 116, 119-35, 139-41, 144, 146, 149, 155-9,
 162-4, 169, 171, 180, 197, 208-9, 213,
 220-3, 225, 228, 239, 241, 245-53, 256-7,
 259-73, 276-80, 286-7
English Nation (at Bruges) 10, 21-2, 54,
 64, 91, 93, 167
Epistles (of Cicero) 129; (of Ovid) 122
Epistolae (of Phalaris) 59, 61
Epitome 7-8, 284
Erfurt 249
Esau 215
Ethics (of Aristotle) 59
Eton College 278
Europe 2, 58, 60-1, 214, 280
Exchequer 49
Exeter, Earl of 55
Expositio symboli 57-8, 278
Ezechiel 216, 221

Fall of Princes 120, 173, 294, 302
Farquhar, J.D. 286n
Fasciculus temporum 286
Fastolf, Sir John, of Norfolk 16, 68, 103,
 176, 207
Faye, C.O. 301
Feast of Nativity of St John the Baptist 38
Feast of St Edward 49

Feats of Arms 13, 15, 32, 122, 177, 248n
Febvre, L. 153n
Festial 108, 115, 128, 219, 295, 302; see also
    Liber festivalis
Field, P.J.C. 201n, 207
Fielding, Geoffrey 49
Fierabras 125
Fisher, J.H. 90n, 187n, 192-4
Five Wiles of Pharaoh 223, 226-7
Flanders 2, 55, 64-5, 69, 86, 167, 177, 232,
    278
Flemish 2-3, 126, 167, 277, 289, 297
Fletcher, B.Y. 301
Florence 278
Flores Sancti Augustini 3, 80
Four Sons of Aymon 15
Flower, D.C. 227
Fox, D. 286n
France 1-2, 12, 15, 24, 64, 69, 71, 167-8,
    170, 178, 181
French 2-4, 10-16, 24, 27, 30, 33-5, 53-4,
    64-9, 72-3, 79, 85-7, 90-2, 96-7, 100-5,
    109-10, 119-22, 124-31, 137, 143-6, 163,
    171-4, 180-4, 197, 201, 204, 207-9, 213,
    220, 223-6, 232, 241, 245, 276, 280, 287,
    289, 296
Furnivall, F.J. 144n, 155n, 157n, 299
Fust, Johan 80

Games of Chess 4, 11-12, 23, 27-8, 34, 66,
    75-86, 94-9, 107, 112, 151, 175, 208, 292,
    296
Gaselee, S. 298
Gaultier, Thomas 260-73
Gaunt, John Duke of 9, 172
Geoffrey of Vinsauf 162
Gerard ten Raem 57
Germanic 132, 139-40
Germany 58, 71, 214
Gesta Romanorum 80, 83-4
Ghent 55, 79, 93, 169
Gibbon, Edward 5, 7-8, 19, 71
Gideon 216
Gilte Legende 15, 195n, 213, 223-4, 226, 228
Gloucester, Humphrey Duke of 179n, 181-3
Godfrey of Bouillon 208, 299
Görlach, M 297
Golden Fleece 86, 97, 168
Golden Legend 15, 23, 27, 32, 61, 70, 105,
    108, 115, 177, 195, 205, 213-29, 289, 296-7
Goldwell, family of 58, 278
Goldwell, James, Bishop of Norwich
    58-61, 278

Gordon, I.A. 134n
Gospel of Nicodemus 299
Gouda 232, 234, 243-4
Gower, John 16, 89-91, 127, 129, 149,
    157-8, 164, 173, 179, 181, 187-98, 207,
    277, 291, 299-300
Greece 214
Greek 137, 208
Greenberg, C. 66n
Green, R.F. 179
Greg, W.W. 154-5
Gregory 218-19, 222
Griffith, R.R. 53, 99n
Güssen, L. 282n
Guido of Colonna 129, 181
Gutenberg, Johan 80, 275
Guy of Warwick 181

Hague, The 113
Hales, Alexander of 59
Halle, Robert 42
Halliwell, J.O. 298
Hammerschlag, J. 145
Hammond, E.P. 173n, 179
Hands, R. 62n, 303
Hannibal 299
Hanseatic League 55
Harowe, John 42, 44
Harpius, Henricus 303
Harris, K. 299
Hartung, A.E. 300
Hastings, William Lord 103, 111
Hawes, Stephen 179
Haywarde 287-8, 295
Heilbronner, W.L. 276n
Heli 217
Hellinga, Lotte 57, 67n, 80-2, 168, 278n,
    280-3n, 287n, 290n, 295
Hellinga, W.Gs. 80-2, 145n
Henry IV 181, 189, 206
Henry V 170-2, 175, 181, 298; see also
    Prince of Wales (Henry)
Henry VI 37-41, 185
Henry VII 13, 51, 177, 296
Henryson, Robert 286
Hesdin 15, 86, 97
Heton, Christopher 42-4
Heton, James 42
Higden, Ranulph 68, 117, 121-2, 128, 130,
    132, 194, 208, 224, 293
Hill, Richard 299
Hilton, Walter 70, 128
Hindman, S. 286n

Hirsch, R. 275n
Historical Library 104, 137, 173
History of Godfrey of Boloyne 241-2, 272n
History of Holy Ware 299
History of Troy 3-4, 9-16, 22, 24, 34, 37, 55-6, 64-8, 73-91, 95-9, 107, 109, 112, 119, 151, 157, 167-8, 170-7, 242, 272-3n, 276, 278, 285
Hoccleve, Thomas 157, 179
Hodnett, E. 279n
Hoffman, E.J. 300
Holland 2, 231, 233
Homer 170
Homiliae in evangelium S. Iohannis 303
Horae 73, 108, 113, 115-16; see also *Book of Hours*
Horse, Sheep and Goose 87, 107, 110, 174, 297
Horstmann, C. 277n
Hospitaller of St John's 12
House of Fame 150-2, 155-7, 160-1, 164, 300
Huizinga, J. 14
Hulbert, J.R. 134n
Hulsterloo 250
Hunt, Thomas 61, 115
Huntington Library 9, 278

Idley, Peter 24
Image of Pity 108, 115-16
Imray, Jean 38n
Indulgence 6-7, 73, 75, 86, 107, 279, 297
Instructions to his Son 24
Ireland 71
Isaac 215
Isaiah 217, 221
Isopes Fabules 174
Israel 216-17
Italian 129, 208, 278
Italy 58, 62, 71

Jackson, W.T.H. 231n
Jacob 215
James, M.R. 227n, 294-5, 302
Japhet 214
Jason 86, 96, 98, 172
Jason 15, 34, 85-7, 96-9, 107, 109, 120, 151, 167, 172-5, 244n, 272n, 297
Jehan le clerc 34, 53
Jepte 216
Jeremy, Sister Mary 23, 213n
Jones, P.E. 43n
Jerome 58, 215, 222
Jerusalem 217-18
Jewish Antiquities 215-16

Job 216, 218-19, 221
Joseph 215
Josephus 241-16, 222
Joshua 216-17, 220-2
Jubal 214
Judas Maccabeus 221
Judith 216, 219, 221

Kane, G. 22n
Kekewich, M. 168n
Kellner, L. 133n, 247, 250, 256n
Kent 24, 53, 90-1, 187
Ker, N. 199n, 303
Kerling, N.J.M. 20n, 243
King Appolyn of Tyre 86
King Arthur 73, 151, 199-211, 221; see also *Morte Darthur*
Kinkade, B.C. 132n
Kipling, G. 67n, 168
Klinefelter, R.A. 297
Knight of the Tower 11, 15, 30, 32, 105, 144, 177, 200, 270n
Knowles, C. 95n
Koch, J. 154-5
Kryekenpyt 249-51
Kuriyagawa, F. 26n
Kurvinen, A. 195, 213n, 229n

Large, John 42
Large, Robert 1, 37, 39, 41-4, 64
Larken, H.W. 47n
Lathbury, John 59
Lathrop, H.B. 25n, 107n, 245n
Latin 10, 14, 58-73, 80, 101, 115, 121-6, 129-32, 137-8, 141, 143, 158-61, 180, 184, 188, 193-7, 213-14, 219-20, 223-6, 249, 277, 279, 291, 296, 303
Laurentius Guglielmus de Saona s.v. Traversagni
Leach, MacEdward 248n
Leeu, Gerard 72, 232-3
Lefèvre, Raoul 3, 14, 64, 90-7, 167-72, 207
Legend of Good Women 173
Legend of Seynt Gyle 184
Legenda 7
Legenda aurea 115, 128, 197, 213, 220, 223, 225, 228
Legenda dorée 105
Legman, G. 270-1n
Leland, John 159-60
Le Morte Arthure 130, 204
Lettou, John 72
Lewis, R.E. 60n

Libellus super Tullanis elegantiis 62
Liber festivalis 60-1, 72; see also *Festial*
Life of Adam 225
Life and Typography of William Caxton 37
Life of Our Lady 108, 113-14, 161-4, 174, 297-8
Life of St Edith 302
Lille 53
Lilleshall (Shropshire) 60
Lindsay, Sir David 298
Lives of Adam and Eve 223, 226
Lives of the Fathers (Vitas Patrum) 4, 303
Logeman, H. 233n, 237n
Lollards 67, 182, 221
London 1-2, 43-7, 57, 61, 64, 67-72, 90, 93, 111, 127-8, 133-5, 150, 175, 180, 183, 201, 243, 249, 276, 280, 292, 303; port of 20; tower of 27, 201
Lot 215
Louis, King of France 284
Louis de Gruuthuse, Earl of Winchester 2
Loutfut, Adam 298
Louvain 3-4, 76, 80-3, 159
Love, Nicholas 116
Low Countries 1-3, 14, 39, 43, 64-5, 76-7, 80, 83, 167, 170, 178, 231, 233, 241
Low German 68, 123, 126
Lucas, P.J. 178n
Lübeck 232
Lutz, C.E. 286n
Lyall, R. 295
Lydgate, John 9-10, 16, 66, 70, 93-4, 99, 101, 108-10, 113-14, 120-3, 127, 129, 149-51, 157-8, 161-4, 167-85, 187-8, 284-5, 294-5, 297-8, 301
Lyndewode, William 59
Lyons 15, 67, 69
Lytleton, Henry 47-8

Macaulay, G.C. 187, 189-94, 300
Maccabees 216, 221
MacCracken, H.N. 183
Machlinia, William de 72
Magdalen College School 59
Magdalene College, Cambridge 289
Mainz 275, 303
Malory, Sir Thomas 11, 16, 22, 33, 128-33, 168, 173, 176, 187, 199-211, 273
Manly, J.M. 150n, 152-3, 291, 294, 301
Mansion, Colard 3, 14, 56, 83, 85, 289
Margaret Countess of Shrewsbury 181
Margaret Duchess of Burgundy 4, 9-15, 19, 55-6, 64, 67-8, 70, 79, 86, 91-4, 97,

119, 151, 167-71, 175-7, 181, 278
Margaret Duchess of Somerset 177
Martin, E. 232-3
Martin, H.-J. 153n
Martin, R.H. 284n
Marx, C.W. 299
Master of Margaret of Burgundy 278
Matheson, L.M. 62n, 294, 298-9, 301
Mathew, Gospel of 218, 222
Mathews, W. 22n, 130n, 201n
Maynial, Guillaume 6-7
McKerrow, R.B. 260n
McKnight, G.H. 259, 267
Meale, C. 301
Medicina stomachi 174
Mercers 1-2, 22, 39, 64, 93, 103, 167
Mercers' Company 21, 37-49, 64, 175; acts of court 38n; wardens' account book 21, 37-49, 64
Merchant Adventurers Company 1, 64
Metamorphoses 34, 289-90, 298
Methodius 214-15, 222
Methuselah 215
Meyer, P. 144n
Middle English Dictionary 141, 226
Miélot, Jean 207
Milan 159
Mirk, John 60, 72, 128, 219, 295
Mirror of the Life of Christ 70, 128; see also *Speculum vitae Christi*
Mirror of World 2, 26-7, 33, 53, 103-4, 108, 110-11, 163, 241, 279
Mish, C.C. 260n
Mitchner, R.W. 197n, 202-3n, 302
Moore, S. 180n
Moral Proverbs 99-101, 143, 151, 177
Morals (of St Gregory) 219, 222
Moran, J. 61n
Morgan, M.M. 302
Morland, William 303
Morte Darthur 11, 16-17, 128, 130, 168, 173, 176, 187, 199-211, 273; see also *King Arthur*
Moses 214, 216, 223-4, 228
Mountgrace Priory 116
Muller, J.W. 231-44
Mynors, R.A.B. 299, 303

Needham, R. 199n
Nembroth 215, 225n
Newbold Revell 22, 201
New College Oxford 153
Newgate 201

Nider, Johannes 301
Nixon, H.M. 276n
Noah 214-15
Norse 125
Norton-Smith, J. 290n
Notary, Julian 72
Nova rhetorica 7-8, 62, 68, 280-1, 284, 298
Nyche, Thomas 42-3

Offord, M.Y. 144, 270n
Of Friendship 103, 128
Of Old Age 68, 103, 121, 128, 176, 207
Oldys, William 37
Olschki, L.S. 279
Olson, C.C. 22n
Order of Chivalry 11, 105, 138-43, 177, 200, 245n, 298
Ovid 34, 122, 129, 165n, 205, 289, 298
Ovid moralisée 187, 197n
Oxford 8, 57-65, 69-73, 115, 159-60, 249, 276, 278
Oxford English Dictionary 140-1, 157, 226, 246n-47, 268n

Pächt, O. 278n
Painter, G.D. 51-6, 75-7, 81, 85-6, 276n
Paris 6, 24, 183-4, 249, 251, 280, 284, 301
Paris and Vienne 15, 109, 205, 248n
Parkes, M.B. 281n
Parliament of Fowls 150-1n, 156-7
Parliament, statutes of 70
Pearsall, D. 179, 182n, 299
Pepys, Samuel 289
Phalaris 59, 61
Pharaoh 215
Philip the Bold of France 15
Phillipps, Sir Thomas 165n, 289
Pickering, John 55
Pierre de St Cloud 232
Piers Plowman 127, 296
Pilgrimage of the Life of Man 182-3
Pilgrimage of the Soul 128, 174
Pius II 80
Plea and Memoranda Rolls 43, 45
Plomer, H.R. 69n, 146n, 234n, 242-3n, 272n
Poggio Bracciolini 137, 143, 145, 208
Pollard, A.W. 109n, 279n
Pollard, G. 281n
Polychronicon 16, 62n, 68, 77-8, 102, 104, 117, 121, 128, 132n, 137-45, 152, 162, 173, 194, 207-8, 224-9, 293, 298-9, 302
Pratt, William 32, 49, 101, 151

Premierfait, Laurence 182, 207
Prince of Wales (Arthur) 124, 177, 296; (Edward) 15, 86, 96-8, 151, 175, 181; (Henry) 171-2, 175, 181-2
Prior, O.H. 279n
Pro Milone 59
Propositio Johannis Russell 277
Pynson, Richard 60-73, 259-73, 301-2

Quattuor Sermones 60, 108, 114-15, 284, 302

Rachel 215
Raynaud, G. 295
Recuyell of the Histories of Troy s.v. *History of Troy*
Redeknape, Edmond 46-8
Redgrave, G.R. 109n
Reffkin, L. 114n
Regement of Princes 157
Register of the Freeman of the Grocers's Company 45; of the Mercers' Company 39, 45
Rehoboam 218-20, 222
Reinaert den vos s.v. *Van den Vos Reynaert*
Renoir, A. 179
Reszkiewicz, A. 257n
Reul, Paul de 256n
Reynard the Fox 27, 68, 77, 108, 116, 126, 145, 174, 231-58, 259-73, 278
Rhodes, D.A. 114n
Richard II 89, 173, 181, 189, 194, 229n
Richard III 11, 51, 177, 200, 206, 287
Rickert, E. 150n, 152-53n, 291, 294, 301
Rivers, Anthony Earl 30, 32, 68, 99-101, 114, 120-1, 128-30, 143, 151, 168, 178, 207, 287-9, 292
Rolle, Richard 59, 128, 135
Roman de Renart 27, 174, 232
Rome 214
Rood, Theodoric 57-61, 115, 278
Rouen 72, 302
Royal Book 15
Rufinus, Tyrranius 57, 278
Russell, John 56
Ruysbroek, Jan van 70
Ruysschaert, J. 69n, 196n, 298
Rylands Library 76, 108, 114, 288

St Albans 57, 61-5, 69-73, 276, 298, 301, 303
St Albans Abbey 61-3, 71
St Andrew 209, 220
St Benet's Chapel 159

St Bonaventura 70
St Elizabeth of Hungary 70
St Katherine of Siena 70
St Paul 171, 217, 221
St Rocke 225, 296
Saint Winifred 277, 297
Salisbury, Thomas Earl of 183
Salve Regina 299
Salter, E. 134n; see also Zeeman
Samson 216
I Samson 217
Sanctorale 219-20, 227
Sands, D.B. 25n, 107n, 149, 231-2n, 234n
Sarum Hours 278; *Sarum Missal* 6-7
Saul 217, 220
Scale of Perfection 70
Scattergood, V.J. 184
Schirmer, W.F. 179, 183n-4
Schoeffer, Peter 303
Scholderer, V. 275n
Schoolmaster-printer of St Albans 61, 63, 71
Scotland 71, 286
Scott, K.L. 289n, 296
Scrymgeour, John 298
Sem 214
Serpent of Division 162, 183
Seth 214
Sex epistolae 7-8, 59
Shaw, Sally 130n, 202n
Sheen 303
Sheffield, John Lord 5n
Sherborne, J.W. 184
Shirley, John 66, 157, 173, 180, 295
Short Title Catalogue 109
Siege of Jerusalem 104, 173-4, 221
Siege of Thebes 163-4, 172, 180, 284-5, 299, 302
Simko, J. 273
Sixtus IV 7-8
Skeat, W.W. 156
Skelton, John 123, 129, 137n, 145, 152n
Socrates 100
Sodom 215
Solomon 218, 222-3
Somerset, Earl of 55
Sommer, H.O. 205n
Spanish 208
Southwark 299
Speculum aureum decem preceptorum dei 303
Speculum vitae Christi 108, 115-16; see also *Mirror of the Life of Christ*
Spurgeon, C.F.E. 121, 158n, 162n

Stanney, John 32, 177
Stans puer 174, 299
Stowe, John 290, 295
Strabo 214
Strassburg 159
Strete, Randolf 42
Suffolk 180
Surigone, Stefano 101, 150, 157-61
Swieczkowski, W. 257n
Swierk, A. 275n
Switzerland 2, 58
Syon monastery 277n

Takamiya, T. 293n
Temple of Glass 174
Temporale 219-22, 227-8
Termuthe 216
Testament 301
Thielemans, M.-R. 53
Thomas, A.H. 43n, 45n
Thomas, H. 23n, 253n
Thompson, E.M. 303
Thorney, Roger 285, 300-2
Thrupp, S.L. 45
Tiptoft, John Earl of Worcester 16, 68, 103, 128-30, 161, 176, 207
Title and Pedigree of Henry VI 181
Tobit 216, 219
Tollemache, Lord 300
Toulouse 280
Tracy, Ralph 303
Trapp, J.B. 283n, 286n
Traversagni, Giovanni Antonio 280
Traversagni, Lorenzo Guglielmo 7-8, 62, 68-9, 280-1, 284, 298
Traylen, Charles 303
Trevisa, John 16, 68, 78, 104, 117, 121, 128, 130-3, 162, 194, 207-8, 224, 227
Triggs, O.L. 301
Troilus and Criseyde 9, 122n, 150-1n, 179, 284
Troy 16, 93-4, 97, 157, 181
Troy-Book 16, 93, 120, 129, 151n, 157-8, 161-4, 169-73, 180
Turin 283

Uppsala 283

Van den vos Reynaert 145, 231-58
Veldener, Johannes 3-4, 65, 76, 80-4, 276
Venice 7-8
Vespasiano da Bisticci 58, 278

Vienne 280
Vignay, Jean de 207, 223
Vinaver, E. 130, 199n, 210n
Virgil 122, 296
Vulgaria 59
Vulgate 213-29

Wales 71, 89-90, 187
Waning of the Middles Ages, The 14
Warkworth's Chronicle 293, 299
Wars of Alexander 296
Warwick, Earl of 170, 181
Watts, P.R. 22n
Webb, C.A. 114n
Wells, James 47
Wells, J.E. 223n
Weiss, R. 159-60n
Welsh 209
Wendelstein, L. 125
Werken, Theodoric 303
Westminster 3, 6-7, 15, 29, 32, 49, 57, 60-3,
    66, 69, 72, 75, 85-7, 90, 96-7, 99-107, 109,
    115, 153, 160, 175, 177, 201, 205, 276,
    279, 284, 289, 292-3, 303
Westminster Abbey 4, 21, 31, 63, 71, 101,
    158-60, 288; Almonry 63
Westminster, Abbot of 122, 142

Whetham, John 303
White Friars 55
Wiencke, H. 144n, 259n, 272-3n
Willem 232
William Caxton: A Bibliographical Guide 72
Wilson, Edward 296
Wilson, R.H. 300
Winchester 16
Wood, W.L. 303
Woodville, Anthony s.v. Rivers, Anthony
    Earl
Woodville, Elizabeth 30-2, 105, 177
Woodward, Margaret 292, 296
Worcester s.v. Tiptoft
Worcester, William 68, 103
Workman, S.K. 137n, 145n, 152n, 234n,
    245n
Wydeville, Anthony s.v. Rivers, Anthony
    Earl
Wynkyn de Worde s.v. de Worde, Wynkyn

Yngilby, J. (Bishop of Llandaff) 303
Yorkshire 90, 187

Zeeman, E. 128n; see also Salter, E.
Zell, Ulrich 275
Zyricxzee 249